PACIFIC NORTHWEST U.S.A.

Publisher:	Aileen Lau
Project Editor:	Catherine Khoo
Assisting Editor:	Emma Tan
Design/DTP:	Sares Kanapathy
	Brian Wyreweden
	Sarina Afandie
Illustrations:	Chua Teck Chai
Cover Artwork:	Susan Harmer
Maps:	Ivy Toh

Published in the United States by
PRENTICE HALL GENERAL REFERENCE
15 Columbus Circle
New York, New York, 10023

Copyright © Sun Tree Publishing Ltd
1994

ISBN 0-671-87897-2

Titles in the series:
Alaska - American Southwest - Australia - Bali - California - Canada - Caribbean - China -
England - Florida - France - Germany - Greece - Hawaii - India - Indonesia - Italy - Ireland -
Japan - Kenya - Malaysia - Mexico - Nepal - New England - New York - Pacific Northwest
USA - Singapore - Spain - Thailand - Turkey - Vietnam

USA MAINLAND SPECIAL SALES
Bulk purchases (10+copies) of the Travel Bugs series are available at special discounts for
corporate use. The publishers can produce custom publications for corporate clients to be
used as premiums or for sales promotion. Copies can be produced with custom cover
imprints. For more information write to Special Sales, Prentice Hall Travel, Paramount
Communications Building, 15th floor, 15 Columbus Circle, New York, NY 10023.

Printed in Singapore

PACIFIC NORTHWEST
U.S.A.

Text by Raymond Chatelin

Project Editor
Catherine Khoo

Prentice Hall Travel

New York   London   Toronto   Sydney   Tokyo   Singapore

C O N T E N T S

C O N T E N T S

Land of People – Festivals & Arts & . Culture 105
Local color - Crown Jewel of Festivals - Music festivals - Oldest Jazz festival - Cultural symphony - Arts explosion - Arts and Crafts - Walla Walla Symphony - Maritime history - Rich cultural traditions - Seattle Center

FOLLOW THAT BUG

City of Destiny – Seattle & Tacoma 127
Wealth of natural beauty - Legacy of the past - City of character - Coffee Talk - Diversification - Culture Industry - Architectural transformation - Magnet for shoppers - Neighborhoods - Core of downtown - Washington State Convention Center - Scenic Waterfront - Commercial district - Bohemian beat - Magnolia - Ballard and Roosevelt - North of the city - Tacoma - Commencement City - Antique Row

Scenic Sound – Puget Sound & The San Juans 161
Complex web - Exquisite beauty - Olympia - Capital's centerpiece - North of Seattle - Mount Vernon - Weekend escape - Gateway to San Juans - Bellingham - Scenic Chuckanut Drive

Ocean Roars – Washington Coast 181
Callam Bay and Sekiu - Neah Bay - Wilderness coast - Ocean shores - Hoquiam - Aberdeen - Salmon Capital of the World - Long Beach - Oyster centers

Salad & Cereal Bowl – Central Washington 199
Rich saladbowl - Okanagan - Molson - Colville Reservation - Chelan - Apple capital - Cashmere - Ellensburg - Tranquil Splendor - Union Gap - Wine industry - Fort Simcoe

"Many Waters" – Inland Washington 215
Veritable gardens of wheat - West of Walla

C O N T E N T S

C O N T E N T S

The exquisite beauty of wild and cultivated

flowers decorate the cities, countryside and national parks of the Pacific Northwest.

of the cities reflect

Highrises and spires

the new prosperity and elegance of Metropolitan Pacific Northwest.

The Pacific Flyway, a highway in the skies for birds on their

"The Pacific Northwest is a place where myth and reality exist side by side, where ancient traditions and contemporary lifestyles have blended into a new culture.

It is a magical harmony of contrasts – of towering mountains, inland ocean channels, cosmopolitan cities, fast-lane resorts, giant fir forests, the rolling hills of the wine country, and the high sandy dunes of the Pacific coast. It is a place of desert and rain forest; of roaring surf and gentle streams; apple blossoms and cactus flowers; powerful volcanos and icy snowfields.

It's hard to believe that just 150 years ago, the great cities of Seattle and Portland were just trading posts on the edge of an enormous wilderness. Even today, the Pacific Northwest is not defined by its cities – though there's much to enjoy in them. Rather, it is still the wild flavor that produces the intense attraction and commitment the region's citizens have for it.

Introduction

1

Welcome to the Pacific Northwest!

The placid beauty of Mount Hood beckons.

The region had always suffered culturally at the hands of eastern America with its large and famous symphony orchestras, opera companies, writers, and artists. The view of the Pacific Northwest as a place where cowboys and lumberjacks dwell, lingered long beyond its time.

Once, people here cared about what the rest of the country thought about them. In their insecurity, they thought it mattered. No longer does it matter now.

A distinct character

A new kind of person has emerged from the Pacific Northwest, one not bound to tradition and establishment. You can see that change in the performing and visual arts, and also in the definition the region finds from the native peoples' cultural traditions.

Seattle and Portland, the two largest cities in the Pacific Northwest, have distinguished orchestras and two vibrant opera companies, plus a variety of dance, ballet, and theater ensembles.

They don't claim to be the world's best, or even the continent's most innovative. But they have used their performing arts as a means to create a distinct character.

The region's cuisine reflects its diversity and the reality of the Pacific Northwest being a gathering of mini-cultures – a cultural brew of the Orient, of native peoples, and a pinch of continental Europe. It's a place where you can find just about anything you want and where numerous ancient natural mysteries vie for the attention of modern Man.

On the northwest coast rests the Olympic Peninsula like a giant thumb rising above the populated Puget Sound. Mountains and shores are often shrouded in fog or rain-laden cloud. Ancient artifacts lie rotting in some forgotten forest and off in the distance the San Juan Islands rise above the ocean water, like jewels adorning the rim of a crown.

By contrast, Seattle, which is virtually next door, is an international city having a relaxed lifestyle spiced by a rich cultural diversity. Major skiing facilities atop nearby mountaintops are

Relaxation is the keyword when touring the Northwest.

30 minutes from downtown.

Blessed with a mild climate, Seattle people like to boast that during the winter months they can play golf or tennis in the morning, sail in the afternoon, and go skiing nearby during the winter months – and it's true.

The Pacific Northwest has undergone a metamorphosis in recent years, growing in substance from a rustic, edge of-the-frontier place with world-wide interest in its vast natural resources, to a sophisticated region attracting international tourism.

It has become a contemporary place without cutting its physical past. Now a center of high-tech and cultural internationalism, it is still dominated by nature.

Celebration of life

The oceans, mountains, and rolling hills have never really been tamed, but they are now being utilized more efficiently. Certainly, testament to nature's domination can be found throughout the region – in the aftermath of Mount St. Helen's volcanic explosion, in the sadly deserted ghost towns of Oregon's dry southeast.

For most of all this is a physical land. People are drawn here for its enormous beauty, an overpowering radiance that is never far away, always beckoning. The celebration of life's renewal is everywhere in abundance throughout the seasons. Wenatchee's

The wonders of nature can be experienced in the many forest parks.

Apple Blossom Festival in Spring is a time of innocence. And later, during fall harvest time, people taste the product of the picturesque vineyards of Oregon's Williamette Valley or Washington's Yakima Valley.

From the middle of April to early June there's a sweetness in the air that can't be found later in summer, as bloosoms herald the coming of the growing season. It's a festive time marked by carnivals, parades, and festivals.

Natural wonder

In early to late October, there is a different celebration of renewal when the spawning salmon return to rivers and streams along the coast. Estuaries become red with writhing fish that have made their way up the Columbia and its tributaries – a natural wonder that is also at the base of an entire industry.

As you'd expect, joggers, skiers, golfers, fishermen, sailors, all make use of the Pacific Northwest's varied topography, a world defined mostly by water – rain, runoff, lakes, rivers, snow, inlets and ocean. Downhill and cross-country resorts spread westward and south. Golf courses are to be found everywhere – in the arid lands of central Washington and Oregon, the high mountain plateaus, and along the west, mild coast.

Compelling Beauty

There are many things that might be obvious to the first time visitor. The mountains are dramatic testaments to an untameable land, the ocean seems overwhelming in its power, and the desert regions seem like remote and vast wasteland unable to support even the most primitve life. But the Pacific Northwest is also a world of little things that bring joy to those who live here. You find it in the micro-breweries that seem to pop up in every city, as adjuncts to inns and pubs; and the small book stores of Portland and Seattle where people gather to sip their coffee and discuss the latest works of unknown authors.

It is also found by walking among the delicate life forms of a tidal pool on the northern shores of Puget Sound

Roses in full bloom at the International Rose Test Garden in Washington Park.

where, in winter, the rain is misty and soft. The ongoing process of life's renewal can be found everywhere in great splendor. Whale watching takes tourists to greet the 20,000 gray whales that pass within a short distance of the Oregon and Washington coasts to and from their way to the Bering Sea twice a year. They go south to mate. They return with the young by their side.

At small towns throughout the eastern portions of Oregon you experience migration and renewal of a different kind, tracing the route of the Oregon Trail that brought thousands of immigrants to settle the west from New York and Boston in the mid-19th century. Many stopped off to create new settlements, some died along the route.

Trip into Paradise

It's not a perfect paradise. There's an ongoing battle between conservationists and developers over the future use of the region's many environments. That balance between nature and jobs is becoming more difficult to maintain.

It's common now to see large swaths of clear cut-on mountains that were once virgin forest. Some of the streams and rivers that were once avenues for spawning salmon are now ravaged by pollution or development. Tourists, anxious to experience a small part of this vacationers dream, are pressuring some popular venues during peak summer months. But, there is still much here

Fast Facts

Between them, Washington and Oregon encompass 165,192 sq miles, an area slightly less than the size of Sweden. Oregon is the 10th largest state in the union and covers 97,073 square miles. Washington's land mass is 68,192 sq. miles.

Oregon's population is just under three million while Washington's is close to one million more. In both states, the populations are focused in the two largest cities.

Seattle is Washington's largest community with a population of 516,000 in the city proper, but with a regional population of 2.7 million. Portland is Oregon's largest city with 350,000 residents and a regional population totaling 50 per cent of the entire state's 2.8 million people.

The state capitals – Olympia in Washington and Salem in Oregon – have relatively smaller populations with 30,000 and 70,000 respectively. But the Olympia figures are a bit deceiving as it sits at the southernmost point of Puget Sound, Washington's most populated region that includes Seattle and Tacoma.

Salem, on the other hand, is isolated from the Portland region and rests in a less populated part of the state, southwest of Portland.

The main industries are varied ranging from land and sea based businesses as fishing, mining, and forestry to high-tech, aircraft manufacturing, and tourism which is now Washington's fourth largest industry and Oregon's third largest. Each state has large farming and ranching industries. In fact, you can split the region into two economic worlds. West of the Cascades the prime industries are logging and manufacturing. East, farming makes up the basis of the economy.

Religious preferences are as varied as the population makeup with Caucasians, African Americans, Native Americans, Asians, Hispanics, and Pacific Islanders comprising the the complex makeup of Pacific Northwest peoples.

So, all major religions are found in the region, though outside the greater Seattle and Portland areas, there are less choices. In both of those cities are found various Protestant, Roman Catholic, and Eastern Orthodox churches, there are numerous Jewish Synagogues, Buddhist Temples, and Islamic mosques.

The usual joke about climate in the Pacific Northwest is that if you travel another 50 miles (80 km) it will change. Indeed, there is no single climate to the vast area. The heaviest rainfall is west of the Cascade Mountains that bisect Washington and Oregon. East of the range, it is much drier and warmer in the summer, colder in winter. Seattle's climate is mild throughout the year. The average high in July - its hottest month - is 62°F (16.6°C) though it can, on occasion reach 85 F (29°C). In Walla Walla, by comparison in the southeast desert region of the state, the average July temperature is 76 F (24.5°C) though it is often 95 F (35°C) and higher. In the south eastern area of Oregon July and August temperatures reach 100 F (38°C).

In January Seattle averages 38° F (3°C) while in Spokane, on the central eastern border of Washington/Idaho, the average is 25°F (-4°C) and is often colder. Wise travelers touring the state, bring a range of clothing to reflect the varying conditions. The mountains, like those elsewhere, are unpredictable and sometimes have snow in June at higher elevations.

Oregon's highest point is Mt. Hood at 11,237 feet (3436 m) and its lowest point is at sea level. Washington's highest is Mt. Rainier at 14,411 feet (4392 m) and it too has a sea level low point.

Washington was admitted to the Union as a state on November 11, 1889. Known as The Evergreen State, its state flower is the Coast Rhododendron and the state bird is the Willow Goldfinch. Its gem is Petrified Wood, its fish is the Steelhead Trout, and its song is Washington, My Home.

Oregon, admitted to the Union on February 14, 1859 is known as the Beaver State. Its flower is the Oregon Grape and its bird is the Western Meadowlark. Its gem is the Thunderegg, its insect is the Swallowtail Butterfly, and its song is Oregon, My Oregon.

The oldest city in the Pacific Northwest is Oregon City, established in 1849 and Oregon is one of only two states without a sales tax.

However, *Money Magazine*, one of America's leading financial news publications, calls Oregon second only to Hawaii as the state with the heaviest tax burden.

Ecola State Park in Northwest Oregon.

that cannot be found elsewhere – still plenty of open space, wilderness, and a sense of community. The region is so vast that unless you're willing to spend months seeing it, you'll never see it in one trip. And its allure is so great you'll want to come back time and again.

There is still the sensation of being alone with nature, beneath the flight pattern of Canada Geese, of seeing Bald Eagles soaring overhead. It is still a unique, often gentle place and now might well be the most perfect time to experience it.

History

The native Indians who inhabited the Pacific Northwest in more recent times were peaceful, fiercely independent, artistic, and self-sufficient. Warfare was rare, and food was plentiful.

Soft wood, especially red cedar, was abundant and easily carved so that transportation between villages was conducted mostly by waterways.

Theirs was an oral history, often sharing similar stories between them as they created moralistic fables that in part governed their daily lives. When they were finally visited by white men, they had none of the defenses needed to ward off either disease or ambition.

In the end they were easy prey to desire and greed, leaving behind essentially only a ghost of what had been their culturally rich societies.

The northern reaches of the Pacific Northwest were virtually unknown to European explorers of the 16th

President Thomas Jefferson, who spearheaded the discovery of the route to the Northwest.

9

Native Peoples

The indigenous peoples were fishing the Columbia River for salmon as far back as 11,000 years ago. Throughout the Pacific Northwest, archaeologists are still finding remains of villages and encampments. The most recent is near Cape Flattery on the Olympic Peninsula where scientists are working their way through a 2,000-year-old village site near the town of Ozette.

The finds are more numerous in Washington State and along the Pacific coast to Alaska, than in Oregon. Coast Indians enjoyed a rich environment and plenty of food from game, berries, and from the seas. Whatever nourishment the Indians couldn't find from the sea, they got from coastal rivers. Because they didn't have to devote all their time in the search for food, they were able to develop a mature, long lasting, and distinct series of cultures.

Cultural diversity

Prehistoric Washington State was the home to several dissimilar Indian cultures from at least four different linguistic groups. Among the coastal tribes were the Makh, Quinalt, Salish, Puyallup, Nisqually, and Skykomish who lived in the Puget Sound area and after whom many of today's towns and regions are named.

The Chinook, Cowlitz and Klickitat lived along the Columbia River. Between them they comprised the most prosperous groups of hunter-gatherer cultures ever known. They were relatively peaceful – with very few tribal wars between them – and they were essentially content people.

In Oregon, the landscape was home to an equally diverse population of Indians - among them the Clatsop, Multnomah, Klamath, Modoc, and Nez Perce whose complex cultures were eventually ravaged by the coming of white settlers to the Pacific Northwest.

The destruction of the native cultures was done over a period of time and in incremental stages. From 1542, when Bartholome Ferrelo caught the first glimpse of the fog-shrouded Oregon coast, to George Vancouver's coastal probing of what is now Washington State, the British and Spanish devoted their imperial activites to the search for a Northwest passage. Later, the search for the passage was replaced by the search for furs.

Territorial immigrants passed through the region via the Oregon Trail and began settling, pushing the relatively passive native peoples out of their traditional lands and influence.

Early white settlers, believing they were entering a world of rampaging red men having a single cultural identity, were initially confused by the peaceful nature of the peoples and by their widely differing cultures and languages.

Coastal tribes

It was the coastal tribes that left the most evidence of their existence. Their main source of food was the salmon that spawned in Washington's many rivers. The predictability of the spawning seasons produced permanent villages within short distances.

century. The Spanish were the primary explorers of the southern Americas and confident in their abilities to hold onto their vast land claims.

There had been — and still are – rumors of Japanese and Chinese voyages to the west coast, and of Russian castaways there in the 17th century. But it was Juan Rodriguez Cabrillo, among the Europeans, who first touched the California coast in 1542.

Sir Francis Drake

When the British captain, Sir Francis Drake, appeared on the west coast of South America in 1579, he threw a scare

discovered the legendary and long sought after Northwest Passage through the North American continent.

There was not, of course, any such passage though it continued to drive explorers in search of it for parts of the next two centuries. Drake didn't like what he found along the coast, as he had a definite aversion to the weather, calling it a "vile, stinking fog".

Other explorers

Archaelogists still cling on to the theory that the first people who populated the New World came through the Pacific North Coast. Though evidence is lacking, they believed the first Americans trekked through Alaska and made their way through Canada into the Western United States.

While the Northwest Passage never did exist, it still managed to draw explorers to the Pacific Northwest, including the Russians, who moved across the Bering Sea and into Alaska before moving southward.

Russian claims

Russian claims to the region were based in part on the fact they had little opposition and hunted Northwest sea otters and other fur bearing animals without interference.

The Spaniards, though concerned about Russian incursions into their zone

Some tribes were highly proficient whalers, using large canoes made from the plentiful and soft cedar trees that could be easily carved and which held up well to water. In that aspect of their lives, they were similar to the Kwakiutl people north in Canada.

Near Cape Alva on the Olympic Penisula are the remains of Ozette, a Makah hunting and fishing village that was burned in a mud slide 500 years ago. It had been occupied for at least 2,000 years and archaeologists have found more than 50,000 artifacts including a remarkable effigy of an Orca. At a fishing station near the mouth of the Hoko River — at the north end of the Olympic Peninsula — artifacts date back 3,000 years.

Many of the region's native peoples were also skilled artists, producing ceremonial masks, decorated boxes, and other objects that today can be found in virtually every regional museum, but especially at the University of Washington in Seattle, and at the Museum of Anthropology located on the University of British Columbia campus in Vancouver, British Columbia.

The tribes of the south concentrated more on trade than hunting and fishing. They used the Columbia River as a water highway to reach tribes located east of the high Cascade Mountains in a region made up of high desert and the rolling hills extending to the Rockies.

These tribes – including the Sanpoil, Yakima, Wenatchee, Spokane, Palouse, and Wallawalla - lived in less permanent settlements than their coastal counterparts. Instead, they established camps where they found food, much like the Prairie tribes further south and to the east.

in the Spaniards who saw the Pacific as their private domain. It also gave hint of what was to come.

Drake plundered ports along the coast, escaping north in his ship, the *Golden Hind*. Drake's mysterious disappearance – the Spanish had expected him to head back around the Cape – made the Spanish believe Drake had

Pioneer Square in Seattle, with an historic Indian totem pole.

of influence, established no permanent settlements on the coast. And the Spaniards failed to follow up on their discoveries along the coast.

The Russians, on the other hand, although they had founded one major colony at what is now Sitka, Alaska, they were mobile in their huntings in the Pacific Northwest.

Subsequent exploration of the region was the result of Juan de Fuca, the fictional name of Apostolos Valerianos, a 60-year-old Greek ship's pilot. He claimed to have been a ship's pilot for

The Oregon Trail was dubbed "The Longest Graveyard" by pioneers.

Walter Raleigh, and others. Explorers 200 years later were still pursuing this northwest passage.

Captain James Cook

Captain James Cook undertook his third circumnavigation of the world for the British Royal Navy in 1776, sailing the Pacific North Coast looking for the Passage he didn't think even existed. The British Government had posted a 20,000 pound prize for the passage's discovery. Cook wanted to prove once and for all, there was nothing to be found. As expected, Cook never did find it, but he did a lot of trading with natives, opening the door to future trade.

the Viceroy of Mexico in the Viceroy's voyages of 1592 in which de Fuca discovered a "passage" just about where the now-named Strait of Juan de Fuca divides British Columbia from Washington's Olympic Peninsula.

The tale – complete with stories about animal-skin clad natives, caught the attention of Queen Elizabeth, Sir

The opening of the Northwest coast

In the late 18th century, two ship captains – the Englishman, George Vancouver and the American, Robert Gray – made discoveries on the Pacific Coast that began the development of the Pacific Northwest.

Vancouver, being in the employ of the British Admiralty, was interested in exploration and in staking a foothold for England in the new world. He had had a long history of service to England, having sailed on Capt. James Cook's second and third voyages and, as a midshipman, he had accompanied Cook on his West Coast expeditions.

He returned to the area aboard his sloop, *Discovery*, after having established his reputation in the West Indies in the early 1780s serving under Admiral George Rodney. His mission to the Pacific Northwest was to take over the territory at Nookta Sound, which had been assigned to England by the Nootka Convention.

Nootka Sound is a natural harbor on the west coast of Vancouver Island, having several protective inlets. The British claimed it 10 years after Cook explored it, by establishing a trading post in 1788.

A year later it was seized by the Spanish and became a point of controversy between the two nations. The settlement of the dispute, via the Nootka Convention, opened the northern Pacific Northwest to British settlement.

Vancouver's second assignment was to explore and survey the northern Pacific Northwest. And he did that in abundance. For three years – 1792-95 – he not only explored the region, but provided most of the names by which almost all coastal regions, especially in Washington State, are now known.

He and his Second Lieutenant, Peter Puget, explored the Strait of Juan de Fuca and the Gulf of Georgia and circumnavigated what is now Vancouver Island.

The impact of his discoveries didn't really have any effect until after the publication of his accounts of the voyage. He died in 1798, before they were complete. But Puget and Vancouver's brother finished the project named *Voyage of Discovery to the North Pacific Ocean and Around the World*.

Gray had talked to Vancouver on a chance meeting at sea, just off the Washington coast. Fur trader Gray was more interested in economic gain from the area than exploration. His past had included taking a rich cargo of otter skins to Canton, China, and he was the first American to circumnavigate the world.

Columbia River

So finding that Vancouver and he were not competing for the same spoils, Gray set sail south aboard his ship, *Columbia*, where he eventually encountered the

Totem Park in Seattle.

John Day Fossil Beds, where the five geological epochs are captured in stone.

mouth of what was later named the Columbia River.

While Vancouver and others had known about the entrance and the huge sandbar that protected it, Gray was the first to bypass the obstacle and sail up the river itself. He was able to collect from the Indians enormous amounts of furs.

Claims to the region

Thus Vancouver's exploration of the Puget Sound and Vancouver Island region, and Gray's establishment of the American presence in the Columbia River set the stage for both country's claims to the Pacific Northwest.

Other nations were laying claim to the region. Spain and, to a lesser extent, Russia, both knew about the fur trade possibilities and attempted to make some claim to the region. But, unlike Britain and America, their claims were limited by their lack of colonization.

Alexander Mackenzie

Britain cemented the Cook explorations and the first dispatches from Vancouver, by sending Alexander McKenzie, in 1783, to cross Canada and to explore the regions of the Pacific Northwest, giving Britain a second claim. McKenzie was in the employ of the Northwest Company, a fur trading establishment that was often the spearhead for British

Crown claims.

North of the 50th Parallel

McKenzie became the first explorer to cross North America north of Mexico. In 1788 he made it as far north as the Arctic in a futile search for the elusive and fabled Northwest Passage. He then followed the Bella Coola River from the Canadian Rockies to just north of Vancouver Island, proving there was no such passage north of the 50th parallel.

But there was still no conclusive claim to the region south of that point. In 1803, U.S. President Thomas Jefferson chose Captain Meriwether Lewis, his former secretary, to explore the lesser known Louisiana Purchase, the land the United States had bought from France for $15 million and which virtually doubled the national domain. Lewis chose as his companion, Capt. William Clark.

But, Jefferson, who didn't really believe the Pacific Northwest would ever serve a useful purpose extended the Lewis and Clark mandate a year later in order to find a suitable route to the Pacific. Jefferson's lack of confidence in the region was overcome by his dislike to the British establishing claims to that part of the continent.

The expedition was arduous, nearly failing many times, especially in the trek across the high Rockies. But, eventually they made their way along a variety of passes and rivers to the Columbia and to the coast, sighting the Pacific on November 15, 1805 and wintered at Fort Clatsop.

To say they didn't like what they found is an understatement. The winter was wet, cold, and the members of the expedition plagued by illness. In spring they headed home with Lewis returning much the same way they had come, and Clark exploring the Yellowhead River to the south. They met up again in North Dakota and in 1806, returned to St. Louis -- from where the expedition had begun, bringing back with them detailed maps, observations, and scientific collections.

Hudson Bay Company

In 1868, the Hudson Bay Company was established by an Act of the British Parliament. It was the most powerful commercial enterprise on the continent, interested in establishing trading posts wherever there was game. The company had already established a string of posts across Canada and was the dominant force in the northwest part of the continent. It had one primary competitor, the Northwest Company, and they competed fiercely for furs and territory.

Canadian explorer, fur trader, and geographer, David Thompson, was the most prolific of the trading post builders. Thompson had left the Northwest Company to join the rival Hudson Bay Company and he not only explored the region, but set up posts in northeastern Washington and northern Idaho to prevent encroachment by American fur traders. He was the first white man to trace the source of the Columbia and to sail all of its tributaries.

In 1810, under Thompson's direction, Spokane House was built, the first trading post in the state of Washington. His bigger plan, however, was to establish Britain claims as far south as the mouth of the Columbia River.

But when he finally arrived, he was shocked to find that American fur trader, John Jacob Astor, had established Fort Astoria in 1811 on behalf of the Pacific Fur Company.

Uneasy alliance

The relationship between the British and Americans during the early 1800s was complex. Since there were no political borders and neither could mount any significant military presence, they agreed in 1818 to share the region in a joint occupation of the territory. Each side, however, knew that the other wanted complete domination.

The British were making their presence felt through the time-tested estab-

lishment of colonies. The Northwest Company and the Hudson Bay Company merged in 1821, forming a huge fur-trading conglomerate. Hudson Bay Company built its temporary headquarters on the north side of the Columbia, 100 miles (161 km) inland at Fort Vancouver across the river from where it met the Williamette.

The settlers planted crops, raised livestock, and made the fort self sufficient, eventually increasing its population to 500. Other posts were created at Spokane, Okanagan, and Nisqually.

Several factors were against the British from the beginning. The fur trade declined, England had difficulty in continuing a far-flung empire, and there was a decided lack of women in a land populated mostly by trappers and explorers. It was obvious that whatever nation could attracted both sexes, would be in a position to populate the region.

Arrival of the missionaries

So, the American government encouraged missionaries, among others, to be sent. The first was Methodist, Jason Lee and he was followed by the Dr. Marcus and Narcissa Whitman two years later, heading a group made up of various New England Protestant churches.

A Boston educator, Hall Jackson Kelley, read the journals of Lewis and Clark and like many others became obsessed with the northwest. He claimed to hear the voice of God asking him to

Mount St. Helens

The eruption of Mount St. Helens had an explosive power of 300 Hiroshima-size atomic bombs.

Compared constantly with Mount Fuji in Japan, Mount St. Helens was popular with hikers, climbers and a variety of outdoor adventurers. It was a volcano that was dormant for 123 years and no one expected it to blow.

Then on March 20, 1980, the mountain known locally as "the ice cream cone" began to rumble and 10 days later, steam was seen coming from two brand new craters atop the 9,677 foot mountain. By April 4, the craters had merged into one huge, 1,700 foot wide fiery chasm.

Finally, after seven weeks of minor earthquakes, the mountain exploded at 8:32 a.m. on May 18 with a fury measured at an explosive power of 300 Hiroshima size atomic bombs. Triggered by an earthquake that measured 5.1 on the Richter scale, the eruption blew 1,312 feet off the volcano's summit in a lateral northeast blast that flattened 230 sq. miles of forests.

The ashen plume rose 16 miles and temperatures 15 miles away immediately shot to 572°F. The blast killed an estimated 70 people, destroyed 220 homes, and 17 miles of railroad.

The wildlife death toll was staggering with more than 5,000 black-tailed deer, 200 black bear, 15 mountain goats, 1,500 Roosevelt Elk, and millions of fish and birds dying either from the initial blast or because of falling ash. The region's rare spotted owl population was entirely wiped out.

Towns in Eastern Washington were covered by up to 3 inches of ash and traces were found as far away as mid-Montana and in Vancouver, British Columbia. Weather patterns were affected around the world.

Mount St. Helens is not the only volcano in the region. The 700-mile-long chain of mountains that make up the Cascades – from north-

propagate Christianity in the region. So, in 1829 after losing his textile business to bankruptcy, he organized the American Society for Encouraging Settlement of the Oregon Territory.

Kelley was a journalist, and among other activities, and he began publishing glowing reports about the region, an area he had never seen. These semi-plagiarized, imaginative reports recruited many wanting to settle in what was called "New Eden". While his own personal attempts to reach his own Promised Land with a flock of followers in hand failed time and again, he generated enormous enthusiasm.

American evangelical enthusiasm was reaching a peak at about the same

ern California to southern British Columbia – are laced with volcanos. Most are larger than Mount St. Helens and include Mount Rainier, Mount Hood, and Mount Baker, all of which are near major population centers. They are part of what scientists call the "Ring Of Fire", some 850 active volcanoes in mountain ranges around the Pacific Rim.

The largest eruption in recent memory was on the Pacific island of Krakatau in 1883. The resulting atmospheric dust cloud colored sunsets around the world for two years, and the resulting tidal wave from the explosion killed 36,000 people in nearby Java and Sumatra.

Mount St. Helens' pyrotechnics were known to Northwest native peoples, some of whom called it the Louwala-Clough, or "smoking mountain". According to Klickitat mythology, Wy'East and Klichitat – the two sons of Sahale, the Great Spirit – fell in love with a beautiful maiden, Loowit, and proceeded to fight for her attention. After they had wreaked havoc by burning villages and forests, Sahale struck down the three lovers and erected mountain peaks in their places. Loowit became Mount St. Helens, with its beautiful cone of dazzling white; Wy'East became Mount Hood, and Klickitat, Mount Adams.

While occasional growls still come from the mountain's core, Mount St. Helens has once again become a prime destination for adventure seekers. Plants and wildlife are slowly returning and hiking trails are being cleared through the monumental devastation that still stuns the senses.

Approach to the Monument

There are three ways of apporaching Mount St. Helens National Volcanic Monument: From the west, at Castle Rock take exit 49 off Interstate 5 and drive 5 miles (8 km) east to the Mount St. Helens Visitor Center at Silver Lake. From the north drive via Morton and Randle, ending at Windy Ridge. From the southwest, the approach doesn't get much publicity, via the Woodland-Cougar area, although it passes through some old lava beds including Ape Cave.

At the $3 million Mount St. Helens visitor center on the shores of Silver Lake in what is now officially the Mount St. Helens National Volcanic Monument, video presentations reproduce the power of the blast. It also has a walk-in model volcano, a mural, numerous displays, and a 10-minute slide show.

In an ironic change of pace, the mountain that used to be an out-of-the-way place with just a handful of mountain cabins and small resort ranches, now attracts upwards of two million visitors a year.

From late June to early September, park rangers give talks and lead nature hikes and car caravans from several points. A permit is required for hikes into the crater or for hiking above 4,800 feet. Hiking onto the crater floor is permitted only when the ground is covered by snow.

time as Kelley's propaganda was making the rounds. The Whitmans had the usual attitude towards the Indians – that they were savages of inferior mental capacity and should be treated like children. They set up a mission near Walla Walla, in what is now the southeast portion of Washington State. Oregon and Washington were one political territory and it was not until 1853 that it would be divided into two states.

Clash with the Indians

While Whitman wasn't much more successful in "converting" the native people, he was convinced they would come

Gold Discoveries

The discovery of gold in California was the catalyst for the Pacific Northwest's own discoveries. In Oregon, especially, gold played an important role in the early growth of the state.

Californian miners, began moving north as the claims in that state were either exhausted or prohibited new gold seekers from staking their own claims. Large nuggets were dug up in 1851 in Rich Gulch and Sailors Diggings and the rush was on. In the decade following the California gold rush of 1848, thousands of miners came to southern Oregon because of gold finds in the Rogue Valley and on the south coast. Gold was found on the beaches at river outlets and in the hills. Miners even struck gold in ocean surf around Whiskey Run, south of Coos Bay.

Along the banks of the Illinois River, which flows northward into the Rogue River, many gold strikes in the early 1850s gave rise to numerous boom towns that flared and then fizzled. Only a few signs are now around to indicate they even existed.

Some have the most intriguing names in Oregon. How did the town of "Wonder" get its name, for example? Lore has it that the village was named by settlers who wondered how a merchant who established a store at that point might hope to make a living.

"Sailor's Diggings"

During the boom days, three towns thrived along the Illinois River – Waldo, Kerbyville, and Browntown. First called "Sailor's Diggings", Waldo still exists as does Kerbyville though the latter's name has been changed to Kerby. Browntown, originally the biggest of the three communities, has vanished without a trace.

The largest nugget found in the area weighed 204 ounces. In those days, with gold bringing in $16 an ounce, it was worth $3,264. Today, at $350 an ounce, it would bring $71,400.

Jacksonville was created in 1851 near a gold-bearing creek and the Applegate Trail became a major thoroughfare for cross-country immigrants. Baker, located in eastern Oregon, was that region's Jacksonville equivalent and was located near the Oregon Trail. Gold was discov-

ered in that area in 1861 and the town prospered through the early 1900s. Between them, Jacksonville and Baker were reputed to be among the wildest towns in the west. That was incidental to the fact that the Union cause in the Civil War was financed in large part by the gold mined in Oregon.

One stretch of Canyon Creek, near Canyon City in the John Day Valley, yielded $28 million in gold for the Union side. Canyon City was the hub of the region's gold activity in the 1860s, claiming 10,000 miners in the town.

During the gold mining era Jacksonville became a major center of commerce. And, in the foothills of Cottage Grove, near the southern tip of the Williamette Valley, gold finds had to lie dormant until the early 20th-century because the technology didn't exist to mine the million-dollar deposits.

The stories about gold have had some odd results. In the 1930's Depression, poverty-weary citizens of Oregon actually tore up their backyards and indeed found thousands of dollars in gold from old claims.

Sumpter

The town of Sumpter is typical of the gold mining towns that emerged in eastern Oregon in the later part of the 1800s. Prior to gold finds, it was a collection of crude cabins, but after a narrow gauge railroad was built from Baker, the town boomed as a deep shaft mining town. It had 3,000 residents, three newspapers, six churches, 24 saloons, sidewalks and even electric lights. It even erected an opera house and in 1902 was called "Golden Sumpter". Today the only evidence of its good times is an 1899 gold vault. The old mining dredge is merely a tourist attraction.

The Yukon Gold Rush of 1897 brought Seattle out of its economic doldrums, even encouraging the then-mayor, W.D. Wood, to resign his post and head north. Seattle merchants sold millions of dollars to prospectors and dreamers – proving once again that you can usually make more out of someone else's dream, than from one of your own.

to his side once they were immersed in a "superior" culture. To ensure they did what they were told, Whitman often whipped them in the manner of punishing schoolchildren of that day.

Unfortunately for the Indians, Whitman they brought disease with their white culture and attitudes. During the outbreak of measles in 1847, Whitman gave the Cayuse Indians who lived around the Whitman Mission some medicine despite warnings that the Cayuse on occasion killed their medicine men – especially the unsuccessful ones. In a matter of weeks nearly half of the Cayuse tribe died –- 198 Indians, mostly children. The Indians, seeing that the white people still lived concluded that the Whitmans had kept the good medicine for themselves and their white children while feeding the Cayuse bad medicine.

The Cayuse War

On November 29, 1847, the Cayuse stormed the mission, murdered the Whitmans and 12 mission residents. Twelve others were kept as hostages. This touched off what was later called the Cayuse War. Federal troops were sent to quickly dispatch the Cayuse, only to find themselves embroiled in a two-year chase around the upper Columbia River.

Given a choice between extermination or surrender, the Cayuse leaders turned over five of their fellows who were the instigators of the killings. They were hanged in a public ceremony in Oregon City.

New Eden

The British didn't discourage easily, even in the face of missonaries and a variety of pioneers scouring the mountains and valleys. In 1839 The Hudson Bay Company formed a subsidiary called Puget Sound Agricultural Company to organize settlement in Oregon country. It was a kind of forerunner of today's public relations firm, formed with the intent of selling the idea of New Eden to England's own citizens and discourage Americans from migrating to the region. But British claim to Oregon country began to wane with the influx of American migrants. It was made worse by the discovery of gold in California in 1848.

The Oregon Trail

Traveling the paved routes across Oregon today gives little evidence of the hardship and trial facing the early pioneers who took the Oregon Trail. It was the artery for 350,000 emigrants who settled the American West by walking and driving their covered wagons 2000 miles to the West Coast in the mid-1800s in search of the fabled gold. More than 53,000 of those people settled in Oregon after traveling the route nicknamed "The Longest Graveyard".

Those making it to the Columbia River in 1846 had only one way into the Williamette Valley - they had to float their wagons, at great expense, down the Columbia from The Dalles onward. Many capsized on the way and died.

Jesse Applegate, a leader on the westward journey and later the leader of a provisional government in Oregon, described the conditions in this last portion of the route to the coast as "a scene of human misery".

Another pioneer, Sam Barlow, heard rumors of an Indian trail across the Cascade Mountains and decided to try a mountain crossing.

He established an overland route into the Williamette, but it was hazardous and impractical. What became known as the Barlow Trail, eventually became the most dangerous portion of the Oregon Trail.

Gold fever

The California gold find of 1848 took an estimated 66 per cent of Oregon's male population in the search for wealth. They returned later not only with gold, but with an awareness of what miners needed and what they would pay.

Wheat, which at one time was legal tender in an economically depressed Oregon, was suddenly worth money to Californians as food and Oregon began a boom time.

Then gold was found in several lo-

Lumber was a prime industry in early Seattle.

cations throughout Oregon and trade began throughout the region. A regular migratory route was established between Jacksonville, a major gold field in southern Oregon, and San Francisco, further opening up trade within the Pacific Northwest and California.

The British eventually got the message that its time was over in this part of the world and the Hudson Bay Company moved its headquarters north to Fort Victoria on Vancouver Island.

Between 1840 and 1860, 53,000 settlers moved into Oregon country to take advantage of free land offered by the federal government, through the Organic Act of 1843 and the Donation Land Law of 1850. Settlers could own 640 acres simply by marking the boundaries.

"Fifty-Four, forty or Fight"

By 1846, only Britain and the U.S. claimed ownership of Oregon country. Americans were clammering for land up to the latitude 54 degrees, 40 minutes and the phrase, "Fifty-Four Forty Or Fight", became part of American lexicon at the time, though the U.S. government never adopted the slogan or its meaning as policy.

Negotiators brought England and the United States to an agreement on a division at the 49th Parallel. That demarcation created a small peninsula that hangs below Canada, but unattached to the United States, known today as Point Roberts.

A regional territorial government was formed in 1848 and Abraham Lincoln, who would later become 16th President of the country, was selected as the governor. He refused the offer because his wife, Mary Todd Lincoln, felt Washington was a safer place.

Instead, the position was filled by Joseph Lane, a Southern racist in favor of slavery and who eventually opposed Lincoln in the election of 1860, running as vice-President on the Southern Democratic ticket with John Breckenridge.

Racial discrimination was an integral and unfortunate part of Pacific Northwest history. Blacks were prevented from living south of the Columbia River even though the law prevented slavery

A reminder of the logging days.

there.

Chinese labor

Young Chinese men, lured by work and gold, came to the region in the 1860s and acquired the name, "Coolies", a corruption of the Chinese term, *ku-li*, or "muscle strength".

The backlash against the cheap, Chinese labor was overwhelming. A bill was introduced in the Oregon legislature that barred Chinese from the territory in 1854, but it didn't pass. Instead a series of taxes placed on Chinese laborers cut deeply into their wages.

By the 1880, anti-Chinese sentiment reached a fever pitch and violent incidents brought death and injury to many. Full scale rioting was prevented, in large part, because of the stance taken by the publisher of Portland's newspaper, the *Portland Oregonian*. He sided with the Chinese who were in Oregon and convinced Oregonians that most of the jobs they had were unwanted by whites.

Oregon and Washington

Residents living north of the Columbia petitioned the U.S. congress for their own territory and were granted their wish on March 2, 1853 when President Millard Fillmore signed a bill creating Washington Territory. At that time, Oregon residents were thinking of statehood. They agreed to join the Union primarily because they thought statehood would give them power to prevent the influx of Chinese, blacks, or even Indians into their territory.

Oregon became the 33rd state on February 14, 1859. When Washington became a territory, its population was 4,000. By the time it became the 42nd state in 1889, its population was 173,000.

California and Oregon were already states when the first settlers north of the Columbia River came ashore at Alki Point, in 1851.

As much as they wanted to, they couldn't find much to name after themselves. Previous explorers, especially Captain George Vancouver, had honored his crew and members of the admiralty by naming just about every-

thing in sight when he explored Puget Sound in 1793.

The naming of Seattle

The first settlers did name the new settlement, Seattle, after a local Indian Chief, Sealth, who had befriended the whites. One of the original settlers to the region, Charles Terry of New York, wanted to call it New York, but fellow residents rejected his efforts.

The relationship with the native peoples was hardly congenial. Chief Sealth's goodwill towards the settlers did not envision being exiled to a reservation which whites wanted to do. After the Treaty of Port Elliott, in 1855, the Chief eloquently summed up his people's plight by saying, "The Indian's night promises to be dark. Not a single star of hope hovers above the horizon."

Unfortunately, he was right. In January, 1856, a band of Yakima and Klickitat Indians attempted to destroy the fledgling town. The settlers took refuge in a blockhouse as a naval vessel bombarded the attackers, forcing them away. That ended any chance of the culturally sophisticated native peoples of Puget Sound ever getting back their land.

As the Great Northern Railroad moved north and west, Seattle hoped to be the terminus. In 1873, the city offered the company $250,000 in cash and bonds, 7,500 town lots, 3,000 acres of undeveloped land, and half the water-

Ku Klux Klan

The Klan, as it came to be called, was originally organized by ex-Confederate troops and sympathizers at Pulaski, Tennessee in December, 1865, to oppose radical Reconstruction and maintain "white supremacy". But, as its influence spread, the organization became more than a Civil War-driven organization. Absorbing many smaller hate groups as it spread, its practices played upon fears and superstitions about blacks.

The Klan was just one of many such organizations of the time. Among them were The Men of Justice, The Pale Faces, The Constitutional Union Guards, the White Brotherhood, and the White Rose. The Ku Klux Klan was the best known and in time absorbed many of the other organizations.

General organization of local Klans was completed in April 1867 and General N.B. Forrest was made its leader. It was successful in keeping local blacks from voting and its influence began to be felt at the legislative level in many states, particularly – but not limited to – the American South. Its strange disguises, midnight rides, silent parades, mysterious language and commands, were found to be effective in generating fear. The riders muffled their horses' feet and covered themselves in long, flowing white robes, their faces covered by a white hood. With skulls at their saddlehorns, they posed as spirits coming back from Confederate battlefields.

The Force Bill

To fight the increasing power of the Klan, the U.S. Congress passed legislation, The Force Bill, imposing severe penalties to Southerners who obstructed Reconstruction. It was further strengthened by later amendments penalizing anyone stopping Blacks from voting and it placed Congressional elections under direct federal control.

On April 20, 1871 – inspired by activities of the Klan, the Act was further amended declaring acts of armed combinations and, rebellion illegal, and it empowered the President to suspend the privilege of *habeas corpus* in lawless areas.

But that didn't stop either the Klan activities or its growth. In the lower Southern states, the dominant Klan group was the *Knights Of The White Camellia*. A second, more militant group was formed in 1915 with its first meeting held in Stone Mountain, Georgia. In addition to its "white superiority" platform, it expanded its hit-list to embrace anti-Catholicism and anti-Semitism. They opposed all forces of "metropolitan morality" which were creating "modern Sodoms and Gemorrahs".

The white, rural Protestants, who for so long had ruled and had been unchallenged as rulers of the nation, were the Klan's members.

By the 1920s, the now-underground radical group was spreading wildly and controlled politics in many communities. Texas, Oklahoma, Indiana, Maine, and Oregon were particularly under its influence. It frequently resorted to lynching, beating, tarring and feathering in its para-legal activities. Leaving burning crosses in the yards of targeted victims or disliked politicians was a common practice.

At the peak of its powers, in the early 1920s, its membership was estimated at between 4 and 5 million. The Klan began to decline as state legislatures outlawed masks and secret societies. And the bad publicity it received for its violence frightened others away, with dwindling membership at about 30,000 in 1930. The Great Depression reduced paying membership during the next decade to virtually zero.

But, by then, it had done severe damage to people whose lives it had destroyed. Some Klan members were arrested, tried, and convicted for their crimes.

After the Second World War, an attempt at revival failed when state after state banned the society. Today it still exists in rudimentary form in regions of the South, but its activities are relatively unimportant.

front. In one of the worst business decisions of the time, the railroad rebuffed the offer and chose Tacoma instead. Nevertheless, the city's population continued to grow. It grew from 3,553 to 42,837 in the 1880s and the railroad finally linked the city to the east. In 1893, the population exploded, reaching 200,000 by 1914.

Fishing and lumber were the prime industries in early Seattle. The city grew up around what is now Pioneer Square cutting lumber and then sending it south to California.

The great fire of 1889

The great fire of 1889 culminated a decade of violence and economic ruin, when it burned to the ground virtually every building in the Seattle's core.

It was a blessing in disguise, ridding Seattle once and for all of rat infested, grungy living standards that by all descriptions were festering conditions for disease and poverty.

The mid-1880s were rough. The city had been hard hit by the national depression and the local fisherman, lumber workers, and miners, found themselves competing for jobs with out-of-work city employees and Chinese laborers who had been recently fired after the area's railroad was completed.

It wasn't a pretty time in Seattle's racial history as resentment that was always just below the surface, exploded in anti-Chinese violence in February, 1886. Five men were shot, Chinese homes and stores were demolished, and 200 Chinese were forced aboard a San Francisco-bound steamship. Eventually, 500 Chinese were eliminated from Seattle and it would be another decade before the Chinese community rebuilt itself to its former numbers.

The Yukon Gold Rush pulled Seattle out of its economic slump during the late 1890s and the city became a boomtown, a transportation gateway and chief supplier to the northward bound prospectors.

In an twist of irony, Seattle's equipment suppliers made more money from the gold rush than most prospectors. By the time the gold seekers reached Alaska and the Canadian Klondike, land claims had already been made and the gold was tied up. The local citizens celebrated their own good fortune by staging the Alaska-Yukon-Pacific Exhibition in 1909. Some of the structures built for that fair still exist on the University of Washington campus.

Seattle became the jumping-off point for later prospectors. And by the time the northern gold rushes had lost their vitality, Seattle was beginning to challenge Portland as the region's biggest metropolis.

Population boom

Portland, though a long time settlement in the region, didn't really grow until railroad and shipping tycoon, Henry Villard established an immigration office in Portland. He wanted to encourage Europeans to immigrate once Oregon became a state.

He flooded Europe with propaganda about the region and soon the continent was swimming in promotional literature. His plan was to increase population in order to protect his investments. The more people in the region, the more opportunities for economic development.

In 1877, 18,000 people arrived in Oregon and there were stories of promoters depopulating whole Russian villages. The region's population increased by almost 500,000 in the 1880s.

Portland had been the Pacific Northwest's largest and most important center and they didn't like Seattle draining off their business. So they staged the 1905 World's Fair, supposedly to celebrate the centenary of Lewis' and Clark's discovery of the area. The fair and its publicity worked, with population increasing to 270,000 by 1910 and with the fair investors making a 21% profit on their investment.

Seattle countered with its own fair in 1909 and a year later its population for the first time exceeded Portland's by 30,000. Together, the fairs from the two cities put the Pacific Northwest on the map.

Discrimination

The Ku Klux Klan reacted violently to the increase in Oregon's black population, a growth resulting from Portland's emergence as a railroad center in the late 1880s. But though the Klan was initially successful and created enormous cultural pain, it eventually collapsed, the victim of internal greed and dissension.

Some Klan members wanted to recall Governor Walter Pierce –– whom the Klan had backed as a candidate in 1922 – for not fulfilling the wishes of the organization. Others opposed the recall. The resulting conflict within the Klan tore it apart and it disintegrated in the early 1920s.

Trade unions had become a political force by 1919 and Seattle became the site of America's first general strike. Thousands of "Wobblies" walked off their jobs on February 6, causing newspapers to call it a revolution. But the strike – one that had many causes – lasted only four days and workers returned to work on Lincoln's birthday. The relationship between unions and management would never be the same.

The Great Depression hit the Pacific Northwest hard, as it did the entire nation. Growth was at a standstill until the Second World War. Again, however, the ugly head of racism arose and persons of Japanese ancestry, American or foreign, were removed inland and their property confiscated.

The move seemed justified when, in June 1942, a Japanese submarine lobbed a 5.5 inch (14 cm) shell in the general direction of Fort Stevens, a Civil War installation near the mouth of the Columbia River. It left Oregon with the distinction of being the only state attacked during the war.

Government here has always been a mix of conservative and radical, with huge swings in social and legislative action from one side to the other. It had in past history, on one hand, instituted some of the most outrageous racial legislation in the West and yet has also been forward looking in many of its social environmental legislation.

The bad old days of official racial disharmony are long past, a victim of American constitutional rulings and of changing attitudes in a world drawn closer by technology and political circumstance.

This land was once one of political extremes, much like its topographical makeup. But nothing any longer is so predictable.

Oregon used to be Republican country, conservative in attitudes and right-wing in its politics. Yet, in the last election it last elected a Demo-

Cows grazing against the backdrop of Mount Rainier.

Government & Economy

Farmer's market in Seattle.

crat as Governor and Lt. Governor. And Washington saw nothing unusual in electing a Democrat as Governor and a Republican Lt. Governor as they did in 1992.

Depression and discrimination

Political history in Washington and Oregon was never smooth. The mid-1880s were especially rough for Seattle. The city had been hard hit by the national depression and the local fisherman, lumber workers, and miners found themselves competing for jobs with out-of-work city employees and Chinese laborers who had become jobless after completing the area's railroad. It wasn't a pretty time in Seattle's racial history as resentment that was always just below the surface exploded in the wake of anti-Chinese violence in February, 1886.

Both Oregon and Washington had tried to rid the Chinese from their shores through a variety of official and unofficial means. At the least, an anti-Chinese reaction by the population was simply ignored by the government.

In November of 1885, anti-Chinese forces in Tacoma marched in the rain to rouse resident Chinese from their homes and herded them onto trains headed for Portland. And a year later, the Washington Legislature passed a law prohibiting Chinese from owning property in the state.

The most overt action came in early 1886 when Seattle residents marched through the town, gathered whatever Chinese they could find and escorted them to the docks. There these people were told that to avoid trouble they should simply leave aboard a ship departing for San Francisco.

The journey was stopped after a court order banned the expulsion. But, that did not end matters. Chinese men were shot, Chinese homes and stores were demolished. Militiamen had to be called in to restore order.

Reforms

Still, in a strange balance of actions and philosophy, Oregon also blazed trails in reform. The Oregon system of initiatives and referendum was formulated in the 1890s and became part of the state's political life in the early part of the 1900s. Oregon also extended suffrage to women in 1912 and in 1921 enacted a compulsory education law.

The 1920s also ushered in large scale union activity that was more tranquil and less violent than elsewhere in the nation.

New Deal programs of the 1930s produced large scale road, dam, and infrastructure development.

And later, Oregon would make certain some of its most prime property would always be in public hands by declaring the entire ocean front to be public property.

The "Wobblies"

With its embracing of radicalism in many forms, it comes as no surprise that the Pacific Northwest was the perfect breeding ground of the "Wobblies".

The Revolutionary Industrial Workers Of the World (I.W.W.) and known as the Wobblies, was organized in Chicago in 1905 by delegates from 45 labor organizations including the Western Federation of Mines.

The objective was to unite in one body all skilled and unskilled workers for the purpose of overthrowing capitalists and rebuilding society on a socialist basis. Its methods were simple – direct action, propaganda, boycott, and the strike. It was, however, opposed to sabotage, arbitration or collective bargaining and to political intervention and affiliation.

The union was especially strong in the lumber camps of the northwest, among dock workers in port cities, and in textile and mining areas.

At the time of the First World War, the Wobblies were anti-militaristic and its members were accused of avoiding the military draft, of fomenting German-paid strikes, thereby crippling wartime production. Many of its leaders were thrown into jail and to this loss was added the large number of leaders who joined the Communist Party after 1917. Infiltrated by federal agents, the union was under constant attack. Members were arrested for distributing anti-war

Legislative Buildings on Capitol Way

The landscaped 55 acres of greenery, the grand buildings that make up the complex, and the many manicured gardens that are strategically located, make Olympia's **Capitol Campus** one of the nation's most attractive legislative centers. Located between 11th and 14th Avenues off Capitol Way, the setting includes an arboretum, a sunken rose garden, and large clusters of rhododendrons. These plants plus cherry trees brighten the grounds with their blossoms in March/April. There's a replica of Copenhagen's Tivoli Gardens fountain, and a cluster of buildings dating to the early 1900s.

Work on the capitol complex actually began in 1893, but the 1890s depression and the political pressures put on the governor stopped the project. It wasn't begun until 1911 when the New York architects Wilder & White took over the project.

The architectural style combined Classic Revival buildings and handsome landscaping. Later additions in the 1920s, 1930s, and 1950s reflect the styles in fashion during those times. The Doric colonnades of the Legislative Building are surmounted by a 287-foot dome encircled by a Corinthian colonnade.

When it was completed in 1928, the dome was the fourth largest in the world. The opulent interior boasts marble, parquet floors, chandeliers by Tiffany & Company, and elegant furnishings. Guided tours of the building are available when the legislature is in session and by appointment.

Buildings of note

Just opposite the Legislative Buildings rises the pillared **Temple of Justice**, seat of the state's **Supreme Court**; and to the west is is the red-brick **Governor's Mansion**, the oldest building on the campus dating to 1908. It has been recently restored

The **Washington State Library** houses a collection of murals, mosaics, paintings and sculptures by Northwest artists, the most prominent of whom are Mark Tobey and Kenneth Callahan.

One of the most popular tourist stops is the **State Greenhouse**, which provides all of the floral arrangements and greenery for the whole capitol complex. The **State Capitol Museum**, housed in a 1920 California-style stucco mansion and just a short walk away from the campus, contains exhibits on native American culture.

North of the state capitol is a group of 19th-century houses and buildings. The **Headquarters of the Board of Education** was formerly the Thurston County Courthouse and an early state capitol. It was designed in Romanesque Revival style by W.A. Ritchie in 1891-92. The **William G. White House** is a Queen Anne villa built in 1893; and the **Bigelow House** is a 14-room Gothic Revival mansion built in 1854 for Judge Daniel Bigelow and has been occupied continuously by the family ever since.

---

literature and some members were even deported.

In a major clash between lumber company representatives in Everett, Washington in 1917, seven members were killed and in another, 31 were injured. Another clash was expected and indeed did come when the Emergency Fleet Corporation in Washington, D.C. refused to settle a threatened shipyard strike in 1919. The corporation warned that it would cut off its supply of steel to shipyards if employers agreed to labor demands. That confrontation led to the general strike of 1919 and to the eventual unionization of many of Seattle industries.

Mass immigration

With the coming of the Second World

Apples, an important cash-crop.

War, the Pacific Northwest began to achieve its ambition of becoming an economic powerhouse. With industrialization, to the dismay of some, came mass immigration. Portland was with 100,000 immigrants, placing strains on its housing and its desire to absorb the many blacks that were part of it.

Japanese who had come into the region made their homes in the Portland and Puget Sound areas. Like the Chinese before them, they were met by many of the anti-foreign property owner laws passed by Washington in 1921 and 1923. After the evacuation of the Japanese and the confiscation of their property, many Northwesterners were openly pleased. Washington and Oregon were designated a military area in which Japanese could be confined and stockades were built at The Dalles, Oregon and at other locations.

Certainly, the prevailing political trend in the Pacific Northwest has been conservative both among the farmers and in business. Yet, in the mid-20th century onwards there was a significant break in what was once considered consistent Republican strength.

In 1932 and 1936, President Franklin Roosevelt carried Oregon. Since then, there has been a regular floating of political thought — left and right – depending on the issues. The labor clashes of the I.W.W. labeled Washington a radical state and it has never completely shaken the term, regardless of its incorrectness.

A special place

However politicians on both side of the spectrum agree — that their is a special place, a green place whose major assets are its gifts of nature. When it could act to restore man-made efforts, they have done so admirably.

The rehabilitation of Seattle and Portland's old towns and the subsequent development of their respective downtown cores have added to the magnetism of the region. Both cities take pride in their relationship to the outdoors, in fact revelling in the opportunities for physical activity.

They are both, in fact, physical cities demanding from its citizens that they adhere to the stated and unstated rules of environmental conduct. It's a conduct that had its manifestation in the 1960s and 1970s as the cities of the polluted East were overwhelmed by anti-Vietnam War protests and by overdevelopment. That's when the rest of the nation looked towards the Pacific Northwest as a place of purity, of fragile and pristine beauty.

Conservation and environmentalism

Over the years, governments on both sides of the Columbia River have enacted a variety of legislation protecting the environment. And both have had to bend with the will of the populations demanding protection of the environment and wildlife. Oregon passed the first bottle bill in the United States in 1971, making demands on citizens to recycle the containers.

The federal government has created three National Parks in Washington and one in Oregon. But each state has created a number of its own pro-

Cattle ranch in Oregon.

tected areas and have placed pressure on the federal government to create National Monuments.

Still, the major cities suffer from the same problems faced by cities the world over – pollution, population pressures, traffic, crime, and infrastructure deterioration. The pressure on politicians to maintain the kind of relaxed and safe environment that drew people to the Pacific Northwest in the first place is enormous. Whether they can indeed meet the challenge is still uncertain. In the Puget Sound area, especially, the

population pressures are profound. Portland, with about 25 percent of the Puget
Sound population has fewer problems
to resolve.

Regardless, politicians know that
they have in their care, a special place.
Even with its problems, Seattle is one of
the most livable places in America offering a comfortable mix of cultural sophistication and natural ruggedness.
Portland remains as close to nature as a
city can be with its boundaries of forest,
river, and mountains.

And the region's smaller cities –
Spokane, Bellingham, and
Eugene, among others
– are human preserves
seemingly cut from the
surrounded terrain, sit-
ting like temporary in-
truders in an otherwise
unadorned setting.

Economy

It was no surprise when *For-
tune* rated Seattle the fourth best city in
America for educated workers in its November, 1993 issue. It was ranked four
slots higher than San Jose, even though
the Silicon Valley is still the epicenter for
information technology.

With 152 research centers; 3,424
patents issued in 1988-92; 29.5 percent
of its 25 years-of-age or older population with a B.A. or higher; and ranking
second in the nation in having innovative firms, Seattle was an easy pick for

the magazine's selection committee.

Technological giants

Boeing is still an imposing corporate
figure in the Pacific Northwest's varied
economy. But it is not alone in developing innovative and advanced technology. Microsoft Inc. is commanding a
growing share of the high-tech spot-
light.

The proximity of two of the nation's
technological giants may be one reason
why the Puget Sound region is considered as having one of the largest con-
centrations of techthusiasts in the
United States.

Techthusiasts are found
in the greatest numbers
where there are universities
and hi-tech companies.
They are three times
more likely than the av-
erage American to buy
new electronic/video
equipment. They also
spend more on new foods, household
appliances, vacations, and recreational
sports. Their appetite for new technology makes them a natural target for
interactive television and for virtual reality. Yes, that's the face of the new
Pacific Northwest economy.

Its original assets and chief businesses — mining, fishing, and lumber –
are in decline though they still provide
a good deal of corporate income and
jobs.

Lumbering, a substantial employer in Oregon's manufacturing sector.

Lumber industry

Still, resource companies have a powerful impact on the region's economy. Washington has five *Fortune* 500 companies of which two are high-tech or manufacturing and three are resource based.

Oregon's five *Fortune* 500 firms share a similar mix. The two states, plus Idaho, supply about 60 per cent of America's total lumber. Oregon is the leader and has been since 1938 and Washington is generally the third or fourth largest producer depending on the year.

Douglas fir, western hemlock, and western cedar are some of the commercially important trees native to the west side of the Cascades.

In 1900, Frederick Weyerhaeuser bought 900,000 acres of prime forest land from the Northern Pacific Railroad for $6 an acre, later increasing his holdings to more than two million acres by 1913. With more than six million acres today, Weyerhaeuser Corp. is now the largest lumber company in the United States.

But, Weyerhaeuser and other companies are beginning to prepare for what's being called "the ripple-down effect" as reductions in allowable forest cuts and exports are implemented over the next decades.

It's expected that emphasis will change to manufacturing of secondary wood products such as furniture parts.

Fishing fleet anchored in Newport.

Nature's harvests

Fishing is important to both states with traditional harvests of salmon and bottom fish continuing even in light of declining stock.

And agriculture is still crucial to the region's well being. Washington's agriculture produces more than $3 billion annually, over 80 percent of which is produced on the "dry side", east of the Cascade mountains. The biggest money crops are wheat, hay, and potatoes followed by livestock, apples, pears, cherries, grapes and other fruits and vegetables. One of the fastest growing crop industries is grapes.

Washington has more than 60 wineries, Oregon has another 85 smaller ones. Oregon produces more than 10 percent of the nation's greenhouse and nursery stock and cattle is its largest argicultural sector.

Micro-breweries

While the wine industry has been around a long time – the first Oregon vineyards were in existence 100 years ago – a new and surprising mini-industry is beer. In fact, there's no better place outside of Germany to experience beer from small breweries.

Prior to 1982, when the first kegs of beer rolled out of the Red Hook Brewery in Seattle, no micro-brew had been pro-

The Space Needle

The 605 ft. (184 m) tall Space Needle is both a symbol and a landmark. It demands attention, not just to itself, but to a city that has transformed itself from basic Northwest industries to a leading edge, high-tech force. Located at the Seattle Center, it opened April 21, 1962 as the centerpiece of the Seattle World's Fair and now has 1.2 million visitors annually.

New economic cornerstone

The theme of the fair was Century 21 and in keeping with that original theme the Needle, with its view of Mount Rainier 75 miles (121 km) away, has come to symbolize Seattle's powerful aerospace and high-tech economy. In a real sense, the fair and the Space Needle heralded the end of the image America held of the Pacific Northwest as merely a provider of wood, fish, and natural resources. It announced that the area was the future cornerstone of a new economy.

Originally constructed for a cost of $4.5 million, the privately owned structure is basically an elegant tripod with a pod atop it. Weighing 3,700 tons with 146,000 pounds (66,225 kg) of steel weld, it sits on a foundation that is 30 ft. (9.1 m) deep and which contains 2,800 yards (467 truckloads) of concrete and 250 tons of reinforcing steel.

It features an observation deck, two revolving restaurants at the 500 ft. (152 m) level (Space Needle Restaurant and The Emerald Suite), four retail gift shops and banquet facilities on the Skyline level at 100 ft. (30.5 m) which accommodates up to 350 people.

As tourist traps go, this is one of the better ones you'll encounter. There are no hucksters competing for your buck and at the end you feel you've had something for your money. It takes 43 seconds aboard any of the three glass enclosed, 25 passenger capacity, elevators to reach the top level. From there — at the 518 ft. (158 m) level — you find a 360° view of the surrounding scenery including the Olympic and Cascade mountain ranges, Mount Rainier, downtown Seattle, Lake Union, and Puget Sound.

Inside the observation deck is an exhibit by Eastman Kodak designed to orientate visitors to more than 60 things to see and do in Greater Seattle. On the same level is the Top Of The Needle Lounge and two gift shops. Eighteen feet (5.5 m) below the observation deck is the revolving restaurant level - turning on a 14 foot-wide turntable, driven by a one horsepower motor, that makes one complete revolution each hour.

The Space Needle Restaurant is a family oriented facility that offers food in an informal setting while the Emerald Suite, opened in 1982, offers more formal, elegant dining. Both feature Northwest cuisine, emphasizing fresh seafood and produce from the Pike Street Market and lamb from Ellensburg in Eastern Washington. At ground level are two shops: Needle 'n Threads features a variety of clothing, and Northwest at the Needle, sells gifts and crafts of the Northwest.

Memorable moments

The structure has had its share of positive and negative, light and heavy moments. The heaviest visitor to the Needle was the King of Tonga who weighed in at 400 pounds (181.4 kg) and had to have a special chair carried up the service elevator.

In the summer of 1974 a "streaker" circled the Needle in a private plane. Restaurant patrons applauded his arm-flapping and leg-waving as he appeared in the plane's open door. There have also been numerous marriages, one birth, three suicides, and a jump by two parachuters in 1975.

And, if the great Pacific Northwest earthquake that everyone is worried about ever does arrive (it has been anticipated for several centuries) the Space Needle just might be the place to be. Although built to withstand a wind velocity of 150 mph (241 kph), the Space Needle closed in 1962 when wind gusts of 83 mph (133.5 kph) were recorded and again in 1973 during a 75 mph (120.6 kph) wind. But, it has withstood earthquakes without damage including the 1965 tremor measuring 6.5 on the Richter scale.

Fishing Industry

While fishing is one of the Pacific Northwest's oldest industries, it has, in recent years, been as much a gamble as rolling the dice in Las Vegas. In Washington state alone, fishing contributes more than $1.5 billion each year to the economy. Commercial fishermen are also the most productive, harvesting more than 2.3 billion pounds of fish and seafood annually, more than half the total U.S. edible catch.

The Pacific Northwest salmon fishery alone now harvests 250,000 pounds of salmon annually, worth between $100-$150 million.

In Oregon, commercial salmon fishing was late in developing, compared to Washington. While native peoples exploited migrating salmon with the seasons, the early white pioneers were preoccupied by lumber, mining, and agriculture. Canning technology first perfected in Alaska eventually made its way down to Oregon in the 1860s. In the modern era, Oregon's salmon fisheries have grown into a megabusiness.

Innovative approaches

Initially, bad planning and poor ecological awareness meant depleted salmon runs in the 1980s. The damming of major rivers like the Columbia interrupted migration; and Asian drift netting is a major contributor to salmon depletion.

Northwest fishermen claim that the miles-long netting rakes off millions of pounds of baby salmon annually that would normally have returned to their home rivers. The salmon shortfall has led to a more innovative approach to the industry. To ensure adequate supplies of the commercially valuable Chinook, coho, sockeye, chum, and pink salmon, Oregon and Washington have developed state fish hatcheries with Washington alone having 26, which annually produce 150 million salmon and contribute to half of the yearly commercial catch.

New and innovative processing methods are being tapped. For example, processors are preparing a new product called *surimi*, a fish protein paste used to make artificial crab, scallop, and shrimp products.

Population demands

Fish such as dogfish, pollock, hake, rockfish, and other flatfish once overlooked by Americans are being harvested to meet population demands. Health conscious consumers have increased per-capita consumption of seafood by 40 percent since 1967. A caviar industry has developed as a supplement to ocean fishing, derived from sturgeon in the Columbia River.

In the early 1980s, Alaskan waters were dominated by foreign fleets and joint-venture boats. But the tide has indeed turned with

duced in America since Prohibition. There are more micro-breweries per capita in Portland and Seattle than in any other city. Thirty of the 150 registered micro-breweries in the country are within 400 miles (643 km) of Portland.

Coming of the railroads

It was also in the 1880s with the coming of the railroads that the Pacific North-west was transformed from a series of local industries to nation-wide suppliers. Portland became a railroad and steamboat hub, maintaining the city as the region's most important city until the turn of the century.

It was with the coming of the railroad in the late 1800s that the Pacific Northwest – especially the Tacoma/ Seattle region –- began to realize its economic power. Seattle was transformed forever in 1916 when William

American factory trawlers harvesting in excess of 350,000 tons of bottomfish.

Salmon fishing, thought to be a dead industry a decade ago, has made a dramatic comeback with Puget Sound's seine fleet yearly increasing its catch. Washington fishermen bring home an estimated 92% of all salmon, bottomfish and shellfish harvested in Alaskan waters. Eighty-five per cent of the bottomfish caught by U.S. fishermen are caught by the massive factory trawlers that moor at Seattle's Fishermen's Terminal.

But, commercial fishing is not the only money maker of the Pacific Northwest's fishing activities. Winter steelhead, Dolly Varden, rainbow trout, eastern brook trout, walleye, sturgeon, catfish, perch, and crappie all can be caught in interior waterways and along the flanks of the Cascade range.

The rivers that drain into Puget Sound – particularly the Nootsack, Skagit, Skykomish, and Snohomish — have steelhead and sea-run cutthroat trout. The other Cascade rivers drain into the Columbia River and all have good trout, walleye, and steelhead fishing. In Oregon, some of the finest salmon fishing ports are at Coos Bay, Depoe Bay, Brookings, Astoria, and Florence among others. South of Florence, the large Dunes lakes provide some of the best bass fishing in the state. Stiped bass are found in the south fork of the Coos River.

Boeing and his friend, Clyde Esterveld launched their first airplane on Lake Union, a float plane designed to deliver mail to Canada.

Flight into the future

World War I had convinced Seattle's business people that shipbuilding was the wave of the future. Boeing, however, had other ideas and while he had made his fortune through timber, he was convinced the future had wings.

As it turned out, Boeing was correct. The end of World War I left the region with more than 30,000 people unemployed with no prospects in sight. But, it did produce the first large high-tech employment pool, establishing the region as a legitimate center of tecnological manufacturing.

And during the war, the area became the center of union activity which, despite the series of confrontations between labor and management during the mid-1910s, established a liberal and progressive political attitude.

With World War II came Seattle's second big boom and the resulting consolidation of its aviation industry. The Korean, Vietnam, and Cold Wars plus the passenger jet era made everyone think the prosperity was endless. But that ended in 1970 when, almost overnight, the industry fell flat and Boeing was required to lay off two-thirds of its employees.

Meanwhile, World War II also produced a change in the regional economy with demands for war machinery producing off-shoot development. So, between the mid-1940s through the 1950s, more than 600 electro-chemical and electro-metallurgy industries sprang up in and around Portland.

Again, with the end of a world war, Seattle and the Pacific Northwest were thrown into a depression. But the Korean War and the Cold War with its demands for B-47 and B-52 bombers,

The pick of the best.

plus civilian needs for the Boeing 707 commercial liner, brought an end to the downturn.

By 1960, the Seattle regional population was almost one million and Boeing employed one of every 10 persons. However, the difficulty in being a one-industry region, as the Boeing dependent Puget Sound area was, has been witnessed in a series of economic recessions notably in 1969-70 when the company reduced its work force by nearly two-thirds.

The impact of the end of the cold war on the war-industry machine is still unknown. Major naval facilities in Everett and in other Puget Sound locations have been pinpointed for eventual closure; and Boeing is becoming more dependent on the commercial airline industry for its long-term orders.

After cancellations of the SST supersonic aircraft and military aircraft, Boeing diversified, creating subdivisions in a wide range of aircraft types including helicopters and hydrofoils. The employment force stabilized at around 70,000 and the company is still the world's leader — though under pressure from Europe's Airbus group — in commercial aircraft production, supplying 180 airlines worldwide.

Economic catalyst

But, more than any other single moment in the Pacific Northwest's history,

The world-famous Wescott Bay oyster farm in the San Juan Islands.

it was the 1962 Seattle World's Fair that defined the modern economy. In a sense it was a continuation of a tradition in the region as it was fairs at the end of the 19th and beginning of the 20th centuries that were the catalysts for previous economic gains. And the most obvious remnants of the fair are located at the 74-acre Seattle Center with its distinctive Space Needle, the five building Pacific Science Center, the Opera House, and the Bagley Wright Theater.

Launching the way to Seattle becoming a major destination city, the fair energized and focused the population and politicians into being — at least for that short 6-month period – the best they could be.

Afterwards, it also generated a need to continue that path and citizens demanded and produced better restaurants and hotels, better lifestyles, better cultural institutions, and better visitor facilities.

Thus, the tourism industry in Seattle had a focus and was ready when the rest of the world made its leisure demands on it. The infrastructure had been established through natural growth and by the luck of ecological fate. Both Oregon and Washington have large, efficient, and compatible economic development departments for tourism devoted to ensuring an ongoing influx of tourists and money. Tourism is Oregon's third biggest industry, generating $3 billion annually and ranking behind forestry and agriculture.

Carriage of goods by barge along the Columbia River.

Boeing Aircraft

Times are changing even for a company as large and dominating as Boeing. And for Seattle – whose economic life depends on Boeing – any changes are suspect. The company that prides itself on being an invisible giant, has found itself in recent years having strong competition in a world that it has generally dominated.

Economic giant

Boeing is a gigantic operation, generating sales of around $31 billion and profits of $2 billion. Its exports account for more than 50 % of the total sales and its business backlog is around $90 though that figure changes fairly often as orders are filled. While it employs around 90,000 in the Puget Sound area, its worldwide figure is 150,000. It owns or leases more than 20 million sq. ft. of office space and its Seattle area annual payroll is $5 billion. Overall one in every four jobs in the Seattle area depends on Boeing. The city survives on its fortunes.

You won't find a Boeing office tower in downtown Seattle. In fact, the company's executive offices are housed in a drab looking, three-story building in an industrial region south of the city. As in most of Seattle's properties, access is limited to employees and scheduled visitors. As you drive from Seattle southward on I-5, you'll pass an airfield with new jets lined up alongside. It's Boeing Field where the company prepares its aircraft for delivery to clients. The company headquarters is on the other side, out of view.

In Everett, where the company manufac-tures the 747-400 jumbo, the 767, and the new 777 series, tours are offered daily. It's the only Boeing site that is open to the public.

World's largest building

The 747 is built in the world's largest building, with the hangars measuring 200 million cubic ft. (5.66 million cu. m.). Instead of a beehive of activity, however, visitors find no more than 700 workers at a time leisurely assembling parts that were manufactured elsewhere.

Seattle discovered in 1970-71 how much an economic downturn could change it. In less than two years, Boeing shrank its work-force from 105,000 to 39,000. Thousands of families picked up and moved out. And the city suffered. A billboard south of town asked the last person to leave to turn out the lights.

The battle to keep the company above the waterline is an ongoing one. A recent order from Southwest Airlines for the purchase of 63 Boeing 737-X twinjets for delivery between 1997-2001 didn't increase the work force, though it meant fewer layoffs.

In 1993, Boeing cut commercial aircraft production by 35 % and laid off thousands of workers because of the world-wide industry slump and defense cutbacks. When the new purchase order was announced, in late November, Boeing had not had a new order for its giant 747-400 aircraft in more than a year.

With the turmoil in the commercial airline industry, Boeing has been increasingly looking overseas for continued sales growth. Closer ties

Shift in economic focus

Change in economic focus is taking place throughout the region. Today, the high-tech industry is the second largest employer in Oregon's manufacturing sector - behind wood products - and is expanding into Washington State.

In the Seattle region, high-tech is moving throughout the suburbs, an industry that includes Microsoft, the computer software company that has made its founder, Bill Gates, one of America's richest men.

But not all high-tech has been an unqualified success. The nuclear power industry, which came on line in the

between the United States and other members of the Asia-Pacific Economic Co-operation group (APEC) offer the chance to redefine the giant corporation's future goals.

Presence in the Far East

The aerospace promethean already has a large presence in the Far East. Japanese airlines operate the world's largest fleet of 747 jumbo jets, and Malaysia Airlines has the largest fleet of 737s outside the United States.

A significant milestone was reached in 1993 when Singapore Airlines took possession of the 1,000th Boeing 747 jumbo.

But that market is changing. As the Asian economies increase dramatically, transworld flights (Singapore to London) are being replaced by regional flights (Singapore-Beijing). That means a cutback from the giant jumbos to something smaller. Boeing forecasts that the fastest growth in air freight between now and 2005 will be flights between the APEC partners. It is putting a lot of its future into the success of the Boeing 777 long-range twinjet. That would place it in a niche between the 747 and 767 and therefore in direct competition with Airbus's new four-engined A-340.

As trade and business with the APEC nations increases, it might also mean a less reliance on Puget Sound workers. Parts for the 737, for example, are already being produced in China. Boeing executives admit there will be more pressure in the future to build parts overseas for future orders.

1960s-70s, has been an acknowledged disappointment.

The large Hanford nuclear power site north of Tri-Cities, was completed in 1981 with a huge budget overrun and public outrage over power fee hikes. Some of the reactors have not been completed and the industry appears to be on hold.

Export Industry

Trade with the Pacific Rim nations of Japan, Korea, China, Australia, and others have created a new, emerging export industry. With the Asian economies thriving and the region having one-half of the world's population, it's an industry whose time has obviously arrived. It means that one of every 6.5 manufacturing positions in Washington is now dependent upon the business of exporting. Seattle is the nearest port and airport to the Orient. Other kinds of shipping have also created a boom in smaller ports like Everett, Port Angeles, Olympia, and Bellingham, from where bulk and manufactured goods are shipped throughout the Pacific Rim.

Telecommunications equipment, clothes, cars and trucks are the primary imports arriving from Taiwan, Canada, Japan, and Hong Kong. Oil tankers arrive in Port Angeles from Alaska to supply the oil refineries in Anacortes and Ferndale. Both Tacoma and Seattle are increasing their already substantial containerized shipping facilities. Oregon's booming food processing and packaging industries are continuing to thrive and there seems no let up in the future.

High tech and tourism owe their reputation to being in the right place at the right time. The region's utility rates are perfect for chip manufacture. With low production costs and high quality products attracting the computer chip industry.

Geologically, the Pacific Northwest is a young land, created over a period of about 200 million years.

We know that the ocean once lapped at the shores of land near to what is now Idaho. Eventually, continental movement created the Klamath Mountains, which stood as a huge island in the Pacific Ocean for millions of years. Volcanic eruption began to develop the outer edge of the coast line.

It was 35 million years ago that the ocean floor sank, driving up a series of volcanoes, the predecessors of today's Cascade Range. The resulting inland sea was slowly filled in by sediments.

Molten basalt filled in hundreds of square miles, creating land, and two million years ago, volcanic eruptions reached their peak with the formation of the Northwest's long chain of fire moun-

The compelling beauty of Crater Lake.

Geography & Climate

51

Untamed fury of Cape Kiwanda, Oregon.

tains that are part of the Pacific Rim's Ring of Fire.

Rivers cut through the geographical mix with the Snake River, on the eastern edge of Oregon, digging a deep path through relatively loose and new land formations. The Columbia etched its way through what we now call the Columbia Gorge.

It's the rain, really, that determines everything. Its presence or its absence determines the kind of animal and plant life that each geographical region would contain.

Land of multiple personalities

The Pacific Northwest is best understood as a series of five micro-climates, and valleys separated by mountains. Moving west to east, each of these valleys record progressively lower rainfall levels until you eventually encounter a desert on the eastern portion of the region which ranges all the way from Canada to Nevada.

What you have is a land with multiple personalities. But it's the rain, really, that determines everything. Those who expect to see only the great evergreens that adorn the 600-mile-long (966-km) Cascade range and are found on their western side are surprised when they drive through the arid, treeless brown hills of eastern Washington and through the lava encrusted desert country east of Bend, Oregon.

There, instead of of lush and wet terrain, they find what often appears to be a lifeless land marked by flora that often barely manages to cling to life. Desert replaces towering mountains and hard lava replaces soft, sand beaches.

Much smaller than the Cascades is Washington's Olympic Range in the northwest corner of the state. Storms created over the Pacific annually dump more than 100 inches (254 cm) of rain in the area which in turn is responsible for the vast rain forests of the peninsula, receiving up to 184 inches (467 cm). But even here, where the rain crashes in from the Pacific, nothing is as it seems. Oddly, on the eastern slope of the range, the communities of Sequim and Port Angeles get only between 12-20 inches (30-76 cm) annually.

Typically west coast weather is mild and wet in the winter, warm and dry in the summer with predictable weather patterns throughout the year.

Columbia River Gorge

The Columbia Gorge, where the Columbia River carved its way into the Northwest.

to her death to ease her broken heart. Granted, that a jump of that magnitude would make her forget her lost love, it's claimed her face can still be seen in the mist of the falls. A lovely old stone lodge houses a naturalist's center.

Beacon Rock, a towering 800 foot (244 m) sheer-walled monolith, on the north side of the river, is the largest formation of its kind in the United States.

The 3,000 foot (914 m) deep, 75 mile (121 km) long Columbia River Gorge is the natural border between much of central Washington and Oregon. Beginning just east of Portland, Oregon's only natural scenic area is the result of fiery volcanoes, lava flows, and Ice Age flooding.

It is the only sea level passage through the Cascade Mountain Range. First navigated by the Lewis and Clark Expedition in 1804-5, the Columbia River surges through high desert, snow-capped mountains, a series of prosperous communities, and fertile farmlands on its Pacific Ocean journey.

Roads follow the gorge on both sides of the border, Highway 14 on the Washington side and Route 84 on the Oregon periphery. These roads allows easy access to each side of the gorge.

From a breathy whisper to a thundering roar, waterfalls on the Oregon side with names like Horsetail Falls and Bridal Veil, grace rugged basaltic cliffs. Multnomah Falls, at 620 feet (189 m), is the second highest waterfall in the United States.

A steep and winding trail through the misty woods leads to the top of Multnomah Falls where it is said that an Indian Princess jumped

Windsurfer's paradise

The Columbia River is a favorite for windsurfers, generating raging winds of 35 mph. (56 kph). Seven months of the year, sailboards and their determined riders ricochet across the water on the tumbling currents that provide the kind of ride surfers love.

From Crown Point, on the Oregon side, you have a 30-mile vista of the gorge with a visitors center and gift shop housed in Vista House.

Forty-four miles (71 km) from Portland, off Route 84, is the Bonneville Dam, completed in 1939 and the first major hydroelectic project on the Columbia River. Named after 19th century explorer, Captain Benjamin de Bonneville, the dam has an elaborate series of ladders to allow migrating salmon to go upriver.

Four miles (6.5 km) east are the Cascade

The stories you've probably heard about rainfall are sometimes true. In January, 1935, Washington's Quinsalt Ranger Station recorded 35 inches (89 cm) of rain in a three-day period.

There is, of course, a purpose; the

Locks, built in 1896 to tame the treacherous rapids that were crossed, often at great peril, by early immigrants to Oregon. Now unused, the locks are commemorated in the Cascade Locks Museum in the town of Cascade Locks.

If you follow the old Scenic Gorge Highway (Rte. 30) at Troutdale, you'll climb past majestic waterfalls, monsterous cliffs, and magnificent views. The old highway, built by lumber magnate Simon Benson in the decade of 1910, is a narrow, twisting 22 mile (35 km) road, which is there for no other reason than sightseeing.

The Dalles

Although many visitors miss it, the Dalles, with its 19th century brick storefronts and historic homes has an Old West character. It was the traditional end of the Oregon Trail, where the wagons were loaded onto barges for the final leg of the journey.

The Dalles was named by the Hudson Bay Company's French Canadian voyageurs who thought the basaltic rocks lining the Columbia resembled flagstones (*les dalles*).

The Fort Dalles Historical Museum boasts a number of intact 1850s structures including the 1856 Surgeon's Quarters, which houses the museum, and the original 1859 Wasco County Courthouse, now housing the visitor center.

At the east end of the Gorge, the Maryhill Museum of Art on the Washington side, is one of the country's finest, drawing more visitors than either the Portland or Seattle art museums. The attraction is a remarkable collection of drawings and plasters by French artist/sculptor, Auguste Rodin.

The museum also features French fashion mannequins, paintings, Russian icons, antique chess sets, and Native American artifacts.

A Stonehenge reproduction — built as a World War I memorial – stands three miles east of Marysville.

drizzle and the clouds that blanket the coastal region during most of the winter and the spring nourish the incredibly green landscape that grows thick and fast and which softens the sharp, alpine peaks. The area is still wild. Whether you travel the mountains or the high desert, your constant companion is the terrain.

Much of the land in the two states is undeveloped. Almost without exception, each of its cities are surrounded by countless outdoor recreational possibilities with mountains, lakes, rivers, and an ocean within fairly quick reach.

Contrasting seascapes

No area so much defines the differences within the Pacific Northwest as the coast that runs from the tip of the Olympic Peninsula to the Californian border.

In Washington, the overall features that most visitors encounter include spectacular sea cliffs, a narrow coastal plain with small estuaries and bays, and a major range of mountains – the Cascades – miles inland as is typical of a young coastal region. The coastline of Washington is highly varied where strong currents have carved out headlands, plus islands and fjords.

Oregon's coast, on the other hand, is basically a long beach that doesn't seem to end. The Oregon coast is fairly regular with only a few offshore monoliths cut from the jagged cliffs. It is marked by occasional river mouths, long stretches of sand dunes along the central coast, and many small resort towns. It's almost as though the Columbia River

Rainforest at Olympic Peninsula, Washington.

– dividing Washington from Oregon – also divides two different coastal worlds. The effect is immediate and dramatic.

Inland Washington and Oregon don't get as much rain. The air blowing over the Coastals mountains loses altitude and dries. A huge rain shadow is just to the east of Oregon's Cascades and extends 150 miles (241 km) inland.

The Pacific border zone along the coast

includes a chain of coastal mountains and a series of valleys known as the Great Trough. The Cascade-Sierra zone consists of a long range of mountains stretching southward from British Columbia through central California, splitting Washington and Oregon almost down the center. The Northern Rocky Mountain range comes down from British Columbia into northeastern Washington while the Basin and Range zones flow into Oregon.

On the dry side of Washington's Cascades are hotter summers, colder winters, more snow and less rain. The Ellensburg Valley and Columbia Basin east to the Palouse River have the driest weather conditions in eastern Washington averaging just 7-15 inches (18-38 cm) of precipitation a year.

Geographic conditions oddly moderate the weather in the two largest cities of the northwest, Seattle and Portland. The wind-swept Columbia River Gorge serves as a conduit through which wet air moves towards Idaho. But the reverse is also true, promoting passage westwards of frigid continental winter winds that produce colder days in Portland.

In fact, below freezing days in Portland amount to temperatures almost three times less than what Seattle residents have to endure, 44 days to 16 days. It is also the reason why summers in Portland are warmer than in Seattle.

The only reason why eastern Wash-

Stark stillness of winter.

Cascade Mountains

The Cascades are more than just another mountain chain. They, in fact, define the Pacific Northwest. Because of the range, Washington and Oregon appear to be two distinct segments joined together by a natural zipper. They're a barrier to both transportation and climate, creating both the physical and atmospheric obstacles that have made the region unique.

In very general terms, western Washington and Oregon are more urban and populated and industrial. The eastern portions are rural and have an agricultural economic base.

The range, about 700 miles (1127 km) long, begins at the Fraser River in southern British Columbia and extends southward through Washington and Oregon and into California just beyond Lassen Peak.

It's a wild, untamed stretch of rock and ice that man has never been able to dominate. For anyone who likes the outdoors, it's a mecca of activities with some of the most beautiful mountain scenery on the continent, much of it preserved by three national parks and numerous wilderness and recreation areas.

Thousands of miles of hiking trails, forestry roads, and narrow paved highways lace the mountains and make access to its physical charms surprisingly easy. In them are found old and abandoned mines, small towns that seem to have little reason for existing, lakes, streams, glaciers, and volcanoes. They are estimated to be about 25 million years old, but the range's volcanoes are much younger — less than a million years.

The only break in the mountains is at the Columbia River Gorge that not only allows the Columbia River to flow through to the ocean, but creates an easy corridor for human travel.

Certainly, neither Washingtonians nor Oregonians like traveling the range during the winter months. Only skiers brave the snow and cold on a regular basis, for in these mountains are the Pacific Northwest's major ski resorts.

Ring of Fire

The most dominant feature of the mountains – part of the legendary Ring Of Fire that circles the Pacific Ocean basin well into Asia - are those 15 volcanos of which Washington has five and Oregon 10.

The most famous, of course, is Mount St. Helens which blew its top in 1980. But, there are more that geologists and seismologists claim could come to a boil and explode.

It's the Cascades that divide the Pacific Northwest into wet and dry regions. While never more than 100-150 miles (161-241 km) from the ocean, they have created two worlds — wet-siders and dry-siders.

West, the rains roll in from the Pacific and are pushed upwards along the mountain edge until they drop their moisture. On the eastern side, the rain-shadow side, the pass is empty of moisture and here the Pacific Northwest is dry, arid, and often inhospitable.

It's not a particularly high range with Mount Rainier standing the tallest at 14,410 feet (4392 m) and Mount Hood at 11,239 feet (3426 m), but most are considerably shorter making access relatively easy.

The most spectacular drive along the range is at the northern end, near the Canadian border, along the North Cascades Highway. The North Cascades Highway hugs canyon walls, plunges into short tunnels, passes countless waterfalls, and through four mountain passes. You virtually ride over the tops of the chain. The scenery is gorgeous. By the time you come down the twisting road to Lake Chelan, you've crossed from the rainy to the rain-shadow side and down into Wenatchee's apple country.

The road to Lake Chelan summarizes the diversity of the Cascades and the flora and fauna that reflects the two sides. The wet, westerly slopes are dominated by the Douglas fir which is a species that requires abundant moisture. The east side is comprised mostly of ponderosa and lodgepole pine forests.

The appeal of the Cascades are not just their physical beauty – which is plentiful — but the promise they hold for exploration, and oftentimes flirtation with danger.

There are 160 parks in the Cascades. Many are linked together by the Pacific Crest Trail that traverses the entire range, from Canada to California.

Hiking up Mount St. Helens to view the gaping crater.

ington doesn't look like a version of the Sahara Desert is because of huge irrigation projects the result, in large part, of the large Grand Coulee Dam-produced Columbia Basin Project that puts water on one million acres.

The remainder of the irrigation water comes from smaller rivers such as the Yakima or from deep wells. A comparison is easily made to eastern Oregon which has virtually no irrigation whatsoever. While Washington has hills of wheat and other grains, Oregon's eastern world is inhospitable and an

Sparks Lake in the Sisters Wilderness area, Cascades.

John Day Fossils

At no other place in the Pacific Northwest is the relationship between Man and Nature so perfectly embraced as at the John Day Fossil Beds National Monument.

It's at once a lonely, wild and unforgiving place of hard volcanic rock and rolling hills and a peaceful, calm location so quiet you can hear your heart in the solitude and silence.

You can browse around the beds on your own or in the company of rangers, enjoy the wonderful scenery and delve into the scientific wonders that virtually lie at your feet. You can even be your own scientist, exploring for fossils that haven't yet been uncovered. It's a journey in time – an unbroken view of what this part of the world was like for a continuous seven million years, the only such collection of fossils in the world to do so.

The John Day Fossil Beds National Monument was established in 1974 in three different sites; Clarno, Painted Hills, and Sheep Rock. Clarno is 20 miles (32 km) west of the town of Fossil on ORE 218; Painted Hills is about five miles (8 km) west of Mitchell and north of US 26; Sheep Rock, two miles (3.2 km) north of US 26 on ORE 19, is the main exhibit and visitor center for all three units.

The visitor center is the converted ranch house of an early sheep grower from the early 1900s. Here, you'll find the information you need for a beneficial tour of the park. Staff members present orientation talks every hour during summer; displays that have been unearthed are supplemented by paintings depicting the park as it might have been millions of years ago; and a fossil preparation lab and bunkhouse museum tells the story of how paleontologists first worked the area.

The fossil beds are among the most frequented tourist spots in all of Oregon. Little wonder. These archives in stone provide a paleontological record of the 70 million years and the five geologic epochs of this planet. What you'll find captured in the rock formations of the three beds are the times of 50-ton dinosaurs and the delicate imprints of ferns and flowers.

The beds, which encompass more than 14,000 acres, were first noticed by Thomas Condon, a Congregational minister from The Dalles, who shipped some of his specimens to the Smithsonian Institution in 1870. During the next 30 years, some of the world's leading paleontologists scoured the region, and after them came amateurs collecting and disposing of thousands of samples.

The Blue Basin has an Island In Time trail that takes you into a canyon with 400 foot (122 m) high walls composed of the 20 million year old clay on the upper formation. Fossil replicas are stationed along the trail in the same position as when they were discovered.

The remains of a saber-tooth cat and a tiny three-toed horse called the Miohippus were important finds. As were the fossils of a small sheep-like herd animal called Oreodont.

The lower, and older formations, preserve fossils dating back 30 million years and are found at the Painted Hills Unit. It's here you'll find the most spectacular scenery of the Monument with sweeping views of the rust-painted hills.

The fossils indicate a much wetter climate than today's. The leaves, seeds, and nuts preserved in the beds indicate a wetter climate, one that changed as the Cascade Mountains rose and created a rain-shadow.

The final unit, the Clarno formations, reveal a land that was once tropical, more in keeping with contemporary India with leaves, seeds, and nuts of plants that grew there 40 million years ago.

agricultural wasteland.

In northeastern Washington, the unstable land began 60 million years ago as a flat, mud sea floor that buckled on the rising shoulders of molten rock when inner earth lurched and stood up.

Magma poured out from vents in the earth's crust, piled on itself, and spread eastwards to be smothered by volcanic ash and by ice sheets thou-

Brown hills in Klickitat Valley.

sands of feet thick. The ice had crawled south from the Arctic and nested as far south as Yakima leaving coarse gravel and sediment before retreating north. The result is the backbone of central and eastern Washington, mountains, foothills, plateaus, and the river valleys of four counties to the Canadian border.

Breadbaskets of the Northwest

The valleys are the breadbaskets of the Pacific Northwest. The Williamette in Oregon and the Yakima in Washington produce much of America's fruit and an increasing number of finished products like wine. Throughout the northwest,

the loveliest regions and most spectacular moments are the result of volcanic activity. While now largely inactive – though the eruption of Mount St. Helens in 1980 was an exception –- the volcanoes that make up the Cascades not only produced the lava characteristic of Eastern Oregon, but also Crater Lake and other marvels.

You could easily spend all of your time – one week or a month – in any of the geographical and climatic zones. The Cascades range is a world onto its own with spectacular mountains, National Parks, State Parks, recreational areas, and areas waiting to be explored.

The desert country of Oregon is marked by lonely roads cutting through an endless horizon. But, here too, are

Nature unexplored in the Olympic National Park.

natural wonders such as fossil beds, caves, and huge lava expanses.

You needn't travel to the most popular and crowded of the Northwest's attractions to find impressive geography.

Intriguing geology

The Snake River cuts through the plateau of eastern Oregon to form a deep path through the earth's crust that today is called Hells Canyon, the deepest canyon in North America, deeper even than Arizona's Grand Canyon.

Some of Washington's most intriguing geology is along the Columbia River Basin. A series of volcanic eruptions, giant floods, and slides have combined to create a dramatic landscape. Traveling through the region you will find evidence of lava flows. The area is laced with cinder cones, submerged pinnacles, high benches, and eroded badlands. The Basin was formed 13 to 16 million years ago. Lava flows erupted through fissures from a very large volcano in the area now called Grande Ronde, located in northeast Oregon and southeastern Washington.

Over and over, these fissures spread nearly level flows of molten basalt north to the Okanagan, west to the Cascades, and east to the Rockies.

Lava flows glazed the huge basins every thousand years or so, with pools of hundreds of feet in places and extending over 2,000 sq miles at a time. The

Hurricane Ridge in the Olympic Mountains.

flows stacked up in layers that are easily visible in river canyons today.

The Ice Ages have had an enormous impact on the geology. Volcanoes may have created the mountains, but the glaciers carved them into their present form. In fact, the withered remains of some glaciers can still be seen on the Cascade Range's slopes. Within the past 10,000 years, a warmer climate has caused much of the ice mass to melt, adding to the power of such rivers as the Columbia which has cut its way into the continental shelf.

It was the wildlife and trees that brought migration to the Pacific Northwest in the first place, and both continue to be one of the major reasons why people live here and come to visit. Mention the Pacific Northwest and chances are people think of big trees and migrating salmon.

The region is known for its forests. The primary low altitude trees are the Western Hemlock and the Douglas Fir. The former was used primarily as a pulpwood species and the latter as prime lumber. The largest of the Douglas Fir rise to more than 300 feet (91.4 m) in the Coast Range outside Coos Bay, Oregon.

Above 3,000 feet (914.4 m), silver fir and mountain hemlock take over the highlands. Big leaf maples are distinguished by leaves that are as much as a foot (30.5 cm) long. Other common trees in the mountains are the western red cedar, black cottonwood, red alder, and vine maple. The larg-

One of the many reasons to visit Portland.

Flora & Fauna

67

Moss-covered logs in a rainforest.

est known western hemlock is grown in the Quinault Valley on the Olympic Peninsula. Opposite ends of the flora scale are found in the Olympic Peninsula rain forests and the sparse shrubbery of the Oregon desert. With only 7 percent of the rainfall experienced on the west coast, Oregon's 24,000 square miles of eastern arid lands are home to largely sagebrush and juniper.

Wheat grows throughout eastern Washington, cranberries along the coast, and apple and other fruit-bearing trees throughout the major growing

Indian Paintbrush.

both Oregon and Washington. It's in the formative years that they learn how to identify evergreens, using a memory device that it is extremely useful.

They use letter identifications – the needles of a fir are Flat and Flexible; Spruce needles are Square, Stiff, and Stick to you; Hemlock needles have a Hammock-like configuration; and the Ponderosa pine Plate-like bark is definitely distinctive.

valleys. As you drive through these regions, you see the demarcation lines between wild and man-made growth.

Tree education

Tree education is an important part of every school child's early training in

Record-sized tree regions

Oregon has a number of record-sized tree regions with the world's largest ponderosa pine outside Bend, the tallest Sitka spruce near Cannon Beach, and

They may not be as spectacular as whales, nor as fascinating as spawning salmon, but a large number of small, sea life live within walking distance of any shoreline.

It isn't easy being the resident of a tide pool. Chances are you're small and you're susceptible to wave action, predators, and marauding tourists looking for shells and souvenirs.

A tide pool occurs where rocky outcrops provide a solid home-base for a variety of sea life. The beauty and diversity of life within the water capture the interest of many coastal visitors every year.

Each species is adapted for conditions in the tidal zone in which it lives. And many of those adaptations are visible to the discerning eye. As the tide recedes, more and more of the unique marine creatures become exposed and are visible.

Talk about harsh living conditions. Residents are forced to live with the possibility of drying out in the air and sunlight. They are open to a continuous battering of waves, especially during severe winter storms; changes in salinity when it rains at low tide; problems of oxygen supply because of being surrounded both by water and air in a continuous, alternating cycle; and temperature extremes.

Tidal zones are a little like an apartment block with residents living everywhere from the basement to the penthouse. An inter-tidal community can be divided into a series of zones based on how long and how often the inhabitants are exposed to air and water.

At the top, being sprayed frequently by incoming waves, are Acorn barnacles, rock snails, and ribber limpets. At the bottom are, among many others, sea cucumbers, ribbon worms, and sea palms. The lower the tide, the greater the number and diversity of sea creatures you'll find.

Tide pools are great to watch because their inhabitants are the only sea creatures humans can see with frequency and at virtually any time. Others, like whales, salmon, sea otters, or seals are seen infrequently. The saddest of all sea-creature cycles is the salmon spawn.

Every year, in four-year cycles, varieties of salmon make their way from the ocean to their spawning streams, returning to the place where they were born.

They aren't pretty to watch. By the time they reach the end of their journey, they are scarred, discolored, and their meat is soft. They spawn and die, and become food for bears and other animals.

Glamor of the ocean

The glamor animals of the ocean, of course, are the Gray and Killer Whales along the coast. As with the salmon, the Gray Whales are migratory, plying the west coast south and north as they swim to the Baja Peninsula for mating and birth and then back to the Bering Strait.

The Killer Whales – or Orcas – on the other

the world's largest cypress in Brookings.

The Rhododendron

The Rhododendron became Washing-

ton's state flower in 1892 when the state felt it needed a flower to represent itself at the Chicago World's Fair. It was matched in a close vote of the population with the clover. The rhody, as locals call it, has about 500 different species

hand, travel in family pods. An offshoot of the porpoise, the males are considerably larger than the females. These are the animals that are rode on in sea zoos like Sea World. They are black with white markings and incredibly docile around people when in captivity.

They're called 'killer whales" because they feed on warm blooded prey. But, like porpoises, they present no danger to man. The only times there have been reports of injury or death is when the Orcas mistakenly took a human for its natural prey. They travel in pods of two to 40 members and are easy to identify. Their dorsal fins rise up to six feet (1.8 m) and can sometimes be seen cutting through the waters of Puget Sound.

There are three resident pods in Puget Sound and along the Washington coast with a total of 80 members. The most frequent sightings are around the San Juans. The Puget Sound area is also the home of the largest species of octopus in the world. Though it grows to 12 feet (3.7 m) across the arms and weighs up to 30 pounds (13.6 kg), it is not dangerous and often plays with divers. The waters of the north coast are perfect for diving. They are clearer than waters in the South Pacific, and the abundance of sea animals makes it a rewarding experience.

Every now and then you can see a brownish-black head bobbing in any numbers of harbors along the coast as one of the 7,000 estimated harbor seals comes up for air. Local fishermen don't like them because they supposedly eat salmon.

California Sea Lions, porpoises, and dolphins are commonly seen in the Juan de Fuca and Puget Sound. But, you'll never really get close enough to any of these creatures to have a conversation – not like with a tidal pool.

The Rhododendron – Washington's state flower.

of colors ranging from yellows to pinks to bright reds and whites.

The Hendricks Park Rhododendron Garden in Eugene, the Azalea State Park at Brookings, and the International Rose Test Garden in Portland are three Oregonian flower parks that draw thousands to see the blooms in mid-June. Seed companies and nurseries are prolific throughout the northwest.

Tulips and daffodils

And in the Puget Sound region you'll find fields of tulips and daffodils in the spring, especially near La Conner and in the Mount Vernon area.

If you miss the tulips and daffodils

that grow wild between California and British Columbia and another several hundred that grow in greenhouses.

It sometimes seems that every garden in the Pacific Northwest has them. And why not? They bloom in a variety

Springtime hails the flowering of tulips.

at Roozengaarde or West Shore Acres in Mount Vernon, La Conner Flats has an assortment of flowers in bloom from March through September. The English country garden features daffodils, dogwood, azaleas, roses, dahlias, mums and heather throughout the period.

Berries galore

As you travel throughout the coastal regions eastwards to about the mid-Cascades, you'll find blackberries. Look for burned out areas and clearings, it

The Pasqueflower, dubbed "Old Man of the Mountain".

You're also likely to run into poison oak, so become familiar with the shiny three-leaf cluster before you walk in the woods. It is everywhere.

Endangered species

Animals of the region have long been the victims of exploitation, sometimes bringing certain species to the point of extinction.

European trappers virtually killed off the beaver; ranchers grazed out eatable grasses for hundreds of species and over killed the gray wolf, the Sea Otter and Mountain Caribou to the point where today they are on the endangered species list.

takes root virtually everywhere alongside other berries like wild strawberries, salmonberries, thimbleberries, currants, and salal. Prime snacking season for all of these berries range from mid-summer to mid-fall. There are many U-pick your own orchards along the roadways of the Williamette, the Hood River Valley and the Yakima.

Sea pens in the Seattle Aquarium.

Today, there are 21 species on either the endangered list (those being eliminated from all or large portions of their former homes) and seven classified as threatened (could become threatened in the near future).

Masters of the ocean

The most easily recognized of the creatures that occupy the Pacific Northwest are the great whales that swim in and around the coast; as well as seals, dolphins, and sea lions.

Twice yearly, the Gray Whales migrate along the western shores from Alaska to the Mexican Baja Peninsula where they breed and then swim back up the coast. Minke whales are more numerous than the easily identifiable Orcas, as are Dall's porpoises that are often mistaken for Orcas because of their similar coloring.

Anyone who has seen a migrating Gray Whale up close cannot forget it. It's a baleen whale, unlike the Orca that eats flesh, and feeds by stirring up mud in shallow water and sucking in organisms. Their faces are usually covered by barnacles and they often lift their heads to about eye level in an action called, "spyhopping". Whale watchers in small boats quite often find themselves eyeball to eyeball with these magnificent curious creatures.

Special museums throughout the west coast, including the Whale Mu-

Sea lions sunning in the Sea Lion Caves.

seum at Friday Harbor on San Juan Island, and exhibits attest to the importance of these animals. Historically, they were treated without concern by whalers from around the world.

Only recently, after decades of being on the endangered species list, have the Gray Whales made a sufficient enough comeback to be declared once again self sufficient. The ecological triumph, however, is tempered by pressure from whaling interests to allow harvesting once again.

Other nearly destroyed species, pro-

There's sealife galore in the tidepools off the Pacific Coast.

tected by law, have made significant comebacks. Otters are seen floating with their stomachs to the sky, in coastal waters and the beaver, though tougher to see, thrive in mountains regions.

Commercial salmon fishing was important to the development of the region and remains so today, though the industry falls on periodic bad times. Sport fishing is making a huge impact on tourism revenue with fishermen coming for the five varieties of Pacific salmon and for flounder, lingcod, trout, bass and many freshwater species.

In summer and early fall, schools of up to 100 Pacific white-sided dolphins enter the Strait of Juan de Fuca traveling as far inland as Port Angeles. The 200 pounders enjoy riding the bow waves of ships and then leap full-length alongside a boat.

Not all sealife swims and jumps in spectacular fashion. Sea anemones are called the flowers of the sea because of their bright colors. Relatives of the jellyfish and of corals, they use harpoon-like threads on their radially arranged tentacles to surround their prey. The pink and green anemones resemble zinnias and they cover rocks on beaches.

The sea star is another common creature of the sea, a five-rayed, rough skinned hunter of shellfish. The largest of the species is a 20 rayed-star that attains a length of 3 feet (91 cm).

The sea urchin is a thorny creature, having bristling thorns much in the likeness of a porcupine. The red urchins

Casting a wary eye around.

Wildlife Sanctuaries

A series of wildlife sanctuaries have been set aside throughout Washington and Oregon, giving some protection to the wildlife of virtually every region. While the state and national parks and recreation areas provide their own natural habitats for wildlife, the sanctuaries are special places.

In Washington state, one of the most solitary is the **Willapa National Wildlife Refuge** which encompasses all of Long Island plus parts of Leadbetter Point State Park and Sholwater Bay, just off the Long Beach Peninsula. You'll need to take a boat there. The resident deer, elk, grouse, and bear are not, unfortunately, totally protected as archery hunting is permitted during certain times of the year.

Near Vancouver, on the Washington/Oregon border, the **Ridgefield National Wildlife Refuge**, just off I-5 in Ridgefield, has more than 4,615 acres of fields, woodlands, and marshes for the preservation of 180 species of birds, plus otters, deer, and beavers.

The **McNary National Wildlife Refuge**, near Tri-Cities in Eastern Washington, next to McNary Dam, has a mile-long hiking trail popular with birdwatchers with species like hawks, golden eagles, and prairie falcons.

Grays Harbor Wildlife Refuge is a 500-acre wetlands wildlife refuge in the northeast corner of the Grays Harbor Estuary on the Olympic Peninsula. It attracts up to half a million migrating shorebirds in spring and fall, 12 species including peregrine falcon and the northern harrier. In the lake country of southeastern Oregon is the **Hart Mountain National Antelope Refuge**, stretching across a high plateau and rising above Warner Lakes. The refuge headquarters is near the town of Plush, along ORE 140 northeast of Adel. The 275,000 acres are home to pronghorns and to bighorn sheep, mule deer, plus 213 species of birds and many smaller animals. A hot springs nearby is open to the public for bathing.

The **Klamath Forest National Wildlife Refuge**, north of Klamath Falls on Highway 97, is a good place during the spring to observe sandhill cranes, shorebirds, waterfowl, and raptors.

Eagles in abundance can be found at the **Upper Klamath National Wildlife Refuge** and the **Bear Valley National Wildlife Refuge** — both of which have trees large enough to support up to 300 eagles a night. But since the eagles don't particularly like being observed, the roosting areas are closed from early November to March 30. A world renowned eagle conference is held in February with lectures and films, field trips, and workshops – held in joint sponsorship with the Audubon Society of Portland. Several bird sanctuaries were established between Salem and Eugene by the federal government in the mid-1960s because of the effect of encroaching urbanization and agriculture on the Canada Goose.

The geese now go to the **Baskett Slough National Wildlife Refuge**, west of Salem, to **Ankeny National Wildlife Refuge** southwest of the capitol, and the **Finley National Wildlife Refuge**, south of Corvalis each October. The wildlife ecosystems mesh forest, crop-land, and other environments also attract hummingbirds, ducks, swans, geese, hawks and sandpipers. There are several trails through the refuges, but

---

prefer deep water while the more common purple and green urchins prefer beaches and calm inlets.

Land creatures

The Pacific Northwest land animals are varied in size and comprise an excitingly diverse group. Sparse human population in most of the region, an abundance of wildlife preserves, and landforms that vary remarkably, explain the diversity.

One of the least pleasant creatures is the slug – the slimy brown banana

these are closed in alternating sequences depending on the needs of the particular birds.

Along the Oregon coast are several wildlife refuges including the **Bandon Marsh National Wildlife Refuge**, the **Rock Creek Wilderness**, the **South Slough Estuary Reserve**, and numerous state parks. The Wallowa Valley has two major wildlife viewing areas; the **Spring Branch Wildlife Area** is an 8-acre area with beaver dams and lots of marshes; the **Enterprise Wildlife Area**, two miles west of Enterprise off ORE 82 is a 32-acre site located just before a fish hatchery and is where marsh wrens, snipe, mink, beavers, and muscrats are located.

The **Sumpter Valley Wildlife Area** is a 158-acre site located between Philips Reservoir and Sumpter on ORE 7. Canada Geese, ring-necked ducks, and Virginia Rails not far from the gold mining town of Sumpter.

Near Portland, the **Oakes Bottom Wildlife Park** is a bird-watcher's paradise and home to the blue and green-backed herons, orioles, swallows, and woodpeckers, among others.

Among the biggest refuges in the Pacific Northwest is the **Malheur National Wildlife Refuge**, south of Burns. Malheur and Harney Lakes, fed by runoffs from the Blitzen and Silvies Rivers, have been a major nesting and migration stopovers for centuries. Approaching the area is quite startling as the dry and arid countryside gives way to a sudden onslaught of lush green marshes. You'll have company as the desert lands bring both thousands of birds and bird-watchers alike. Take time to pull over and watch Canada Geese, pelicans, teals, mallards, and other waterfowl.

and the black slugs are the plague of gardeners. When they are not eating plants, you'll see them crawling along on sidewalks or on forest trails.

More attractive is the continent's fastest animal, the pronghorn, that is able to run at about 40 mph. (64 kph). The mountain lion shares the same ter-

A ground squirrel heralds the beginning of spring.

rain, the low brushlands of the eastern cascades.

Grizzlies and Brown Bears

Bears are plentiful in the mountains and in the remote forests and black bears are the most common, found throughout the Cascades. Weighing up to 300 pounds (136 kg) and about 6 feet (1.8 m) tall, their main foods are berries, nuts and fish. Generally, they are wary of humans, but they are wily and highly intelligent and are always open to offers of food. Hikers in the mountains should always beware of keeping food too close to tents at night.

Grizzlies and Brown Bears are rarely

Llama farm in Goldendale, Washington.

found in Washington and Oregon though some can be found in Idaho, in the Selkirk Mountains. The large Grizzlies once roamed the Pacific Northwest, but there are now an estimated 1,000 in remote areas of Idaho, Montana, and Wyoming and they are considered a threatened species.

If you're hiking in the forests, don't be bashful. Make noise. If you do encounter a bear, don't run. Bears may look slow, but they're as fast as a racehorse. Instead, look for a tree that offers a quick climb to at least 12 feet. Drop

Redwood in Olympic National Park.

your pack or your jacket to distract it. As a last resort, roll into a ball and pretend you're dead.

If hunting is something you do, there is plenty of big game, especially deer. Both states have large supplies of Mule deer, so named for their large ears. There are also white-tailed deer, elk, antelope, moose, cougar, and moun- tain goats that range the remote moun- tainous areas, and the common chip- munk and squirrel are everywhere. These common scavengers, along with opos- sums, raccoons and skunks, are even found in the most urban of the Pacific Northwest's cities. Chances are you'll be encountering them in the woodsy neighborhoods, often around garbage cans, in parks, and near picnic areas. Gardeners are most frequently visited and driven crazy by moles.

The largest collections of many spe- cies are native to certain regions. The Roosevelt Elk, for example, is found on the Olympic Peninsula, inside the boundaries of the Olympic National Park and it is given refuge within the park's borders.

The feathered species

More than 300 species of birds live in the Pacific Northwest for at least a part of the year. Easily accessible mud flats and estuaries throughout the region provide refuge for tufted puffins, egrets, cormorants, loons and other migratory water fowl that make their way along the Pacific Coast. Hundred of pairs of bald eagles nest and hunt among the islands of Washington and British Columbia and they winter along the Oregon coast along with blue herons and cormorants. In the old-growth regions you find red-tailed hawks and spotted owls.

Many bird sanctuaries have been set aside, especially in Oregon with the Williamette and the Mulheur regions having the largest. These refuges provide migration homes for Canada Geese, Snow geese, kingfishers, cranes, and others species.

As with the larger animals, a number of birds are now on the endangered list including the White Pelican, Brown Pelican, Peregrine Falcon, Sandhill Crane, and the Spotted Owl.

The need for large old growth forests for the Spotted Owl has meant restricted logging in much of the Cascades. There's little doubt that the creature is the bird of the hour, at least in Western Washington. Old growth forests — 150 years or older – are filled with food for owls and with broken branches, snags, and fallen trees that make great nesting grounds. Scientists believe that

the Spotted Owl — now estimated at only 2,500 pairs – will disappear in 30 years if clear-cut logging continues at current rates.

Bald eagles have made a great recovery in recent years and have been one of the more positive ecology stories of the recent while. About 300 pairs make their permanent homes in west-

Wild deer are plentiful in the national parks.

ern Washington while another 1,600 birds live there in winter.

They are drawn by the enormous numbers of dead salmon lying on the edges of rivers. Eagles are scavengers, and prefer dead animals to anything that moves on the hoof. They are ag-

gressive and often you'll see them diving after other birds – sometimes seagulls – in an effort to take away their catches. Such gorgeous thieves.

Mature bald eagles, with their distinctive white heads, are easy to spot when they perch on tree branches. The

Birding in the Pacific Northwest – by Morten Strange

Trumpeter Swan.

live there as well.

Typical birds to look out for in these parts include Blue Grouse, Band-tailed Pigeon, Black Swift, Vaux's Swift, Hammond's Flycatcher,

It actually starts in the northern part of California but up in Oregon you can experience it in its full magnitude, the temperate rainforest. It is a habitat of rich forests, mainly fire and other conifers, in the warmer parts there are also some deciduous trees like the giant Redwoods. The habitat depends on the warm currents from the Pacific Ocean; the moist winds blow in from the sea and are swept upwards and cooled down by the coastal mountain range just behind the seashore. This is the wettest part of the whole of the U.S., often 2,500 mm and locally as many as 4,000 mm of precipitation are being unloaded onto the slopes each year.

The cool and damp rainforests that have developed here as a result are richer and denser than the spruce belt vegetation behind the coast and in Canada. It is a unique environment stretching from the Pacific Northwest up through British Columbia in Canada and along the Alaskan Panhandle to Anchorage.

Much of the forest has been cleared by logging activities and logging is still going on, the huge trees around these parts are particularly valuable. The Spotted Owl has become something of a mascot for the campaigns by local environmentalists to preserve these forests. It has a limited distribution in exactly this area and it is very particular about where it settles; it is therefore a good so-called indicator species, if it occurs the habitat is unspoiled and authentic and other typical species are likely to

Varied Thrush and several woodpeckers like Black-backed and White-headed Woodpeckers and Red-breasted Sapsucker.

Also look out for some small passerines like Hammond's flycatcher, Townsend's Warbler, Hermit Warbler and maybe most numerous of all the Chestnut-backed Chickadee. They are all characteristic birds that you will have a hard time finding anywhere else in the United States. There is even a hummingbird occuring exclusively in this northernly terrain, the Rufous Hummingbird which in fact can be found all the way up the Pacific coast far into Alaska.

Other species like several owls: Great Grey Owl, Northern Pygmy-Owl, Western Screech-Owl and Great Horned Owl plus Ruffed Grouse, Sharp-shinned Hawk, Pileated Woodpecker, Grey Jay, Cedar Waxwing, Golden-crowned Kinglet are also numerous in the temperate rainforest. But they all have a much wider distribution and can also be found other places all the way to the east of the continent. The cryptic Hermit Thrush has its stronghold here but is a very difficult bird to see well.

On the higher slopes behind the coastal rainforest the mountains extend up into alpine zones resembling the arctic tundra, the tallest peaks are snow-covered year-round and produce glaciers. White-tailed Ptarmigan, American Pipit and a few hardy songbirds like Mountain Bluebird and Rosy Finch are some of the scarce creatures you will find in this environ-

Great Grey Owl.

Blue Grouse.

ducks, swans, grebes, White-faced Ibis, Sandhill Crane and many shorebirds gather, especially during the spring and summer months. Many migrant passerines and often rare species also occur in nearby patches of woodlands. Further north in the state of Washington the **Turnbull National Wildlife Refuge** offers a similar habitat and is renowned for holding such western resident specialities as Yellow-headed Blackbird, Wilson's Phalarope and Red-necked Grebe, apart from large numbers of migrants during the winter season.

Nearer the coast in Oregon just west of Eugene is the Fern Ridge Reservoir which has many ducks and gulls particularly but which is also well known for the rich variety of landbirds and birds of prey which can be seen in surrounding woodlands and cultivated areas. In the northern part of the state, Savie Island in the Columbia River has a variety of habitat and is popular with birders all through the year, but especially so in fall and winter when thousands

ment close to or above the tree-limit which is here just above 2,000 metres elevation.

In Washington, the 358,640-hectare **Olympic National Park** has probably the best sample of rainforest in the Pacific Northwest and further inland the 96,793-hectare **Mount Rainier National Park** has forests but also some vulcanic peaks rising steeply to 4,380 meters. It is an imposing and magnificent landscape unmatched in splendor by anything else you will ever see. And there are about 140 different birds respectively on the local checklists to look out for.

Wetlands and Coastlines

Behind the coastal mountains the winds having deposited all their water content on the western slopes are completely dry and something like desert conditions prevail. Here and in the populated valleys of the Pacific Northwest the wetlands are often the best birding spots.

The **Malheur National Wildlife Refuge** in Oregon on the dry side of the mountains is such an oasis where huge numbers of waterbirds like

Sandhill Crane.

...Birding in the Pacific Northwest – by Morten Strange

Yellow-
headed
blackbird.

of waterfowl gather in the wetlands. In the extreme south of Oregon, the Klamath and the Tule National Wildlife Refuges are well known as "duck factories".

In the United States the status of the waterfowl birds is a bit sensitive and if you are just visiting you should be aware of this. There is a strong hunting lobby campaigning for more liberal laws and a longer shooting season often opposing the bird-watchers who typically call for more restrictions on the killings. The two sections however also sometimes join hands and work together to preserve a vital natural habitat for the waterbirds and special protection for endangered species.

The Pacific Northwest coastline itself is something else again, a rugged terrain with often steep cliffs, rocky islands close offshore and patches of sandy beaches in between. Mudflats and saline marshes have developed in just a few sheltered places. It is a harsh environment but also very productive, the sea and the beach is teeming with fish and invertebrate lifeforms that many birds thrive on. A few shorebirds like the Black Oystercatcher are residents but many more visit and stay during the winter when their breeding grounds in the arctic are frozen over. Surfbird, Rock Sandpiper and Black Turnstone are some of the western specialists to look out for here, they do not occur on the eastern shores of the United States, but several other species show up often giving the birders trying to identify them a real headache.

Several species of gulls and cormorants fly and feed just off the Pacific Northwest beach but typical pelagic families like petrels and auks only come up onto land briefly during the summer months to breed and then only on the most exposed and isolated cliffs facing the sea.

In Oregon, the South Jetty at the mouth of the Columbia River is a perennial gathering point for birders trying out their proficiency in picking out and naming seabirds often viewed at long distances. Just south of here the Tillamook Bay area is another famous site for winter birds, both seabirds approaching the shore and landbirds found just behind the coastline. In Washington the San Juan Islands are especially good for offshore birds like auks and wintering loons, and taking the short ferry ride from Seattle to Victoria on Vancouver Island you are bound to turn up exiting coastal bird sightings. Vancouver Island is another worthwhile birding destination, but lies outside the U.S.A. jurisdiction.

More Information

The key element in birding is your skill in identifying all the birds you see. And there is only one way to learn: to spend time at the best birding spots while studying your field guide closely during each trip. In the Pacific Northwest one of the most popular guides is the *Field Guide to the Birds of North America* by the National Geographic Society, 1983. The classic volume *A Field Guide to Western Birds* by R.T. Peterson who pioneered this format for modern identification guide books is still used by many.

There are birds everywhere to watch, even outside your office window if you look for them, but most birders soon want to venture out to the best places to see large numbers and different kinds. Location guides are a great help here, *A Guide to Bird Finding West of the Missisippi* by O.S. Pettingill covers all of the western United States if you plan to travel widely. Specifically for Oregon *The Birder's Guide to Oregon* by J.E. Evanich, 1990 is available and north of here the *Guide to Bird Finding in Washington* by T.R. Wahl & D.R. Paulson, 1991 applies.

It is always a good idea to consult the local experts for advice when you visit a new state. Or if available you should call a hot-line number for information on the latest news regarding rarities spotted and the best sites to visit right now; in Oregon call: (503) 292 0661, in the State of Washington : (206) 526 8266.

Wild Turkey.

somewhat similar golden eagle has white patches on its tail and underwings.

The great Blue Heron is frequently seen along harbors, rivers, or lakes, and the belted kingfisher is seen in the Puget Sound district. In the Cascades the mountain bluebird is found in abundance at the town of Bickleton in the Horse Heaven Hills of southern Washington where several dozens of birdhouses throughout the town give homes to the bird. Shore birds are found along the entire coast line of both states. Gulls are common, as are dunlins, whimbrels, plovers, and killdeers along the mud flats. Offshore are coots, scaups and buffleheads sitting on the water and eating floating plants.

Three Arch Rocks National Wildlife Refuge is the site of Oregon's largest seabird colony, home to 200,000 nesting common murres and other species including tufted puffins, storm petrels, and cormorants. Along I-5 in Oregon's Williamette Valley, you'll see red-tailed hawks sitting on fence posts and American kestrels, a falcon-like bird, on phone wires. Further south turkey buzzards circle the dry areas in the warmer months. Vultures are commonly sighted above the Rogue River.

In 1989, the Twighlight Eagle Sanctuary was established along the Lower Columbia River near Astoria. And those motoring on Sauvie Island near Portland will find a protected wildlife refuge with more than 200 species of birds flying through on their migration.

Like its terrain, the Pacific Northwest is a mix of varying human groupings. The first ones here, of course, were the aboriginal tribes who occupied every region of the Northwest each having their own peculiar adaptations to terrain and climate.

Historians claim Native Americans crossed over to Alaska from Asia at the end of the last ice age when the region of the Bering Sea was 300 or more feet (91.5 m) lower than current levels and was passable. Once on the North American side, they migrated down into the Pacific Northwest.

Though they occupied the Pacific Northwest for centuries, it wasn't long after the arrival of white immigrants that the Native Indians lost both their lands and their identities.

People & Religion

89

Hitching a ride.

Plateau Indians

In Central Washington, the inhospitable terrain was home to the Plateau Indians – the Yakima, Columbia, Okanagan, Nespelem,

Got the sun in my eyes.....

and others. Their struggles with new white settlers were fierce and continued long after they had signed away their lands in treaties with Washington's territorial government in 1855.

In recent years, the population has once again undergone a change.

Neighborhoods and colleges that were almost all-white 20 years ago, are more like a giant United Nations meeting room as American Blacks, Hispanics, and Southeast Asians – along with Native Americans – provide a mosaic of colors and origins.

The Pacific Northwest is rich in
character and characters.

Ethnic groups

The population demographics of the past 20 years indicate that Hispanics are the fastest growing ethnic group in the United States, with 100,000 of the estimated 20 million actually residing in Oregon.

According to the 1990 U.S. census, Washington is still overwhelmingly white 88.5 percent of the population. Blacks accounted for 3.1 percent; Indians 1.7 percent; Asians, 4.3 percent; and Hispanics were 4.4 percent of the population. Oregon has a somewhat similar population breakdown with whites making up 92.8; Blacks, 1.6; Indians, 1.4; Asians, 2.4; and Hispanics, 4.0 percent.

The region, however, is more complex than a simple percentage breakdown of population. Rather, it is made up of highly individualistic people and this new American melting pot is creating its own identity – rich is character and characters.

Attitudes are shaped by a number

The Hispanics

Although now considered the fastest growing minority in the Pacific Northwest, identifying the Hispanic population is an elusive exercise. The Hispanics are a mixed group, encompassing a variety of origins. This elusiveness has precluded them, in part, from establishing the same kind of identifiable neighborhoods as have the Chinese, for example.

Between 1980 and 1990, the U.S. population in total grew by 9.8 percent, but the number of Hispanics grew by 53 percent (7.8 million) giving them a total of 22.4 million in the United States.

The growth has been in specific regions, mainly, such in the Los Angeles, New York, Miami, San Francisco, and Chicago areas. In Washington, D.C. the Hispanic population grew by 136.7 percent in that time; and in Dallas-Fort Worth, by 109.4 percent, making them the 16th and ninth ranked cities in terms of total population.

While the growth in the Pacific Northwest was measurable and impressive, the numbers were relatively small. In fact, no Pacific Northwest city comes close to ranking in the top 25 of U.S. Hispanic concentration.

Seattle had the most with 18,341 and there were 214,570 throughout the state. The state figures were exceeded by Washington, D.C.'s 224,786.

Eighth Biggest Asian City

By comparison, Seattle-Tacoma's Asian population increased by 110 percent during the decade, ranking that city as the eighth biggest Asian city in the United States.

Broadly understood, the term Hispanic refers to people of Spanish or Spanish-American origin. The majority trace their roots to Mexico, Puerto Rico, or Cuba.

However, every Spanish speaking country is represented in the U.S. Hispanic population. Brazilians are not counted in the group, as their language is Portuguese.

In recent years, political upheavals and extreme poverty have led El Salvadorans and other Central Americans to emigrate to the United States in increasing numbers.

Contrary to common belief, the Spanish speaking countries are not homogenous, but varied and complex. The populations incorporate Spanish and other European influences as well as Indian and African traits. In the Caribbean, Panama, and the coast of Venuzela, Columbia, and Equador, African culture has left a strong influence. In Mexico, most of Central America, and the Andean countries, diverse Indian cultures have had an impact.

One characteristic of the Hispanics is that intermingling in some areas has made it impossible to distinguish one race from another. In others, the race is very clearly defined. Argentina, for example, has a white majority of 99.6 percent, mostly of Italian, German, or English extraction.

Despite the diversity, many factors unite the Hispanics including language, religion, customs, and attitudes towards self and family. Language is the most powerful unifier, but there is doubt that alone will continue to bind these diverse peoples.

Large numbers of second generation Hispanics are primarily English language speaking, and 85 percent of U.S. Hispanics speak the language. Although Spanish continues to be a strong unifying force among immigrants, surveys suggest the impact diminishes quickly with the second generation.

Largest minority

It is projected that Hispanics will become the largest minority in the country, surpassing blacks, within the next 25 years. The total number of Hispanics is expected to be 31.2 million by the year 2000, making up 11.6 percent of the U.S. population, while blacks will constitute 13.3 percent.

The Census Bureau forecasts that by the year 2025, the number of Hispanics could reach 60.9 million or 20.2 percent of the population although these figures could change if fertility and immigration patterns change. More conservative projections estimate the Hispanic population at 39.9 million by 2025.

Children of the Northwest.

of factors and rare are those who, on the eastern side of the Cascades, share the same views as those on the coast.

Dry-siders and wet-siders

The Cascades divide the region into dry-siders and wet-siders. Those on the rainy coast view those who live in the dry interior as mainly red-necked farmers who like country music and television sitcoms. Those in the eastern regions look at those pinko coasters who live in rain and noise as nothing but whiners and polluters.

Generally speaking, the wet-siders are more politically liberal than the dry-siders, though that's an easy image to perpetuate. The land and its harshness has created a no-nonsense life-style on the dry side that most wet-siders view as restrictive.

The two largest cities, Seattle and Portland, are both on the wet side, so it's no surprise that the region is also split along population patterns as well. City dwellers, who cross the Cascades only when necessary, view the plains, deserts, and dry conditions as a foreign, inhospitable land. It's surprising, really, that the different worlds have survived in relative harmony. Some think it's because each side accepts mavericks, those who work outside the system. The land is big enough to absorb them and the history of the region has, in large part, been defined by them.

Idealistic communities, survivalist communities, religious communities, and tree-huggers have always been an intregal part of living here. The relationship has not always been a harmonious one – as with the acrimony unleashed in Oregon's experience with the Bhagwan Shree Rajneesh in the 1980s when the sect leader and his band of merry wierdos almost succeeded in taking over an entire county. (See: Bend and Southern Oregon p.303).

The Williamette Valley and central coast in particular are fast becoming a melting pot. Each year more and more Asians and Hispanics join the original settlers from the east coast and midwest, with those from Germany and Scandinavia. Among recent arrivals are a group calling themselves the Russian Old Be-

North Coast resident with a hefty catch.

Survivalists

Like Wagnerian Valkyries preparing for their calling, the Pacific Northwest's survivalist communities await their Gotterdamerung. They are one of the more frightening consequences of the Cold War and the economic differences that have produced wide divisions in class and economic structures.

In their more harmless form, the survivalists are merely strange recluses found in small groups on communes in the Cascades. Worried about the effects of nuclear attack on the United States, they moved to the Pacific Northwest during the 1970s and '80s to raise families and keep their collective head down. Others have taken a more aggressive approach, arming themselves with exotic weapons and have created para-military organizations.

Broken dreams and ambitions

The Pacific Northwest has always been a gathering place for broken dreams and ambitions. Crossing from east to west you drive past abandoned mining camps, deserted gold trail towns, and ranches that never saw success.

But the legacy of the Survivals may be less passive. The followers of Bhagwan Shree Rajneesh, for example, were originally thought to be nothing more than a bunch of radical fakes. By the time they had made their move to politically take over the community of Antilope, Oregon in the mid-1980s, they had purchased a variety of assault weaponry. For what purpose it serves, it remains unclear, but they managed to scare the locals out of their wits.

Most of the current crop of survivalists have grouped around Grant's Pass in Southern Oregon close to the California border. The theory, of course, is that the place is far removed from any "targetable" site – south of the Puget Sound's Boeing facilities and north of the Silcon Valley near San Jose.

The so-called survivalist communities – ranging in size from 10 to scores – may be coming to an end, or at least changing their focus.

The Cold War, after all, is over and the major threat to society is now unclear. Perhaps, to their thinking, however, that's reason enough to continue their preparations for a societal holocaust. Like other similar groups in California and in the American south, these people think that society as they know it will collapse, bringing anarchy and mayhem to America. While the primary reason for the collapse has been nuclear attack, any reason for these people will do – floods, earthquake, inflation, or government corruption.

In a sense these groups are like the cast of a bad horror movie, stockpiling supplies of dried peas and ammunition. Rifles, handguns and even military equipment like hand grenades and machine guns are a part of the survivalist preparation.

In response to criticism, they view the rest of society as nearsighted fools who will come to them when the emergency hits them. But, make no mistake, these groups are not benevolent societies. They are more intent on protecting themselves than in throwing out life preservers. However, they are part of the strange collection of misfits and oddballs that make up the Pacific Northwest. Unless you happen to mistakenly cross one of their well-marked perimeters of defense, they're simply another nail in a large house of characters.

lievers, religious colonists who began arriving via China and South America in the 1960s. Hard-working and colorfully clad, the Old Believers keep mainly to themselves, although each year more and more of their young people break away from tradition.

The Yakima Valley has long been a place where East and West have mixed with European-American settlers relying on workers from the Pacific Rim to clear the forest, help build the transpor-

Siberian husky puppies with a Northwest girl.

tation and irrigation systems, and to work the land.

The fate of these people, however, has not always been good with itinerant workers sometimes being treated in the past as semi-slaves with poor living conditions, hard work, and poor pay. That has changed because of civil rights legislation, farm workers unions, and general attitudes towards people. Instead of being treated as outsiders, these workers are today an indispensable part of the land. An offshoot of that acceptance has been a rich diversity of cultural traditions and a mixing of life styles.

The American adventure in Southeast Asia produced an unexpected migration after 1975 into America. With Seattle and Portland as entry points from Asia, large numbers of Vietnamese, Cambodians, have flocked into the region.

Northwesters have never been as solid believers in the Great American Dream as their eastern counterparts. Throughout American history, there have been movements to reorganize, recreate — indeed redefine – their part of the world. Whether it's the acceptance of maverick personalities or its distance from the central government, the Pacific northwest has always been attracted to separation. And, in recent times, to restricted entry.

Cascadia

The idea of a land called Cascadia,

A wet-sider's view.

encompassing northern California, Idaho, Oregon, and Washington, has been discussed for years. It embraces the values of the region – of a new country that is pragmatic and environmentally sound.

Is this any different than the illusions that drew the utopians earlier, or the racists that viewed the Northwest as a white enclave of Christian values? Probably not, and while the garden-variety theorists and quacks get their publicity and what artist Andy Warhol called the "15 minutes of fame", none of the movements are ever long lasting.

In the 1970s, Oregon Governor Tom McCall said that the world should visit his state, but don't stay. There were even billboards plastered around the state

At peace with nature.

proclaiming his edict.

Of course, people came and did stay and continue to do so. McCall's declaration may have generated exactly the opposite to what the governor had intended. What was it, after all, that McCall was trying to protect? If it was that good, it might be worth seeing, went the reasoning. At various times in Oregon's history, there have been attempts to create new states – usually between northern California and southern Oregon. Inhabitants of this region have tried on several occasions to secede

ted Owl, a bird indigenous to the old growth forest areas of Washington and Oregon. Fearing for its survival, environmentalists petitioned the federal government and the courts to declare the endangered bird's habitat — in which one mating pair needs 1,000 acres of old growth to feed and survive – off-limits to loggers.

They won, stopping the harvest of millions of acres old growth forest. Ask a logger what he thinks of environmentalists who have endangered their livelihood, and you're likely to hear an inventive combination of expletives.

That's only normal for this part of the world.

Religion

The Pacific Northwest has always been a spiritual land. The Native Peoples saw the place as a land stalked by a series of spirits, positive and negative, that influenced their lives and the land. Later, missionaries saw a different kind of spirit – one firmly entrenched in the Christian brotherhood.

Christianity in the Pacific Northwest was evangelical and oppressive. Natives were viewed as desperately ignorant child-like creatures in need of Christian education and salvation.

Of course, the underlying philosophy was that the white culture was far superior to the Indian's. This attitude was not far removed from the kind of ignorant oppression that was to follow

– in 1852, 1953, 1854, and 1941 with the last drive for independence in the 1960s dramatized by a roadblock of U.S. 99 at the Oregon/California border.

Still, some movements do have a lasting effect, especially those that effect the fragile environment. Environmentalists stopped the logging industry in its tracks with their concern for the Spot-

Utopian communities

The Pacific Northwest – the end of the route westwards — has attracted more than its its share of weird and strange societies, communities, and colonies. The latest – and one of the most documented – was the takeover of Antelope, Oregon, by followers of Bhagwan Shree Rajneesh in the mid-1980s.

While the media rushed to cover the story and helped in elevating a minor mystic to a major personality, the Raj was only one in a long history of such charasmatic figures who convinced people to follow him into the forests and deserts. It's no coincidence that the Pacific Northwest is where the environmental movement is the strongest, and where protectors of the Spotted Owl attained loyalty usually reserved for Saints.

In fact, this passionate commitment to the conservation movements of the Pacific Northwest are in keeping with the region's history of combatting the status-quo. This has always been a place where individualists have not only found comfort, but in some instances, have had followings.

In Washington, it is estimated that no less than six utopian communities have sprung up since the late 19th century. Not all have been on the lunatic fringe. In fact, some have made an enormous positive impact on the region.

The Puget Sound Cooperative Colony is probably the most successful and has the most impact on both the economy and life style of the state. Founded in Port Angeles, on the north coast of the Olympic Peninsula on the Strait of Juan de Fuca in 1887, it helped establish that town as a viable commercial center.

Not all have been so successful as most have been anti-establishment and/or protest in nature. Those we see today have usually been formed for religious reasons rather than for philosophies of sharing. Most of these groups find little sympathy from local residents and they have never become an integral part of their nearby communities.

Oregon has always been an attractive place for utopians of one kind or another led by unconventional characters.

The town of Aurora, about 30 miles (48 km) south of Portland was founded in 1857 by a German immigrant, Prussian-born William Keil who has been described by historian John E. Simon as a tailor, doctor, preacher, pioneer, dictator, mystic, and fanatic. Keil was apparently so obsessed with the vision of an ideal community that he placed the body of his recently dead son in the lead wagon of the train to Oregon as a symbolic guide to the new land.

His philosophy for a communal society was that every man and woman owned nothing individually. As he put it, "...every man owns everything as a full partner and with an equal voice in its use and its increase and the profits in the form of the various racist attitudes. Eventually, the Ku Klux Klan and the anti-Chinese oppressions later in the century would seem a logical outgrowth of this attitude.

There was also a more political reason why the federal government gave a de-facto approval of missionaries being sent westward. Missions were an important method of establishing white settlements in the region, giving credence to American claims of sovereignty.

Caught in the crunch between the Bible and international land possession were the Native Peoples.

"Book from Heaven"

The first overt attempt at Christian domination, oddly enough, was the direct result of the Indians themselves taking the initiative. Four Nez Perce Indians arrived in St. Louis, Missouri, in 1832.

occuring from it. But in no other way do we differ from our neighbors. As a community we are one family."

He had tried this in Missouri and had left after seven years — having had a fairly successful commune – because of disease, the slavery question, and local unrest.

He made his way westwards complete with barrels of home-made liquor, making friends with Indians along the way by constantly feeding them. After failing to establish a colony on the Washington's coast, he and his followers of several hundred established Aurora Mills.

Midway between Salem and Portland, the town couldn't fail. It was an ideal place for a restaurant and a hotel which the group built. Shops and small businesses rose and prospered and farming supplied most of the colony's money.

Keil became more and more dictatorial and his will was supreme. People began to leave. After his death from a stroke in 1877, the colony dissolved. What remains today are five preserved buildings filled with tools and materials of everyday life.

His fate and that of the colony follow a general pattern of past and modern communal living. First comes the vision, then the colony, and finally dissolution and rancor. Only rarely, as in the case of the Puget Sound Cooperative Colony, do they succeed in the long run.

They were members of a tribe who had encountered the Lewis and Clark expedition and were told by them that the White Man had a "Book From Heaven" that described how to reach the happiest of hunting grounds.

At that time Clark was in charge of Indian Affairs for the Far West, the four tribesmen told their old friend that they wanted to learn about the white man's religion. Little did they know they were opening a Pandora's Box. When given the stories of the Bible, they were disappointed, having come to St. Louis more in search of a road map than Christian dogma. Two of the members died in St. Louis and their story reached the public.

Talk about bad timing. Evangelical enthusiasm was reaching a peak and missionaries were willing to go anywhere on earth to reach wayward souls. They took up the Pez Perce request with a vengeance.

Early missionaries

The first missionary in Washington, Jason Lee, was sent by the Methodist Church in 1834 to introduce Christianity to the Native Americans. But instead he spent most of his time and resources ministering to the whites.

He wanted to reach the Nez Perce, but passed the dry tribal grounds of the eastern Palouse and settled in the Williamette Valley, a much more generous growing region.

Unfortunately, the White Man's diseases of smallpox, measles, and influenza wiped out most of the Indian population and Lee was left with mostly whites. Most of them were Catholics, French Canadians who had previously been employees of the Hudson Bay Company and had since settled around the region of French Prairie.

Because of many French employees of both American and British fur companies, much of Oregon has French names. In fact, the distinction of being the first permanent white settler in Oregon country belongs to Joseph Gervais who settled along the Williamette River in 1828 near the town later named after him. As it turned out, Lee's major contribution to missionary and political settlement in the area was through his writing and eastern lecture tours about this "New Eden".

The Whitman's and their tragic Mission near Walla Walla followed soon after the Lee attempt, which was also followed by the Reverend Henry H. Spalding, who made his home further north and was responsible for converting the Nez Perce to Christianity.

Old Joseph

Nez Perce Chief Tu-eka-kas, Old Joseph, converted to Christianity in December, 1838, when Spalding took him into the Presbyterian Church. When his son was born in 1840, Old Joseph asked Spalding if he could pass on his Christian name to his son. Of course, Spalding answered, if the chief promised to raise the child according to the tenets of the church. He would, answered Old Joseph.

Later, Young Joseph was told by his father, he related years later, "When you go into council with the white man, always remember your country. Do not give it away. The white man will cheat you out of your home. I have taken no pay from the United States. I have never sold our land."

The Catholics

The Methodists were followed by Father Fancis N. Blanchet who arrived in St. Paul, Oregon in 1838 to attend the needs of the Catholic population. He also attempted re-christianizing the natives who had been christianized by the Methodists in the Williamette Valley.

In turn, the good father started a feud between the two Christian camps, confusing local Indians about the meaning of Christianity. It should have given them realization of what to expect down the line. Later, they would discover exactly what the white man's religion meant. It was designed for and by white people wanting to colonize the west to white standards. This was to be a land of white Christian values devoid of the evil influences of the east and it would be eternally reserved for white tradition.

Racism

It was also a value system that established racism as a foundation to its gospel. There was something about the missionary movement westwards that attracted the worst attitudes to Oregon, attitudes that remained well into the 20th Century. For example, the 14th Amendment to the Constitution – guaranteeing citizenship to blacks barely passed the Oregon legislature which afterward twice voted to rescind its ratification. The state didn't ratify the 15th Amendment – black suffrage – until 1959, 89 years after the government had declared its ratification nationwide.

In the West the Ku Klux Klan was at its most powerful in Oregon in the 1920s with an estimated 25,000 active members in 1922, the Klan's influence was strong enough to influence legislation, closing all Catholic schools. And it was instrumental in having the ensuing referendum vote passed, though it was later declared unconstitutional by the U.S. Supreme Court.

Utopian communities of various persuasions have been a part of Pacific Northwest lore, many of them today as offshoots of the visionary movement westward in the mid-19th century. The Puget Sound Cooperative Colony, founded in Port Angeles, on the north coast of the Olympic Peninsula in 1887 established itself as a positive force. Others, like the one established near Antelope, Oregon in the 1980s by Bhagwan Shree Rajneesh, were collections of weirdos and nut-cases.

Chautauqua Offshoot

One of the most positive quasi-religous movements westward was the Chautauquas. Formed in 1874, in Chautauqua, New York, it was an offshoot of the Methodist Episcopal summer Sunday School institute, an enlightened summer program of study into arts, science, and the humanities.

Other communities were encouraged to organize their own Chautauquas through their own Methodist Societies and several hundred were organized across the land, including the Northwest. The Chautauquas had something of the spirit of a revival meeting mixed with a bit of a country fair.

In 1912, the movement went commercial and continued bringing the arts, sciences and some of the world's leadings artists and writers to out-of-the-way communities. It ended in 1924, but its mark had been made. The Methodist Society, for example, fought long and hard to ensure that Ashland was part of the Chautauqua circuit. And that same society was responsible for beginning a library and the educational facility that would eventually become Southern Oregon State College.

Every jazz, classical, theatrical, rodeo, or blue grass festival takes place in a setting where you can do things – fish, hike, play tennis and golf. There's nothing highbrow about summer opera in the Pacific Northwest, nor low down about country and western fiddlers festivals. They are just good times.

Festivals in this part of the world reflect their environment. There are desert festivals, mountain festivals, and oceanside festivals each one having a unique sense of place and setting.

There are festivals for the mind and some for the senses. Most take place when the rains disappear along the coast and when the snows melt inland and in the mountains. But there are many festivals and celebrations that occur dur-

Making a statement.

Pendelton Roundup

Pendleton is a quiet place for most of the year, content to be a ranching and wool manufacturing center in eastern Oregon where its 15,000 population lives a fairly straightforward existence working the land most of the year. One of the largest towns in the region, it's an economic factor because of vast wheat fields, green peas, world famous woolen mills, and tourism.

But, in September shouts of "Ride'em Cowboy" ring out as the community celebrates its Pendleton Roundup, a week-long celebration of cowboys and the Western myth.

Begun in 1909 as a Fourth of July cowboy gathering, it is now one of the country's major rodeos, with local white and Indian cowboys competing with one another for modest purses in bronco and bull riding, bulldogging, wild horse racing, and other events. But, because summer is harvest time, promoters decided to hold it in September and, except for 1942/43, it has been held every year in September. It has become as important a rodeo as the Calgary Stampede in Alberta.

Jackson Sundown

The Round-Up Hall Of Fame reflects the history and stars of the event. Oldtime Western film stars and stunt men such as Hoot Gibson and Yakima Canutt regularly competed. So did a Nez Indian named Jackson Sundown whose story is what myth is made of.

The Treaty of 1855 in the Walla Walla Valley established an 800-square-mile reservation in the foothills of the Blue Mountains just east of Pendleton.

Three related Indian tribes – the Umatillas, Walla Wallas, and the Cayuses – plus the Nez who had received their own reservations – were horse-loving ranchers in their own right.

So, when the Pendleton Roundup began, Indian contestants more than held their own. But it was Jackson Sundown, whose native name was Blanket Of The Sun, who set an age standard never equaled.

When he won the title of World Champion Bronc Rider in 1916, he was 50 years old – by standards even then, an old man in a young man's activity. Judges were reluctant to give the award to a middle-aged Indian and made him do several rerides. The crowd began chanting "Sundown" until the judges relented and awarded him the prize.

Horses have made the Hall as well, the most notable being "Midnight" who was ridden three times in different rodeos and never broken. The cowboy who rode him was thrown five times.

Today's Roundup has more activities than just riding and roping and includes Happy Canyon, a night show that now draws enormous crowds on its own. Afterwards the Happy

ing the harsh weather months as well.

Larger cities throughout the region average at least one major event each weekend during summer and early fall. Some, like the Oregon Shakespeare Festival, the Oregon Bach Festival, Portland's Rose Festival, the Seattle Opera's Wagner Festival, and the Pendleton Roundup draw visitors from around the world— people who plan months ahead to attend.

Local color

Others, like the the Cannon Beach Sandcastle Contest in May, the Blessing Of The Fleet in Garibaldi, Oregon (May) and the Hot Air Balloon Stampede in Walla Walla, Washington, also in May, are examples of local color.

The Belly Dance Recital in Corvallis (May), the Moonlight Madness festival

Canyon Dance Hall provides dancing, gambling, and drinking. Pendleton was, after all, once called the Entertainment Capitol of the Northwest with its 32 saloons and 18 bordellos. While the form of diversion has been toned down, the tradition still lives. There is a Country Western concert that in past years has brought in such greats as Reba McEntire, Ricky Skaggs, the Oak Ridge Boys, Randy Travis, George Strait, and Brooks & Dunn. A barbeque, Western Art Show, and other activities are fringe action to the rodeo itself.

At the Round-Up Corral the starting gun goes off at 1:15 p.m. and seven professional events are held every day on the grass arena, plus pony express, wild horse, and baton races on the circular track.

If you tire of the wild cow milking contests or the eating, the town itself offers a wide range of possibilities including 27 historical points. The Rivoli Theater, Bowman Hotel, Hendricks Building, Temple Hotel, City Hall, and Columbia Hotel are just a few buildings that date from the turn-of-the-century or before.

The Pendleton Underground Tours takes you through the tunnels underneath the historic district where much of the gambling halls card rooms and bordellos were located. Golf at the Pendleton Country Club, saddles and clothing at Hemley's Western Store, and a tour through the Pendleton Woolen Mills are highly recommended.

Bavarian dancers keeping step in Leavenworth village.

(July), the Little Ole Opry in North Bend (August), and the Muddy Frogwater Festival in Milton (August) are a few of the off-the-wall fests you'll find in Oregon.

The Oregon Shakespeare Festival in Ashland, takes place in an outstanding theater setting with the Elizabeth Theater being the centerpiece. The design and dimensions of the space are based on the Fortune Theater of 1600 in England. The productions – staged between February and October — are well known for their authentic stagings, adhering to the original texts as Shakespeare wrote them. The Black Swan (150 seats) and the Angus Bowmer (600 seats) round out the three-theater complex near downtown on South Pioneer Street.

The Country Fiddlers Contest brings together fiddlers from throughout the Northwest in a mix of music making and good food, participating in the old spirit of the west. Held in Enterprise, near Wallowa in Northeast Oregon in the third weekend in July, the contest treats old-time western music lovers to music and cowboy festivities.

The Wallowa Valley Festival of the Arts, in April, has wine-tasting parties, a silent auction, a quick-draw competi-

The unforgettable Bing Crosby in Gonzaga University in Spokane.

Brewer's Festival, Oregon.

tion and a cowboy poets' festival.

And if you still need more fiddle music, there's the Festival of American Tunes (July) at Fort Worden, near Port Townsend, Washington. If the place looks familiar, it's because this was the location for the Richard Gere/Debra Winger film, *An Officer and A Gentleman.*

In LaPush, on the West side of the Olympic Peninsula, Quileute Days (August) celebrates with dugout canoe races and a parade. Bring your own food as people come from miles around and there's only one cafe in town.

In Oregon's Williamette Valley, two festivals draw thousands to the celebrations - the Brownsville Pioneer Picnic (June), Lebanon's Strawberry Festival (June) and Albany's World Champion-

ship Timber Carnival (July 4).

Crown Jewel of Festivals

The Pioneer Picnic is Oregon's oldest celebration, dating from the 19th-century. But the crown jewel of festivals is the one-day Timber Carnival with lumberjacks competing in a wide range of activities, an olympics of logging that includes scaling, chopping, log-rolling, axe throwing, and sawing. As part of the Lebanon contribution to the festival, an 8-foot (2.5 meters) high and 1,000 pounds (450 kilos) strawberry cake helps quell appetites.

Artistic Director Helmuth Rilling has turned the Oregon Bach Festival in

Eugene into more than a Bachian experience (June 25-July 10). The two dozen or so concerts feature musical styles ranging from composers of the Baroque era to 20th-century and jazz.

While the works of major contemporary international composers are always on the festival's programs, the staples are always played yearly. So, works like Bach's many Cantatas, the St. Matthew's Passion, and the Brandenburg Concertos are regular staples of the world-reknowned German conductor's festival.

Often overlooked is the Peter Britt Music Festival in Jacksonville, Oregon (June-September) which features an array of music, dance, and theater. Set among the Ponderosa pines and the native Madrones, the hillside estate of the pioneer photographer is a natural amphitheater for the outdoor festival of special food and cultural arts ranging from Japanese Taiko Dojo to Brahms.

As the self-proclaimed apple capitol of the world, Wenatchee, Washington, seems the most appropriate place to hold an annual Apple Blossom Festival (April). The 10-day festival event starts at the end of April and is followed in late September by the Wenatchee Valley Arts Festival. Sandcastle Days transforms Cannon Beach, Oregon into a sculpted wonderland of sand creatures and miniature buildings.

Long Beach, Washington, is the site of the International Kite Festival (August), but there's more to it than a few pieces of paper on the end of a string.

The festival includes competitive contests for handcrafted kites, children's stunts, and illuminated kites all soaring above the water off the 28-mile (45-km) long beach. At the World Kite Museum and Hall Of Fame, are exhibits of kites from around the world –- Japan, China, Thailand –- with displays of stunt, military, and advertising kites.

Oregon has its own kite festivals in the Puffin Kite Festival (April) in Cannon Beach; and the Rockaway Beach Kite Festival Kite Festival and Salmon Bake (May) in Rockaway.

Music festivals

The Olympic Music Festival (June 26-Sept. 5), is staged in a turn-of-the-century barn. This is salmon country so while the music of the resident ensemble, the Philadelphia String Quartet, brings satisfaction to the soul, you might also try your luck along Juan de Fuca Strait. The program has the mainstream of chamber music with Mozart, Haydn, Beethoven, and Brahms.

Also on the Olympic Peninsula is the Port Townsend Jazz Festivals that take place in February and in June. During May, however, many of the towns historic and pleasant Victorian-style houses are open to the public. The International Folk Dance Festival is in August and the Port Townsend Rhododendron Festival takes place in spring, usually March/April when the blossoms appear.

Wenatchee Apple Blossom Festival

The annual festival isn't really about apple blossoms. That's just the excuse. It's real objective is to unite the entire region in a two-week event that celebrates community creativity.

Its real name is the Washington State Apple Blossom Festival, thereby putting the celebration into a state, rather than a local, context. The Washington State version originated from a spring festival held annually in New Zealand. The wife of the region's first apple shipper and a native of New Zealand, Mrs. E. Wagner, suggested beginning a similar one in the Wenatchee Valley.

The Ladies Musical Club produced the first one, then called "Blossom Days", in 1920. It lasted one day and was held in Wenatchee's Memorial Park. The events involved song, speeches, and a street dance.

The event was such as success that the ladies lost their jobs. The Commercial Club, the forerunner of the Chamber of Commerce, took over sponsorship of the celebration. The first parade was held in 1921 and the first-ever Apple Blossom Queen, Florence Kratzer, reigned over the festivities.

Today, the Apple Blossom Festival draws well over 100,000 visitors from around the world. It lasts 10 days and continues to boast the distinction of being the first apple blossom festival in the country. The speech, the song, and the street dance of the original event, have given way to 50 events that take in virtually every interest.

There's an old-fashioned square dance, musical theater, apple baking contests, historical exhibits, a food fair, a carnival, arts and crafts fair, band concert, car show, handball tournament, model airplane show, golf tournament, a series of competitive runs, a precious gem mini-festival, and many other kinds of people-gathering excuses.

The North Central Washington Museum is both a showcase for regional art and a cultural center featuring a variety of concerts, art displays, and apple blossom traditions.

The Chelan County Museum brings out its special displays during the 10 days, and there is a national juried art exhibit featuring works from artists around the country.

There's even something about apples at the Washington Apple Commission Visitor Center. You learn how the state's 4,500 apple growers produce more than seven billion apples annually - more than 50 percent of all the fresh apples grown in the United States.

Legend's Games

A new event kicked off in 1993, the Washington State Apple Blossom Festival Games at the Walla Walla Point Park softball and baseball complex. An assortment of basketball, softball, and volleyball games culminate in the Legend's Games, a reunion of former local fast-pitch softball greats.

The town becomes a madhouse of community involvement with few residents untouched by the largely volunteer generated activities. Much of the events are free. The University of Washington Coaches Tour is the most expensive with golf and dinner at the Wenatchee Golf and Country Club costing $55.

You can get more information about the events by writing to the Washington State Apple Blossom Festival, P.O. Box 850, Wenatchee, WA 98801 or by telephoning (509) 662-3616.

Clarinetist David Shifrin's Chamber Music Northwest festival (June 22-July 25) usually features 35 performers in 25 concerts taking place at Reed College and Catlin Gabel School in Portland. The Emerson String Quartet has as the ensemble-in-residence and artists include some of the biggest names in music.

The Seattle Chamber Music Festival season (June 29-July 24) takes place at the Lakeside School near Lake Wash-

Having a swinging time at the Rose Festival Fun Center.

ington where artistic director Toby Saks has put together a program utilizing 30 musicians. Seattle is also the site of numerous festivals including the Bumbershoot Arts Festival (September), the most popular of the city's gatherings. Plays, art exhibits, music of all kinds, and crafts take over the Seattle Center. Salmon Days in Issaquah (October) features a salmon bake, races, and live entertainment.

Other Seattle festivals include the colorful Chinese New Year parades in the International District (late January

Oldest Jazz festival

Bellevue, on the eastern shores of Lake Washington, has its own Jazz Festival (July), held on the Bellevue Community College Campus with three stages hosting players from throughout North America in the oldest jazz festival in the state.

The city (the fourth largest in Washington with a population 87,000 and essentially a bedroom suburb of Seattle) is also home to the Northwest Arts and Crafts Fair featuring a jury-selected list of artists displaying their work.

Art In The Park in Everett (August) and the Mount Vernon Tulip Festival which varies in time depending on the season, are two popular near-Seattle gatherings.

The list of festivals, musical, theatrical, community, is extensive. Virtually every town and region has several during the year. Contact the Oregon and Washington state tourist departments for complete lists. Or you can write to regional tourist boards listed in the Directory.

Cultural symphony

Artists and performers are given more latitude in failing or succeeding than their counterparts in either New York or Chicago.

Perhaps that's because the cultural identity of the region is still being de-

or early February); Fat Tuesday (February) a Mardi-Gras style fest; a Seagull Calling Contest (March); Worldfest (April) in which the characters of 20 different cultures are celebrated; Northwest Folklife Festival (May); Bon Odori (July) a celebration of Seattle's Japanese community; Winterfest (November) is Seattle's pre-Christmas festivity.

Centrum Festivals

One of the most influential arts organizations in the state is not based in Seattle, but on the northernmost region of the Olympic Penisula in Port Townsend. Some of the most inspired chamber music is presented on a wooden stage at the Fort Worden State Park Beach in Port Townsend every August.

It's not so much the music making that inspires confidence in the future of the genre, but the audience — made up of the best young musicians in the northwest.

Most Northwesterners know Centrum from its Jazz Port Townsend weekends, or because of the bombastic Festival of American Fiddle Tunes and the many other concerts that the organization unfolds during the summer season. But Centrum, which was founded in 1973, is devoted to ensuring the future of music by educating youngsters in a series of educational programs. In 1981, it worked with 2,000 children and in 1992 that figure was up to 12,000 plus more than 1,200 teachers.

The workshops bring gifted students from around the state for a week of exploring their special talents. The instructors are professional and their disciplines range from standup comedy to jazz to poetry to chamber music.

While the organization continues to increase its work with children, it is also increasing its number of concerts, events that inevitably draw large crowds to the peninsula. The performances not only provide public access to the arts, but would also bring in money to continue the education program.

The fort's old First World War blimp hanger is the site of the concerts. The renovated building was constructed to house dirigibles that were never used in combat.

The $2.4 million renovations produced the McCurdy Pavilion with huge sliding doors that open onto expansive Littlefield Green where audiences sit on chairs or blankets.

The music extends well beyond the summer months. Chamber Music Port Townsend, for example, is presented in the last weekend of January with internationally noted musicians.

The same site is used for a Centrum and Port Townsend Film Company sponsored feature film industry conference in October. The conference brings hundreds of film industry people together to talk with one another about trends and industry matters.

Among the favorite public festivals are Readings from the Port Townsend Writers Conference, two weeks in July; Jazz Port Townsend in late July; Marrowstone Music Festival Orchestra presented in collaboration with the Seattle Youth Orchestra throughout August; World Beat Festival presenting mambas, rhumbas, and lively Latin jazz in September.

Any listing of Centrum events, however, is guaranteed to be outdated by the time it reaches the public. For current information, contact the organization directly at P.O. Box 1158, Port Townsend, WA 98368 or telephone (206) 385-3102. Fax (206) 385-2470.

---

fined. There are fewer sacred cows to gore and the major organizations are relatively young with histories that would definitely pale when compared to the giant cultural industries of New York, Chicago, or Philadelphia.

This lack of cultural baggage does allow for flexibility. The Seattle Symphony's music director, Gerard Schwarz, for example, convinced his board of directors that the orchestra should embrace the music of certain 20th-century American composers. So, the Seattle Symphony is now generally recognized nationwide for its brilliant interpretations of neo-romantic American music from David Diamond, Howard Hanson and others.

While the 1962 Seattle World's Fair is an acknowledged land-mark for the region's economy and for its moving into a technological universe, it was also a major point of reference for cultural activity.

Until the fair, the Seattle Symphony's only competition for artistic endeavors was from the Seattle Art Museum. There was no professional opera, theater, or dance, very few art galleries, a part time orchestra, and three museums with limited exhibitions. It was, in short, a cultural wasteland, perfectly representing what eastern Americans thought of the Pacific Northwest — all trees, no brains.

Arts explosion

Then almost overnight, the arts began an explosion that has carried over to today. Simultaneously with the closing of the fair, Seattle Opera and the Seattle Repertory Theater were created, and within the next decade the Pacific Northwest Ballet, and many smaller groups made the city culturally livable. Performing arts, however, are not the only cultural expression in Seattle. Sometimes it comes in small, untrumpeted and downright unusual packages.

A two-level shop in Seattle's Pioneer Square area, the popular and eclectic Eliot Bay Book Company, is gener-

ally accepted as the nerve center of the city's literary life.

To someone coming from the large metropolitan regions of the mid-west or east coast, the idea of a bookstore being the focal point for a city's writers and thinkers must seem odd, indeed. But, the literary world is a working one in Seattle, unlike New York which has major publishing parties with the media and cultural figures meeting in a common purpose, rubbing elbows and clinking wine glasses.

While authors abound, here, they generally fade into the background, bound to their word processors. In fact, there is as yet no large collection of work that can be identified as "Pacific Northwest" as there is of "Southern" or New York".

Tickets for readings at the Eliot Bay are free, but quickly snapped up. The Eliot Bay Cafe downstairs, provides strong coffee and its annex serves as the literary cradle for readings to take place.

Outside, on Pioneer Square, large crowds mingle on nights that famous authors come to read.

Another book store in another part of the Northwest has made a different kind of impact. In Portland's Powell's City of Books, you encounter what has

Portland Center for the Performing Arts.

been claimed to be the largest collection of saleable books in America.

With more than one million new and used titles, customers are encouraged to pick up a map at the door to find their way through an elaborate maze of aisles. Powell's too has its coffee-shop

reading room.

Art and craft

As one would expect in a land where Aboriginals produced fine art, the North-

Northwest Folklife

Nationally acclaimed as one of the most diverse and grand ethnic festivals, the Northwest Folklife Festival attracts nearly 200,000 visitors and hosts 6,000 participants representing at least 100 countries.

Held over the Memorial Day Weekend in May, the festival stages about 1,000 dance and music performances on 22 stages. While Seattle hosts a series of folk festivals year round reflecting the city and the Pacific Northwest's ethnic mix, it is this festival that focuses the region's attention.

Among the annual attractions are Japanese *taiko* drums, Russian folk music, Eastern European dances, African *marimbas*, Old-time fiddle music, Native American groups, and a diverse collection of cultural ensembles. Each year the festival works with a different ethnic community to present a major program relating to that group's arts and heritage.

In 1994, for example, the African American and Alaskan native communities are invited to highlight elements of their folk cultures. The ethnic communities use their arts and traditions to provide an understanding about their lifestyles. While the impact of African Americans is fairly well known, even though they make up just 12 percent of Seattle's population.

Washington State is home to 1,400 Alaska Native Peoples, many of whom came to Washington for better education, artistic opportunity, or as a result of the Alaska Natives Claims Settlement Act in 1971. In addition, the most direct passage between Alaska and the lower 48 is through Seattle primarily via Alaska and Delta Airlines.

Other programs at every festival include the Traditional Artists area where 14 master artisans from around the world demonstrate skills ranging from Hmong basket weaving to Norwegian rosemaling. The International Children's Village offers visitors hands-on activities, performances, and family dance workshops throughout the weekend.

Since 1972, the festival has been held annually on the grounds of the 74-acre Seattle Center which has a huge variety of performance and eating space.

Uncommon Market

The facilities are perfect for one of the Pacific Northwest's largest and finest crafts markets. The festival's Uncommon Market, as they call it, presents more than 80 booths with a wide array of handmade, ethnic and imported products from Africa, Asia, Europe, and the Americas. In the Crafts Marketplace, jewelry, clothing, ceramics, and leather goods from 139 selected artists are on sale.

The Northwest Folklife Festival also has the world's largest musical instrument auction, 35 international food booths offering inexpensive ethnic foods prepared by some of the region's finest chefs, a roadhouse with square, swing, and contra dancing, plus workshops in a variety of disciplines.

During the four-day weekend celebrations, there is little unused space on the Seattle Center grounds. The free event draws enough people to create a carnival atmosphere and it's one of the truly joyous Pacific Northwest experiences.

There's more to Seattle's folk music and cultural activity than this one festival. Seattle's biggest fair of the year, Seafair, is a three-week long extravaganza of crafts, arts, parades and ethnic festivals culminating in the unlimited hydroplane races on Lake Washington in early August. The Pacific Northwest African-American Festival celebrates Black history with a parade, arts and crafts, also in early August. The Chinatown International District Festival is held in mid-July to celebrate Chinatown's unique diversity with Asian and Pacific Island dancers and foods.

west's art and craft galleries are active. On the first Thursday of every month, for example, the galleries in Seattle collectively stage an open house of their newly installed exhibits between 4 p.m. and 8 p.m. and a flow of people move in

Maryhill Museum in Goldendale, Washington.

and out of the art spaces.

It's as much theater as art with Occidental Park openings appearing to be mini-festivals – bands pounding out their music while gallery owners/managers hawk their exhibits.

The Northwest Gallery of Fine Woodworking on First Avenue is a showcase for amazing woodworking. Warm hues of exotic woods in furniture, sculptures, vases and bowls will make you dissatisfied with your own collections.

Every town and city has at least one museum of local, regional, national, or international status.

Westerners are, by nature, collectors of their past, probably because their history is so short, and their efforts reflect local and regional identity.

Walla Walla Symphony

But the cultural activities of small-town Northwest are more than just historical artifacts. The Walla Walla Symphony was established in 1907 and is the oldest continuous symphony orchestra west of the Mississippi with programmes that ranges from Bach to Shostakovich; Mozart to Howard Hanson and contemporary composers such as Marvin Schluger and Steve Heitzig.

Modern Seattle is defined by the Museum of Flight at Boeing Field, a combination of art and technology. Centered in a dramatic piece of glass and steel architecture called the Great Gallery, are 22 aircraft hung from the

Jazz

Jazz is a growth industry here. You find it at festivals in the mountains, near the ocean, and in any number of pubs and bars in Seattle, Portland, Spokane, and Eugene. To list every one in the Northwest would take a book. But there are some venues that are unusual enough to take a detour to hear.

No one has ever adequately explained why jazz has always been popular in the Northwest. It just has been. The mix of free and structured rhythms seems suited to the lifestyle, attracting both traditionalists and the free-spirited to its multiple identities.

Oregon's biggest and splashiest of the festivals is the Mount Hood Jazz festival which isn't held on Mount Hood at all, but rather at Mount Hood Community College in Gresham, a suburb of Portland, the first weekend of August. This is the music event of the year for local jazz lovers. But it attracts more than just the locals. You hear a myriad of languages being spoken during the two, nine-hour concerts that make up the fest.

Started in 1982 by a group of Gresham businessmen, the festival capitalizes on the healthy jazz environment in town. Lou Rawls, Count Basie, Stan Getz, Wynton Marsalis and Grove Alexander Jr. are just some of the musicians who have headlined the event in recent years.

The crowds are made up of people who view jazz as an art form in itself. Write to the festival and ask when tickets go on sale, because they're snapped up in a day once the schedule is announced. (Box 696, Gresham, WA 97030, tel: (503) 666-3810).

Each summer and Autumn, the Washington Jazz Society in Seattle charters the ancient but appealing passenger boat, *Virginia V*, for a combination jazz-concert and Puget Sound tour. Don't look for avant-garde music here, because the organizers want to appeal to a broad cross-section of music lovers. But, the music is often exceptional and is always well presented. Again, tickets are in demand. The Washington Jazz Society offers information at P.O. Box 24284, Terminal Ennex, Seattle, WA 98124.

While there have been some closures of popular jazz clubs in the past few years, Portland is still a jazz-active city. You have a choice of live and recorded music, and because of the genre's reputation, you're likely to see jazz greats playing at main stream jazz outlets.

French food and live jazz are found nightly at Brasserie Montmartre on SW. Park Ave. This clientele is strictly middle-class, well dressed, and proper.

A different view of the world can be had at Parchman Farm on SE Clay Street. This club features a music library of more than 1,000 jazz albums. It's a quiet, casual place to hear music. It attracts the kind of audience that gets up on stage and starts jamming with the evening's musicians. At The Hobbitt, there's live music six nights a week featuring local and national acts. And every Sunday afternoon there's a jam session that attracts local jazz musicians.

The Traditional Jazz Society of Oregon is based in Eugene (P.O. Box 7432, Eugene, OR 97401. Its objective is the perpetuation, preservation, and promotion of traditional jazz and its lively concerts are attractive alternatives to Eugene's Opera, Symphony, Mozart, and the Bach Festival.

ceiling as if in full flight. In all, 45 aircraft – many of them rare – reflect more than 75 years of aviation.

Maritime history

The Museum of History and Industry on 24th Avenue has Seattle's best early-day collection and pays tribute to Puget Sound's rich maritime history. Do not miss, too, the Columbia River Maritime Museum, on the Oregon Coast, which features among others, the fully operational US Coast guardship *Columbia*.

In Eugene, at the University of Or-

Seattle Art Museum.

egon, the Museum of Natural History is one of the best ways to orient yourself to the state's geology and anthropology. Permanent exhibits cover Oregon's fossil history, and Northcoast art.

The Washington State Historical Society Museum in Tacoma houses items on state and Puget Sound history and collections of Northwest Indians.

Rich cultural traditions

Major cultural groups have had a mix

the Ashland Shakespeare Festival; or the large museums like Portland's Art Museum and Tacoma Art Museum with their vast collections of European and American art. The Portland Art Museum owns the finest and most extensive collection of Native American art in the country, much of which is displayed on a rotating basis. In addition, there are galleries of Asian, African, and Pre-Columbian art. Between the extremes of traditional and aboriginal are many forms of art and culture, each with its clientele and many reflecting the region's own dynamic culture.

Much of Portland's major cultural activities are essentially centralized, like Seattle's, in an attractive downtown location, the Portland Center For The Performing Arts. Included are the Arlene Schnitzer Concert Hall, the Intermediate, and the Winningstead theaters.

The Schnitzer Concert Hall has expanded Portland's downtown musical scene in spectacular fashion. Not only is it the home of the Oregon Symphony Orchestra (OSO), but also the scene of the Chamber Music Northwest's summer season and the magnet for popular showbiz stars. Originally known as the Rapp & Rapp Paramount Theater, it was built as a vaudeville place in the 1920s. Now, fully restored and on the list of National Historic Landmarks, it's a jewel of a hall. The OSO was founded in 1896 and is the oldest symphony orchestra on the west coast, older even than San Francisco's. The season that runs from September to June, has the

of traditions from which to draw – migrating immigrants from Asia and Europe, plus an indigenous native culture that had defined itself through its art and song.

Thus, there's a mix of cultures to be experienced in many forms. There are the large European-based cultural institutions like the Seattle Symphony and

Ashland

In 1935, when the entire country was deeply into the Great Depression and everyone was broke, the people of Ashland decided to build an Elizabethan stage. The idea was to celebrate July the Fourth by staging two of Shakespeare's plays, an idea only slightly watered down by the stipulation of local merchants that a boxing match be held the same day to cover any losses from the theater.

To everyone's surprise, not only did the Shakespearean adventure make money, it made enough to cover the losses from the boxing match. From that day, Shakespeare became an important element in everyday Ashland's life. Today, with the exception of Stratford-on-Avon in England, and Oberammergau in Germany, no specific city is as closely identified to cultural activity as is Ashland with its Oregon Shakespeare Festival.

But its activities go well beyond the borders of Ashland. For six months the festival stages five plays in Portland as well. In total, the festival presented 878 performances in 1992 (723 in Ashland, 155 in Portland) on a yearly budget of more than $12 million, 79 percent of which is realized through earned income.

Each year more than 100,000 theater lovers head to Ashland to experience not just the plays, but a style, and a sense of intellectual well being. Combined with the Peter Britt Music Festival in nearby Jacksonville, two miles (3 km) north, both events garner a potpourri of music and theater enthusiasts in a cross fertilization of arts disciplines.

The beginnings

Ashland was founded in 1852 on Bear Creek, at the southernmost end of the Rogue River Valley. Mining, logging, wool production, and agriculture became its main industries. In the early 20th-century, businessmen tried to promote the city as a mineral springs resort. The venture failed, but mineral water rich in lithium, sulfur, sodium, and chlorine still bubbles from fountains in the city's main plaza and in Lithia Park.

A walk through Lithia Park is a must with 100 acres of trees with name tags, shady paths, and picnic tables along Ashland Creek. Two special areas, the Japanese Garden and the Sycamore Grove, offer inspiration through their quiet radiance. Along Main Street to the Plaza and Lithia Park, Victorian and turn-of-the-century houses create a specific ambience that's in keeping with the festival. The Southern Historical Society runs a museum in the restored Colonial Revival, Chappell-Swedenburg House, built in 1904-05. Exhibits focus on the history of the region's development. The Lithia Springs Hotel, now called the Mark Anthony, is a nine story building that was once the tallest structure between San Francisco and Seattle and is a National Historical Landmark.

Ashland Festival

The festival itself – which brings in more than $45 million into the local community – is actually three separate theaters with 11 plays in repertoire, three of them by Shakespeare and held outdoors on the Elizabethan Stage. It sits on the site of Ashland's Chautauqua Dome. It's a lovely site, but keep in mind that sitting very close means craning your neck and it can get stiff. Dress warmly and invest in renting pillows and lap blankets. Eight plays are split between the large indoor Agnus Bowmer Theater with its computerized sound and fabulous acoustics; and the smaller, Black Swan where modern and experimental theater is the norm.

Shakespeare isn't the only act in town with the Actors Workshop, Lyric Theater, Studio X, Children's Theater, the Oregon Cabaret Theater, the State Ballet of Oregon, and Southern Oregon State College's theater department offering their own work.

usual variety of classical, children's and pop concerts.

The Portland Center Stage is a north-ern offshoot of the Oregon Shakespeare Festival in Ashland while the Portland Repertory Theater continues its year-long season of standard, quality theater. Storefront Theater is known for taking risks and the Artists Repertory is the place for off-broadway performances.

The Portland Opera Company is housed in the old Civic Auditorium along with the Oregon Ballet Theater. The opera company stages four productions a year ranging from mainstream Italian to light and contemporary opera.

By comparison, the Oregon Ballet Theater is new, formed in 1989 from two popular Portland ballet companies and is now stronger than either of its predecessors. Traditional ballets such as *Romeo & Juliet*, and *The Nutcracker* are its staples, but new works are also performed frequently.

Seattle Center

Seattle Center is located on the old Seattle World's Fair grounds in Belltown. Boasting more than 8 million visits a year to its 74-acre grounds, it's not just the entertainment center of the city, but its cultural heart – the home of the Seattle Symphony, The Northwest Ballet Company (famous for its annual Christmas stagings of Tchaikovsky's *The Nutcracker*) and Seattle Opera which gained a worldwide reputation in the 1970s for its productions of Wagner's *Ring of the Nibelung Cycle*. It still stages the four-opera event, though irregularly.

More than 100 performances by professional companies from six continents entertain families during the six-day Seattle International Children's festival in May and the Northwest Folklife Festival, on Memorial Day weekend, is the largest of its kind in the nation.

The center hosts more than 5,400 performances annually in its Opera House, Playhouse, Coliseum, and Bagley Wright Theater. The Arena, and Exhibition Hall are home to a number of cultural events throughout the years. The Space Needle towers over the center, but the city's symbol is only one of many innovative designs. A series of arches, designed by architect Minoru Yama-saka – who also designed the IBM Building downtown – identifies the Pacific Science Center.

The Seattle Art Museum, the Frye Art Museum, and the Henry Art Gallery are Seattle's traditional galleries, having superb collections, and presenting them in traditional, time-worn ways.

On The Board, and the Center of Contemporary Art (COCA) are the city's leading new expression cultural centers. COCA brings shock therapy to the city's art traditionalists a couple of times a year with exhibitions that try to break new ground; On The Board stages contemporary dance, music, and a multi-

Semiahmoo

A merge of old and new at the Inn at Semiahmoo.

A piece of history, a slab of culture, The Inn at Semiahmoo sits on a mile-long wooded spit of land at Blaine that juts into Puget Sound.

The four-story Inn is 110 miles (177 km) north of Seattle and 40 miles (64 km) south of Vancouver on a site that was once an important site for the Semi-ahmoo Indians ("those who eat shellfish").

The Inn is part of the $200 million Resort Semiahmoo – an 800 acre development that incorporates a marina, an 18-hole Arnold Palmer designed golf course, a lighthouse square waterfront village, villas, condominiums, and homesites.

The hotel has been constructed on a major piece of Pacific Northwest history, sitting on a site where 3,000 years ago, Salish Indians thrived on the shores of Drayton Harbor. The $33.5 million hotel and conference complex is a prime example of how past and present cultures can merge in a single location.

Built by Atlas Hotels of San Diego, the 200 room complex opened for business June 13, 1987 and has become a major player in northwest Washington's tourism.

The Semiahmoo Inn has indoor/outdoor tennis courts, racquetball, weight training, a spa, an indoor running track, a 15,000 sq. ft. conference center that can accommodate groups of up to 800, restaurants and bars.

It has a 175 seat theater, board room, additional exhibit space, nine to 16-foot ceilings for the use of video projection equipment.

Fishing is a major ingredient of the hotel and there's an extensive bicycling path around the wooded peninsula, beach paths, jogging and horseback trails, and five miles of oyster and clam beaches.

Its Arnold Palmer golf course was rated as the finest new resort course in America by Golf Digest, and has become the focal point of the meandering, rolling landscape.

More recently, the location saw a series of salmon canneries – the last one, owned by Alaska Packers, closing in the middle 1970's. Sailing ships called it home and its steam-driven engines turned day and night.

For nearly half a century it was the site of one of the world's most productive canneries. Prior to the resort being built, the site was a collection of rotting buildings, and a deteriorating dock.

Many of the old cannery buildings have been refurbished and remodeled for hotel use. The old boiler room is now the Inn's bakery; bricks from the boiler room were used to build the two-story fireplace in the hotel's lobby; the cannery bunkhouse is the site of a museum.

Many waterfront buildings have been restored to house a 80-shop village of shops, galleries, pubs, markets and restaurants. The fish-processing plant original to the site became the Inn's 80-seat bar while the cannery has become a more formal, full service restaurant.

The Spokane Opera House dominates the downtown skyline.

media mix of expression. There is a rich tradition of jazz and country music with the former scattered throughout every major city and the latter a way of life in the interior of Washington and Oregon.

In Seattle, Dimitriou's Jazz Alley is the place to go. Cool and sophisticated, Dimitriou's books only the best performers. In Portland you'll find many restaurants that have piped in jazz, but if you want live entertainment, it's to be found at Brasserie Montmartre with the well dressed crowd, or at Parchman Farm for more relaxed jamming.

Seattle & Tacoma

The people who live here are not only well-read, they're optimists. Some say it's because of the rain. Seattle is where citizens brag about their book stores and where more sunglasses per capita are purchased than in any other city in America even though much of the year is defined by low, water saturated clouds.

There are few cities in America with as distinguished a recent past as this one. Since 1975 it has yearly been chosen America's "best" in many magazines and in many categories including best bicycling city, most livable, best city to locate a business, best hotels, best place to visit by a variety of magazines, books, and even by America's Mayors.

Travel up the Space Needle for a bird's eye view of the city.

It's certainly a place where its citizens partake in its good fortune. It is ranked fourth in America in sales at eating and drinking establishments, fourth in frequency of opera performances and in spending

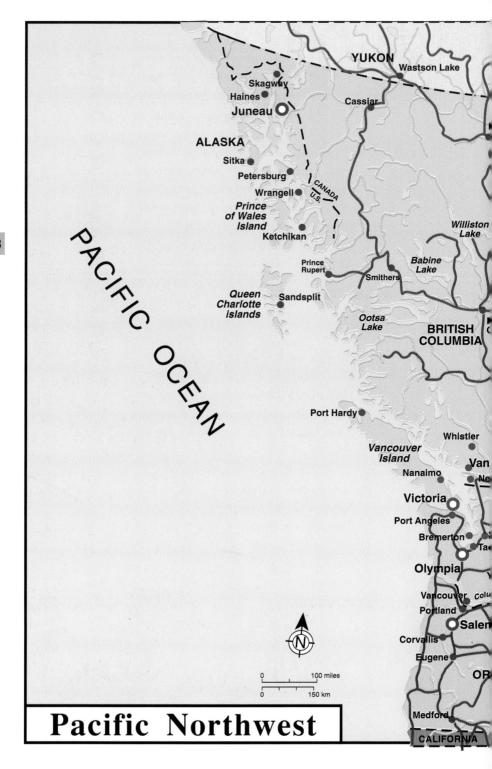

PACIFIC OCEAN

YUKON

Wastson Lake

Skagway

Haines

Juneau

Cassiar

ALASKA

Sitka

Petersburg

Wrangell

CANADA
U.S.

Prince
of Wales
Island

Ketchikan

Williston
Lake

Prince
Rupert

Babine
Lake

Smithers

Queen
Charlotte
islands

Sandsplit

Ootsa
Lake

BRITISH
COLUMBIA

Port Hardy

Whistler

Vancouver
Island

Van

Nanaimo

Ne

Victoria

Port Angeles

Bremerton

Ta

Olympia

Vancouver

colu

Portland

Salen

Corvallis

Eugene

OR

Medford

CALIFORNIA

0   100 miles

0   150 km

Pacific Northwest

money for its libraries, and it has more theater performances annually than any other city except New York. And Seattle definitely gorges on its sea culture at restaurants beside Puget Sound, Union Lake, or Lake Washington.

Yet, hardly any of this was ever planned. It just sort of happened because Seattle is a city that makes itself up as it goes along.

People here just do things differently. You notice it as soon as you land at **Seattle-Tacoma Airport**, known as SEA-TAC, 14 miles (22.5 km) south of the city.

People here seem to talk more, to begin with, and the city somehow seems less of a tourist ghetto than any other American destination.

One explanation might be because this is a place where tourism and living are integrated, where nothing has been imposed, and where virtually every interesting place is there for a reason. So there are no artificial Disneylands out in the suburbs where you have to drive to experience character.

In fact, there just may be fewer tourist traps per square foot in Seattle, than anywhere in North America. The short tourist season, generally July through September, has kept it from becoming tacky.

Wealth of natural beauty

First-time visitors are usually astonished at the wealth of natural beauty in and

The Courthouse and Municipal Park.

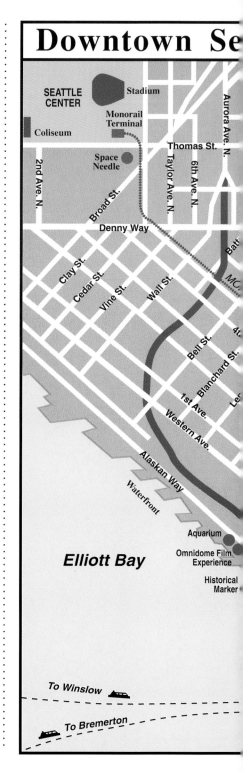

around Seattle. Literally touching the city's boundaries are thousands of square kilometers of evergreen forest and salt and freshwater shorelines.

Bracketed east and west by freshwater Lake Washington and saltwater Puget Sound, the city occupies a north-south corridor, slender at the waist and embracing several hills.

Most of Seattle's best sights, frankly, can't be appreciated from a tour bus. The best are clustered in pedestrian-scale sections best savored on foot. Downtown business district buses are free and the Monorail speeds quickly between downtown and the **Seattle Center**, the city's cultural crown jewel. Not even the popular **Pioneer Square**, the city's preserved historic district, with its active

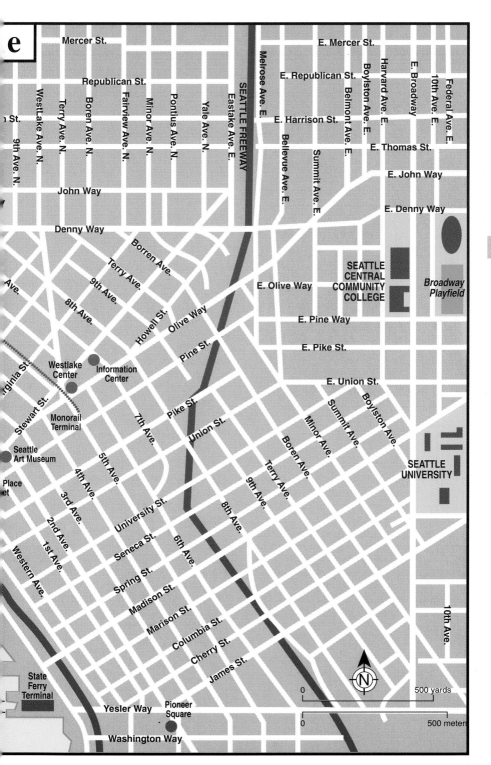

Mercer St.

E. Mercer St.

Republican St.

E. Republican St.

E. Harrison St.

E. Thomas St.

Melrose Ave. E.

SEATTLE FREEWAY

Eastlake Ave. E.

Yale Ave. N.

Pontius Ave. N.

Minor Ave. N.

Fairview Ave. N.

Boren Ave. N.

Terry Ave. N.

Westlake Ave. N.

9th Ave. N.

St.

Bellevue Ave. E.

Summit Ave. E.

Belmont Ave. E.

Boylston Ave. E.

Harvard Ave. E.

E. Broadway

10th Ave. E.

Federal Ave. E.

John Way

E. John Way

Denny Way

E. Denny Way

Borren Ave.

Terry Ave.

9th Ave.

8th Ave.

Ave.

E. Olive Way

SEATTLE
CENTRAL
COMMUNITY
COLLEGE

Broadway
Playfield

E. Pine Way

Howell St.

Olive Way

Pine St.

E. Pike St.

Westlake
Center

Information
Center

Virginia St.

E. Union St.

Monorail
Terminal

Stewart St.

7th Ave.

Pike St.

Boylston Ave.

Summit Ave.

Seattle
Art Museum

Union St.

Minor Ave.

Place
et

5th Ave.

4th Ave.

3rd Ave.

Boren Ave.

Terry Ave.

9th Ave.

SEATTLE
UNIVERSITY

2nd Ave.

1st Ave.

University St.

8th Ave.

Western Ave.

Seneca St.

6th Ave.

Spring St.

Madison St.

10th Ave.

Marison St.

Columbia St.

Cherry St.

James St.

State
Ferry
Terminal

N

Yesler Way

Pioneer
Square

0   500 yards

0   500 meters

Washington Way

Pioneer Square

Pioneer Square, the city's preserved historic district.

Long before European settlement, it used to be an Indian village. Now Pioneer Square Historical District is the place where lawyers have small offices and where the residents of the fashionable Magnolia district buy their art.

And it's where Seattle began back in 1852 after the original settlers abandoned Alki Point– where they had landed a year before – because of the hard, cold windy winters and poor moorage for visiting sailing vessels. Today, the only reminder of the original Tlingit Indian village that preceded Pioneer Square is a 60-foot totem pole and a bronze bust to Chief Seattle at Pioneer Place Park.

Original Skid Road

Resting adjacent to the site where the present Kingdome hosts NFL football and American League baseball, Pioneer Square district is where loggers built the original Skid Road (along Yesler Way) to ski logs downhill to the waterfront. Constructed by Henry Yesler, the skid was designed to transport logs from the steep surrounding hills down to the waterfront where Yessler had a sawmill.

It became known as **Skid Road**, a term that was eventually absorbed into American lexicon as "skid row" to denote a city's run down area, the home of derelicts and winos. Locals are as sensitive to the use of "skid row" as San Franciscans are to their city being called "Frisco".

Pioneer Square's handsome red brick buildings – most of them recently restored – were built after the great fire of 1889 consumed the flimsy shacks that occupied the region.

The buildings stand on the pleasantly irregular 20-block grid – that begins at triangular Pioneer Square (First Ave. and Yesler Way) – which is the result of the city's founders, Arthur Denny and David Maynard, not agreeing with each other on whether the streets should parallel the shore of Elliott Bay or run north and south by the compass.

Underground city

After the fire, **First Avenue** was raised to reduce the incline of the hill. Since rebuilding had already begun, the first story of some commercial buildings ended up below the street level, accessible by stairs.

The shops that remained below ground were eventually condemned in 1907, but that didn't stop their economic activity as the boulevard-below-ground had already become Seattle's brothel and gambling center.

You can tour this underground city beginning at Doc Maynard's Public House at First Ave. and **James Street** where guides from Bill Speidel's Underground Tours provide humorous anecdotes and local history during a one and-a-half hour tour.

Above ground can be found the ornate ironwork, the brick sidewalks, small side streets, and intimate buildings that define the area.

In the early 1960s, Pioneer Square was a human dump, occupied by degenerates and drunks. It was saved from being turned into parking lots and high rises when locals defeated an urban renewal plan.

Even today, you'll find some of the city's homeless congregating around **Occidental Park** with its Alaskan totem poles. But, despite the fact that political leaders don't really know what to do with the park, this seems to only add to the eclectic mix of boutiques, missions, art galleries, book stores, sidewalk cafes, upscale condos, and carpet stores.

The 42-story **Smith Tower**, constructed in 1914 at the corner of Second Avenue and Yesler, was once the tallest building west of the Mississippi. From its observation floor the low, red buildings contrast with the glittering high rise towers hemming in the area.

At **Ishii's Bookstore** on First Avenue, David Ishii has a vast collection of books that reflect his own interests – fly fishing and baseball and the city's largest collection of out of print, scarce, and used books on the subjects. Nearby is the **Eliot Bay Book Company**, one of the finest in the Northwest – you can use the cafe downstairs to read newspapers.

Seattle's Art Gallery Center

The Pioneer Square area is Seattle's art gallery center where, on the first Thursday of every month, the galleries open late and restaurants and other stores gear up for the onslaught of buyers and gawkers.

The **Northwest Gallery of Fine Woodworking** has furniture by local woodworkers, and the **Sacred Circle Gallery of American Indian Art** is where you'll find contemporary native people's art. In the Grand Central Arcade, a converted hotel, you can watch artists and artisans at their crafts.

After a *Mariner's* or *Seahawks* game at the Kingdome, which anchors the southwest side of the district, F.X. McRory's Steak, Chop and Oyster House, on Occidental, is the watering hole of choice.

Sneakers is a long, narrow sports bar across the plaza from the Kingdome and is filled with sports memorabilia.

night scene and 30 art galleries, seems out of place.

The downtown commercial core is about 15 blocks north to south and eight blocks east to west. Dominated by the 76-story **Seafirst Columbia Center**, it's the financial hub of the Pacific Northwest and it hosts the city's conventions with the **Washington State Convention and Trade Center** and the 74,000 capacity **Kingdome** as the major convention sites.

The major hotels – The Hilton, Four Seasons Olympic, Alexis, Westin, Mayflower Park, Holiday Inn Crowne Plaza, Stouffer Madison, Seattle Sheraton – are within a six-block area.

While this is obviously a city rejuvenating itself with contemporary towers, Seattle has also refurbished many old buildings, converting them into shopping malls such as the **Grand Central Building** and **Court In The Square**. They give the downtown core a sense of continuance and ambience.

Legacy of the past

Fishing and lumber were the prime industries in early Seattle and that past is today's fashion. The city grew up around **Pioneer Square** and today it's a chic gathering place for artists and artisans, where the city's most current in-restaurants are located.

The city's strong maritime traditions are still visible at **Fisherman's Terminal**, near the Ballard Locks, home

Old-town ambience in Pioneer Square.

Strong maritime traditions at Boat Locks.

to the U.S. North Pacific fishing fleet it has moorage facilities for 700 boats.

The Lake Washington Ship Canal connects Puget Sound with Lakes Union and Washington.

The **Hiram M. Chittenden Locks**, near the western entrance to the canal, offers a fine vantage point from which to watch the bobbing procession of tugs, fishing boats, pleasure craft, barges, and research vessels as they are raised and lowered 21 feet (6.4 m) between fresh and salt water.

City of character

Seattle is a place of muted colors, where gray isn't simply a dulling of other, more vivid hues, but instead a series of constantly changing shades of watery light. Yes – and let's be frank about it – it rains here. But, not nearly as much as Seattle's reputation suggests. And the kind of weather Seattle endures still allows for year round outdoor activities.

Coffee Talk

It's also an excuse for staying indoors – which might explain Seattle's love affair with coffee shops. Everywhere you walk, you find one – people just sitting around, reading newspapers, talking, staying out of the rain. (Seventy percent of the coffee sold in Seattle are specialty coffee, about 10 times the amount of

Aerial view of Seattle.

other cities).

If that sounds as though the locals are a bit schizophrenic, trying to decide between indoor and outdoor, you're right. When it rains, they complain. When it doesn't they miss it - and complain. That's also part of the Seattle character. The average yearly rainfall is 36.2 inches (92 cm) which, locals agree, is a lot more than the 19.5 inches (50 cm) that falls in San Francisco. But it's less than the 39 inches (99 cm) that falls on Washington, D.C. and the 40.3 inches (102 cm) New York has to endure.

International District

It's not a Chinatown though many of the original Chinatown motifs still dot the International District that lies northeast of the Kingdome and borders Seattle's Pioneer Square district.

There are none of those bright, neon-lit streets that characterize large North American Chinatowns in San Francisco, Vancouver or New York; it's not a mini Hong Kong nor is it meant for tourists. That makes it refreshingly honest. The International District population is about one-third Chinese, and one-third Philippino, with the balance coming from all over Asia plus a dusting of whites, blacks, and American Indians. The area became home to the Chinese after they had completed work on the trans-continental railroad and it has remained fairly intact despite anti-Chinese riots during the 1880s and even after the internment of Japanese-Americans during the Second World War.

It's a place of small stores, southeast Asian restaurants, herbalists, massage parlors, acupuncturists, and scores of private clubs where residents gather for gambling and socializing. The **Wah Mee Club** on Canton Avenue gained notoriety in 1983 for a multiple murder that was linked to gangs and gambling interests.

The **Uwajimaya** emporium at 519 Sixth Avenue is the largest Japanese grocery-department store on the West Coast. The centerpiece of the neighborhood, it's a tiled, Japanese-style gourmet's delight with anything Japanese you care to buy – china, fabrics, housewares, and a variety of gifts. At Okazuya, the Asian snack bar in Uwajimaya, you can buy a variety of noodle dishes, *sushi*, *tempura* and other Asian dishes for carryout or for inside eating.

The **Nippon Kan Theater** (628 S. Washington) was once the focal point for Japanese-American activities including Kabuki, and was renovated and reopened in 1981 as a national historic site. Today, it's the performance hall for Asian productions and is the site of the Japanese Performing Arts series in October through May. In mid-July, Pacific Island dancers, Thai musicians, dragon dancers from China, Taiko drummers, and others celebrate the district's diversity at **Hing Hay Park.**

At the **Wing Luk Museum** (407 Seventh Avenue), named after the first Asian ever elected to office in Seattle – as a City Council member – exhibits emphasize Asian history and culture.

An acupuncture exhibit shows how needles are inserted at various body points to generate energy, eliminate pain and to heal. The permanent exhibits include costumes, fabrics, crafts and traditional medicines. **King Street** is where most of the Chinese activity takes place and it is where you can buy shark fins, trussed poultry, herbs and ingredients known only to residents of the area. One of the best *dim sum* in town is to be had at the House of Hong on Eighth Street with its purely Cantonese cuisine and choice of 75 *dim sum* items. Even simple classics like ginger beef dumplings and "*ha gow*" are flavorful and are brought in piping hot.

"Little Saigon"

The **Asian Plaza** at Jackson and 12th Avenue has been referred to as "Little Saigon" because it houses many of the 450 Vietnamese-owned businesses in Seattle. At the **Viet My restaurant** on Prefontaine Place, the owner, Chau Tran serves authentic Vietnamese dishes and an incredible seafood soup, is a one-woman operation. Nearby is **Lao Charean**, a small, usually overcrowded restaurant that serves Laotian and Thai food with "*gai yargn*" (chargrilled chicken marinated in coconut milk and spices) being the house specialty.

Its rain reputation is because Seattle's climate is more focused with major rainfall between November and February with virtually nothing in July and August. Most days the rain falls in a misty haze. It has to rain longer to accumulate significant measurements of the stuff. What takes an hour to accumulate in Chicago, might take three days in Seattle.

Seattle's skyline, with Kingdome a prominent part of it.

Diversification

While Boeing is still the major employer in Puget Sound, the city has done its best to diversify in the past two decades. Puget Sound's top 15 public companies now include heavy duty trucks, insurance and financial services, retail fashion stores, computer software, airlines, and discount warehouses. It has become a major league city in every sense of the word. Its professional baseball and football teams, the *Mariners* and the *Seahawks*, can be seen playing at The Kingdome, Seattle's professional sports arena next to Pioneer Square.

But it is also the most dominant major city in the Pacific Northwest in other ways. As the leading commercial center the city offers the visitor a wide range of shopping opportunities whether in the large shopping malls of Northgate Shopping Center, Westlake Center, Alderwood Mall, the University Village or the Westwood Village.

Culture Industry

Its culture industry is active with the Seattle Symphony, Seattle Opera, Pacific Northwest Ballet, Seattle Repertory Theater, and smaller other theater companies; choral, chamber music, theatrical, art galleries, museums, and dance companies providing a daily menu of intellectual nourishment.

Seattle has undergone an architectural transformation.

Street scene in Seattle.

Architectural transformation

The tourism people have given the name of Emerald City to Seattle which, of course, virtually everyone hates. You'll never hear the name used by anyone who works outside the convention and tourism bureau office. If there's one thing Seattle people dislike, it's being pigeon-holed, labeled.

There has been an architectural transformation in the past decade that has been both physical and cultural, especially in the downtown core. As a result large areas that were unattractive and even dangerous, are now considered desirable for living and visiting.

Areas you wouldn't walk in after dark are now model examples of inner-city facelifts. Along First Avenue, just up from the Pike Place Market, a series of new constructions have meant a vast change.

New stores, restaurants, a clothing district, and small hotels have sprung up in recent years in the lower downtown where before broken down buildings and derelicts once dominated.

Oddly, you never feel that the city and its environs are ever impersonal or even big, as its regional population of 1.5 million suggests it should. Instead, it's a city of parts, small enclaves that have their very own distinct identities and unique character.

The old monorail station terminal on Pine at Fifth Avenue was an embarrassment for years. Around it, crumbling streets and buildings were a symbol of a city that was decaying and which still seemed to be living off its glory years of the early 1960s.

No more. If you haven't visited the city in the past 10 years, you're in for a surprise. Westlake Center personifies that change giving a new face to Seattle – new, bright, young, innovative, and service orientated.

Magnet for shoppers

Adjacent to downtown Seattle department stores (The Bon, Nordstrom's) **Westlake Center** shops are a magnet for shoppers and visitors alike. The plaza

Vintage Melbourne trolleys offer a lot of character and charm.

is a central draw for outdoor concerts, for meeting people, for brown-bag lunches, and for people watching.

In 1989, four 1927 trams from Melbourne, Australia were put into service, extending the city's tram route from along the Seattle waterfront through Pioneer Square to the International District. Now, for the first time, the city's entire transit system is linked. True, while the old trams are kind of neat and cosy, they are not quite the same as San Francisco's romantic system. But they do offer their own character and charm.

The Seattle waterfront is accessible. It's where commuters board the Washington State Ferry system that sails the inner channels of Puget Sound, feeding passengers to various suburbs. In fact, a cheap and delightfully different way of seeing the city is by taking the hourly ferry to Bainbridge Island from Pier 52. At the Bainbridge pier walk up Windslow

Way to the Streamliner Diner for the salsa omelet.

Neighborhoods

Seattle is split into three general neighborhood districts - south and north of the strait that connects Lake Washington and Puget Sound. The north section includes the neighborhoods of Ballard, Greenlake, Lake City, North Seattle, Greenwood, Fremont, Wallingford, Roosevelt, and the University. South are Magnolia, Queene Anne, Capitol Hill, Seattle Center, First Hill, Pioneer Square, International District, Madison, Denny Regrade, Georgetown, and Downtown. East on the shores of Lake Washington are the communities of Mercer Island, Bellevue, Kirkland, and Bothell, areas that are growing but which few tourists have the time to explore. Yet, there is plenty to see and do. Lake Washington, which separates the main city from the eastern communities, has a series of parks and recreational areas.

Southcenter, at the southern confluence of Interstates 5 and 405 is one of Seattle's largest covered shopping malls, sitting on 92 acres and housing 125 stores. The new $29 million **Meydenbauer Center**, a convention and performing arts center, has opened in downtown Bellevue, nine miles (14.5 km) east of Seattle and 17 miles (27 km) from Sea Tac Airport. Facilities include a 410-seat theater, a 36,000 sq. ft, (3344 sq. m) exhibit hall. The performing arts theater

Reliving the past in Pioneer Square.

showcases performances by the Bellevue Philharmonic Chamber Orchestra and Issaquah's Village Theater. Nearby attractions include the shops at **Bellevue Mall** and the **Chateau St. Michelle Winery**.

Georgetown is the industrial section south of downtown and the location of the **Museum of Flight** and its world-class **Great Gallery**. This is every airplane buff's dream with 35 original Boeing aircraft – including a B-29 – hanging from the ceiling.

Seattle's neighborhoods are a direct result of its history. Built on seven hills it is virtually surrounded by water – the ocean, Union Lake, Lake Washington.

And because of the terrain, the street system outside the downtown area is somewhat confusing. It isn't helped by street signs that often change names several times along the route. Nonetheless, distances between points are relatively short and even if you get lost, who cares. Getting lost leads to discovery and there's plenty to discover.

Core of downtown

Your first experience of the city is likely to be downtown, a large, walkable region that includes some of the city's most famous sites. If you're in the Sheraton, Westin, or any other of the core hotels, you'll be close to either the Westlake Center, Pike Place Market and the waterfront, Seattle Center, or Pioneer Square. The skyscrapers downtown

Pike Street Market

mime artists. You can, in fact, spend most of a day walking through the 250 permanent shops or going through the wares of more than 200 artists and artisans.

If the Space Needle is the symbol of Seattle's economic outlook and its most obvious landmark, and the Seattle Center is its cultural heart, then the Pike Place Market is Seattle's soul and its sense of smell and taste. Certainly, if the role of great markets like London's Covent Garden, Paris' Les Halles, and Jerusalem's Triple Bazaar is to make you eat, then come prepared to partake in a feast.

What was once simply a farmer's market has expanded over the years to become the oldest continuing working market in the United States and it is filled with delightful characters hawking their fresh fish and produce in a dozen accents.

Located at the foot of Pike Street and Western Avenue, the cultural mix of foods and peoples that rest at the city's watery edge is a menagerie of competing sensual pleasures, a social statement defining the region and its people. This is one of Seattle's most cherished places, one that residents prefer never to change. Here visitors and residents buy the freshest seafood and produce in town.

But it's more than just a place to buy a salmon and a head of lettuce; stall owners bark to passing clients and every corner has a spot occupied by street musicians, puppeteers, or

City within a city

It began in 1907 as a place where farmers gathered to sell their produce to city dwellers, but the market has grown into a city of its own. As the number of farmers decreased as the city expanded to overtake farm land, artists and craftsmen moved into the vacated stalls along with restaurants, antique shops, and a variety of speciality businesses and even a modern bank. Warren-like lower levels with steps and ramps at what seem like unplanned intervals invite visitors to browse its bowels.

Farmers in the market have to meet a strict set of rules. They must gross (or try to) at least $2,000 a year from their farm. They must grow or gather everything they sell, with the exception of a specific list of vegetables that they can buy for resale during the winter months only.

They must also process all jams, vinegars, and similar products themselves, and they must produce the main ingredient themselves. All farms are inspected to ensure that the farmers really grow the crops they sell.

Go early in the day on foot (parking is at a premium) and revel in the colors. The high stall

are fairly recent, dating primarily from the 1980s. The 76-story Columbia

Seafirst Center, 44-story Pacific First Center, the 62-story AT&T Tower, and

The United States's oldest continuing working market.

area is flanked by mountains of red tomatoes, green cucumbers, glossy purple egg plants, and orange carrots. Silvery salmon on beds of ice, Dungeness crabs, oysters, clams, cod, bockwurst, liverwurst, cheddar cheese, mocha-java, orange pekoe and hundreds of other foods greet your eyes and nose at every turn.

Since the market is built primarily on stilts over the edge of a bluff, the restaurants offer a vantage point found in few places around the city. Morning coffee or lunch at any of the several restaurants provide a view of Elliot Bay.

Across the street from the market is the small, intimate, and elegant 65-room hotel, **Inn At The Market. The Pike Place Hillclimb** takes you down several flights of stairs from the bluff on which the market is built, to Piers 52 to 70.

other core buildings have been a boom to local and international sculptors.

In 1973, the city passed an ordinance outlining art requirements for new structures. Henry Moore's sculpture, *Three Piece Vertebrae*, outside the Seafirst Center predated the law, but the bank has more than 1,200 pieces of art in its collection.

The $27 million **Seattle Art Museum** at University and First, is a fairly recent addition to downtown. It allows the original site in Volunteer Park, to display its unrivaled collection of Asian art better. The new gallery's permanent collection represents a wide range of expression from ancient Egyptian sculptures to contemporary American painting. In addition to the permanent and touring collections, the new gallery includes classrooms for several disciplines, hands-on activities, a cafe, and an expanded museum store with one of the best selections of art books on the west coast.

Washington State Convention Center

The Sheraton is flanked by the **Washington State Convention Center** whose architecture resembles a series of green glass tubes. Stop off to visit the ground-floor tourist office and then visit the structure's second floor bells which come from each of the state's 39 counties. The bells are controlled by a computerized system and are played on the hour.

The **Seattle Center** is where you can attend the city's major cultural

One of Seattle's most cherished places.

events – the opera and symphony – and the basketball games played by the Sonics. The grounds contain the Space Needle, Opera House, Pacific Science Center, and a Fun Fair that includes a laserium, arts and crafts centers, amphitheater, and several theaters. A Children's Museum is in the Central Hall.

Scenic waterfront

The **waterfront** takes in several neighborhoods, including the Pike Place Market, and is defined by its pier numbers. The Washington State Ferry Line is at Pier 51 with its Joshua Green Fountain outside the entrance; sightseeing boats run to Alaska from Pier 70; the new B.C. Ferries ply to Victoria, British Columbia from Pier 69; Seattle Harbor Tours leave from Pier 56; and Gray Line Cruises from Pier 57. Most of the piers have been transformed into shopping centers, especially piers 55 & 56. The Omnidome and the Seattle Aquarium share Pier 59; Pier 54 is the home of Ye Olde Curiosity Shop and Museum and Ivar's Acres of Clams, owned by colorful local businessman, Ivar Haglund, who has made a fortune selling clams at several regional restaurants.

Commerical district

Capitol Hill, which lies just east of down-

The best seat in Waterfront Park.

town, is home to Seattle's gay and lesbian population though the region is sexually mixed. A large number of apartment blocks supplement the mansions of Millionaire's Row on 14th Ave. East. But the district's major attraction is **Broadway**, the neighborhood's major business street and Seattle's leading commercial district.

Broadway is Seattle's restaurant and boutique row and where casual walkers are out as late as midnight in a nonthreatening environment. It's the hangout of punk fashion. Opus 24 (225 Broadway) has fashions and items from all over the world; Northwest Native (815 E. Thomas) is where you find gifts and sportsware with a Northwest motif. Check out B&O Expresso on Belmont for the best coffee house in the city.

The Egyptian and Harvard Exit theaters are leftovers from the golden age of 1920s theater architecture. The new multi-level Broadway Market is worth a stopover. It's a veggie restaurant and one of the city's great people-watching places. A block east is the major store of REI (Recreational Equipment, Inc.), the country's largest co-op selling outdoor equipment.

At **Volunteer Park**, originally a cemetery for the city's original residents (it was moved in 1887), you have one of

the finest views of the Space Needle, Puget Sound, and the Olympic mountains. In the grounds are the 1932 Art Deco building that houses the Seattle Art Museum's Asian collection and the Volunteer Park Conservatory's three greenhouses.

Eastlake is separated from the rest of Capitol Hill by Interstate 5. William Boeing made his start in a hangar at the foot of Roanoke Street, building seaplanes that he tested on the lake.

Union Lake fronts on Seattle's working waterfront. A colorful houseboat community is moored at the northern end near the University district. The Residence Inn-Marriott's $25 million hotel complex is nearby. The Center for Wooden Boats at the south end of the lake has a wonderful collection of 75 rowboats and sailboats, many of which can be rented. Several restaurants front the lake. One of the most popular is the Lakeside restaurant, a mirrored, tri-level establishment overlooking Lake Union with the city skyline rising in front of you.

Bohemian beat

The **University** area, northeast of Union Lake, has several blocks of what once would have been called Bohemian character with small ice cream shops and coffee houses on streets filled out by small shops catering to exotic tastes in clothing and art.

Among the campus highlights are the **Drumheller Fountain** with its view of Mount Rainier, Red Square, Husky Stadium, the Thomas **Burke Memorial Museum** with its excellent North Coast Indian collections, the **Henry Art Gallery** with its 19th and 20th-century art, the **Museum of history**, and the **University Book Store** billed as the continent's largest university book store.

University Way North is the main drag. Locals queue up at the Varsity Theater for the latest Hollywood flicks and then go to the Big Time Brewery and Alehouse afterwards.

Magnolia

In Magnolia, Discovery Park covers 400 acres of beaches and wooded areas. Daybreak Star, an Indian cultural center, presents craftspeople at work, music and dance. Known locally as Pill Hill because of its concentration of major hospitals, First Hill has the **Charles and Emma Frye Art Museum** which houses permanent exhibits of 19th and 20th-century painters.

Ballard and Roosevelt

Ballard is a neighborhood that reflects its Scandinavian origins. **Golden Gardens Park** divides the area into two sections.

The **Nordic Heritage Museum** graphically describes the legacy of every Nordic country. The **Owl Cafe** is the oldest bar, established in 1902. Wonderful jazz clubs and antique shops abound in the **Ballard Historical District**.

Located north of the university area, **Roosevelt** is largely residential with homes dating from the the early decades of the century. The **Kirsten Gallery** has cutting edge exhibits exploring new-age aesthetics. A few blocks west of Roosevelt, **Green Lake** is Seattle's main recreational section. You can feed the ducks at the **Waldo Waterfowl Sanctuary**, play nine holes at the **Pitch 'n' Putt Golf Course**, or catch a play at the **Bathhouse Theater**.

Home of the Woodland Park Zoological Gardens, **Phinney Ridge** and greenwood blend without differentiation. Antique shops, and art galleries are generously located along Seattle's "Antique Row" on Greenwood Avenue. The Poncho Theater offers children's productions.

North of the city

North of the city is what's becoming known as **Technology Corridor** with seven business parks between Bothell and Everett along Interstate 405. The best known of the technological giants in the area is Microsoft.

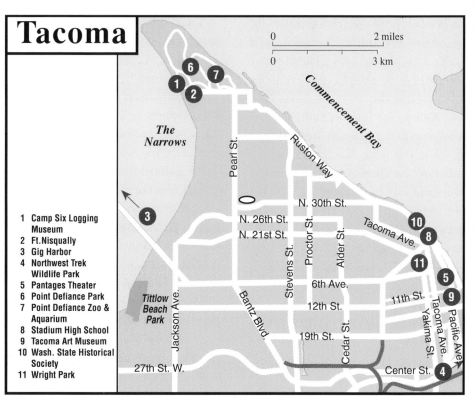

Tacoma

0 — 2 miles
0 — 3 km

The Narrows

Commencement Bay

Ruston Way

Pearl St.

N. 30th St.
N. 26th St.
N. 21st St.

Stevens St.
Proctor St.
Alder St.

Tacoma Ave.

6th Ave.
11th St.
12th St.
19th St.

Tittlow Beach Park

Jackson Ave.

Bantz Blvd.

Cedar St.

27th St. W.

Center St.

Tacoma Ave.
Yakima St.
Pacific Ave.

1 **Camp Six Logging Museum**
2 **Ft. Nisqually**
3 **Gig Harbor**
4 **Northwest Trek Wildlife Park**
5 **Pantages Theater**
6 **Point Defiance Park**
7 **Point Defiance Zoo & Aquarium**
8 **Stadium High School**
9 **Tacoma Art Museum**
10 **Wash. State Historical Society**
11 **Wright Park**

Northgate, the west coast's pioneer shopping center opened in 1950 as the first shopping mall west of the Mississippi. **North Seattle Community College** and the 18-hole **Jackson Park Municipal Golf Course** are nearby.

Tacoma – City of Destiny

It has only been in recent years that Tacoma has come out of the large shadow cast by its northern neighbor, Seattle, an hour's drive away.

Throughout its history, Tacoma never quite lived up to its billing as "The City Of Destiny" and has had to endure endless jokes about its industrial char-

acter, unfavorable life-style comparisons, and the acrid odor coming from the nearby Simpson Tacoma Pulp Mill which manufactures cardboard and other paper products.

But those days of bad jokes and second-class citizenship have fairly well passed as Seattle's southern neighbor now has developed its own share of attractive sites, fine restaurants, cultural activities, sports teams, and enshrined historical regions. Sided by Commencement Bay and the Tacoma Narrows, and backed by Mount Rainier, the city has been undergoing a cultural revitalization over the past decade. The city once known for its hostility to the arts is now, in fact, a home to them.

Autumn in the City of Destiny.

Commencement City

Originally called Commencement City, because of its location, the city was renamed in 1869. The name Tacoma comes from the Indian word "Tahoma", which means Mother of Waters (their name for Mount Rainier). In 1855, city fathers gave the city it the title, City of Destiny, in the hope that this encouragement would boost its growth.

Alas, the future was not as bright as

civic leaders had hoped. The first settlers were lured in the 1850s and 1860s to the vast lumber potential. Among them was Nicholas De Lin, a Swedish immigrant and entrepreneur who built a water-driven mill and eventually opened a brewery, barrel factory, and salmon packing plant.

Tacoma was a small village until 1873 when the Northern Pacific Railroad chose it as its western terminus and from that time onwards it competed with Seattle for dominance on Puget Sound. For the next decade, Tacoma's population erupted, increasing from 1,000 to 36,000 as the railroad brought industrial development (it is now 170,000).

The president of the railroad, Charles Wright, was a free spender, donating money for parks and schools. The resulting housing construction gave the city elegant homes and neighborhoods, many of which are still standing. The stately homes and cobblestone streets in the north end of Tacoma are often used as sets for Hollywood films, and students still use Stadium High School, a turreted, chateau-like structure. Designed as a luxury hotel in 1891 for the Northern Pacific Railroad, it was converted into a high school after a fire left only the outer shell. Tacoma's stability was seriously

The Northern Pacific Railroad chose Tacoma as its western terminus, contributing to its industrial development.

shaken in the depression of 1893 and its commercial universe folded quickly. That was the same year in which another rail company, the Great Northern Railroad, chose Seattle as its western terminus.

Although the city rallied with the Klondike Gold Rush, its growth slowed down considerably by the turn of the century and in the 1920s, the Northern Pacific moved its western headquarters to Seattle.

Although it is still a blue-collar town, Tacoma has retained its past while em-

flourished in the railroad town at the turn-of-the-century. The Old Tacoma Hall was built in 1893 in a style described by its builders as "Italian Renaissance", it now houses offices.

The nearby **Northern Pacific Headquarters Building** is a handsome Italianate structure built in 1888. The Elks Temple, constructed in 1916, is in the Classic style.

The 1889 **Bostwick Hotel** is a classic example of a triangular Victoria "flatiron", while the Union Depot was designed by the same architects who created New York's Grand Central Station. Located in the warehouse district on Pacific Avenue, the station is an heirloom from the golden age of railroading and is one of Tacoma's most cherished sites.

Among the museums in town are several that fit the "unusual" category including the Children's Museum of Tacoma, the Tacoma-Pierce County Sports Museum (in the Tacoma Dome), Karpeles Manuscript Library Museum, the Bair Drug and Hardware Living Museum, the Fort Lewis Military Museum, and the Puget Sound Mariner's Museum in Gig Harbor.

Antique Row

"Antiquing" is a favorite pastime of locals and Antique Row, located in the heart of Tacoma's historic district, provides ample opportunity to enjoy this activity. There's a unique blend of speci-

barking on a cultural Renaissance. From the **McCarver Street Bookstore** in the Old Town district, to the waterfront's avante-garde public arts project, "Trestle: Ancient", to city-subsidized artists housing in the historic warehouse district, the arts have become fashionable.

Downtown, the **Old City Hall Historic District** reflects the activity that

Tacoma Dome

Nothing illustrates the difference in character between Tacoma and Seattle as their respective domes. Seattle's Kingdome is large and made of cement, The Tacoma Dome is considerably smaller and made of wood. And while the Kingdome is the venue for major league professional football and baseball and can squeeze in about 70,000 for rock concerts, the Tacoma Dome is the home of only the minor league *Tacoma Rockets* of the Western Hockey League and can pack in 25,000 enthusiastic concert goers. The Tacoma Dome is a record holder and holds bragging rights to being the most unique dome in the Puget Sound region.

Largest wooden dome

It is the largest wood domed structure in the world, measuring 530 feet in diameter and is 150 feet tall – equal to a 15-story building. And it covers a land area of 6.1 acres. There are 288 triangular wooden sections supporting the Urethane composition roof, and each weighs 5,000 pounds.

Owned by the City of Tacoma, the Tacoma Dome is truly a multi-purpose entertainment facility. Since its opening in April 21, 1983, the $44 million facility has hosted a number of events as varied as the Billy Graham Crusade and the NCAA Women's Basketball Championships. During the 1990 Goodwill Games, it was a major venue for ice hockey, figure skating, and men's and women's gymnastics.

Excellent acoustics

The Tacoma Dome is getting a lot of the business that used to be the exclusive domain of the Kingdome. Musical events prefer the Tacoma Dome's excellent acoustical qualities and its efficient operations. A major key to the flexibility of the Tacoma Dome is the 16 basic seating configurations available.

Seating configurations include 16,000 movable sideline and end-zone seats, which readily convert the facility from large-scale stadium events like soccer, to arena events like concerts and ice-shows.

The Tacoma Dome also has the added advantage over its Seattle competition of having an adjacent 30,000 square foot Exhibition Hall that can host events like concerts, and antique shows.

Subdivided into five soundproof rooms, separate events can take place at the same time. The Arena and Exhibition Hall have 130,000 square feet of total exhibition space. If it has one disadvantage, it's the fact it is somewhat removed from the downtown.

Located just off Interstate-5 to the southeast of the downtown core, however, it is near Freighthouse Square and its Public Market and within several blocks of the Visitors Center.

The location, however, does allow for easy access into and from the 2,900 capacity parking lot. So, unlike Seattle, major events don't tie up traffic for blocks around downtown.

ality shops with more than a dozen antique collectible stores.

At **Pantages Center**, the restored 1,100 seat Pantages Theater, originally designed in 1918 by B. Marcus Priteca, is the focal point of a restored downtown cultural life, holding stage, music, and dance performances. The building is an example of early 20th-century Greco-

Roman music hall architecture, similar to old Orpheum theaters across the continent with classical figures, ornate columns and arches. Now the home of the Tacoma Symphony, it was a stop on the Vaudeville tours. W. C. Fields, Mae West, Will Rogers, Charley Chaplin, Bob Hope, and Houdini all appeared there.

If Bing Crosby excites your curios-

City children keeping their cool with ice cream in the summer.

ity, the Pantages Building around the corner from the main entrance, houses the Bing Crosby Historical Society with memorabilia of the crooner's life. Born in Tacoma, he just might be the city's most famous son. There is another display in Spokane where the crooner once lived. The **Tacoma Art Museum**, in a former downtown bank building, houses a large collection of American and French paintings, Chinese jades and Imperial Robes. Among the collection are works by Renoir, Degas, and Pissaro. It has a permanent children's gallery and a glass art collection.

The **State Historical Museum** has valuable Native American artifacts including canoes, baskets, and masks from British Columbia and Puget Sound. The

University of Puget Sound, in the north end, and **Pacific Lutheran University**, in the south, each provide a variety of cultural programs and art events open to the public.

Ruston Way waterfront, along the south shore of Commencement Bay, has beautiful walks with the wide expanse of the bay framed by steep cliffed islands, the Olympic and Cascade ranges, and Mount Rainier.

This people place attracts locals to its many restaurants, trails, piers, and parks. A promenade for pedestrians and bicyclists stretches the length of the two-mile (3.2 km) waterfront.

The city's most famous landmark is the 700-acre Point Defiance Park that encompasses **Fort Nisqually Historic**

Tacoma Victorian Houses

If cities are defined by their architecture, then Tacoma is decidedly eclectic - historically speaking – with a good supply of intriguing old houses. Tacoma was a small mill town that was changed into a sophisticated city in a very few years by Eastern capitalists involved in the railroad, the shipping industry, mining, timber, and land. Their tastes varied greatly and many of the owners demanded designs that set them apart.

Several factors contributed to the eclectic architectural styles of the mid-1800s to 1900. The Post-Civil War era evolved from the traditional Greek Revival to Victorian picturesque. And the opening of the Orient brought influences from new sources and provided a wider range of inspiration.

So, diverse sources were drawn upon by architects to produce houses that included fish-scale shingles, bay windows with curved glass, pillars, pilasters, terra-cotta tiles, stained glass and leaded windows, cupolas, wrought iron fences, gothic arches, dormers, gables, and quoins.

And that's not all. The glitzy stylings included brackets, pendants, dentils, corbels, tall chimneys, projected porches, cornices, and pediments until nothing more could possibly be added.

This wealth of detail could be found in the most modest of cottages as well as in pretentious mansions. All of these influences are rich examples of what Tacoma once was and much of it still exists.

Most of the homes have been restored by private owners, are currently being lived in, and cannot be visited except by a drive-pass. But there are some unique architectural examples worth a visit even if it is at arms-length.

The **William Laird McCormich House** (509 North Tacoma Ave.) is a stone example of Italian Renaissance; the post-Victorian mansion that once belonged to Henry Rhodes, Tacoma's most famous mercantilist, stands at 701 North J Street; the post-Victorian **H.F. Alexander House** (502 North Yakima) has a series of Ionic columns and ornate corbel trim that recalls an opulent past.

The colonial mansion that once belonged to William R. Rust (1001 North I Street) is known as "Tacoma's Greatest Town House" because the interior of the majestic sandstone structure has been divided into apartments.

Site at the northern tip of the city. Within the park are also the Point Defiance Zoo and Aquarium. When Captain George Vancouver and his entourage stumbled on Puget Sound in 1792, Peter Puget was ordered by Vancouver to sail past Point Defiance and the Narrows. In 1833, members of the Hudson Bay Company built Fort Nisqually which has since been reconstructed. Another sea captain, Charles Wilkes, surveyed the sound in 1841 and gave his starting point the name it still bears, Commencement Bay. The original structure was on the Nisqually Delta and was relocated at Point Defiance in 1935 as part of a WPA project during the Great Depression.

There are 10 buildings including the Factor's House (1854) and the Granary (1850), the only surviving original example in Washington State of the French Canadian post-and-sill construc-

Vista Trail at Fort Nisqually Historic Site.

tion used in the Hudson Bay Company's forts of the period. A museum features exhibits on the role of the fort in Puget Sound history. The **Camp Six Logging Logging Museum**, also part of the site, is a 20-acre museum featuring restored bunkhouses, hand tools, and historic logging equipment. It features a Dolbeer donkey steam engine, a restored water wagon, and a ride on an original, 90-ton Shat steam locomotive.

The **Tacoma Narrows Bridge**, connecting Tacoma to the Olympic Peninsula, is the fifth largest suspension bridge in the world. The original, dubbed the "Gallopin' Gertie" because of its undulating motion in windy weather, collapsed in a wind storm within four months after its completion in 1940.

The current structure spans 5,979 feet (1822 m) and was completed in 1950. It doesn't sway. Across the bridge is **Gig Harbor**, a delightful harbor town with old-styled shops and plenty of restaurants plus bed and breakfast inns.

Across the Sound is **Vashon Island**, a 15-minute ferry trip from Defiance Dock, and its most enduring charm is its rural character with plenty of cows and is perfect for bicycle touring. For an even slower pace, Anderson Island might be for you. The last ferry is at 6:30 p.m. and if you miss it, you'll have to sleep under someone's porch as there are no motels.

The **Western Washington Fair**, located in Puyallup is the sixth largest fair in the nation. Every September, for 17 days, the fair has a variety of carnival, rodeo, and arts events.

Tacoma is also home to the largest amateur owned observatory in Western Washington with the **Pettinger-Guiley Observatory** run by the Tacoma Astronomical Society. And the Daffodil Festival, spread two-weeks throughout the Puyallup Valley, includes a golf tournament, a "most magnificent mutt" dog show, and a boat parade — as well as free daffodils everywhere.

Sea-Tac was incorporated as a city in 1990, chiefly because of its proximity to Seattle-Tacoma International Airport. South of it, the Duwamish River becomes the Green River, made infamous by the scores of bodies of young women found along its way during the 1970s/ 80s. Till today, the Green River murders have still not been solved.

On a map it looks as though Puget Sound and the San Juan Islands merge into a single geographic and cultural organism. Just the opposite is true. The further north you travel, the more isolated, the less populated, and the more it becomes physically and spiritually private.

That gradual change produces a series of mini-cultures that can appeal either to those seeking city-spawned sophistication or island solitude.

And, frankly, getting around Puget Sound is not always easy. It often takes advance planning, a combination of driving and ferries, and research beforehand before you reach your island or out-of-the-way retreat.

It can be crowded on busy weekends, destroying the illusion of pristine isolation, especially within the central Puget Sound area where King, Snohomish, Pierce, and Kitsap counties have a combined population of 2.7 million.

Peace and quiet awaits the visitor to the San Juans.

**Puget Sound &
The San Juans**

161

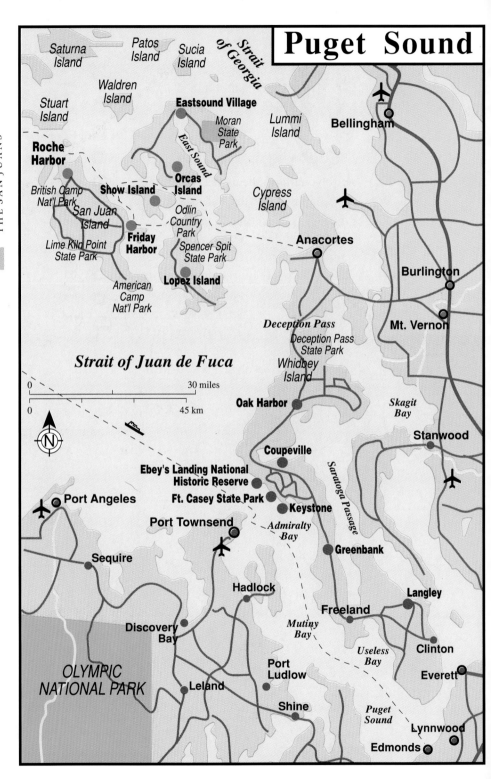

Puget Sound

Saturna
Island

Patos
Island

Sucia
Island

Strait
of Georgia

Waldren
Island

Stuart
Island

Eastsound Village

Moran
State
Park

Lummi
Island

Bellingham

**Roche
Harbor**

East Sound

British Camp
Nat'l Park

Show Island

**Orcas
Island**

Cypress
Island

San Juan
Island

Odlin
Country
Park

Anacortes

Burlington

Lime Kiln Point
State Park

**Friday
Harbor**

Spencer Spit
State Park

Mt. Vernon

American
Camp
Nat'l Park

Lopez Island

Deception Pass

Deception Pass
State Park

Strait of Juan de Fuca

Whidbey
Island

0   30 miles

0   45 km

Oak Harbor

Skagit
Bay

Stanwood

Coupeville

Saratoga Passage

N

**Ebey's Landing National
Historic Reserve**

Ft. Casey State Park

Keystone

Port Angeles

Port Townsend

*Admiralty
Bay*

Greenbank

Sequire

Langley

Hadlock

Freeland

**Discovery
Bay**

*Mutiny
Bay*

Clinton

**OLYMPIC
NATIONAL
PARK**

Leland

**Port
Ludlow**

*Useless
Bay*

Everett

Shine

*Puget
Sound*

Lynnwood

Edmonds

Ferry boat landing on Orcas Island.

Complex web

Officially, Puget Sound includes the area between the entrance to Hood Canal and the southern tip of the sound. But, in popular usage it includes most of the inland sea to the north. At its southern end it looks like a complex web of watery fingers intruding on the land mass.

The Sound is an enormous glacially carved scar on the earth's surface. Typically in this region, the bottom drops off abruptly after a short distance from shore and the narrow sand, gravel, or cobblestone beaches are frequently below sand and gravel bluffs. The southern end of Puget Sound is anchored by Olympia, the state capital on Com-

mencement Bay while the northern portion of the San Juan Islands stretch to the Canadian border to the north.

Exquisite beauty

Between them is shared an exquisite beauty, a lifestyle defined by water and a geography so diverse and varied that it often confuses the first-time visitor. Seattle itself rests at the top of southern Puget Sound and from almost any location along the city's oceanside waterfront you can watch the large ferries delivering people from and taking them to any number of islands, towns, villages, and cities that rest along the waterways.

Rain Forests

A sense of stillness pervades the atmosphere in a typical rain forest.

It's unusual to find rain forests outside the steamy jungles of southern latitudes. In the mind's eye, at least, they are in keeping with the writings of Somerset Maugham and James Michener whose stories from the South Pacific bring to mind images of heat and sultry air. But, on the Olympic Peninsula, rests the largest rain forest in North America and one of only three official rain forests in the entire world – the other two being in Chile and New Zealand.

In **Olympic National Park**, on the west side of the Olympic Peninsula, the Hoh, Queets, and Quinault Valleys make up most of the Olympic rainforest.

Only about 150 inches (381 cm) of rain falls yearly here, as compared to more than 400 inches (1016 cm) on the island of Kuaii in the Hawaiian chain, for example.

But, it does the job. Some of the largest trees in the world are here including the world's largest western hemlock (in the Quinault), the largest Douglas fir (in the Queets), and the largest red alder (in the Hoh). The four major species that grow in the rain forest – the Sitka Spruce, western red cedar, Douglas fir, and western hemlock – average 200 feet (61 m) with the tallest being in excess of 300 feet (91 m) high.

The park is a primeval place where glaciers drop off sheer cliff faces into the rain forest below; and where America's largest herd of Roosevelt Elk roam virtually unseen. While the largest mountains on the peninsula are not particularly high, the tallest being 8,000 feet (2438 m), they do capture the moisture laden clouds that sweep into the coast at the end of a 2,000 mile (3218 km) trip.

Rain forests create their own ambience – a pillow of silence in which the smells and silence are almost smothering. These areas have never been logged so life itself has been uninterrupted since prehistoric days with nature growing upon itself generation after generation.

Enormous trees grow out of long-decayed "nurse trees" that serve as a breeding ground for new life; club moss drapes eerily over branches and hangs down like uncut hair; ferns and mosses, skunk cabbage, lichens, bunchberry, and vanilla leaf cover nearly every inch of the forest floor so that you won't hear your own footsteps. In winter, the rain is constant, yet there is little sense of dampened enthusiasm as you walk through the many trails, the best of which fan out from **Lake Quinalt Lodge** on the edge of the lake.

In summer, the sunshine seems out of place, delightful as it might be. At the **Hoh Rain Forest Visitor Center**, about 19 miles into the park, vast amounts of information is available about the wildlife, botany, and history of the region.

From the Lake Quinalt Lodge, near glacial Lake Quinalt, it's a short hike to Big Acre, a thicket of old-growth trees.

The Olympic National Park is the largest rain forest in North America.

The Washington State ferries are as much a cultural institution as they are a means of transportation. In fact, no self-respecting West Coaster believes the ferries are just a way to get to places even if they do belong to the nation's largest ferry system with 25 ships serving nine routes. Among the most popular car-carrier routes are those to Bremerton (Olympic Peninsula) and Bainbridge Island, and the non-automobile vessels to Bremerton (50 minutes), and Vashon Island (35 minutes).

Once aboard either the small 55 car or the large 206 car capacity ferries, the hurried pace of everyday life comes to an end. Inside, there are restaurants offering beer, wine, and fast foods and a solarium for anyone wanting fresh air during the winter months.

Standing outside in either rain or sun, the sea smells, the sounds of lapping water, mixes with the views of passing tree-covered islands and the engine noise combine to produce a local music for the senses.

Olympia

Like capitol cities the world over, Olympia defines itself by its power structures. But, unlike many other centers of political decision making – and in keeping with the Pacific Northwest's softer, more gentle lifestyle – the state capital building is not its most popular attraction. It takes second place to the Pabst Brewing Company, just off Interstate 5 at exit

Welcome to Port of Friday Harbor!

103. And little wonder, at the end of every plant tour, there's free beer.

Olympia was settled in the 1840s by pioneers attracted by the industrial potential of nearby Deschutes Falls. But the town of **Tumwater** – from the Chinook word "Tum wa ta", meaning waterfalls – rose first just a few miles south of what is now the city center.

The first permanent American settlement on Puget Sound, Tumwater was a financial success with sawmills and gristmills in the mid-19th-century and later the development of a brewery in-

Capitol's centerpiece

As expected, the capitol's centerpiece is the **Washington State Legislative Building**. Lavishly fitted out with bronze and marble, this striking Romanesque structure houses the offices of the Governor and other state executives. Sessions of the State Senate and the House of Representatives can be viewed by visitors.

Directly behind the Legislative Buildings is the **State Library** that boasts a unique non-objective mural by Washington's most famous painter, the late Mark Tobey, plus artifacts from the state's history.

Downtown, on Seventh Avenue between Washington and Franklin Streets, the restored **Old Capitol** with its pointed towers and high-arched windows suggests a medieval chateau. And adjacent to City Hall, just off Plum Street, is the **Yashiro Japanese Gardens** that honors one of Olympia's sister cities.

The **Washington Center for the Performing Arts** (on Washington Street between Fifth Avenue and Legion Way) has given the downtown core new life. In the same block is the **Marianne Partlow Gallery**, a major outlet for contemporary painting and sculpture. The **Capitol Theater** provides a showcase for live theater and musicals.

Not far from Olympia is the **Nisqually National Wildlife Refuge**, a diverse mix of conifer forest, deciduous woodlands, marshlands, grasslands,

dustry. Today, Olympia Beer is still brewed in Tumwater and beer brewing is still a major industry along with manufacturing and government. Olympia, originally called Smithfield after its founder, Levi Smith, became the seat of government in 1853 when its name had been changed to Olympia after the majestic mountains to the west.

San Juan Islands

Float plane ready
to whisk visitors to
the San Juans.

The San Juan Islands have been called the jewels of Puget Sound, but that description tries to place a value on a priceless part of this region. They are less gems than a misty collection of rainswept islands that are, for the most part, inaccessible to many of the vulgarities of tourism. They simply sit there as a symbol to a part of the region that can never be civilized and they seem to thumb their noses at those who might try.

Coming to grips with the essential character of these islands isn't an easy task because of their isolation. Of the 172 islands with names, only four – Orcas, San Juan, Shaw, and Lopez – have any sizeable population and are served by Washington State Ferries. No bridges span them.

Most of the others are private and can be reached only by sailboat or motor launch. And, to be frank, the last thing the residents – virtually all of whom are there because they want to escape humanity – want to see are tourists and visitors.

Commercial hub

Although the islands are only 50 miles north of Seattle, it takes several hours to reach them. **Friday Harbor**, on San Juan Island, is the commercial hub of the region with a colorful, active waterfront, with shops that cater to tourists and a collection of small, waterfront restaurants.

A short walk from the dock is the **San Juan Historical Museum** (with its collection of local artifacts) and the more interesting Whale Museum with an Orca painted on the side. Unlike most such museums, there's no attempt to grab your cash with trinkets. Instead, there are full skeletons, sound shows and videos that provide information about the species.

Official Whale-Watching Park

Six miles from Friday Harbor is **Lime Kiln State Park**, the first official whale-watching park in America and the place from where the occasional Gray Whale or Orca can be seen. At the San Juan Island National Historic Park are two camps that attest to the island's history and chronicle the Pig War.

The British camp on the northwest corner of the island (eight miles from the ferry dock) has a blockhouse, commissary, and barracks while the American camp (on the southeast side and five miles from the dock) has the armaments from the era.

At the northern end of the island, **Roche Harbor** seems like a bit of suburban fashion with houses having manicured lawns, rose bushes, cobblestone roads, and polite fencing while flower boxes grace the dock. On the third weekend in July both Roche and Friday harbors stage the Dixieland Jazz Festival.

Roberto's servings of pasta in his restaurant

A room with a
view on Orcas
Island.

seum has a collection of
relics from 1880s pio-
neer days.

on San Juan are outstanding. Roche Harbor Resort, at 107 years of age, is the venerable old gal of the islands. Ask for the harbor view at Hillside House, Fridays, and visit Lonesome Cove Resort, both are popular and good choices. The latter has about 30 per cent newlyweds at any given time.

Orcas Island

Orcas Island is the hilliest of the four ferry stops and a favorite of nature lovers. Moran State Park, which covers 5,000 acres is the largest in the San Juans. From the summit of Mount Constitution, which rises 2,409 feet above the sound, you get a spectacular view. The **Orcas Island Historical Mu-**

Lopez

Lopez is the best for cycling and the most openly friendly as waving to passing strangers is a quirky pastime of the locals. Wave back or be classified a tourist.

Shaw Island

Shaw Island, the least visited of the ferry stops, is best know for the Franciscan nuns (in habits) who operate the ferry dock and the general store, "The Little Portion", named after Saint Francis of Assisi's Chapel in Italy.

Fishermen's Bay,
Lopez Island.

A 10-day tulip festival in Puget Island is an event not to be missed.

mudflats and the meandering Nisqually River. Within the 3,780 acres is one of the last pristine deltas in the United States.

North of Seattle

If you drive north of Seattle, the Puget sound opens up. It can be entered on the west side through the Olympic Penisula or along the east side by driving north on I-5 towards Vancouver, B.C.

In **Everett**, the economy of this 57,000 population city that's located 25 miles north of Seattle, can be summed up in a single word – Boeing. The giant 747/767 plant is the city's largest employer and the world's largest (in vol-

ume) manufacturing plant. Strategically located at the crossroads of Puget Sound, **La Conner** is located midway between Seattle and Vancouver, B.C. across the water from Fidalgo Island. Getting its start as a trading post, the town still remains a fine example of American life at the turn of the century with many well preserved homes and buildings from the mid to late 1800s. A historical walking tour guide is available from the La Conner Chamber of Commerce.

Many of the historic structures along the waterfront now house boutiques, galleries, and restaurants. The **Gaches Mansion** – a grand Victorian structure filled with period furniture – is preserved as a museum. The **Skagit County Historical Museum** holds a collection of automobiles, vintage clothing and artifacts. It's a popular destination. Lodgings of choice are the Heron in La Conner, Hotel Planter, Dewney House, Rainbow Inn, and the La Conner Country Inn.

Mount Vernon

Founded on George Washington's birthday in 1877, **Mount Vernon** was named after Washington's plantation. Today the farming region produces 40 per cent of the nation's peas.

The 10-day tulip festival, held annually in April in a joint effort by Mount Vernon, La Connor, and Anacortes is one of the Sound's most anticipated festivals with Skagit River trips, a rugby tournament, crafts displays, and community involvement. After March 1 get a map of daffodil, tulip, and Iris fields from the Chamber of Commerce.

Weekend escape

Whidbey Island, the longest island in the lower 48 states (supplanting New York's Long Island which was declared a peninsula by the United States Supreme Court) is both the site of a major naval base and a weekend escape for Seattle

residents who use the dozen or so inns and rural seashore atmosphere to escape city life. Unlike most of the islands in Puget Sound, you can drive to it from the mainland.

No spot anywhere along its 45-mile length is more than five miles from the sea. The slender, serpentine stretch of land is filled with a rolling patchwork of loganberry farms, pasturelands, sprawling state parks, hidden heritage sites, and small farming and fishing villages.

The island is named after Joseph Whidbey, master of Captain George Vancouver's flagship, the *H.M.S. Discovery*, who stepped ashore at what is now Coupeville in 1792. Local Indians at that time made Whidbey strip to the waist to prove he was really as white as he appeared to be.

Today, Whidbey is one of Washington's biggest tourist attractions so be prepared for crowded conditions during the summer. Attendance at Deception Pass State Park rivals that of Mount Rainier.

The small community of **Langley** is an artistic hamlet near Whidbey's southern tip and an ongoing hot spot for weekend escapes from Seattle. Langley is the jewel of Whidbey's many small towns. Shops lining the streets of this small artists' community make it the perfect place for browsing. The Cascade

Whidbey Island is one of Washington's biggest tourist attractions.

Cut-out murals adorn the walls of Anacortes' historical buildings.

Mountains and the Saratoga Passage make a perfect backdrop. It's the home of the Island County Fair, held in late August with a logging show and a show of local talent.

Coupeville is part of a National Historic District, one of the largest such districts in the state. The restored town with its Victorian homes is filled with maritime lore. The Captain Whidbey Inn is a favorite weekend getway. Oak Harbor is the busiest town on the island because of the Naval Air Station, Whidbey's largest industry.

Gateway to San Juans

On the northern tip of Fidalgo Island,

Anacortes is known to locals as the gateway to the San Juan Islands because of its ferry terminal. An easy drive from Seattle, the island itself is a good place to enjoy folk art, to ride a charming miniature excursion train, and to see impressive murals at the Anacortes Mural Project.

Forty life-sized murals are attached to many of the historical buildings. They are reproductions of turn-of-the-century photographs depicting everyday scenes and early pioneers of the town.

The San Juans begin midway up the Strait of Juan de Fuca and end at the Canadian border where they blend into British Columbia's equally picturesque, Gulf Islands. It's tougher to get to the woody and rocky San Juans than to

Roche Harbor Resort in San Juan Island.

other regions of Puget Sound. But it's the difficulty that attracts people and is the reason why the islands are filled with writers, artists, and eccentrics.

Estimates of the number of islands in the chain vary – from as little as the 172 that have names to as many as 700 that show some surface at low tide and 438 at high tide.

The San Juan Islands are the crown jewels of the Sound. Americans can thank a hungry pig for the fact that the islands belong to the United States. Due to a badly worded treaty between England and the United States, the islands were the focus of an international incident called "The Pig War".

Captain George Vancouver claimed the islands for England in 1791 and

Capt. Charles Wilkes did the same thing for America in 1841. So, the islands were occupied by both nations' citizens and military – a prescription, even today, for calamity.

The British built a stockade and encampment on the west side of San Juan Island on a gorgeous cove while the American built their camp on the exposed, windy, southern tip. Both camps are now a part of the San Juan Islands National Historic Park.

The military arrived because in June of 1859 one of the 25 American settlers on San Juan Island shot a British-owned pig rooting in his garden.

The Englishman demanded payment, the American refused and then the Englishman demanded the Yank be

Pabst Brewing Company

English camp on San Juan Island.

It's all in the water, goes the commercial. Maybe they're right. Pabst Brewing Company's operation is in Tumwater Falls, the historic heart of the Olympia region, the home of Olympia Beer.

Pabst is the major brewer of the Pacific Northwest and the brewing company garners more visitors to its plant than to any other attraction in the capitol city, including the Legislative Building. Located off Interstate 5 at exit 103, it's the home of several brands of beer including Olympia Gold, Hamm's, Hamm's Special Light, Buckhorn, Pabst Blue Ribbon, Olde English 800, and Olympia Light. A privately owned company, Pabst bought out the Olympia line in 1983 after a 87-year history of being a purely local operation.

Daily tours, during working hours seven days a week, allow you to watch the complete brewing process. While there's always samples at the end of the tour, films tell the story of the history and process on weekends.

"Special" water

It was while on a business trip to Olympia in 1896 that Leopold F. Schmidt decided to open a brewery. The 49-year old, German-born brewmaster from Montana listened as a barber told him about the water from popular artesian wells. Laboratory analysis confirmed the water was indeed "special" and he decided to stay awhile.

He bought the land on which the water was located and began construction of his brewery – against local advice not to try during the wet and soggy winter months. After several construction delays, brewing began in July and on October 1, 1886, the first bottles of Olympia Pale Export were siphoned by hand from wooden barrels.

The going price for a 31-gallon (117 Liter) barrel of beer at that time of ongoing beer wars was $3.25. Leopold, however, stunned his competition by asking $8 a barrel for his "premium" beer. He got it and thereby established a tradition of upscale beers and pricing in the Pacific Northwest, a tradition that continues today in the small house-breweries that dot the Puget Sound area.

As the population increased, demand rose, and offshoots of the original recipe were devised, the brewery has undergone several expansions, with new equipment brought in to handle each label.

brought to trial in Victoria.

The Americans refused to participate and the soldiers stood at arms-length until the matter was settled by arbitration 13 years later by Kaiser Wilhelm I of Germany who gave the

Tours of the Pabst operation take you through every aspect of the process, beginning with the preparation of the grains. Selected barley malt is allowed to steep in the mash tub while rice from the Sacramento Valley, or finely ground corn from the Midwest, and water go into the cereal cooker for boiling.

The cereal cooker mash is added to the barley malt, forming the main mash. Natural fermentation creates fermentable sugars which are then added to a type of strainer.

The extract – called "first wort" is then allowed to filter off. Later hot water is sprayed over the grains to extract remaining sugars and create the second wort for the remainder of the brew.

The wort is then transferred to the brew kettle and brought to a furious boil. A blend of hops is added in stages – robust hops first, milder ones last – while the brew is boiling. Here the brew takes on full hop flavor and aroma.

Hops are removed in the hop strainer (spent hops are used for fertilizer and spent grains for dairy cattle food). The brew is then cooled to 50 degrees F (10 C).

The chilled brew is transferred to a startling tank where pure yeast is added. After fermentation the beer is then moved to large storage tanks for aging and mellowing.

Following one month of aging, the beer is passed through several stainless steel filters to remove the yeast and give the finished product clarity. The beer is keg filled, canned and bottled in the packaging center.

A gift shop offers many ways to loosen your purse strings with shirts, old truck models, shorts, gold towels, glass pitchers, golf putters, and wooden trays – among other items – available for purchase.

Nearby is the Tumwater Recreational Area, and the Tumwater Falls Park situated next to the brewery. A few blocks away is the State Capitol Museum.

San Juans Islands to the United States. The pig, as it turned out, was the only casualty.

Bellingham

Located on Bellingham Bay with Mount Baker as its backdrop, **Bellingham** with its population of 54,000, is the last major city before the Washington Coastline meets the Canadian border. The broad curve of Bellingham Bay was charted in 1792 by Capt. George Vancouver who named it in honor of Sir William Bellingham. When the first white settlers arrived, forests stretched to the edge of the high bluffs along the shoreline.

Timber and coal played major roles in the town's early economy, but the Lummi and Nooksack Indians had for centuries fished the local waters. Today the town, situated on three rivers flowing into the bay, has been rediscovered - and little wonder. It's full of fine old houses, stately streets, lovely parks, and Squalicum Harbor's busy 1,700 commercial and pleasure boat marina is the second largest in Puget Sound. Passenger ferries leave for whale watching cruises, tours to Victoria on Vancouver Island, and cruises to the San Juan Islands and to Alaska.

The downtown area is a lively mix of restaurants, art galleries, and speciality shops in low-slung, brick buildings that date to the late 19th-century. The oldest, the **George E. Pickett House** (10 Bancroft Street) was built in 1856 for Captain Pickett, who erected a stockade in Bellingham to protect against Indian attacks from British Columbia. He later went on to fame for leading a gallant, but futile Confederate charge at Gettysburg.

The **Whatcom Museum of History and Art** is in a building originally built in 1892 in the Second Empire style as a city hall for which it was used until 1940. It has been beautifully restored and is home to Eskimo and Northwest Coast native artifacts as well as pioneer exhibits.

The 224-acre **Western Washington University**, on Sehome Hill south of downtown, is a fine expression of the spirit of West Coast architecture that combines natural backdrops with echoes of European design and there are many internationally acclaimed sculptures in its gardens. The **Sehome Hill Arboretum** offers wonderful views of the San Juan Islands.

Scenic Chuckanut Drive

Driving south of town on seven mile-long **Chuckanut Drive** you will find yourself on one of the most scenic roads in the state, hugging the shoreline. Spectacular views of the islands are to be found from small oyster and seafood restaurants along the way.

At nearby Lummi Island in mid-June, the Lummi Indians celebrate the Lummi Indian Stommish, a festival similar to the ancient potlach. Potlatch was a ceremony in which native peoples celebrated life and often gave away their possessions.

A 7-mile road travels the island perimeter – the island can be reached by a 7-minute ferry ride from Gooseberry Point on the Lummi Indian Reserve.

To the north of Bellingham are Ferndale, Birch Bay, and Blaine. **Ferndale** is Main Street USA with one main drag, a few motels, some bars, and

All set for a ferry cruise around the islands.

one major industry – an ARCO Petroleum refinery. **Birch Bay**, by contrast, is one of the State's oldest resort towns and now draws thousands of tourists, especially young people, between Memorial Day and Labor Day.

At **Blaine**, the reason for stopping is the Inn At Semiahmoo, situated on Semiahmoo Spit across the inlet from the Canada/US border. An Arnold Palmer golf course, several specialty restaurants, and a convention center draw large numbers of Vancouver and Bellingham residents on weekends.

Much of Washington's Pacific Ocean coastline remains virgin wilderness, especially in the north where few roads allow accessibility to any but the most enthusiastic backpackers.

Further south, from Moclips (at the southern edge of the Quinalt Indian Reservation) to the Columbia River, almost the entire shoreline is composed of fine sandy beaches interrupted occasionally by rocky bluffs. And wherever Razor Clams dig in rapidly at the surf line, there's a tourist town.

The coastline begins at the northern tip of the Olympic Peninsula where rain forests and coastal mountains make access difficult. By taking Route 112 to Neam Bay and Cape Flattery then Route 101 south and a side-road to La Push, you begin to understand why the Olympic National Park was

Hecata Lighthouse on the Washington Coast.

Washington Coast

181

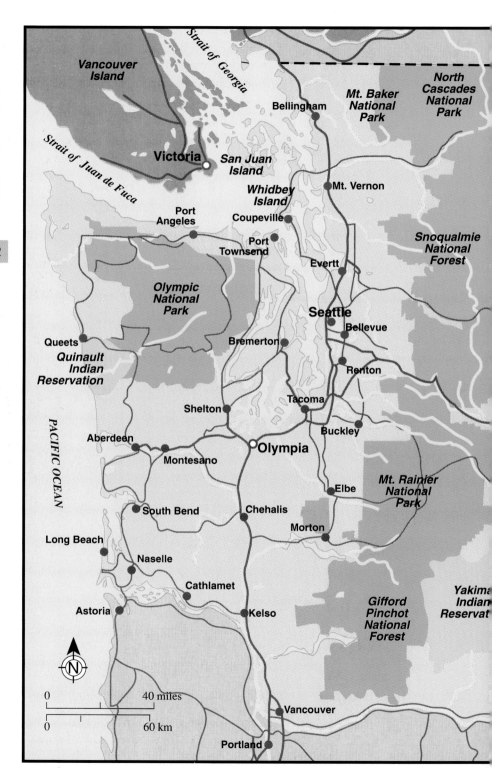

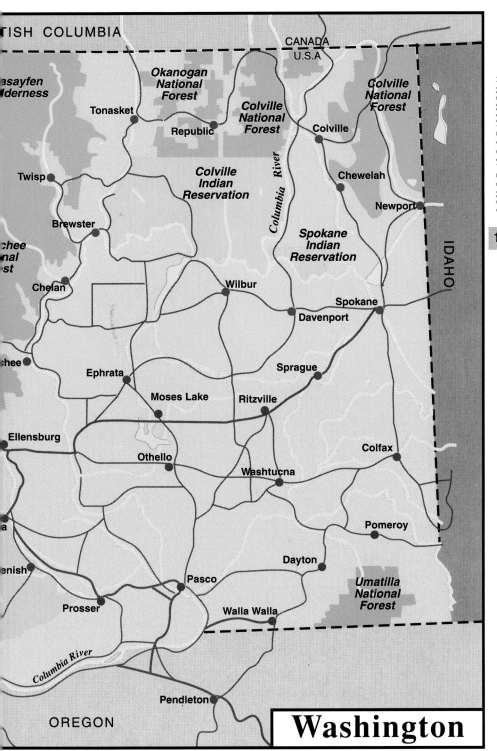

[ISH COLUMBIA

CANADA
U.S.A

asayfen
Iderness

Okanogan
National
Forest

Colville
National
Forest

Colville
National
Forest

Tonasket

Republic

Colville

Twisp

Colville
Indian
Reservation

Chewelah

Newport

Brewster

chee
nal
st

Chelan

Wilbur

Spokane
Indian
Reservation

Spokane

Davenport

chee

Ephrata

Sprague

Ellensburg

Moses Lake

Ritzville

Colfax

Othello

Washtucna

Pomeroy

enish

Dayton

Prosser

Pasco

Walla Walla

Umatilla
National
Forest

Columbia River

Pendleton

OREGON

Washington

Columbia River

IDAHO

Straits of Juan de Fuca off Sekiu.

created. Largely undeveloped, the Olympic Coast is home to American Indian research centers, archeological preserves, maritime sanctuaries, and pristine beaches.

Developers haven't been able to tacky-up the region and it's almost totally uncommercial. Ocean Shores, at the south end of the Peninsula – almost due west of Olympia, was developed as a summer resort in the 1960s and 1970s. But even that town does not have the feel of the ocean-side resorts which you'll find in California or in Florida. That might be due to the climate which is generally overcast, wet and windy in the winters and cool in the summer.

Callam Bay and Sekiu

Fifty miles due west of Port Angeles on Route 112, where the Strait of Juan de Fuca approaches the Pacific, are the twin towns of **Callam Bay** and **Sekiu** (pronounced C-Q).

If you travel northwest at **Slip Point**, you can see some of the finest tidal pools in the region and just west of Sekiu, at the mouth of the Hoko River, you can view the remains of a 2,500 year old Makah Indian fishing village at the **Hoko Archaeological Site.**

Neah Bay

Neah Bay has been the home of the Makah tribe for thousands of years and at the Makah Museum, Cultural and Research Center are the prehistoric artifacts discovered at the Hoko and Lake Ozette digs including baskets, whaling and sealing harpoons and canoes. There is also a replica of a 15th-century longhouse. The facility houses the largest collection of Northwest Indian artifacts in the world. Also the home of a commercial fishing fleet, Neah Bay offers charter fishing excursions.

Route 112 ends at **Cape Flattery**, the northernmost point in the lower United States. The road at times runs within feet of the water, providing spectacular blufftop views of the Strait of Juan de Fuca, a great location for whale watching between March and May.

Wilderness coast

A short trail at the end of the road leads to the shore and the end of the continent. Beach hikers can find some of the last wilderness coast in Washington south of here. **Shi-Shi Beach** presents a

Lighthouses

Lighthouses have long been a sea-going tradition in the Northwest.

The lights are still on, but the romance has been dimmed in the lighthouses that run the length of the Washington and Oregon coastline. The era of the manned lighthouse has virtually drawn to a close.

From the tip of the Olympic Peninsula, where the Cape Flattery lighthouse protects the entrance to the Strait of Juan De Fuca and Puget Sound, to the California border, lighthouses have been part of the sea-going traditions of the Pacific Northwest.

The romantic notion of the isolated lighthouse keeper protecting oncoming ships from shoals and disaster, is a part of coastal living – one that began in 1716 in Boston Harbor and lasted for 274 years.

In 1800 there were 24 lighthouses in the country, all on the east coast. A century later, 650 stations dotted the shores and legends grew about keepers who braved storms, isolation, loneliness, and illness to save lives and property.

Today, all lighthouses and fog signals are automated and no longer require a keeper's care. Yet, much still remains of the early lighthouse history along the west coast. Though some early lighthouses have been replaced by modern towers and satellite navigation systems, many remain in their original condition as reminders of another time.

Since 1972, vessel traffic from the Strait of Juan de Fuca to Tacoma has been monitored by the Puget Sound Vessel Traffic Service operated by the U.S. Coast Guard. Similar to air traffic control systems, it combines radar stations and two-way voice communication.

Washington State has 25, most of which are in the Puget Sound, Olympic Penisula area. Fifteen lighthouses are accessible by car and ten are open to the public.

History

The lighthouses were built for two functions – to warn maritimers of danger and to provide relatively comfortable living conditions for the keeper. In the more remote areas, keepers and their families received supplies and food by boat or, later on, by helicopter. Some even brought livestock with them.

In the beginning, light warnings were given by primitive lanterns – some just kerosene – hand-held or on posts. As technology improved, lenses with flames in front of them were used to warn incoming ships.

Different fuels to light the flames were used including whale oil, rapeseed oil, olive oil, porpoise oil, lard, and eventually kerosene. Soot from these fuels meant keepers were constantly busy polishing lenses.

At Point No-Point lighthouse, the oldest on

dramatic view of jagged off-shore rocks and a smooth beach that runs for 3

miles (5 km).

The region is known as the grave-

Puget Sound and located on the Sound's west side on a spit near Hansville, people still take an active part. It's one of six lighthouses in Washington with resident Coast Guard personnel. They mow lawns, paint buildings, plant flowers, maintain equipment, act as tour directors, and even rescue boaters now and then.

The **Point No-Point Lighthouse** is one of the few where you can still see what life was like at a life station 100 years ago. Its first light, a household kerosene lantern, was lit on New Year's Eve in 1879. It gained its unique name from an naval officer who, in 1841, saw the point of land and thought it bigger than it really was – a fact he discovered upon sailing to it. Indians called the spit Hahd-skus, or long nose. The name never appeared on navigation charts.

One of the easiest lighthouses to reach is **West Point Lighthouse** at the foot of Seattle's Magnolia Bluff in Discovery Park at one of the busiest vessel traffic intersections in Washington waters. It was the last lighthouse in Washington State to be automated, in February, 1985. The lighthouse and dwellings are original, it's operation typical of lighthouses throughout the system. A fourth generation Fresnel lens (a focusing lens that concentrates light into a narrow beam) rotates in a 27 foot (2.13 m) tower flashing alternate red and white. The white beam is visible 19 miles away and the red from 16 miles distant. A coast guard keeper and his family live there to conduct tours and tend the grounds.

Oregon's lighthouses are not as numerous or concentrated, but no less historic. Near the Oregon Dunes National Recreation Area, stands the "second" **Umpqua River Lighthouse**. The "first" was built on the dunes at the mouth of the river in 1857, but lasted only four years before a vicious storm blew it over.

It took 33 years before local residents were able to build another, but it's still standing on a bluff overlooking the south side of Winchester Bay, still flashing its warning signal once every five seconds.

yard of ships. Nine miles south of Ozette, the **Norwegian Memorial** acknowl-

Playing in coastal waters.

edges seamen who died in an early 20th century ship wreck; and 6 miles further south – 3 miles north of Rialto Beach opposite La Push – the **Chilean Memorial** marks the grave of 20 South American sailors who died in a 1920 wreck.

The largest town on the Olympic coast is Forks, with 3,000 people, 277 miles (43 km) south of Callam Bay on Route 101. Mushroom gathering, steelhead fishing and timber are the big industries. The **Forks Timber Museum** is filled with exhibits of old-time logging equipment and photos. Here too is the **South North Garden**, a surprisingly good Chinese restaurant in the middle of logging country.

On the coast, 14 miles (8.6 km) west of Forks, is **La Push**, an 800-year-old

Skirting the Pacific.

Indian fishing village and the center of the Quileute Indian Reservation. An abandoned Coast Guard station and lighthouse here are used as a school for resident children. La Push is a quiet, friendly village which during the summer is jammed with tourists. Located on a beach strewn with driftwood, the roar of high breakers rolling in from the ocean is a constant sound. In August, another sound dominates the region with the Quileute Days celebrations.

South of La Push, Highway 101 moves inland until, just north of

the single strip road.

The southwest coast extends from Moclips to the Columbia River and is totally unlike the shoreline of the Olympic Peninsula with sand beaches drawing tourists. The smallest community is **Moclips**, the largest is Ocean Shores. Between them the towns become larger as your drive south – or small as you go north.

Ocean shores

At the southern tip is **Ocean Shores**, a 6-mile (9.6 km) long, 6000-acre peninsula that was a cattle ranch before being purchased for $1 million in 1960 by a group of investors. Today, it would be impossible to place a dollar figure on the strip of condominium style hotels and second homes, many of which lie along a series of canals.

As the closest ocean beach area to the Seattle-Tacoma metropolitan region, hotels are booked early and throughout the summer. During off-season, hotel prices are considerably less and the region is comatose quiet. The region used to be Indian clam-digging grounds and is still used for that purpose by invading tourists who arrive not for sightseeing, but for rest and relaxation and golfing.

One of the few attractions is the **Ocean Shore Environmental Interpretive Center**, four miles (6.4 km) south of the town center with exhibits describing the peninsula's geological formation and anthropology.

Kalaloch, it again runs along the shore to Queets before making a wide detour around the Quinalt Reservation which has forbidden public access to its beaches.

Well inland, the road will eventually take you to the junction of Route 109, at **Hoquiam**, where you can then drive west to the coast and then north on

Hikers on the beach of Olympic National Park.

The drive north to Moclips is a scenic, deliciously soothing experience. **Capolis Beach** and **Ocean City** are home to the Razor Clam and the State Department of Fisheries sponsors clam-digging clinics throughout the summer at Ocean City State and at neighborhood schools to prepare you for the short, intense, clam season.

Ocean City State Park stretches for several miles along the coastline with horseback riding, clamming, picnicking, and surf kayaking being popular pastimes. Birdwatching is popular. But

Ilwaco

Ilwaco sits on the head of the Columbia River, protected from the onslaught of winter storms by Cape Disappointment and the isthmus that separates it from the Pacific. While today its lives off tourism and some fishing, at one time the village of 600 was one of the most notorious along the coast. From 1884 to 1910, gillnetters and trap fishermen fought one another for the ownership and rights of access to the rich fishing grounds. Everything and anything was used – knives, rifles, lynching threats – to get their respective messages across to the enemy.

It's a more peaceful community these days and the only evidence of the near-riot conditions that prevailed at the turn-of-the-century can be found in the **Ilwaco Heritage Museum** which uses wonderful dioramas to illustrate the history of southwestern Washington.

Beginning with the Native peoples and their influence, the presentation moves on to the influx of traders, missionaries, and pioneers, concluding with the contemporary industries of fishing, agriculture, and forestry.

Clamshell Railroad

The museum also houses a model of the peninsula's "clamshell railroad", a narrow-gauge train that once transported passengers and mail along the peninsula to Oysterville. The railbed on which tracks were placed, was composed of ground-up clam and oyster shells, hence its name.

The town is now home to salmon, tuna, crab, and charter fishing. A 1926 Presbyterian church was restored and converted into The Inn At Ilwaco where guest rooms now occupy the old Sunday School rooms. The sanctuary is now a playhouse, welcoming concerts and theater, wedding receptions, reunions, and other activities.

One of the town's gathering points is the Reel-Em-In Cafe where locals and tourists alike drink coffee, brag about their catches and near-misses, and watch the harbor activity unfold through the windows.

---

if you swim, be careful of the riptides.

Be prepared to fight a lot of traffic during the summer and much of it will be trailers. You won't have problems finding either lodging and eating possibilities which are plentiful.

Ocean Park is the commercial hub of the north peninsula, founded as a camp for the Methodist Episcopal Church in Portland in 1883, which passed laws prohibiting saloons and gambling. They no longer exist, but the Taylor Hotel does. Built in 1892, it now houses retail shops and is the only structure in town from that period open to the public.

On the way further south of Ocean Park, you'll have to come back out along Route 109 and through the Grays Harbor area including the twin cities of Aberdeen and Hoquiam with a combined population of about 38,000.

It's a surprising place – firstly because of its industrial nature, and secondly because of its handsome mansions built by lumber barons.

Hoquiam

Hoquiam's Castle is an aristocratic, 20-room mansion built in 1897 by Robert Lytle, which has been restored to its original Victorian luster complete with furnishings. Tiffany lamps and cut-crystal lamps provide an unspoiled 19th-century image.

Polson Museum, housed in the former 26 room mansion of Alex Polson, is filled with Gray Harbor history and logging past. Surrounding the house is a small park and rose gardens.

A couple of miles west of town is the **Grays Harbor Wildlife Sanctuary** that attracts a half-million migrating shorebirds that visit the basin including the western sandpiper, dunlin, red and the short and long-billed dowitcher. The arrival of the birds is reason enough for the Festival of Shorebirds.

Hoquiam's Loggers Playday, held the second weekend of September, is a fair of lumberjacks who throw axes, climb trees, and show off their log-chopping skills.

Aberdeen

In Aberdeen, a major attraction is the **Grays Harbor Historical Seaport** where crafts people at this working replica of an 18th-century shipyard, have constructed a replica of the *Lady Washington*, the brigantine in which Captain Robert Gray sailed the region in 1783.

Route 109 from Aberdeen around Grays Harbor, meets the Pacific coast again in an area known as "the Cranberry Coast", as the region grows most of the state's berries. They come from plants that were imported from Cape Cod in the early 1930s.

Salmon Capital of the World

Westport, the principal cranberry coast city, calls itself the "Salmon Capital Of The World" and it sometimes seems as though there's nothing else to do but fish or eat salmon at the many restaurants. It's a marina town filled with colorful boats and lively conversation. There's even a 1,000 foot (305 m) walking pier that allows the non-boater a chance to fish.

The old Westport Coast Guard Station has been rehabilitated as the **Historical Maritime Museum** preserving relics of Westport's past. At **Westhaven Beach Park** – also known as Agate Beach – shell hunting and driftwood collection eases high blood pressure.

Festivals in the area include the Driftwood Show (March), the Blessing of the Fleet (May), the Cranberry Blossom Festival (June), the Westport Kite Meet (June), and the two-week-long Saltwater Festival (June/July).

The drive south around **Willapa Bay** reveals broad, flat, swampy ground, bogs, and mud flats that make up the Willapa National Wildlife Refuge, an important sanctuary for a wide variety of shorebirds. They also make the region's productive oyster farms possible.

Long Beach

Officially designated the "North Beach Peninsula", but more popularly known

Westport, billed as the "Salmon Capital of the World".

as **Long Beach**, the 28 miles of long, flat sandy beaches on Washington's exposed southwest shore, provide some of the state's most popular vacation spots. The economy of the Long Beach Peninsula is based on tourism, cranberries, and oysters. Sometimes you need a crowbar to separate one from the other. The long expanse of sand comes to an abrupt halt at North Head, a rocky headland south of Seaview. A glance back up the peninsula reveals large breakers along a ribbon of sand backed by low, grassy dunes. From the **Cape Disappointment Lighthouse**, the oldest working one on the west coast, you watch ocean waves fight the currents of the Columbia River.

Cape Disappointment was named in 1788 by British fur trader, John Meares, who tried several times to pilot his ship across the rain-swept and treacherous Columbia River Bar. Certainly, if the entrance to the river had been less turbulent, there's little doubt a large city would today sit on the headland on the north side of the river. Instead, the area is still quite unpopulated.

The **Fort Columbia State Park and Interpretive Center** is a former coastal defense fort built in 1903 to house 200 soldiers. Many of the fort's 30 structures have been restored. A hike up the hill behind the fort, offers – on a clear day – a breathtaking view of the peninsula and the Columbia.

The small town of **Ilwaco** sits at the head of small spit whose major attraction is the **Canby State Park**. The Lewis and Clark Interpretive Center displays

Long Beach thrives on its cranberries.

the journals and entries of the famed expedition of 1804-06 that ended at that spot. The nearby Coast Guard Lifeboat Station and Surf School is located in one of two lighthouses on the Cape.

As you drive up the peninsula – drive one way up Sandridge road that takes you along the Bay, and back along the ocean on Route 103 – it's easy to understand the attraction. It's a perfect place to walk the beaches, rent a cabin or stay in one of many out-of-the way inns. The Shelburne Inn, Klipsan Beach Cottages, and Sou'wester Lodge are three worth considering. The Lightship Restaurant and Columbia Bar offer both views and good food.

Naturalists love the peninsula for bird-watching, beachcombing, and hik-

An Jlwaco mural.

ing, while history buffs can delight in 18th-century grave sites and 19th-century houses.

It is not, however, the place to swim, with rogue waves being known to drag unsuspecting bodies out to sea and signs continually warn tourists about the dangers. Believe me when I say, "Don't ignore them." And don't ignore the traffic on the beaches as locals drive their off-road vehicles and motorcycles up and down some areas of the longest uninterrupted beach in North America. **Seaview** is a favored tourist spot with old-fashioned cottages and an historic inn, The Sou'wester. But it has been overshadowed by the town of Long Beach, just north, for some time. To celebrate Washington's Centennial in 1989, 16 artists

painted murals throughout the Long Beach Peninsula and they can be seen on the sides of many buildings.

Oyster centers

Oysterville is the northernmost settlement and was once the oyster capital of the state. The town (established in 1854) didn't however, survive the end of the industry that fished to extinction the native shellfish.

But, Oysterville has made a comeback thanks to restoration. **Leadbetter Point State Park** occupies the northernmost tip of the peninsula and is a bird-watchers' paradise. Another oyster center, **Nahcotta**, is a good place to

Long Beach

Dramatic coastline of the Long Beach Peninsula.

china and glassware.

Kites galore

Part of the Long Beach Peninsula, Long Beach town outwardly seems somewhat out of place with the pristine flavor of what has been called the largest unpopulated estuary in the country. Lying just a mile north of the junction of Routes 101/103, the town's principal new attraction is a 2,400 foot (731.5 m) wooden boardwalk that runs from South 10th to Bolstad streets.

Elevated 40 feet (12 m) above the dunes, the boardwalk allows people to make an easy walk to the high-tide mark. The beach that runs in front, is open to driving on the upper sands as well as to clam digging, beachcombing, and surf fishing. Obviously, vigilance is required.

During the summer months, it's a crowded place filled with tourists and has the usual beachfront services such as bike and moped rentals, candy stores, an amusement park, and Marsh's Free Museum, which is essentially a large souvenir shop. This one has the world's largest frying pan (so they say) and a variety of music boxes.

Pastimes is a collectibles shop and expresso bar at S. Fifth and Pacific Hwy. where antique collectors can find a wide assortment of clocks,

But the biggest enterprise in town is the **World Kite Museum and Hall of Fame**, a result of Long Beach's week-long International Kite Festival in late August. Kites from everywhere in the world hang from the ceilings, mounted on stands.

Kites is what Long Beach is all about. Kites of all kind with short tails, long tails, box, square and diamond shaped. As long as it flies it can show its stuff.

If you happen to arrive in town without your kite in tow, drop by **Ocean Kites** at 511 Pacific Avenue S. where kites of all shapes and colors are available.

A couple of galleries break the kite fixation. The **Charles Mulvey Gallery** is open weekdays selling Northwest coast watercolors while the **Potrimpos Gallery** features watercolors, sculpture, and photography in a Victorian House.

In October and early November, cranberries take over the region; most of the fields which are harvested are owned by Ocean Spray. The **Washington State University-Long Beach Research and Extension Unit** on Pioneer Road offers free tours of the cranberry bogs during harvest.

view Long Island, home of an old-growth cedar forest in the Willapa National Wildlife Reserve. It's the largest estua-

rine island on the Pacific coast, and is home to bear and elk but the reserve can only be reached by boat.

Totem poles at an abandoned Indian village.

Once you cross the Cascades and reach Central Washington you also cross into another cultural zone – one dominated by open space, large farmlands, and bone-dry hills that are covered by snow in the winter. The Central highlands reach from the Canadian border to the Columbia River and include the state's richest growing area.

The north of this region is dominated by the Okanagan Valley which also reaches into British Columbia to its fruit valleys and recreational areas.

The Yakima Valley in the southern portion of the central state, is the primary winery center with 40 different wineries, and is Washington's biggest growing area. The wine industry, in particular, has spawned an active and productive tourism industry.

Yakima County ranks first nationally in the number of fruit trees; first in the

Pipples are cash crops in Yakima County.

Central Washington

Deserted barn near Wenatchee.

production of apples, mint and hops, and fourth in the value of all fruits grown.

Rich saladbowl

When you cross the Cascades into the Okanagan, along Highway 20, the Northern Cascades Highway, you drive down the rain shadow, past Mazama, Winthrop, and into the heart of Okanagan County through the Okanagan National Forest.

The scenery changes quickly and dramatically as you pass into the Methow Valley. As you descend the east slope of the Cascades, the thick fir forests give way to smaller pine tree with

no undergrowth. The mountains are bare and it seems as though you can see forever.

In fact, without the Grand Coulee Dam in the heart of the northern section, the entire region would be totally inhospitable to farming. Instead, because of irrigation by sprinkler systems, a rich salad of fruits, vegetables, and

Windsurfing is one of the many pleasures in the Methow Valley.

wheat have been created.

In the northern-most section, however, there is more water than one would normally expect. Farmers and ranchers in the four northern counties use an estimated 1.5 billion gallons every year to irrigate their land. Every year enough runoff traverses the underground regions of the land to fill two Kingdomes.

When you reach **Winthrop** you wonder if you've crossed over into a Wyoming western town film set because of the false-fronts, the saloon doors, hitching rails, wooden porches, and cowboy ambience.

The **Shafer Museum** is housed in an 1897 log cabin built by the town's founder, Guy Waring. Displays include pioneer artifacts, a stagecoach, and horse-drawn vehicles.

The valley itself offers a variety of physical pleasures including rafting, cross-country skiing, fishing, and hiking along the many trails.

Okanagan

The town of **Okanagan**, at the end of Highway 20, is one of the main entry points into the Grand Coulee Recreational Area. And if you drive along Route 95, you'll reach the Canadian border and Oroville.

Fort Okanagan, an important part of America's fur trade, is primarily an interpretive park. Set above the junction of the Okanagan and Columbia Rivers it has a visitor center on the bluff overlooking the original site, but is now under the waters of Wells Dam's backwaters.

On the way you'll pass Omak where the famous and controversial Suicide Race is part of the Omak Festival held over the second weekend of August. At the end of the four rodeos that take place over the three-day weekend, a surge of horses and riders sweep down a steep embankment, across the Okanagan River, and into the arena.

While no human has ever been killed in the event that was first started in 1933, many horses have broken their legs and have had to be destroyed, hence the name Suicide Race.

On a more positive note, the festival attracts Indian tribes from all over the Pacific Northwest to celebrate their heritage.

A teepee Indian village is constructed and traditional games and dances are performed.

Molson

Near Oroville, settled in 1858 by Hiram Okanagan, is **Molson**, one of the west's finest ghost towns. The old town is now an outdoor museum.

Osoyoos State Park is one mile north of Oroville and stretches along the shores of Osoyoos Lake.

One of the most popular parks in the area, it is heavily used by Canadians and Americans alike as the lake straddles the border.

You can take Highway 20 across the top of the state almost to the Utah border. You'll pass through endless rolling hills, following a path along valleys and streams and past rambling ranches.

Columbia River Valley en route to Wenatchee.

Colville Reservation

To reach the Grand Coulee area, however, take Highway 155 from Omak. At Nespelem, on the **Colville Reservation**, is the final resting place of the celebrated Chief Joseph of the Nez Perce whose life spanned the period of major white immigration to Washington.

The Chief Joseph Memorial is a monument with the chief's face in relief at the head of his grave in a reservation cemetery. Though initially well disposed to white immigrants – he had been educated by missionaries in his youth – he was forced into a savage war that he lost in Oregon's Wallowa Valley. After a time in Kansas at Fort Leavenworth, he was transferred in 1885 to the Colville Reservation.

The recreation area is barely developed, an obvious plus for those interested only in boating, fishing, and camping. But if you're looking for fine dining and nice hotels, you're better off continuing south once you've seen and toured the dam.

Chelan

At the bottom of the Methow Valley, on the way to Wenatchee along Route 97, you go through the small town of **Chelan** which sits at the south end of Chelan Lake. It's a tourist town that serves the throngs who come to the 55-mile (88.5-

Molson

It began with a gold mine and a lot of hope, but today the town of Molson, east of Oroville and along a dirt road, is a testament to lost glory – almost a ghost town. Since the Poland China Gold Mine, 2 miles south of the Canadian border, was located on land too rugged for a town, buildings were put up 4 miles west of the mine. It was a place with rolling hills, a seasonal stream, and a supply of wood within walking distance.

John Molson, of the Canadian brewing family and a heavy investor in the mine and promoter George Meacham pooled their money to build the town. With $75,000 put up by Molson, builders put up a drugstore, a newspaper, and the three-story Tonasket Hotel.

But, while people did originally flock to the town, the mine was a bust – there were no precious metals. While the miners left, settlers arrived and fairly soon a store and a grain warehouse were built along with a general store – When a small railroad was built to the town, its future seemed assured. It had eight saloons and a sheriff to keep the peace.

Legend of Old Molson

But, J.H. McDonald came to town and filed for a homestead of 160 acres including nearly the entire town of Molson and the hotel. It seems that no one had bothered to file any of the land upon which Molson was built. McDonald, who now had the town in his clutches, gave out eviction notices. So, shopkeepers moved a half-mile north where they built a new town. By 1906, the old town and the new one were about the same size and the hatred between the two towns was deep.

McDonald fenced the entire town of Old Molson. Someone tried building a bank, but McDonald wouldn't deed him property. So the banker put it on skids and moved it every day. Depositors had to walk down Main Street every day to locate their money.

The rancor between the two towns and citizens continued year after year. The only truce was when they got together to build a school since neither town had enough money to finance the project alone. The school was built halfway between the two towns and quickly became became Central Molson, a sort of buffer zone between two warring camps.

But, the rivalry intensified. When one town built a theater, so too did the other. The same thing happened when big homes were built and even with automobile dealerships.

By the 1960s, the town – by that time there were three of them – was virtually a ghost town. Today, Molson consists of only a few scattered buildings and farm equipment in an open-air museum.

It's a testament to what greed and ego – and inattention to detail – will bring.

Ohme Gardens, rated one of America's best.

km) long and up to 1,500-feet (457-m) deep lake. The **Lake Chelan Museum** displays some early farming and orchard equipment and native Indian artifacts. Among the more interesting exhibits are apple labels and stone lithographs from the early 1900s.

Campbell House was built in 1901 and is now a hotel; the **Log Church** dates to 1898; and the 1890 **Whaley Mansion** is now an inn.

On the way south to Wenatchee you have the choice of driving on either side of the Columbia River, crossing

Cultured harmony in Ohme Gardens.

over Chelan Falls to use the lesser traveled Route 151 through the orchard town of Orondo to East Wenatchee. The main route, Highway 97, follows the Cascades foothills.

At **Rocky Reach Dam**, 28 miles (45 km) north of Wenatchee, visit the viewing room where migratory salmon and steelhead swim by the windows. The dam also has a museum tracing the natural and human history of the Columbia River and the Gallery of Electricity with its hands-on exhibits that allow you to create electricity.

Apple capital

Wenatchee is the self proclaimed apple capital of the world and everything in this region relates to that fruit. The **North Central Washington Museum** features permanent and temporary exhibits on the region's history, geology, archeology, natural history and fine arts. The museum also has an exhibit on a unexpected airplane landing. In 1931 a plane left Misawa, Japan on the first non-stop trans-Pacific flight from Japan to the United States. Forty-one hours after take-off, the plane made a belly-landing at Wenatchee.

Ohme Gardens, just north of Wenatchee, covers 9 acres and is one of America's most highly acclaimed gardens. Fifty years of weed-pulling and watering has transformed the barren hillside of sagebrush into evergreens, grass, ponds, and waterfalls.

Twelve miles (19 km) west of Wenatchee is Mission Ridge, the area's largest skiing facility with four chairs serving 33 runs.

Cashmere

The town of **Cashmere**, settled in 1856 by the Oblate Fathers – among the region's first missionaries – offers has a pioneer village on the grounds of the Chelan County Historical Museum that has an archeological collection of artifacts that date back 10,000 years.

One of the highlights of Cashmere's Founders Days festival is the Stillman Miller Hill Climb. It's the result of an early resident who claimed he could pour himself a beer in the local tavern, run up Numbers Hill, and be back before the head settled.

From Cashmere, Routes Two and 97 follow the Wenatchee River and 97 turns left before reaching the Cascades. You can follow the winding highway all the way to Ellensburg or take the summer-route road, the Old Blewett Pass Highway – a switchback road with sweeping views of the Cascades.

If you take Route 97/2 all the way into Leavenworth, be prepared to think Bavarian. It's one of the major tourist areas in the Cascades and all of the town's architecture is in Bavarian style.

Another spectacular road south of Wenatchee is the **Colochum Pass Road**. Recommended for recreational vehicles only, it's an adventurous two-lane route

Gingko Petrified State Forest Park, Washington.

over the top of the foothills.

Ellensburg

Ellensburg's biggest claim to fame is the popular Labor Day weekend rodeo.

The quiet town with a population of less than 12,000 maintains a finely preserved historical district of nearly 20 buildings. The **Kittita County Museum** maintains local artifacts.

The city began as a trading post and was once called Robber's Roost, the

Olmstead Place

The Olmstead State Park Heritage Area celebrates the legacy of the family farm. Located 4.5 miles (7.2 km) southeast of Ellensburg, the park gives the visitor an idea of what farm life was like back in the late 1800s.

The log cabin and farm buildings (on the National Register of Historic Sites) are part of a total-experience tour that includes a walk along the Altapes Creek Trail that runs from the red barn to the Seaton Cabin Schoolhouse.

The original Olmstead cabin dates from 1875 when Samuel and Sarah Olmstead crossed the Cascade Mountains on horseback with their young family. Like many early residents, the Olmsteads were attracted to the Kittitas Valley by the tall grass that provided feed for their livestock; the rich soil and suitable climate for farming, and the plentiful water supply.

Their farm was one of the first homesteads in the valley. Though simple and rugged by today's standards, the Olmstead cabin was considered large and comfortable in 1875.

Newspaper lined the walls for insulation and a fireplace provided heat. Constructed of Cottonwood logs from the Yakima River Canyon, the logs were squared with a broad ax, dovetailed at the corners and held together with round pegs made from a small tree.

Lumber was cut with a whip-saw and windows were freighted in from the Dalles. The restored cabin has been furnished with articles from the period between 1875-1890, the time it was occupied by the Olmsteads.

It was in 1900 that the farm entered its period of greatest development. It has a milkhouse, dairy bar, wagon shed, granary, and toolhouse. Cream was made, then made into prize butter for the Seattle market. Crops from the farm included hay, wheat, and oats.

The red barn was built in 1908 and a new residence was built. The large five-bedroom house saw more than 70 years of family life and changes and is furnished just as the family left it, reflecting the heritage of several generations.

The Seaton Cabin Schoolhouse was constructed in the 1870s and originally stood in a meadow miles away but was reconstructed at Olmstead Place in 1980. It was here that the Olmstead children and other nearby families learned to read and write.

Mr. & Mrs. Charles Terry lived in the cabin that would later serve as a schoolhouse. Graduates of a teacher's college in Pennsylvania, the Terrys knew the value of education and started a private school in their home. Each of the 10 school children paid one dollar for three months of education. The school had few books - one speller, one reader, and a dictionary donated by Samuel Olmstead.

Every child had a pencil and a tablet made from brown wrapping paper. On warm spring days, the children would eat lunch in the school yard. Their tin lunch pails were filled with every day foods - fried sage hen, roast beef or ham sandwiches, pink radishes, leaf lettuce, and dried apples or wild berry pie.

As time moved on, the old cabin was used for the storage of hay and sacks of grain. In 1949 the farm was sold and the Seaton family moved away to another property. In 1979, it was dismantled and erected at Olmstead Place State Park after being donated to the Washington State Parks and Recreation Commission.

The farm and all of its buildings was deeded to the state in 1968 by the granddaughters of the Olmsteads.

name of the original building. The beautiful Ellensburg Blue agate, found nowhere else in the world, is fashioned into earrings, necklaces, and rings at local jewelry stores.

Hidden Valley Guest Ranch, off Highway 97, is the state's oldest dude ranch. For those who want to experience the joys of bouncing on the back of a horse, you can indulge all of your cowboy fantasies.

On the way to Vantage, you'll pass Oldstead's Log Cabins enroute to **Gingko Petrified State Forest Park**. Fifteen to

Lenore Caves

Sun Lakes is one of the most popular areas in Washington.

since it is an equalizing reservoir for Grand Coulee Dam, preserves an illusion of the area being wild and untamed. It is not, of course, having been man-made.

A series of recreational areas and state parks lie south of Grand Coulee Dam including Steamboat Rock, Sun Lakes, and Summer Falls State Parks. The region, especially Sun Lakes State Park, is one of the most popular state parks in Washington, especially during the summer.

South of Sun Lakes State Park and north of Soap Lake a short, uphill hike will take you to Lake Lenore Caves. These caves, carved out of coulee's walls by melting rush waters during the ice age, served as temporary shelters for prehistoric man during hunting trips. The park and Lenore Caves are in the Banks Lake area that lies outside the national recreation area on the southwest side of the dam. Banks Lake is a 31 mile (50 km) long, wide, clear-blue gem that is surrounded by the steep sides of the coulee. Public access to the lake,

Indian landmark

Steamboat Rock State Park is an exception to the no-access problem. Steamboat rock looms 1,000 feet (305 m) above the lake and it was a well known landmark to Indians and early fur traders.

There are plenty of picnic areas in a 900-acre park, a boat launch and moorage area, and a trail that leads to the top of a butte that's a wildflower preserve.

As well as being a popular recreational alternative to Lake Roosevelt, the large lake behind

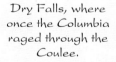

Dry Falls, where once the Columbia raged through the Coulee.

Coulee Dam, known as Banks Lake, irrigates more than a half-million acres of farmland south to the Oregon border.

Not everything in the region is wilderness, however. The relatively new – started in 1984 – Banks Lake 9-hole Golf Club is situated on a mesa above the huge lake. A vivid contrast of lush green set against the parched and arid surroundings, it's worth the short drive from Electric City. Not nearly as large as Banks Lake, **Sun Lakes State Park** lies 7 miles (11 km) southwest of Coulee City on Highway 17. It's most famous for its "dry falls".

When the Columbia ran free through the coulee, Dry Falls was 400 feet (122 m) high and 3.5 miles (5.6 km) wide. Now, it's dry, controlled by Dry Falls Dam. But it is still an awesome sight as you stand where the water once raged down to the coulee floor. High above the coulee, on the east side of the road, the visitor's center offers the best view of the falls.

Soap Lake, Washington.

20 million years ago the area was covered by lakes and swamps and then by lava. The beauty of the park is revealed by walking the trails. You'll see 250 species of petrified wood including the prehistoric petrified gingko tree which is on display in the interpretive center.

Tranquil splendor

A pleasant route to Yakima is through the Rattlesnakes Hills (believe it!) along Highway 24 after driving south on 243. En route you will pass through the northwest corner of the U.S. Department of Energy Hanford Site and travel about 43 miles (69 km) on a good two-lane highway over spectacularly dry, rolling hills.

The Yakima area is the highlight of the entire region. If you get off the freeway at any point between the town of **Yakima** and **Tri-Cities**, you'll discover scenery of tranquil splendor. Settlers arrived in the region in the late 1850s and early 1860s. By 1880, nearly 3,000 people resided in the county. In 1886, North Yakima was incorporated and named the county seat.

Union Gap

It was not until 1918 that the prefix "North" was dropped from the name. At that time, the original Yakima City, four miles (6.4 km) to the south and commonly referred to as the "old town" officially adopted its name, Union Gap.

The secret's in the crop – a Yakima Valley vineyard.

Many still refer to Union Gap as "old town".

Wine industry

The wine industry has greatly expanded since the region's first vineyards were planted about 30 years ago. A northwest taste has emerged – bright, fruit flavors underscored by crisp acids. The white wines are mostly dry and heavier than whites from the Sonoma Valley in California while the reds are rich and textured. Prices have remained fairly low, though the better labels can command more.

The Yakima Valley Wine Growers Association has a series of vineyard and winery tour suggestions. Among the vineyards open to visitors and part of the many regional vineyard tours are Vin de l'Ouest, Bonair, Hyatt Vineyards, Covey Run, Porteus Vineyards, Horizon's Edge, Eaton Hill, Tucker Cellars, Chateau Ste. Michelle, Yakima River, Hogue Cellars, Chinook, and many others. The Yakima Native Indian Culture Center, which is located on the ancestral grounds of the 1.4 million-acre Yakima reservations provides a tour. Native Indian cuisine is available at the Heritage Inn Restaurant, complete with tribal dancing.

Fort Simcoe

An original 1920 Vintage Car Diesel Engine Steam Train takes travelers along the valley. **Fort Simcoe** is one of the best preserved frontier military outposts in the northwest. Historic buildings and an adjacent brick museum contain exhibits depicting the story of the fort and the Yakima tribes.

In **Toppenish**, south of Yakima, the Toppenish Murals cover 25 large walls. The murals, some more than 100 feet (30 m) long, are painted by the Northwest's top artists.

The whole town is an art gallery. Clusters of Western shops, antique stores, and galleries make strolling the streets a real pleasure. In Yakima proper, the **Front Street Historical District** includes a 22-car train that houses shops and restaurants, and the renovated **Pacific Fruit Exchange Building** holds a local farmer's market.

The **Wine Cellar** is a fine place to sample regional wines, the **Inter-urban Trolley** is a restored 1906 trolley that gives rides around downtown Yakima in the summer.

The **Yakima Valley Museum** has handsome pioneer pieces including collections from Yakima's most famous son, Supreme Court Justice, William O. Douglas.

North Front Street is a premier shopping and tourist attraction; **Yakima Arboretum** features 40 acres of various plants and woods; the **Capitol Theater** is home to the Yakima Symphony. Restored to its original 1920s Orpheum-style glory, the hall produces a gorgeous, natural sound.

The valley of the Walla Walla is an important historical region in Washington. It was here that Lewis and Clark voyaged in 1805, where fur trappers set up a fort in 1818, and where Marcus Whitman built his ill-fated medical mission west of the present town.

The region has had its share of Indian wars, boom and bust cycles, and fast-growing immigrant centers. Like most of Washington and Oregon, it's not a simple matter to identify the inland regions in a single geographical or economic region.

There are vast farmlands, dry regions, low hills, massive irrigation systems, towns and cities that border the Columbia River, and some that seem to rest in the middle of nowhere.

The missionaries who settled near Walla Walla in the 1830s discovered the fertility of the land, but were ignorant of

Wheatfields in Eastern Washington.

Inland Washington

Waterfall in Walla Walla, meaning "many waters" in Indian terminology.

the Indian peoples who lived there.

Walla Walla – which means "many waters" in Nez Perce – was a rendezvous place for many tribes. The missionaries who came in the 1830s and followed later by the first wagon trains over the Oregon Trail which followed them, managed to generally alienate all of the tribes.

Real settlement began in the 1860s after the Indian wars with miners who were swarming to the gold and silver fields in the Blue and Wallowa mountains and to northern Idaho.

It became the first real agricultural market the Northwest had outside of San Francisco. Many gold seekers discovered what Oregonians and Seattleites would also discover – it was more profitable feeding miners than being one. The early agricultural development spread northward into the Palouse region which was originally considered a barren, useless wasteland because of its dust covering.

Veritable gardens of wheat

But, it was discovered that the surface was only a few feet deep and beneath it was rich, fertile soil as much as 150 feet (45.7 m) deep below which was a lava base. This discovery is what turned the Palouse region, and the lands west of Spokane, into the vast wheat fields they have become.

Walla Walla itself looks as though it were taken from a New England setting and transplanted with weeping willows and maple trees. As well as the two colleges – Whitman and Walla Walla College – there are many ivy-covered buildings and quiet streets with old frame houses. Whitman College was founded in 1865 as a memorial to Marcus Whitman and the missionary movement.

Throughout the entire region, except for its cities, there appears to have been little in the way of human settlement. Perhaps that's because vast tracts of land were utilized for farming, not building. And whatever was left in the process was swept aside as this part of Washington was quickly developed.

All around Walla Walla are wheat fields. The **Fort Walla Walla Museum** on the west side of town has a collection of 14 old buildings and pioneer artifacts. **Whitman Mission**, 7 miles west, sketches out the story of the mission and its massacre of 1847 when Whitman and his wife Narcissa – after a notorious "re-educating" of the native people to

Christian values – were killed by the Nez Perce during a measles epidemic that destroyed the tribe.

Kirkman House and the **Frazier Farmstead Museum**, just south of the Washington/Oregon border on highway 125/11 in Milton Freewater, are two mid-1800s leftovers. Kirkman House was built in 1880 and is one of Walla Walla's outstanding Victorian style structures. The Frazier Farmstead Museum is an authentic turn-of-the-century farm, established in 1868.

In addition to its famous Walla Walla red onion, the region also has some of the state's most brilliant wineries including Woodward Canyon which produced a cabernet in 1987 that was judged one of the top ten in the world by *Wine Spectator*. Others are L'Ecole No. 41, Leonetti Cellars, and Waterbrook Winery. The Whitman Inn and Merchants Ltd. are arguably the two best restaurants in the town and the Pony Soldier Motor Inn, near Whitman College, is a popular inn.

West of Walla Walla

To the west of Walla Walla are the Tri-Cities communities of Kennewick, Pasco, and Richland, all in the middle of the biggest wine producing regions of the Yakima Valley. **Richland** was a "hidden city" in the 1940s because of work being done on the atomic bomb. The Hanford Science Center tells a bit of the atomic energy saga with informative energy displays.

Pasco was the first of the Tri-Cities (so named because they virtually overlap one another's borders) and was started as a railroad town in 1884.

Kennewick's East Benton County Historical Museum has exhibitions from the pioneer days in the tri-Cities region and in Paco, the Franklin County Historical Museum has exhibits detailing early Indian culture.

You have several choices driving northward from Walla Walla or into Oregon. The southern drive will take you into the Umatilla National Forest and eventually to the Wallowa Mountains and Hells Canyon Wilderness.

Moses Lake is a crossroads almost in the middle of the dry side. Drive north along Highway 17 and you'll reach the Grand Coulee Dam and recreational area. East on I-90 and you'll reach Spokane, the largest city of the dry side.

Moses Lake has been called the recreational capital of the state and with justification. But you needn't bring your camper to find lodging. It's laced with motels, one of the most pleasant being the Lakeshore Motel on the lake. It also has one of the best kept golfing secrets in the form of the 6,772 yard Warden Golf Course just south of town.

You can avoid the hordes of RV and camper traffic along I-90 if you take a series of roads northward of Walla Walla and follow the eastern border of Washington/Idaho, stopping off at Clarkson and neighboring Lewiston, Idaho – and Pullman plus a series of small commu-

The many beauties of Inland Washington.

nities on the way to Spokane via Highway 12/195.

Dayton, which lies on the road from Walla Walla to Clarkson has the restored Dayton Historical Depot, the state's oldest existing railroad station built by the Oregon Railraod and Navigation Company in 1881.

Now a museum, the building is furnished with railroad memorabilia and period furnishing. The **Columbia County Courthouse** was built in 1887 and is Washington's oldest courthouse.

Pullman

Pullman is the site of Washington State University, the arch rival of Seattle's University of Washington. Originally known as Three Forks, Pullman is supposed to have been rechristened in honor of the inventor of the railroad sleeping coach in 1881. The university dates from 1891, is now 600 acres large and has a number of museums such as the Museum of Anthropology and the Jackson Collection of Petrified Wood.

Like all university towns, there are bookstores and small galleries though the town retains much of its original cowboy image. The Nica Gallery exhibits eastern Washington artists. Bruised Books often has rare first editions.

The town's annual Huskies/Cougars football game is one of the year's major sporting events, alternating between Pullman and Seattle.

The 12,000 seat Beasley Performing Arts Coliseum stages events from rock concerts to operas; the new Pullman Summer Palace Theater in Daggy Hall performs in June and July. The Connors Museum of Zoology has the largest public collection of animals and birds in the Pacific Northwest. Oddly, one of the most popular tourist attractions is Ferdinand's Bar in Troy Hall, a soda fountain run by the university's agricultural school. A nine-hole golf course on the campus is open to the public.

Three Forks Pioneer Village Museum, six miles (9.6 km) north of Pullman has a rare fortepiano from 1875. The museum has 15 restored buildings from the late 19th and early 20th centuries including a log cabin whose parlor has the piano which was shipped around

Grand Coulee Dam

Twice as high as Niagara Falls and nearly one mile (1.6 km) long, the Grand Coulee Dam is indeed an imposing sight.

For decades it was the largest cement structure in the world. Now, besides holding back the waters of what is now the 161 mile-long (259 km) Roosevelt Lake and generating electricity, it's the site of a spectacular laser show that uses spillway as a screen.

The total generating power of the dam is 6.5 million kilowatts, enough to serve the entire Pacific Northwest and still have power left over for sale.

Transmission towers march away from the dam stick- like figures, their arms extended and lines shimmering against the stark landscape. The irrigation system includes 333 miles (536 km) of main canals, 1,959 miles (3,153 km) of lesser canals, and 2,761 miles (1,716 km) of drains and wasteways.

The dam was built over a number of years beginning with the authorization of Congress in 1935. Developed while the country was in the grips of the Great Depression, the idea was to use the dam as a symbol of recovery and opportunity under President Franklin D. Roosevelt's New Deal. Opposition to the dam was fierce. Farmers and existing power companies, organized labor, and many members of the Congress doubted the nation's need for such a visionary project.

But the process had an even earlier beginning. As early as 1903, federal agencies had considered proposals for a dam or irrigation system by tapping into the Spokane River.

Natural gorge

Grand Coulee itself is a natural gorge, carved out of the earth during the glacial period. In 1918, another plan was proposed to use the Grand Coulee canyon as a natural storage area by creating a dam. That eventually grew into what is now there.

It's hard today to understand the opposition. By harnessing the swift currents of the Columbia River, the dam has helped transform the parched deserts of central Washington into rich farmlands.

And, as a by-product, the dam produced one of the most varied recreational areas in the Pacific Northwest, the Grand Coulee National Recreation Area.

The dam's first turbo-generating units were completed in 1941, just in time for use at the atomic power works at Hanford. The dam's water was not used for irrigation until 1951. The dam was extended along the north wall of the canyon in 1976.

The backwaters of the dam reach north almost to the Canadian border and east into the Spokane River system. For the irrigation project, a chain of lakes and smaller dams were built to hold irrigation water for distribution south and east of the dam.

The dam system irrigates 500,000 acres. Water is pumped 280 feet (85 m) up the canyon wall to fill Bank's Lake reservoir and from there it is moved through pipes and canals to the farmland.

Cape Horn to the Uniontown Opera House.

Pullman is the center of Palouse country, a wide ranging series of wheat, peas, soybean, rape and other crops. The Palouse is differentiated from the rest of the dry-side by the increasing amounts of rainfall further east because of the gradual elevation gain.

Tourism is not a major factor in this part of the state and in most of the towns. That's good because you can expect lower prices and straightforward, unpretentious clean, cheap motels and restaurants. Here is where you get mama's cooking.

That's also the case in Pullman itself where lodging is modest. Check

Touring the Dam

Any visit to the recreation areas has to begin with a self-tour of the dam proper.

A film is shown every hour at the dam's visitor arrival center. A highlight of the tour is riding the glass incline elevator to the face of the third powerplant for a spectacular view of the spillway from an outside balcony. An artifact room displays the Indian tools and arrowheads uncovered during the dam's construction.

Water is released over the top of the dam for about a half-hour daily at 1:30 p.m. The evening laser shows begin at 9:30 p.m. and is held from Memorial Day through Labor Day.

As you drive around the region, you will probably be confused by the similarity of many town names. The communities of Grand Coulee and Coulee Dam are both at the site of the Grand Coulee Dam itself; Coulee City is 30 miles (48 km) at the southern end of Banks Lake; and in the same area are two small towns, Elmer City and Electric City. In Coulee Dam, the Colville Confederated Tribe Museum, Gallery and Gift Shop, shows authentic villages and fishing scenes, coins and metal artifacts dating from the 1800s.

Fish are constantly being fed into the system with trout and kokanee projects beginning to yield results. An Eastern Washington University scientist has tagged some of them and has discovered many in the lower Columbia River, indicating that fry have gone through the Grand Coulee's giant turbines without injury.

out the Quality Inn Motel which has the best accommodations in town. The Hilltop restaurant serves steak and seafood and has the finest views of the town, though not much atmosphere. The Seasons is acknowledged as the town's finest dining experience. Rusty's Tavern is popular with students. By the time you reach Spokane, you'll probably be ready for an urban experience after driving through Colfax (where you'll find the Perkins House, an 1884 Victorian mansion with four balconies).

Spokane

Spokane is a surprisingly active city with a population of 172,000, whose economy is driven by agriculture. Its outlook is distinctly contemporary. It has an attractive downtown section with abundant indoor shopping along several blocks of converted old buildings linked together by connecting bridges. The largest city in the Inland Northwest, Spokane is 18 miles (29 km) from Idaho and 118 miles (190 km) from the Canadian border.

Before 1800, the city's setting was a favorite Spokan-ee Indian fishing ground with the powerful falls on the river as the focus of their settlements. The Indian wars and the American Civil War slowed the progress of development in the area until the arrival of the Northern Pacific Railway in 1881. At that time the town of Spokane Falls had a population of less than 500.

The town's name was changed in 1891 to Spokane after reaching a population of 19,000 by 1890. With the aid of the railroad, and its ongoing expansion into the northwest, Spokane became the major trading center of this part of the state. It still is the trade center of a 36-county region covering eastern Washington, north Idaho, western Montana,

Contemporary Spokane downtown skyline.

and parts of Oregon. Spokane is an active community.

Riverfront Park is the city's centerpiece, a 53-acre green region that was the site of the 1974 World's Fair. Now, it's the focal point for a number of attractions and activities. The park has

replaced an ugly network of disused railroad tracks, yards, and stations which is what the park was for years. Part of the railroad history is still evident with the clock tower from the Great Northern Railroad from 1902.

On the grounds of the park, the

Big Red Wagon in Riverfront Park.

1909 Loof Carousel with its 54 horses modeled after New York City firetruck horses of that era, is a local landmark, hand-carved by master builder Charles Loof. There's a skating rink, an IMAX theater, and plenty of meandering walking paths.

Other Spokane parks include **Manito Park** on the city's South Hill featuring the Duncan Gardens, Rose gardens, Lilac Gardens, a Japanese Garden, and the Conservatory. **Riverside State Park** offers wilderness-like nature trails, picnic areas, and camping facilities just minutes from downtown.

The area's newest attraction is the **Spokane River Centennial Trail** which, when completed, will be a 39 mile (63 km) long path up to 12 feet (3.6 m) wide.

Off-limits to all motorized traffic, it begins at the meeting of the Spokane and Little Spokane Rivers and ends at the Idaho border. Most of it is now completed and will soon link up to the Idaho Centennial Trail for an additional leg into downtown Cour d'Alene.

The three blocks on W. Riverside Avenue between Jefferson and Lincoln Avenues, contain some of the finest old structures in the city. The **Spokane County Courthouse** is a Loire Valley clone, built in 1895 by Willis A. Ritchie. The area is all that's left of Spokane's railroad boom years with few buildings having survived the great fire of 1889. Seattle, Ellensburg, Vancouver and Washington were also struck by fires in that same year. The sole surviving struc-

Handcrafted carousel by Charles Looff.

ture is the Crescent Building. Post-fire structures are the Spokesman Review Building (1891), the Davenport Hotel (1914), and the Matador Restaurant (1908).

Browne's Addition Historical District and **The Hill** are elegant residential neighborhoods where the city's richest residents built their homes. The Hill is the site of the city's highest lookout point, Review Rock in **Cliff Park**. The **Austin Corbin II House**, now converted into offices, is a fine example of the Colonial Revival style. Corbin, the general manager of the Spokane and Northern Railroad, spent the then-princely sum of $35,000 on the 17-room mansion of buff brick.

Two natural areas outside the city limits offer great ways to see nature. The Little Spokane Natural Area, the Spokane Fish Hatchery, Dishman Hills Natural Area, and the Turnbull National Wildlife Refuge all offer back-to-nature experiences.

Dedicated to the arts

Downtown is the cultural core of the city with the **Spokane Opera House** the home to the Spokane Symphony, traveling Broadway shows, and top name entertainment. The **Metropolitan Performing Arts Center** is a more intimate setting for smaller performances of opera, jazz, plays and musical events. The **Spokane Civic Theater**,

The Centennial Trail is off-limits to all motorized traffic.

Interplayers Ensemble, and the **Valley Repertory Theater** each produce a series of stage plays during the year. An annual free Labor Day concert in **Comstock Park** by the local symphony orchestra draws thousands of picnicking concert goers. Riverfront Park is the venue for numerous jazz and small music ensemble concerts in summer.

The **Museum of Native American Cultures** contains one of the most comprehensive collections of Indian archives in the country. Nearby is the **Crosby Library** on the Gonzaga University cam-

Bloedel Reserve

Sandhill c·anes and deer in the Bloedel Reserve.

Bainbridge is a contradiction. Just 30 minutes by ferry from downtown Seattle, it's a combination of wild place and suburban sophistication – a semi-rural island-haven for city professionals who want a taste of the woods in their hectic lives. Deer forage the island, eagles soar high overhead, and fresh fruit farms produce the same raspberries and blackberries they have for the past century. It's the perfect setting for one of the northwest's great collection of flora, the Bloedel Reserve.

It is 150 acres of lush, tranquil gardens, woods, meadows, and ponds. Plants from all over the world make the grounds a horticulturalist's dream at any time of the year. It is also one of the best kept secrets in Seattle.

You understand why reservations are required and limited – taken Wednesdays through Sundays only – the moment you drive along the entrance road on the north end of the island and you come to the wide gate that keeps the public at bay. The garden is unlike anything on the continent. Half of the acreage is in a constant wild state with alder, firs, cedars, hemlock, and native shrubs, moss and grasses. The wildness, left untouched, houses waterfowl, hawks, insects, and small animals.

The balance of the reserve is cultivated with formal, broad lawns and elms near the three-story, French Chateau style house. There's a Japanese garden, a moss garden that resembles the floor of a rain forest, a rhododendron and wildflower glen under the trees, and a man-made pond planted with cattails and other native species to provide habitat for waterfowl.

It's a fascinating mix of gardens that blend into the next. Trails lead through the woodlands and a footbridge over a ravine boardwalk takes you over otherwise untouched wetland.

Summer Camp

The land was once a Suquamish Indian summer

camp. The land had previously been clearcut with the giant trees being logged off in the 1860s. Fire from slash-burning destroyed the second growth by 1910. Prentice Bloedel and his wife, Virginia Merrell bought the property in the 1930s after it had already been developed and the Chateau built by its former owner, Angela Collins, the wife of Seattle's sixth mayor.

Bloedel once wrote, "...We discovered that there is grandeur in decay; the rotten log hosting seedlings of hemlocks, cedars, huckleberries, the shape of a crumbling snag."

The respect for nature that Bloedel – a forest industry millionaire – wanted to instill in humans, is obvious from the time you enter the reserve. The gardens are meant for meditation with every corner an isolated preserve. The raked-sand and stone Japanese garden is a serene place where light and shadow mimics water. It was once a blue-tiled swimming pool, but was installed with geometric planes, then graded and set with basalt boulders.

The reserve is an undergoing constant refinement. Now overseen by the Arbor Fund, a masterplan was developed in the 1970s and is being adhered to today. The Arbor Fund is a nonprofit making organization created to ensure the reserve's perpetual care as it turned from private to public ownership. Virginia Merrill Bloedel died in 1989 and is buried on the property.

Botanists and other specialists continue to shape the preserve. Future plans include a plan-

Deer graze undisturbed on the lush greenery.

tation of fragrant viburnums and honeysuckle near the bird marsh to attract butterflies – painted ladies, red admirals, tiger swallowtails, tortoiseshells, and azures – all native to Puget Sound.

Reservations are required and tours are available with advance arrangement. For more information contact the Bloedel Reserve, 7571 NE Dolphin Drive, Bainbridge Island, WA 98110-1097; (206) 842-7631.

Rhododendron glen in the reserve.

Bloomsday Running Statues, contemporary sculpture worth a second look.

pus which singer Bing Crosby financed and which now contains gold records, an Oscar, and other memorabilia. The **Cheney Cowles Memorial Museum** displays mining and pioneer relics and is the home of the Eastern Washington State Historical Society.

Golf is very big here attracting golfers from throughout the Pacific Northwest. Not only are there several of the nation's finest golf courses – including Hangman's Valley Golf Course, and Indian Canyon Golf Course, but the prices are real bargains at $15 and less

racing, horse racing, drag racing and a number of college team sports round out the spectator activities.

There are many fine restaurants in the area, among which are Morelands, Milford's Fish House and Oyster Bar, The Downtown Onion, and Niko's Greek and Middle Eastern Restaurant.

Among the hotels are the Sheraton Spokane, next to the convention center, the recently renovated West Coast Ridpath Hotel, Waverly Place, and Cavanaugh's Inn At The Park. Northeast of the city, on the way to the airport, are numerous motels.

Because of its proximity to Spokane, **Cour d'Alene** is almost a suburb and locals commute between the two communities without much fuss and bother.

In the furthest reaches of northeastern Washington is **Republic**, amid the pines and firs of the Colville National Forest which you can reach via Highway 25/20. Stonerose Interpretive Center lets visitors dig for fossils on hillsides at the edge of town. The site is named for the extinct rose fossil found there.

The **Knob Hill Mine**, which spurred the region's gold economy in the mid-1930s is still one of the northwest's largest gold producers. In the **Colville National Forest** are the remains of Old Toroda, and **Bodie** where a stamp mill plant processed ore from the mines through the 1930s.

In Orient, on Route 395, and in nearby Curle with its 1890s Ansorge Hotel, are old buildings and preserved mining town artifacts.

(for seniors) a round. This is a sports-active city with major minor league teams – the Spokane Indians Basball team, and the Spokane Chiefs hockey team. The city is also home to an excellent polo club which features matches on most summer weekends. Stock car

Washington's Mountains

Washington's major mountain chains are the Olympic Mountains that run north to west long the Olympic Peninsula, and the Cascades that runs the length of the state and through Oregon. Mount Olympus is the highest in the Olympic Range at 7,765 ft. (2,428 m). The Selkirk Mountains rise in the Northwestern corner of the state, and the Blue Mountains dominate the southeastern corner.

Punctuating the Cascades, like candles on a cake, are five snow-capped volcano cones – Mount Baker at 10,775 feet (3,284 m); Glacier Peak, 10,541 ft. (3213 m); Mount Rainier, 14,411 ft. (4392 m); Mount St. Helens, (2,550 m); and Mount Adams, 12,267 (3,739 m).

While the vast dry lands to the east with their cattle ranches and sprawling

Liberty Bell on Highway 20 in North Cascades.

wheat fields make up the majority of the total state land mass, the mountains are what almost everyone talks about when defining Washington.

The mountains, quite simply, are spectacular. You may first see them as your inbound flight swings past the icy crown of Mount Rainier or you might first see the ragged peaks of the Cascades while driving along the Interstate. Regardless, you will want access to them and to partake in their many pleasures whether skiing, hiking, camping by a lake, or just relaxing in a mountain lodge.

Weather patterns are the result of Washington's mountains. The Olympics create a downwind rain shadow responsible for the relatively balmy weather in the San Juan Islands and parts of the Olympic Peninsula where you'll find the only rain forests in the contiguous 48 states.

The Cascades trap much of the moisture on the west side of the state, creating relatively arid conditions in Eastern Washington. Five good highways cross the Cascades and one circles the Olympic Peninsula and the base of the range.

Touring the Peninsula

Any tour of the Olympic Peninsula should really begin at Olympia and continue along Highway 101 which in turn leads you either along the Hood Canal or splits at highway 3 through the Kitsap Peninsula.

The Kitsap is often confused as being a part of the Olympic Peninsula, but it isn't since it is separated by the Hood Canal. If you decide to take the Kitsap into the Olympics, you can either take the ferry from Seattle across to Winslow or Bremerton; or you can drive.

Bremerton

Bremerton is surrounded on three sides by water, but from there you find sweeping views of the Cascades and the Olympics. The community's one great claim to fame is that it was chosen as America's most liveable community in 1990 by *Money Magazine*.

Since it is a major naval facility, home of the Puget Sound Naval Shipyard, there isn't much for the tourist to see except for the Naval Shipyard Museum which has American and Japanese naval artifacts.

The waterfront **Wilcox House** is the 1936 former home of Colonel Julian Wilcox. Once described as the "grand entertainment capitol of the Canal region", the oak-floored house is now a B&B. Sinclairs and the Heathstone are moderate-priced eating places where the food is robust but not overwhelming.

As you drive through the Kitsap, you will find a series of attractive small communities – Port Orchard, Silverdale, Blake Island. **Silverdale** is the Kitsap's commercial center and is located at the northern tip of Dyes Inlet. Bangor An-

Sack River on Mountain Loop Highway.

nex, just north of town is a nuclear submarine base.

Silverdale's Whaling Days, held in late July, is the town's biggest event with boat races, and a general carnival atmosphere. The Kitsap Mall has some 200 shops including the major department stores.

The Marine Science Center at Poulsbo is a major attraction in the region. In Suquamish, on the east side of the Kitsap, the **Suquamish Museum** is an award winning museum of the Suquamish and Port Madison Indian reservation. Chief Seattle's grave overlooks Puget Sound in a small cemetery on the Madison Indian Reservation. His place is marked by painted canoes high above the headstone.

Chief Seattle Days, an annual weekend affair held in August at the downtown Suquamish waterfront park, has traditional Indian dancing, story-telling and a salmon bake.

East of the Canal

It's on the east side of the Hood Canal that most of the action takes place. This is, after all, easy access for Seattle people when they want to get away from the tempo of the city. Kingston, Port Gamble, Port Ludow and Bainbridge island are all focal points for activity.

Once home to the west's biggest sawmill operations, the 4 by 12 mile (6.4 by 19 km) island is now largely a suburban community in which 85 per cent of its residents take the ferry to work in the morning.

The family operated **Bainbridge Island Winery**, a few hundred feet from the ferry terminal, is the place to buy limited production wines including their superb strawberry wine.

The Four Swallows is an unpretentious restaurant known for its fine pork. You might also try the Pleasant Beach Grill, tucked away in a Tudor house on the south end of the island. It's a favorite with locals for its cozy, fire-place atmosphere and lately for its seafood dinners.

The 6,471 ft. (1,972 m) Hood Canal floating bridge connects the Kitsap to the Olympic Peninsula. The Hood Canal is not really a canal but a tidal inlet. At its head is the town of **Hansville**, the acknowledged best place on the Sound to catch salmon. It is also where you'll find the **Point No-Point Lighhouse** where you can take daily tours.

The highway, always at the foot of the Olympics, then takes you into the charming town of Port Townsend and onto Port Angeles, the entry into the

A new morning in North Cascades National Park.

Olympic National Park and from where you can catch the ferry to Victoria.

Cascades

While the Olympics have their charm and fascination, the Cascades are the major league of mountain chains. You get 400 miles (644 km) of two-lane highways, mountain lakes, three mountain passes, and climates that vary from snowfall to searing heat.

And the most scenic part of that

A helping hand along North Cascades Highway.

drive is via Highway 20, the scenic North Cascades route, the newest of the trans-Cascade routes, finished in 1971 (though actually begun in 1896), and which begins at Burlington at the junction of I-5 and continues up and over the mountains to the dry side. (See National Parks Section).

In reality, as soon as you cross east from Seattle, you're in the general influence of the Cascades. While Highway 20 is the most scenic, others will give you an equally pleasurable experience.

Interstate 90 is the route most Seattle skiers take into the Cascades, traveling slightly southeast into the major ski areas. You begin climbing into the mountain within 30 minutes of leaving downtown.

At just about the 47 mile (76 km) mark, you'll reach **Snoqualmie Pass** with its four ski areas. The town of **Snoqualmie** is home to the Puget Sound and Snoqualmie Valley Railroad which makes a 10-mile (16-km) trip through the Snoqualmie Valley. Nearby is the Snoqualmie Falls, with a small park, observation area, and trails leading beneath the 268 ft. (81.6 m) waterfall.

Twin Peak's Ambience

If you watched the hit television show, Twin Peaks, you're likely recognize both **Mount Si**, which rises behind the town of North Bend, and the 91-room Salish Lodge at Snoqualmie Falls, used as the

Rosyln, famed for where the television serial Northern Exposure was filmed.

primary building in the series.

The Salish Lodge sits on the edge of a cliff overlooking the falls and is one of the most dramatic settings in the Pacific Northwest for a hotel and restaurant.

If you continue along the I-90 route, you'll eventually exit at Ellensburg at the north end of the Yakima Valley.

One of the few places to stay at Snoqualmish Pass is the Best Western. Cle Elum, mid-way between Snoqualmie Pass and Ellensburg has The Hidden Valley Guest Ranch, The Moore House, the TimberLodge Motel. The town's best restaurant is Mama Vallone's Steak House and Inn.

The **Cle Elum Historical Telephone Museum** has a collection of old telephones, switchboards, and other communication equipment. The 25 mile-long (40 km) **Iron Horse State Park** is a section of former railroad right-of-way with the rails removed and which now has a smoothed-over path for walking, jogging, and bicycling.

The small town of **Roslyn**, three miles north, is used for the set of Northern Exposure, another popular television show.

A more remote route, but one that brings you closer to the land, is via Highway 2, north of Redmond which takes you through the heart of the Cascades into Wenatchee.

From Seattle, you drive past the small communities of Gold Bar and Sultan which had their origins as gold towns.

Leavenworth's attention to its design detail has drawn international acclaim.

A Bavarian welcome at Leavenworth.

A Bavarian town

But if you continue along the Highway you eventually come to the jewel of the Central Cascades, **Leavenworth**. This is a town that draws tourists primarily because of its Bavarian atmosphere. Get set to be in one of the major tourist spots in the Cascades, but it's worth the hassle and hustle. Almost everything is centered around the Bavarian theme – architecture, hotels, restaurants, and annual events.

The town was originally founded on the Great Northern Railway and lumberjacks. When the Great Northern switchyards were moved to Wenatchee, the town tried to survive on its apple orchards. But by the 1960s, it was obvious the town needed more than apples, so it devised a remodeling job and a fall festival.

The town, now drawing international acclaim for its attention to design detail, is a center for a variety of activities ranging from skiing to river rafting.

The Bavarian Village has plenty of shops, taverns, and restaurants all with intricately carved wood adornments. Obertal Mall contains galleries, craft and gift shops. Throughout towns are shops that sell wooden toys, clocks, and Hoelgaard's Bakery will destroy the best of intentions. The new Leavenworth Brewery on Front Street has seven locally prepared brews.

Cross country skiing in winter is big

Quaint village appeal.

in Leavenworth. Visit the Leavenworth Nordic Center just east of downtown for lessons, rentals, and for teaching your children how to do it right at the Kiddies Camp.

If you're looking for European-style accommodation, try the Haus Rohrbach Pension. A real escape can be found at the Mountain Home Lodge, a half mile into the Cascades from Leavenworth. And there are a number of motels in the region.

The Great Bavarian Ice Fest in January, the Malfest on Mother's Day week-

Washington Skiing

Skiing is a family affair in Washington during the winter. It's not unusual to hits the slopes and see a 4-year-old skiing downhill at what seems to be breakneck speed, passing a 70-year-old making a long, gliding S-turn on a well groomed slope.

There are 9 major areas that cater to a wide range of skills. The best areas are along the Cascades from Mount Baker to Mount Rainier with snow on the western side being heavy and wet while some ski areas on the east side have dry powdery snow.

But if you're driving the mountain in the winter, watch for local ski hills that might not be on anyone's "best" list, but which offer unique conditions. It's often a great way to meet locals and to find your way around.

Ski areas

Crystal Mountain, 40 miles (64 km) east of Enumclaw is Washington's largest ski area, a family orientated resort that features a relaxed, European atmosphere and stunning views of the Cascades from the summit.

Most of the skiing – 80 percent – is rated for advanced or expert skiers. Snowboarding – the latest craze – and night skiing are also available on the vertical drop of 3,100 feet (945 m). It has 10 chair lifts, ski shop, rentals, school, lodge, food services, lounges, hotels, condominiums, and groceries.

One of the most popular areas for Seattle skiers is **Snoqualmie Pass**, 47 miles (76 km) east of the city, with four major ski areas in a space of about two miles (3.2 km) – Alpental, Ski Acres, Snoqualmie, and Hyak.

The average summit elevation is 5,400 feet (1646 m) and a base at 3000 feet (914 m) and a vertical drop of (670 m). The four have 25 chairs between them and 11 rope tows. Snowboarders are welcome only at Ski Acres and Snoqualmie. All have ski shops, day lodges, food service and buses to the area.

Mount Baker is 56 miles (90 km) east of Bellingham and serves both northwest Washington and southern British Columbia with seven double chairs and three rope tows on an elevation range of 3,500 feet (1,067 m) to 5,040 feet

(1536 m).

Stevens Pass is 80 miles (129 km) east of Seattle on Route 2 and has an elevation of 3,800 to 5,800 feet (1,158-1,768 m) with a vertical drop of 1,800 feet (548 m). It has 10 chairs, a ski school, shop, rentals, restaurant and cafeteria.

White Pass is 20 miles (32 km) east of Packwood on Route 12, southeast of Mount Rainier. It has a summit elevation of 6,000 feet 1,828 m) with the base at 4,500 feet (1372 m) and a vertical drop of 1,500 feet (457 m). It's an all-inclusive area with condominiums, food and other services.

A dirt road leads to **Echo Valley**, 10 miles northwest of Chelan off Route 150 where you find an elevation of between 3,000 to 3,500 feet (914-1,066 m). Basically a beginner's slope, it has a poma lift and two rope tows.

Leavenworth Ski Hill is another small slope – 1,300 to 1,850 feet (396-564 m) – and having two rope tows. For dry snow on the eastern slope of the Cascades, skiers head to **Mission Ridge**, 13 miles southwest of Wenatchee on Squilchuck Creek Road. The area features mostly intermediate level runs though more proficient skiers can use off-trail glade and bowl skiing.

It has four chairs, two rope tows and snow-making machinery for a facility ranging in height from 4,600 to 6,740 feet (1,402-2,054 m) with a vertical drop of 2,140 feet (652 m). It has a shop, school, eating facilities, and lodge. Accommodations can be found in Wenatchee.

Cross country skiing

Cross country skiing is becoming quite popular and most resorts have at least some trails. It's especially popular on the eastern slopes of the Cascades because of the drier snow conditions and the sunny days. Some of the best is in the Methow Valley where 93 miles (150 km) of trails have been cut. It has been voted the best Nordic area by at least one state magazine.

Heli-skiing, popular throughout Western Canada, has only one large operator – North Cascades Heli-skiing operating out of Mazama. Skiers are dropped off at varying elevations up to 8,000 feet (2,434 m).

The awesome crater of Mount St. Helens.

end, the Washington State Autumn Leaf Festival in September, and the Christmas Lighting Festival are the town's biggest events. At Red-Tail Canyon Farm and Eagle Creek Ranch, hay and sleigh rides through the region's picturesque areas are popular attractions.

To reach both Mount Rainier and Mount St. Helens you drive south and east out of Seattle and Tacoma along a choice of roads, though some – like Highway 131 to Mount St. Helens – are closed during winter months.

Around Mount Rainier, route 706

Port Townsend

Former German consulate in Port Townsend.

If you're looking for the picture-perfect postcard, you'll find it in Port Townsend. It's not just a tourist trap town. It's a working artists' colony, restored by writers, artists and other preservationist minded citizens into one of the most livable communities in the state.

Situated on the northwestern corner of the Olympic Peninsula, where the Strait of Juan de Fuca meets Puget Sound, it sits in full view of the Olympic Mountains.

Founded in 1851, a few months before Seattle, it was soon crawling with sawmills and gold seekers. Anticipating a linkup with the transcontinental railroad – after building its own rail line – the community was soon the home of elegant Victorian mansions and a series of commercial buildings.

Strolling through town, you have the impression that time has stood still. Yet, this is no tacky collection of tourist-traps. It is a refined restoration of old homes that have become bed and breakfast inns, a place where antique shops line the streets, and where grand old mansions are open for viewing.

It was in 1961, just prior to the opening of the Seattle World's Fair, that residents decided to do something about the decaying town and set about restoring its old buildings. By 1976, they had achieved enough to be granted status as a National Historic District. The only way to see the town at its best is to walk through it.

Downtown

The downtown district is centered on Water Street. Here is where you'll find good northwest art galleries, craft shops, and antique stores as well as an unending series of small delis and restaurants.

The locals eat at the Landfall, but for one of the really fine experiences, the **Manresa Castle**, located in an 1897 hilltop inn that overlooks the town, is the one to try.

Much of the town was erected at about the same time as Seattle's Pioneer Square, so there's a similarity in architectural styles. Most notable are the **Daniel Hogan House**, **Bartlett House**, and the **Ann Starett Mansion**. Stop off at the Port Townsend Chamber Of Commerce visitor information center (2437 East Sims Way) for historic site maps.

The **Jefferson County Historical Museum** at the end of Water Street is open for tours as are

takes you through the town of Elbe which has the Mount Rainier Scenic Railroad, a steam powered train that makes a 14-mile (22-km) trip through the forest and across high bridges to Mineral Lake.

Centralia

A quick route is south via I-90 and then east along Highway 12 and to Highway

Ann Starett's Mansion was erected at around the same time as Seattle's Pioneer Square.

the City Hall, Customs House, Jefferson County Courthouse, and Bell Tower.

Needless to say, Port Townsend is a festivals site. The Rhododendron Festival in May is the oldest in town and the Centrum Summer Arts Festival is one of the most successful cultural programs in the state.

The Wooden Boat Festival in September is a combination of sailboats and eclectic design; and the Poverty Playhouse provides film and live productions throughout the year.

There are a number of wonderful Victorian house restorations in the uptown district atop the hill. The multi-colored homes can be seen in Port Townsend's biannual house tours in May and September.

The Rothschild House has been restored with original furniture and is regularly open to the public. Built in 1868, it's a good example of the Greek Revival houses that were prefabricated in New England and transported to Pacific Coast settlements.

On Water Street you'll find a wild collection of stores for virtually every interest. Earthenworks deals in ceramics, the Captain's Gallery has expensive kaleidoscopes, Imprint Book Store has books for every taste, and Phoenix Rising offers New Age cultural items. The Port Townsend Antique Mall has some 40 shops under one roof, certainly enough to create cobwebs in anyone's mind.

If old things aren't what you had in mind, there's the Back Alley Tavern for live music and a lot of local color. The historic Town Tavern has an assortment of pool tables, a huge bar, and fine music. And Aldrich's is an authentic 1890s general store with an upscale inventory.

There's lots of lodging in the region ranging from motels to elegant living. The latter grouping includes the James House B&B, a Victorian conversion of 12 rooms. The former German Consulate residence, Hastings House/Old Consular Inn and Heritage House also offer character settings.

If you want newer digs in which to rest, the Ravenscroft Inn was built in 1987 with seven modern rooms though the antique collection in the inn is formidable.

7. That route will not only give you the option of going to either Mount Rainier (north) or Mount St. Helens (south), it will take you to **Centralia**, the only city in Washington founded by a black man, a former slave who was named George Washington.

Set free, he bought the land where Centralia now sits for $6,000, planted a town, sold lots, built a home, and do-

Glacier on Mount Rainier.

The sublime beauty of winter in the mountains.

nated a parcel of land for the establishment of George Washington Park.

End of the "Wobblies"

It was in Centralia that "Wobblies" leader, Wesley Everett, met his death. In 1919, lumbermen decided to rid the town of all "Wobblies", the militant labor organization. On Armistice Day in 1919, American Legion members marched through the streets and stormed the union headquarters. Everett shot into the crowd.

The resulting chaos eventually ended up with Everett being hanged and shot and a riot that left four Legionaires dead. Only "Wobblies" were tried for the killings.

Fourteen murals decorate the outside of Centralia buildings, modeled after historic photographs.

The **Magyar Museum** has displays of Indian artifacts, wood carvings, and antiques. The Pacific Power and Light Company is a coal-fired plant that has guided tours. Lumber baron, J.P. Gurrier's old mansion, is now the Candalite Mansion B&B.

Fort Vancouver

At the Columbia River, the Cascades are interrupted by the Columbia Gorge. On the Washington side, across from Portland, is Vancouver, where Fort Vancouver is a National Historic Site.

The only fully restored row of officers' homes in the nation is at **Vancouver's Officers' Row National Historic District**. The city paid $10 million to restore these 21 turn-of-the-century homes. The most famous are the Marshall House and Grant House, named for one-time residents General George C. Marshall and President Ulysses S. Grant.

The **Clark County Historical Museum** has a 1890 country store, a 1900 doctor's office, and the first piano in Washington Territory, built in 1836.

The **Covington House**, 1848, is one of the state's oldest log cabins; and the **Pearson Air Museum** has a series of operating vintage aircraft. Just north of town is the **Salishan Vineyards**.

Portland

Portland doesn't really want to be a city. It wants to stay what it thinks it is, a small town that just happens to have 350,000 residents. It has grown cautiously, protective of its natural riches. The state's largest city sits on the banks of the Williamette River, just south of its junction at the Columbia. To the east are the Cascade Mountains and Mount Hood, and to the west is the Coast Range.

During the past 10 years Portland has itself a new vitality without destroying its rich past. While it has been discovered by high technology industries, young urbans, and tourists anxious to taste its innocence, the city has developed a personality reflecting its natural environment and its desire to appear human scaled.

249

The allure of autumn in Portland.

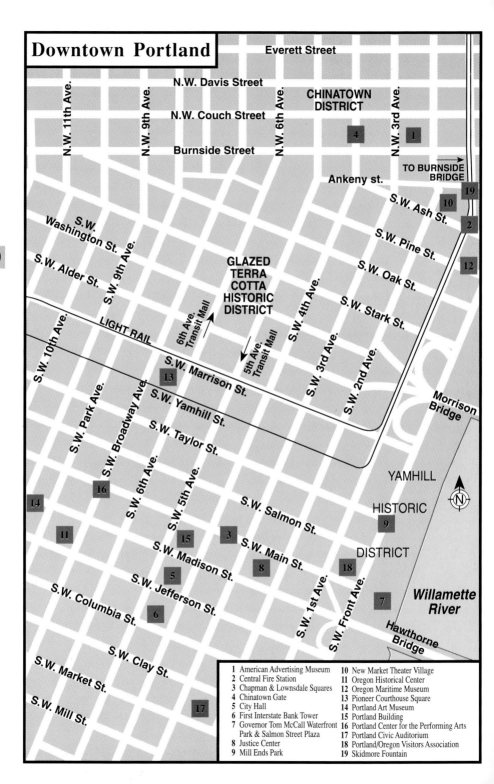

Portland sits on the banks of the Williamette River.

Unpretentious Sophistication

It has 150 parks, a major arts center, an accessible waterfront, and city blocks that are half the normal size. Residents and city officials alike hardly ever mention per capita income or industrial growth. Rather, they emphasize neighborhoods, its music, and the pro basketball team, *The Blazers.*

The city was the first in America to develop a comprehensive energy plan; it has preserved large tracts of land in the city core for green space; there are height and spacing restrictions so that views are unrestricted; and it is foot friendly. Bus travel in the downtown area's Free Fare Zone has meant fewer cars and more walkers.

While it was always a livable place, it didn't always claim to be the most friendly. During the First World War, patriots rooted out dissidents and changed German street names; during the 1920s when lumber and shipping made Portland a boom town, the Ku Klux Klan had success in recruiting members. Now, however, those blemishes are footnotes to a city that truly tries hard to be the perfect people place. In recent years an influx of immigrants, many from Southeast Asia, has given the city an added Asian character.

Though not nearly the numbers nor the overall impact as Asians have given Seattle, Portland is now a place

South Downtown is best explored on foot.

Japanese/American Heritage Park
along the seawall.

where it's easy to find shops that sell Asian-made goods and different Asian restaurants.

A walk through Downtown

Downtown contains three distinct business and retail districts – Heart of the City, Historic Old Town, and South Downtown. Each has its unique character setting it apart from the rest of the city and each is easily explored on foot, sometimes overlapping one another. **Morrison Street** is the primary shopping area in the city core, Chinese restaurants are commonplace in the Historic Old Town, and the Oregon Symphony plays at the Arlene Schnitzer

Salmon Street Fountain along Tom McCall's Waterfront Park.

Concert Hall in South Downtown.

Starting at the Portland/Oregon Visitors Association at Front and Salmon Streets, where you can find helpful maps, you can walk the entire downtown area in a single, well planned day – though that's rushing things a bit.

Peaceful and quiet **Waterfront Park** and **Salmon Street Plaza** are directly to the east of the Visitors Association offices. The **Justice Center** on Third Avenue at the end of Lownsdale Square, contains the Police Museum. The **Portland Center for the Performing Arts** at the corner of Main and Broadway is the city's cultural heart. Within the complex are two theatres and a concert hall. Grand Opera is staged in the Portland Civic Auditorium's 3,000-seat hall.

Two blocks away, across South Park (a stretch of land shaded by old Elms and accented by plants), is the **Portland Art Institute** which includes the Portland Art Museum featuring outstanding collections of Native American, African, Asian, European, and contemporary art. Included in the complex are the Pacific Northwest College of Art and the Northwest Film and Video Institute.

Across the South Park Blocks is the **Oregon Historical Center**, announced by murals of Lewis and Clark and the Oregon Trail. The state's history – prehistoric and contemporary – is housed in a variety of innovative displays.

The **Metropolitan Center for Public Art** is on the second floor of the Portland Building at Madison and Fifth,

Upbeat way to store an unused canoe.

a building marked by the 36-foot (11-m) hammered-copper statue, Portlandia. The statue, created in 1983, is the second largest such sculpture in the world, following the Statue of Liberty.

City Hall, built in 1895, is across the street from the Portland Building and is a marked contrast, architecturally, to its neighbor. While the Portland Building generates intense opinion about the bluish ribbon-like crowned top, the old classic-columned City Hall generates only a sense of familiarity.

Pioneer Courthouse Square centers the region. The site of the first school and the Portland Hotel, it also has one of the strangest weather announcers in the world. At noon a "weather machine" blasts a fanfare and is followed by a shining sun, stormy dragon, or a blue heron to announce the days' weather – which everyone knows anyway.

Heart Of The City contains all major downtown department stores – Meir & Frank, Nordstrom, Saks Fifth Avenue plus Galleria and Pioneer Place shopping centers. And it abounds with speciality shops and high fashion goods. Pioneer Courthouse Square is alive with public art from fountains to rock sculptures. At the nearby Heathman Hotel, a collection of Andy Warhol paintings, "10 Endangered Species" are featured in the lobby.

Historic Old Town is the hot-spot of Portland with ethnic restaurants, nightclubs, and Chinatown attracting

Snack time at Pioneer Courthouse Square.

thousands into the area. At the Saturday Market are artists who create jewelry and woodcarvings and discuss with passersby how they do it. Among the historical items are the Skidmore Fountain, Oregon Maritime Museum, and American Advertising Museum.

In **South Downtown** is the city's business and cultural heart. The Performing Arts Center Civic Auditorium, and the galleries in the Yamhill Historic District are interspersed among the many restaurants. The Yamhill Marketplace is an open-air produce market.

Historic Districts

Yamhill, Skidmore/Old Town, China-

town, 13th Avenue, and Glazed Terra Cotta make up the city's historic districts and they sometimes overlap into the downtown sections.

The **Yamhill District** is near the south end of Portland's earliest commercial core, which ran along Front, First, and Second Avenues and today encompasses a six-block area. After the fires of 1872 and 1873, that destroyed almost everything, merchants and businessmen built a number of High Victorian Italianate structures with ornamental cast-iron facades.

When the open air Carroll Public Market opened in 1914, with stalls on Yamhill Street, the area began to revive after the flood of 1890 had brought growth to a standstill.

Saturday market activities around the fountain square.

In the 1950s, buildings were destroyed to make room for parking lots and construction of the Morrison Street Bridge wiped out additional structures and effectively isolated this part of the city from the Skidmore/Old Town further north.

But, the district has undergone a rebirth during the past two decades with buildings – Centennial Block (1876), Williamette Block (1882), Strowbridge Building (1878), Franz Building (1880), Poppleton Building (1866 & 1873) – being restored and rehabilitated.

Northern end of Tom McCall's
Waterfront Park.

Yamhill Market for four blocks and you'll
reach the **Skidmore/Old Town district**
where Portland was born. The 20-block
area, anchored by Skidmore Fountain,
runs parallel to the Williamette River
and was once the commercial heart.
Being located next to the river has always been a danger since periodic floods
– especially that of 1894 – demolished
buildings and weakened structures.

In the 1940s and 1950s many of the
old buildings were destroyed for new
development but since 1975, when declared a historic district, it has been
revitalized. There are still vestiges of its
old "skid row" character and night walking is not encouraged.

The main mast of the battleship,
Oregon, stands at the foot of Oak Street

Historic street lights, flower baskets,
and street signs adorn the roadways
and the new **Yamhill Marketplace** on
SW Taylor is where to go for Oregon-
made jewelry, clothes, and gifts, and
fast food outlets. North and south, along
Second Avenue, are galleries featuring
local art.

Walk north up First Street from

Portland City Hall

The next great restoration project facing Portland appears to be its near 100-year-old City Hall. Completed in 1895, it is one of Portland's few remaining links between the horse-and-buggy era and the information age.

The city almost lost the landmark building in 1970 through an enormous bomb blast that blew out windows, shook the building, and shattered the massive columns under the east portico. No trace of the bomber was ever found even though the FBI and local authorities pulled out all the plugs. Blame was put on either left-wing or right-wing terrorists, or a monumental prank gone out of control. Regardless, the $170,000 repairs put the old building back in operation even though it's showing its age and a movement is growing to renovate it. The old building, one of the few 19th-century structures left in downtown Portland, sits on SW Fourth Ave. between Jefferson and Madison.

Unusual Mayors

Not only has it had its share of unusual political discussion within its walls, so too have there been unusual mayors. One of the most recent was Bud Clark, a tavern owner, neighborhood activist whose campaign slogan, "Whoop, Whoop" led him to victory in 1985.

To call the former mayor – he was succeeded by Vera Katz – flamboyant, is an understatement. He could well greet visitors in lederhosen or a semi-formal suit.

But, Clark represented the kind of politician that Portlanders want – casual, enthusiastic, accessible, and colorful. His wife is a member of the Oregon Symphony and operates an antique shop. He usually rode his bicycle to City Hall. There is little doubt that Clark brought a sense of smallness to the city, shaping a city of small and identifiable neighborhoods, small businesses, and limit the infusion of large industry. City Hall was placed on the Nation Register of Historical Buildings in 1974. But, the old building is now at a historical cross-roads, a moment in time that will test the resolve of local tax payers. Renovations, especially any that will restore the old building back to its original glory while bringing it up to modern standard including making it earthquake-proof – will cost millions. Is it better to build a new one someplace else, one that will be designed for today's needs and use this building for other purposes?

It's question that Portlanders have grappled with in the past, saving much of its historical districts when development choices had to be made. It cannot be easy working in the old place. The Oregonian reported that many employees work in 100°F (38°C) temperatures, and sprinkler heads have been installed but never hooked up.

Still, Portlanders have a strong sense of time and place and past. Any town, after all, that elects a lederhosen-wearing tavern owner as its mayor must be doing something right.

while the **Oregon Maritime Museum** on Front Street houses models of old ships. Next door is the Central Fire Station with old pumps and antique equipment and nearby is the Skidmore Fountain, built in 1888.

The fountain square is the gathering place for the **Portland Saturday Market** – also open on Sundays – March through Christmas. The New Market Theater, on First Avenue, was considered the finest theater in the west after its 1875 grand opening and contains today three floors of shops and restaurants. The **American Advertising Museum** claims to be the only museum catering entirely to advertising and it exhibits a small, but intense collection of memorable campaigns and ads.

Chinatown is next to the Skidmore

Totem pole along Terwilligee Boulevard in Southwest Portland.

district, filling 10 blocks along Fourth Avenue and in most ways is similar to Chinatowns everywhere in America with small stores, shops and restaurants signalled by Chinatown Gate at Fourth Avenue and Burnside.

Adorning it is five roofs, 64 dragons and two lions. The bilingual street signs, red and gold street lights and banners add to the atmosphere. The **13th Avenue Historic District** is a seven block area between Northwest Davis and Johnson north of Chinatown and is primarily a former warehouse area converted into loft housing, artist's studios and galleries, antique shops, and micro breweries. Blitz-Weinhard Brewing Company on West Burnside offers a beer processing tour and free suds afterward.

The **Terra Cotta District** has a large collection of buildings faced with decorated glazed terra cotta, a hard-baked and fine grained composite clay. Details such as lions heads, classical motifs, griffins, and so forth, can be extremely ornate. Buildings from the late 1890s to mid-1910s such as the Journal Building, Meier & Frank Co., and the Oregon Hotel are concentrated in the area between S.W. Fifth and Sixth Streets bordered by Oak and Yamhill.

West Portland

On the west side of the Williamette are several important areas, driven to along S.W. Canyon Road or on the Tri-Met

Full bloom in the International Rose Test Garden.

Line buses.

The most important is **Washington Park**, covering 322 acres of Portland Hills which embraces the Washington Park Zoo, the **Hoyt Arboretum**, and the **Pittock Mansion**, the latter being a 1909 house combining French Renaissance and Victorian architecture and was built by former Oregonian editor, Henry Pittock. Nearby, at the park's southern end, are the **Oregon Museum of Science and Industry** which includes a hands-on computer display, and the **World Forestry Center** with its collection of old wood and equipment.

The **International Rose Garden** – the oldest continuously operating rose garden in America – is to the east of the park on Kingston Avenue next to the Japanese Gardens that has traditional gardens throughout its 5.5 acres.

East Portland

The region east of the Williamette was slow in developing and but today contains some of Portland's major attractions such as the **Oregon Convention Center** with a matching pair of glass and steel spires rising 250 feet (76 m). Art is everywhere in this 490,000 sq. ft. (45,521 sq. m) facility. The interior features art (even in the washrooms), dragon boats, and a bronze pendulum.

A mile south of the Convention Center is the Oregon Museum of Science and Industry, a 240,000 sq. ft. (22,296

Oregon Convention Center, Portland's classic masterpiece.

sq. m) facility that opened in 1992 with six exhibition halls offering displays on science, space, earth and life. It has an Omnimax motion picture theater and an outdoor science exhibit.

Nearby is the **Lloyd Center** shopping mall, the **Carousel Courtyard** and the **International Museum of Carousel Art**, and the **Cowboy Museum**. The Cowboy Museum is a one-of-its-kind with several exhibits that traces the evolution of the American cowboy. A focal point in the museum is a 100-year-old chuck wagon, equipped just as it was on a trail drive in the days of the Old West. Hands-on experiences are possible.

Two popular shopping districts, **Hawthorne Boulevard** from 30th to 40th Avenues, and **Sellwood** along 13th Avenue offer different specialities. Hawthorne is known for its used books and offbeat antiques, while Sellwood is an antique center.

Near the Portland International Airport is **The Grotto**, on 85th and Sandy Boulevard, a 62-acre Catholic sanctuary with beautiful ponds and gardens, shrines, and paths leading through flower gardens and with gorgeous views of the mountains.

Festivals

Symbolic of the city's character, the Portland Rose Festival burst into life for 25 days in June with involvement from the entire Pacific Northwest as far south as

Mount Hood

Trillium Lake in Mount Hood.

Named after Samuel Viscount Hood, an English admiral of the West Indies, Mount Hood stands at 11,239 feet (3,426 m) and the once volatile crater is the recreational playground for Portland's enthusiastic outdoors set.

On a clear, crisp winter's day, Mount Hood rises high above Portland's skyline, almost like a film set backdrop. The relationship between the city and the wilderness at the city's doorstep is unconditional. Not only does Portland receive its water from streams that flow down its slopes, but the mountain draws the city to its glaciers, switchback hiking trails, and flowered meadows. There's little doubt that Portland enjoys America's most dramatic backdrop with Mount Hood one hour's drive away, and the rest of the Cascades looming off in the distance – Rainier, Adams, Jefferson, and St. Helens with the latter twice blanketing the city in two inches of volcanic dust since 1980.

The Barlow Trail winds between Government Camp and Trillium Lake.

Indians knew that Hood, known to them as Wy-east, and the brother of Mount St. Helens in Washington State, should be respected and feared. They believed it was home to both good and evil. It was, they thought, a single spirit, not merely a mountain, but a Chief and the son of the Great Spirit. French trappers knew it as "an old acquaintance". The Mount Hood of the 1990s is sprinkled with ranger stations, ski runs, hiking trails and little villages like Zig Zag, Government Camp, and places like Frog Lake and Little John Snowplay.

Portland's backyard

Activity in Portland's backyard is a conglomerate of diversity – picking huckleberries, digging mushrooms and fishing for trout are popular;

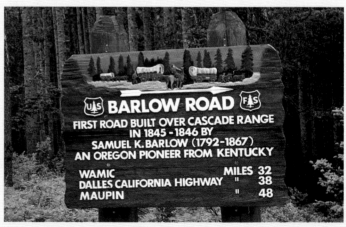

Walking in the rain....

blackberries and fiddlehead ferns find their way to the area's most elegant restaurants.

Cross country ski trails follow the Oregon Trail. The **Barlow Trail** named after Sam Barlow – an Oregon pioneer who in 1845 built a toll road along the mountainside – winds between Government Camp and Trillium Lake. The Barlow Trail winds around Devil's Half Acre and provides access to the grave site of Pioneer Woman, in memory of an unknown woman who died and it is a place still honored by visitors today. Thousands of climbers register each year to climb Mount Hood, which is no easy feat. Climbers need full equipment to navigate the technically treacherous routes. It is second only to Japan's Mount Fuji in its number of climbers.

On the mountain's north side, the **Hood River Valley** is Oregon's largest fruit growing district with almost 15,000 acres of apple, pear, and cherry orchards. More than 185,000 tons of fruit are harvested each year.

The 40-mile (64-km) **Mount Hood Loop** meanders around the base of the mountain and provides a playground for the senses. In the springtime, the valley is alive with blossoms and fragrances. The **Mount Hood Railroad**, built in 1906, takes passengers up impressive grades, through blooming orchards and steep canyons, transporting passengers in restored vintage railroad cars. The railroad was built to haul lumber out of the Mount Hood National Forest to Hood River mills. But since 1988 it has been carrying passengers through the valley to Parkdale. Parkdale has the **Cloud Cap Inn**, the oldest mountain resort in Oregon, built in 1889 at the 6,000 foot (1,828 m) level on the north slope. People from Portland traveled by boat up the Columbia, then by stagecoach or wagon to sample its charm. To withstand the tremendous wind of winter storms, it was anchored to the ground with cables. It is now used by mountaineers and a rescue group.

Cool way to beat the heat.

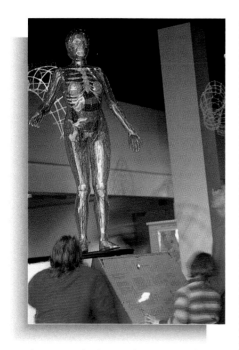

The age of robotics has arrived in Portland.

office buildings, and restaurants – roses accent each and every structure.

It's only one of many annual festivals. July has the Scottish Highland Games and Clan Gathering, the KWG Neighborfair Folkfest at Waterfront Park; August sees the Mt. Hood Jazz Festival at Mt. Hood Community College, the Waterfront Classics music festival at Waterfront Park, the Tualatin Crawfish Festival; Artquake in August, Octoberfest, and Wintering-In-Harvest Festival, and the Ping Golf Championships. November brings the Wine Country Thanksgiving, and the annual Thanksgiving Wine and Art Show. And so it goes on, month after month. The city's arts scene is prolific with major arts organizations like the Oregon Symphony being augmented by smaller organizations such as Nancy Matchek's Contemporary Dance Season at Portland State University.

San Francisco and north to Vancouver, Canada. It's a "something for everyone" gathering with 70 events including an airshow, an Indy car race, two parades and a hot-air balloon race. U.S. and Canadian naval ships line the seawall, and skiers compete on the upper reaches of the Mount Hood icefields.

Mostly, though, it's the roses that the two million festival-goers come to see every year, such as the Grand Floral parade in which floats are draped in roses of every color. And everywhere in the city – parks,

Major downtown hotels are in the middle of the arts action. The Benson, The Heathman, The Governor Hotel, Hotel Vintage Plaza, RiverPlace Hotel, Marriott Residence Inn, and the Red Lion are major lodgings within easy access of many of the arts outlets. For romantics, Glamour Magazine recently called the London Grill at the Nelson Hotel one of the six most romantic restaurants in the United States.

Them Plains Indians, never having seen the ocean, referred to it in legend as "the river with no shore". When Sacajawea, the Lewis and Clark Expedition's Shosh-one guide first laid eyes on the Pacific Ocean, she vowed to tell her people of the plains that their legend was indeed true.

Hyperbole aside, this "river" indeed does have a shore – 360 miles (579 km) of it and every grain of sand is owned by the people of Oregon. Unlike California, the state designated its beach-coast public property in a 1913 proclamation by then-Governor, George Oswald.

The Oregon coastline is exposed to the longest stretch of open ocean on earth and more than 70 state parks and other amenities – lighthouses, viewpoints, bays, and beaches – dot the shoreline. The constant expanse of sand is broken up by a dozen major rivers that flow from the mountains into the sea, from the

Ecola State Park with Cannon Beach in the background.

The Oregon Coast

267

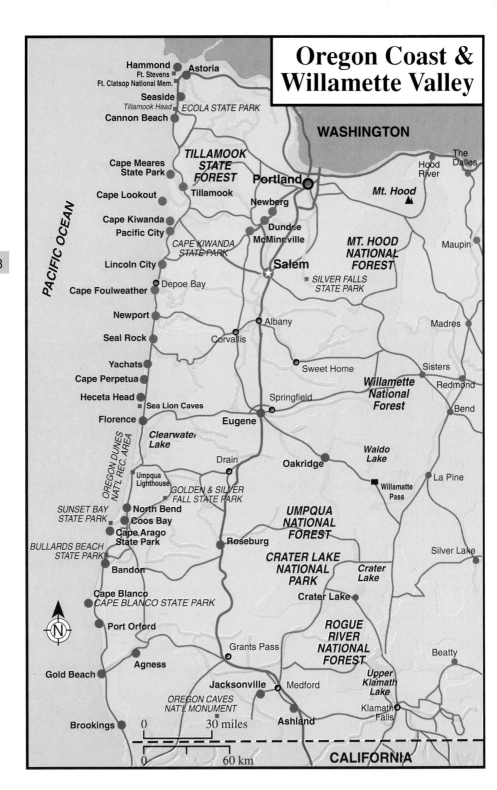

Oregon Coast & Willamette Valley

WASHINGTON

Hammond
Ft. Stevens
Ft. Clatsop National Mem.
Astoria

Seaside
Tillamook Head
Cannon Beach
ECOLA STATE PARK

TILLAMOOK STATE FOREST

Portland

The Dalles

Hood River

Mt. Hood

Cape Meares State Park

Tillamook

Cape Lookout

Newberg

Cape Kiwanda
Pacific City

Dundee
McMinnville

MT. HOOD NATIONAL FOREST

Maupin

CAPE KIWANDA STATE PARK

Lincoln City

Salem

PACIFIC OCEAN

Cape Foulweather
○ Depoe Bay

SILVER FALLS STATE PARK

Newport

Albany

Madres

Seal Rock

Corvallis

Yachats

Sweet Home

Sisters

Cape Perpetua

Springfield

Willamette National Forest

Redmond

Heceta Head
Sea Lion Caves

Bend

Florence

Eugene

Clearwater Lake

OREGON DUNES NAT'L REC. AREA

Drain

Oakridge

Waldo Lake

La Pine

Umpqua Lighthouse

GOLDEN & SILVER FALL STATE PARK

Willamette Pass

SUNSET BAY STATE PARK
North Bend
Coos Bay
Cape Arago State Park

UMPQUA NATIONAL FOREST

BULLARDS BEACH STATE PARK

Roseburg

Silver Lake

Bandon

CRATER LAKE NATIONAL PARK

Crater Lake

Cape Blanco
CAPE BLANCO STATE PARK

Crater Lake

Port Orford

ROGUE RIVER NATIONAL FOREST

Beatty

Grants Pass

Upper Klamath Lake

Gold Beach

Agness

Jacksonville

Medford

OREGON CAVES NAT'L MONUMENT

Ashland

Klamath Falls

Brookings

0   30 miles

0   60 km

CALIFORNIA

Kite flying at Lincoln City beach.

It's a long journey to the North Pole!

Klamath Mountains in the south and the Coast Range in the north.

U.S. Highway 101 extends the full length of it, making access to towns that hang on to its shores a simple matter. Despite a booming tourist industry – the coast is one of the finest recreational playgrounds in the United States – much of it is still pristine and unspoiled.

Indicative of its access, a bicycle route follows U.S. 101 and while it might be for everyone, it's the best way of getting on intimate terms with the broad sandy beaches, sand dunes, sheltered coves, and rocky headlands. A free copy of the Oregon Coast Bike Route Map is available from coastal info-centers and Chambers of Commerce. You get information about services from Astoria in the north to the California border – accommodations, bike repair shops, wind speed, and temperatures.

The coast is most dramatic in winter, when huge waves dramatically crash on the shore and the wind emphasizes the region's wildness. The coastal climate is mild with wet winters and reasonably dry, sunny summers. Temperature extremes are rare. But the kindest weather is between April-September though mid-June brings a 2 to 3 week rain spell.

North Coast

The north coast lies between Astoria, at the mouth of the Columbia River, and

Rescue boat in the Clatsop Spit, Astoria.

Lincoln City, just south of the intersection of ORE 18. Typical of the region are wind-swept beaches and unhampered surf. Paralleling the shoreline is a sand dune area several miles wide, though the major dunes site – Oregon Dunes National Recreation Area – is in the southern portion between Florence and Coos Bay.

Oregon's oldest city

Astoria is Oregon's oldest city and is connected to the Washington shoreline at Megler by the four mile (6.4 km) long Trans Columbia Bridge. In 1805 Lewis and Clark arrived and built Fort Clapsot nearby. In 1811, representatives of John Jacob Astor's Pacific Fur Company founded the first permanent settlement and named it after their employer. Arguably the richest man in America, he actually made most of his massive fortune in New York real estate.

A number of Victorian homes have been restored to their original condition and are open throughout the city. One of the finest is **Flavel House** (441 Eighth Street), a Queen Anne

For a slice of history re-enacted, visit Fort Clatsop.

Clamber up the Astoria column for a magnificent view.

mansion built in 1885 by a Columbia River bar pilot for his family, members of whom lived in it until 1933. It is now the Clapsot County Historical Museum.

A visit to the **Astoria Column** – a 125-foot (38 m) monolith atop Coxcomb Hill and patterned after Trajan's Column in Rome – is a must for anyone wanting a 164-step walk up for a view of the city, Coast Range, and Pacific Ocean.

The newly opened **Fire Fighters' Museum** is the city's latest attraction, but the city's centerpiece is the outstanding **Columbia River Maritime Museum**. It is divided into seven galleries that depict the Columbia River heritage. The 128 foot (39 m) ship, *Columbia*, which was the last active lightship on the coast, is moored outside.

Peter Iredale, the ship that ran aground at Fort Stevens.

Fort Clatsop National Memorial has a replica of the original Lewis & Clark stockade where details of daily life are enacted. The explorers' journals sparked the first real interest in the area and helped initiate migration from the east.

A thriving commercial seaport, Astoria's waterfront is lined with cruise and fishing charters and downtown is an active place with fine seafood restaurants and small shops. The Ricciardi Gallery (108-10th Street) offers a fine selection of regional art.

Shipwrecks

Between 1725 and 1961 there were 200 shipwrecks in the vicinity of the mouth of the Columbia River where competing currents create treacherous navigation. One of the most visible wrecks can be seen on the beach in the **Fort Stevens State Park** – the Peter Iredale, a 2,000 ton cargo ship that ran aground on October 25, 1906.

The Park, 10 miles west off U.S. 101 is the site of a military reservation that guarded the mouth of the Columbia from the Civil War until the Second World War. It has the distinction of being the only military installation in th Lower 48 states to be fired upon by a foreign enemy since the War of 1812. On June 21, a Japanese submarine – in a symbolic gesture – fired a few shells in the fort's vicinity, causing no damage.

Gearhart

The resort town of **Gearhart**, just north of Seaside, could win the prize for having the most examples of Oregon Coast architecture with large, bleached homes in shades of weathered gray and white. Many are owned by Portland's wealthy whose "cottages" are sometimes larger than most homes.

Gearhart Golf Links, opened in 1892, is the second oldest in the West with a 6,089 yard (5567 m) course built on sandy soil that covers 100 acres of dunes.

Seaside

Seaside is Oregon's largest beach-side resort that during the summer is packed with tourists. It is also a favorite with Portland residents.

Crowds mill along Broadway, looking at the tourist amenities available, and then walk along the two-mile-long (3.2 km) cement "boardwalk" that fronts the beach.

In July, beware of the Miss Oregon Pageant and in February the Trail's End Marathon – both bring in hoards of people. Of interest in town are the Seaside Convention Center, the Unknown Sailor's Grave, Seaside Historical Museum. Tillamook Head Lighthouse, and Ecola State Park – with its spectacular ocean views – are south towards Cannon Beach.

Carmel of the Northwest

If Seaside is for tourists, **Cannon Beach** – 10 miles (16 km) south – is for the more cerebral. Called by many the Carmel of the Northwest, it's an arts community with strict building codes that prohibit

Haystack Rock, one of the world's largest coastal monoliths.

neon and ensures architecture of weathered cedar and wood products.

Galleries abound and can be browsed through along Hemlock Street. Like Carmel, it's a monied place. But, the Haystack Program In the Arts is offered through Portland State University – arts workshops co-ordinated with family vacation plans without costing a fortune. Coaster Theater Company hosts summer plays as well as a variety of year 'round productions.

Haystack Rock, one of the world's largest coastal monoliths, dominates

Dunes National Recreation Center

Harsh landscape at Oregon Dunes National Recreation Center.

Mountains and near the shore where terrain is eroded and carried to the sea by numerous streams and rivers. Ocean currents from the west then wash the sand up onto the beaches where it dries and is then blown inland at low

Few samplings of nature in the Pacific Northwest are as elegant, graceful and unexpected as the sand dunes of Oregon. They are unexpected and they dominate the mind long after you've left. Extending along the coast from Coos Bay north to Sea Lion Point, a distance of 53 miles (85 km), they reach inland as much as 3 miles (5 km) and pile as high as 500 feet (152 m), taller than those in the Sahara Desert.

They seem frozen in time and space – bleak, desolate, windy, harsh, sterile and always overwhelming. Yet, these are not static spectacles, constantly changing in form and substance as winds and erosion change their character almost daily.

Like everything else in nature, the dunes – which scientists say were formed over the past 12,000 to 15,000 years – have their own cycle, beginning as sandstone in the Coast Range

tide by the prevailing winds. Following its long tradition of preserving its coast for everyone, the state government in 1972 established a 47-mile (75-km) long stretch from Florence to North Bend as a national recreation area.

Sand dune playground

Averaging 2 miles (3.2 km) in width, the area is managed by the Siuslaw National Forest and has become a sand dunes playground with hiking, boating, riding, and sightseeing in dune buggies.

The most spectacular dunes landscape within the 32,000 acres park are found 9 miles south of the Reedsport Dunes visitor's center, at **Umpqua Dunes** where – after a hike of 500 yards through coastal evergreen forest – you're

the long sandy beach and is probably the most photographed location in town. It's also the best place in America to see tufted puffins.

There are plenty of places to stay and eat. Lodging can be had at The Cannon Beach Hotel and the Argonauta Inn; while restaurants like Cafe de la

Mar, The Bistro, and the Lazy Susan Cafe offer better than average menus.

The route to Lincoln City

A series of small towns and state parks dot the coast on the way to Lincoln City.

greeted by large, spectacular dunes.

The dunes are hidden from the coastal highway, U.S. 101 and the most commonly asked question at the visitor's center is, "Where are the dunes". To help in the search the park service created a lookout 10 miles (16 km) north of Reedsport where viewing decks on three levels provide vistas of the dune and local vegetation.

But once you've found them, you're in for several surprises, the most unusual of which is the rapidly changing climatic conditions. Summer fogs and winter warmth are not uncommon; neither are varying hot and cool "valleys" between the dunes.

The lack of distinct trails means it's easy to get lost among the dunes that look alike. But the sounds of surf and traffic define west and east.

Besides the dunes, the area also encompasses 32 freshwater lakes – created when dunes blocked river access to the ocean – the mouths of the Umpqua and Siusla Rivers, and numerous marshes, estuaries, grasslands, and forests. Only the tops of dead trees poling through the tops of some dunes like wooden skeletons provide evidence of forests that formerly occupied these sites.

While there are about 400 different species of life throughout the dunes region, the only dangerous element comes from dune buggies flying over the top of a dune. But offroad vehicle areas are well marked so you should be able to avoid them.

More difficult to avoid are ghetto blasters from the thousands of young people who walk the edges of the dunes during the summer.

Manzanita is another flourishing arts community and has two impressive state parks, Nehalem Bay, and Oswald West. At **Mohler**, inland from Nehalam, the Nehalem Bay Winery offers sampling and purchase of its Pinot Noir and blackberry desert wine.

Tillamook is the home of Oregon's

Sunset at Oceanside, west of Tillamook.

largest cheese plant and other dairy industries. The Tillamook County Pioneer Museum is housed in the 1905 County Courthouse. The old Second World War U.S. Navy blimp hangars are south of town, 1,000 feet (305 m) long and 170 feet (52 m) high.

Three Capes Loop

Be certain to drive the 22-mile (35.4 km) **Three Capes Loop** on the way south to Lincoln City. It's one of Oregon's most beautiful strips of seaside. The narrow road skirts Tillamook Bay, climbs over Cape Meares, and then follows the shore of Netart's Bay. It scales Cape Lookout (the westernmost headland on the Or-

Sealife is abundant on the northern shores.

egon Coast) and passes through the dairy country of Kiwanda.

Central Coast

Lincoln City marks the end of the northern coast. Between it and Coos Bay are sandy beaches and the vast dunes areas that make up the character of the mid-coastal region. The city is formed by the merger of five coastal towns and is a bustling strip of tourist shops, motels, a factory-outlet shopping center and an attractive golf course, Gleneden Beach Links. In town are several art galleries including the Oceans West Gallery that offers work from 200 Oregon artists. The Bay House is an exceptional restaurant.

Fishing harbor in Depoe Bay, south of Lincoln City.

Whale Watching

"Thar she blows".

Like a fantasy come true, the words were out of my mouth before I even knew it was a possibility that I'd make a fool of myself. But no-one aboard the whale watching boat even noticed. Likely, they had all been thinking the same thing.

"I always wanted to do that," I said, sheepishly to the man standing next to me at the railing watching the vapor spout from a Gray Whale begin to fade several hundred yards off the starboard bow of the boat. "Wish I had said that," he replied.

Along the Oregon coast, whale watching is as part of winter as the coastal rain. Between December and early April, coastal headlands and beaches provide vantage points for viewing the migration of California Gray Whales.

They travel their 12,000 mile (19,300 km) route between Baja California in Mexico, where they breed, to the Bering Sea in the Arctic for their summer feeding. It's the longest migration movement by land or sea of any animal. It's cold and wet and you'll need to be properly dressed. And the wise landlubber prepares for bouts of seasickness.

A variety of ships from bases along the coast – Harbor, Fort Stevens, Ecola State Park, Charleston, Newport, Depoe Bay – offer offshore viewing trips. The companies are carefully monitored to make certain the whales aren't disturbed on their journey. And on a clear day, air excursions over the migration track will provide a vision of spouting whales over the horizon.

The animals are quick on their southern migration, anxious to get on with mating. On the way back north, they're most leisurely in the travel and takes place in two pulses. First, the immature whales of both sexes including females that did not give birth to a calf, and then are followed – usually not until May – by cows with calves at a much slower pace.

The whale birthing process is amazing and has been witnessed several times by researchers. A female midwife pushes the pregnant mama above the surface of the water and rolls her on her back so that the newborn can be born into the air.

If that seems slightly implausible, keep in mind that whales are acknowledged to have the most sophisticated language system on earth next to humans.

The newborns are about 12-15 ft. long (3.5-4.5 m) and weigh about 2,000 pounds (907 kg). They grow about the same length during the next year, nursing on milk that contains 13 times more butterfat than cow's milk. Females typically give birth every other year and whales live to about 60 years.

Since whales are community and family animals, when you see one spout, you'll find many others. Because the whales migrate along the coast, they have to veer westward to get around caostal headlands that extend into the ocean. It's from those points they are best seen.

Upper Drift Creek covered bridge is southeast of Lincoln City. Built in 1914, it is now open only to foot traffic and is the oldest remaining covered bridge in Oregon.

Depoe Bay, a charming village south of Lincoln City, has the world's smallest navigable harbor. Nearby Highway 101 rises to 450 feet (137 m) above the ocean at Cape Foulweather, offering the highest viewpoint along the coast. At the outer end is **Devil's Punchbowl**, a collapsed sea cave that resembles a giant pot and which boils and spouts seawater at high tide.

Newport

At Newport, the Hatfield Marine Science

Spotting the whales

The Mark O. Hatfield Marine Science Center, an extension of Oregon State University, operates a program for whale watching that includes trained volunteers at popular spots along the coast including Fort Stevens, Cape Lookout, Yaquina Head, Cape Foulweater, Umpqua Lighthouse, Shore Acres, and Harris Beach State Parks among others. Early morning is the best time because winds cause whitecaps later in the day. But, whatever inconvenience this means is easily made up for when one of these 50 ft. long (15.2 m) whales that weigh in at 100,000 pounds (45370 kg) rise from the waters and flop on its side just yards away from the boat.

Wrapped in seaweed and covered by barnacles and other parasites, these large animals look gentle with eyes that are remarkably soft and forlorn.

Depoe Bay bills itself as the whale-watching capital of the world and there are many charters available to the migration areas. Charters are highly competitive and you might find that times and costs greatly vary. These boat captains are good at getting you to the whales, which must regularly come to the surface to breathe. And the whales themselves are a curious lot. When they do come to the surface, they often seem as though they're looking directly at you – a sort of people-gazing break from the mundane routine of swimming north.

Center is a working whale research center. The Oregon Coast Aquarium opened in 1992. The Oldtown bayfront intersperse canneries with restaurants featuring clam chowder, salmon and crab. Art galleries and specialty shops have no off-season.

The oceanfront Arts Center displays the work of local painters and sculptors, and Newport's 400-seat Performing Arts Center offers a repertoire from Shakespeare to modern jazz. The Lincoln County Historical Museum and Burrows House both exhibit Native American artifacts.

The Whale's Tale restaurant and the Sylvia Bach Hotel are good stopping off spots.

If, by the time you've reached Newport you're tired of tourist towns, stop at **Yachats**, a nearby retreat for those seeking a quiet, oceanview cabin and dramatic surf views – especially in winter.

Florence

In Florence, the sand dunes begin just out of town. The city, known as a rhododendron center has an annual festival for the flowering bushes in May. The **Siuslaw Pioneer Museum** examines and chronicles how the Siuslaw tribe sold their land to the federal government, but never received their payment. The **American Museum of Fly Fishing** has thousands of attractively framed examples of the art.

Downtown is a blend of old and new. Walk along the Waterfront, on Bay Street, where the town's oldest buildings have been restored.

Florence's most exciting elements are outside the community. **Hecata Head Lighthouse**, 12 miles north, offers the best postcard shot on the coast; and the nearby Sea Lion Caves is the only known mainland breeding colony of the Stellar's sea lion. The Toy Factory

Standing solitary but tall, the Yaquina Bay Lighthouse.

Wild stretch of beach near Newport.

Yaquina Bay Bridge in Newport.

has locally made toys and the Indian Forest has buffalo and deer grazing near authentic models of Native American structures.

South Coast

Even though the 50 miles (80.4 km) of Highway 101 south between Florence and Coos Bay doesn't follow the ocean, your eyes will nonetheless be drawn westward by the mountainous dunes, the biggest of which make up the **Oregon Dunes National Recreation Area**.

Of the 14,000 acres of dunes, about half are open to off-road vehicles. Tours can be arranged with a commercial dune-buggy operator. You can walk

Bandon, the "Storm Watching Capitol of the World".

among the dunes – being careful about buggies – and trails and roads lead to Woahink, Siltcoos, and Tahkenitch lakes. The dunes halt north of Coos Bay and the coastline turns rugged offering some of the state's least explored beaches.

Coos Bay

Coos Bay has the largest natural harbor between San Francisco and Seattle and has long been a busy port. The waterfront and downtown have been remodeled in recent years as the town seems to want more tourists.

It hosts the Oregon Music Festival (July), the Blackberry Arts Festival (Au-

gust), and the Bay Area Fun Festival (September). The Coos Bay Art Museum, Coos County Historical Museum, and the Marshfield Sun Printing Museum reflect local history which developed from logging.

South Slough National Estuarine Reserve is a 4,300 acres (1,740 hectare) preserve of fresh and salt water marsh. **Cape Arago**, west of Coos Bay and south of Shore Acres State Park, has three tidal pool viewing areas at North Cove, Middle Cove, and South Cove.

Bandon-By-The-Sea

Another Carmel-like artists colony exists at **Bandon-By-The-Sea** which pro-

A country romp is a pleasant way to start the morning.

claims itself the "Storm Watching Capitol of the World". The **Old Town** is an engaging neighborhood where you can shop for cranberry treats or pottery. The region is also Oregon's cranberry capitol so you'll have plenty of cranberry foods.

Of interest is the Bandon Cheese Factory, Bandon Lighthouse, Bandon Historical Museum and the West Coast Game Park Safari. The Professional Sports Hall of Fame has, among 5,000 items, Steve Garvey's and Roy Campanella's LA and Brooklyn Dodger uniforms.

On the way south to the California border, **Port Orford Wayside State Park** is a great whale watching promontory.

Gold Beach is a wilderness entry point where you can arrange jet-boat trips up the wild Rogue River one of only 10 designated Wild and Scenic Rivers in America. Major hiking, camping, and river expeditions leave from Gold Beach.

It's a surprisingly pleasant place, a favorite with author Zane Grey. It has one of the loveliest lodges on the West Coast – the Tu Tu Tun Lodge – and the Gold Beach Resort.

And in **Brookings**, six miles (9.6 km) from the California border, the Oregon coast comes to an abrupt end. But it's such a delightful entry/departure point. It's the nation's major producer of Easter lilies and daffodils. The Chetco Valley Historical Museum has a bronze cast of a face that many claim to be that of Sir Francis Drake in 1579.

W hen you get here you'll be faced with over-choice, deciding what to do and where to go. Here you'll find the end of the Oregon Trail, the capitals of Oregon's provisional and modern-day governments, the state's two largest universities, and a choice of vibrant, livable cities surrounded by the farmland of Oregon's green belt.

Williamette Valley

The Williamette Valley has acres upon acres of fertile countryside.

Wineries Galore

Traveling to the Williamette Valley you will expect to see the wineries. More than one-half of Oregon's 85 wineries are in the Williamette Valley. In the 1940s and '50s, scientists at the University of Oregon said the climate and soil were wrong for wine grape. They were wrong, thankfully, and today some of the finest wines in America come from this region. In fact, Oregon's wine growing country now ex-tends from Portland all the way to the

The spills and thrills of Indian rodeo.

Californian border with the greatest concentration in Yamhill County.

The fertile valley

The Indians who were here prior to the white migration never used the valley for farming. But they did constantly burn to provide browse for deer and soils for grasses and berries. Those centuries of burning cleared the land of many trees and it exposed the alluvial soils for later farming. And did they ever farm!

The Oregon Trail.

to reach into the thorny bushes.

Destination of choice

The Williamette River Valley was the Oregon destination of choice for the early settlers – first for gold and later for farming. After the trials of the Oregon Trail, the rich, fertile lands here must have seemed like the Eden they had been promised. John McLoughlin, of the Hudson Bay Company, established the first settlement near the present site of Oregon City in the winter of 1828-29. Close behind were a variety of missionaries who thought they were there to convert Indians, but ended up merely claiming the land for the United States

The Williamette Valley contains the majority of the state's 34,000 farms producing an endless variety of crops – broccoli, cucumbers, beans, corn, grapes, and much, much more.

The harvest lands begin above the valley, in the Cascades, where blackberries and huckleberries are available to those patient and thick-skinned enough

The beginning of the scenic route.

against British claims.

Today the region is a lovely combination of small river towns, well designed and gracious larger cities, dense forests, and abundant water.

Oregon City

Driving south from Portland, the first major city you hit along I-5 is Oregon City, really a part today of the greater reaches of the Portland metropolitan region. The city sits on two levels with the lower level being the site of the original settlement. Here you'll find a number of late 19th-century commercial buildings along Main Street, the most significant of which is the **Bank of**

Commerce building, constructed in terra cotta and brick Classic Revival style.

In the upper level, where the residents built their homes are John McLoughlin House, Barclay House, and the flat-roofed Ermatinger House. The End of the Oregon Trail Interpretive Center is on Washington Street and it contains exhibits on the pioneers who journeyed the 2,000 miles (3218 km) from Independence, Missouri.

Aurora, south of Oregon City, is where a Harmonite communal settlement of Pennsylvania Germans was established in 1856 by Dr. William Keil. What's left is a well-preserved turn-of-the-century village with several Victorian homes and numerous antique

Traversing the Williamette Valley.

shops. The **Old Aurora Colony Museum** contains the town's historical items, and Chez Moustache is the major restaurant.

Scenic routes

I-5 runs the entire length of the Williamette Valley with major highways intersecting with the freeway to connect the region's urban centers with the coast and the communities east of the Cascades. If you want to experience the best of what the valley has to offer, be prepared to do a lot of zig-zagging.

The **99W Scenic Route** travels 122 miles (196 km) past rivers, lakes, parks, museums, historic sites, golf courses, and wineries from Portland and follows the general route of I-5 though it avoids the latter's high-speed pace as it routes through small towns. Keep in mind that Highway 99W is the state's official wine road. This is where you want to be if you're thinking vineyards; Yamhill County is in the northern part of the valley.

But, if you want a real closeup view of the Valley, try taking the 195 mile (314 km) **Williamette Bicycle Loop** that crosses uncongested roadways through Oregon's prime farmland and forest, covered bridges and golf courses. Commercial airlines serve Eugene and Salem.

Newberg, the entrance into wine country, has a number of wineries including Veritas, Rex Hill, Autumn Wind,

Salem's centerpiece, the Capitol Building.

Oregon Bridges

In the 1920s there were more than 450 covered bridges in Oregon thanks to the accessibility of Douglas Fir on the west side of the Cascades. Today there are only 54, preserved and restored by the Covered Bridge Society of Oregon.

Lane County in western Oregon, is known for its collection of preserved bridges. In this rugged wooded country visitors will find 20 covered bridges, more than any county west of the Appalachians. Eighteen of Lane County's bridges are listed in the National Register of Historic Places.

Oldest and Newest

They were originally constructed to withstand heavy rains, ice storms, and salty sea air. With names like Goodpasture Bridge, Unity Bridge, Coyote Creek Bridge, and Wildcat Bridge, they reflect the diverse life found around these romantic covered bridges. The oldest covered bridge in Oregon is the **Upper Drift Creek Bridge** built in 1914 in Lincoln County. The newest addition, constructed in 1963, is the **Rock O' the Range** in Deschutes County.

Many of the bridges are still open to vehicular traffic and are in use daily. Others are open only to pedestrians. Most of the foot bridges have been bypassed by newer, concrete structures. You'll need to get off the main highways to see most of the state's covered bridges, traveling through scenic country with interesting historical sites.

Myrtle Creek, just south of Roseburg, has two of them. The 42 ft. (12.8 m) **Neal Lane Bridge**, one mile (1.6 km) east of town, is the only bridge in the state with a King Post truss. The other is located in town adjacent to the city park. Built in 1930 and originally located off Horse Creek on the McKenzie River, the 110 ft. (33.5 m) long bridge was painstakenly reconstructed by community volunteers.

Oregon's southernmost bridge is the **McKee**, located southwest of Medford. You take ORE 238 through Jacksonville to the small, rural town of Ruch and head south on the country road. In its prime, the bridge was used as a reststop halfway between Jacksonville and the Blue Lodge Copper Mine.

On the Oregon coast, a short 9 mile (14.5 km) trip west and north of Yachats is a must. The short, 42 ft (13 m) **North Fork of Yachats Bridge** with its bright red flared sides, is nestled in a picturesque stand of alder trees. The arched portals and short ribbon openings under the eaves provide interior lighting.

A highlight in the Cottage Grove area is **Chamber's Bridge**, a rare covered railroad span. In the same region, south of Dorena Reservoir, is **Dorena Bridge** with nearby barbeque pits and tables.

Douglas County has a number of fine spans including the **Roaring Camp Bridge** off Route 38 west of Drain. The **Rochester Bridge** west of Sutherlin was saved in the late 1950s when local residents, armed with shotguns, stood an all-night vigil to keep away county highway workers who were threatening to burn it down.

An indispensable guide to Oregon's covered bridges can be had by telephoning the Covered Bridge Society of Oregon at (503) 246-2953.

and Elk Cove. Throughout the region you'll find upscale and middle of the road wineries catering to a number of tastes. Check with the Oregon Winegrowers Association in Portland for a guide.

President Herbert Hoover spent his youth in Newberg and Hoover memorabilia is located at the **Hoover-Minthorn Museum** (his former house) and at his alma mater, **George Fax College**.

The International Pinot Noir Celebration in late July is held in McMinnville on the campus of Linfield College, southwest of Newburg. It's also the home of Lavender's Blue Tea Room

The streams around Salem are a challenge to anglers.

and Nick's Italian Cafe, both superb eating establishments. The old town has 52 preserved buildings.

Salem

The Youngberg Hill Farm Inn is in a spectacular setting at the crest of a 650 foot (198 m) hill with a view across the wine hills of the region. On the east side of I-5, just north of Salem, **Mount Angel Abbey** is a 100-year-old Benedictine seminary atop a butte the Indians considered sacred. The library is considered an architectural jewel designed by Finnish architect Alvar Aalto.

As you would expect, Salem's centerpiece is the **State Capitol**, built in 1938. Don't expect the usual kind of state capitol, however, with sterile white walls and boring office doors. Instead, the marble halls of Oregon's government building is adorned with murals, paintings, and sculptures representing important events and moments in the state's history.

On Court Street, the Vermont marble building is a modern structure that has a sharp, symmetrical facade and a fluted, cylindrical central dome topped by a 24-foot (7.3-m) gold-leaf statue, *The Pioneers*. From the top of the dome, you can have a bird's-eye view of the surrounding valley.

Attractive parks are part of the Capitol complex. **Wilson Park** and **Capitol Park** have a variety of statues and artifacts including the Corinthian columns from the old capitol building that was destroyed by fire in 1935.

Williamette University

Across from the Capitol is **Williamette University**, the oldest institution of higher learning west of the Mississippi. It began as the Oregon In-

Williamette National Forest, where nature reigns supreme.

Silver Falls, where park paths allow the visitor to go behind the falls.

stitute in 1943, founded by missionary Jason Lee to instill Christian values among the settlers. Today, the campus is a pleasant combination of old and new buildings. In Collins Hall, crystals and exhibits show Oregon's glacial past. The **Botanical Gardens** on the east side of the campus is small, but well cared for.

Mission Mill Village, across the road from the university, and is an impressive 4.5 acre cluster of restored buildings from the 1800s that includes the Jason Lee Mason house and the Methodist Mission Patronage both built in 1841. The Salem Visitor's Information Center is part of the complex and has material about the many old buildings including Bush House and the Gilbert

Oregon Wine

Where the choicest Oregon wines come from.

If Washington's Yakima Valley wines have suffered for decades from being the poor cousin to California's Sonoma and Napa Valley's products, Oregon's products have had an even tougher marketing hill to climb. Oregon's wineries are primarily found on the cool, moist side of the Cascades, primarily southwest of Portland along the length of the Williamette Valley. They grow in the Williamette, the Rogue Region and in the Umpqua.

Pinot Noir, Chardonnay, Pinot Gris, Cabernet Sauvignon, Gewurztraminer, Saivignon Blanc, and Muller-Thurgau are the grapes grown in Oregon. Wine is made from a variety of berries: raspberries, blackberries, and boysenberries.

Most of the wineries are family owned with vineyards situated on 15 to 20 acre plots of land. If you visit one, you're likely to meet the person whose name is on the label. And the state is heavy into truth in labeling with winemakers having developed the strictest wine label regulations in the country.

Wines must contain 95 percent minimum of the stated vintage; 100 per cent of the grapes must be from the stated area; and varietal wines must be 90 percent from the stated variety. Also, foreign names are prohibited so don't look for "Champagne". The standards are all the more impressive when one realizes that federal regulations demand far less percentages. For example, federal regulations demand wines contain 75 per cent minimum of stated vintage.

However, the size of the wineries, according to noted French wine writer and vintner, Alexis Lichine, has retarded the reputation and potential of the industry. While parts of the state have the same positive growing conditions as the Napa and Sonoma, he says, not enough grapes are being grown to make a significant impact on world supply.

Nonetheless, Oregon wines are delicate and rich with a straightforward and fruity character. The **Hillcrest Vineyard** at Roseburg is the pioneer wine-making enterprise in the state, its owner has been experimenting with vineyard sites since 1963. Although Hillcrest is known for

House Children's Museum.

The **Reed Opera House Mall** at the corner of Court and Liberty was once the venue of minstrel shows and other pioneer cultural activities. Now filled with boutiques and restaurants, it's a good place to take a break. Made In Salem is

a good place to go for local artistry.

Mahonia Hall is the governor's residence and is named in honor of the state flower, the Oregon Grape (*Mahonia aquifolium*). A tudor mansion built in 1930, it was given to the state in 1988 and is open to tours by appointment.

its excellent Reislings and bottle-aged Cabernet Sauvignons, other varieties develop bottle-aged flavors.

Highway U.S. 99W, west of Portland, is at the same latitude as the world's great wine-growing regions. So, Yamhill County - on the northern cusp of the Williamette Valley - produces Pinot Noir and Chardonnay grapes that regularly compete with some of the world's best.

Oregon's wine claims to fame began in 1975 when an Oregon Pinot Noir beat out dozens of Burgundies. Like Washington, which has been experimenting with cool weather west of the mountains, Oregon is beginning to develop a new wine district along the Columbia River in the east central part of the state.

Wine tastings

Attending vineyard wine tastings is an adventure. While most have drop-in tasting rooms, some like the superb **Adelsheim Winery** in Yamhill County are open only twice yearly by invitation. Amity Vineyards specializes in Pinot Noir, while Eyrie Vineyards, established in 1966 in the hills of Dundee, is best know for both its Pinot Noir and Chardonnay.

The Umpqua Valley is also a source of wine with Girarder and the Henry Estate Winery considered among the best. This is also the region where Hillcrest's White Reisling grows. Owner Richard Sommer, was the first Oregon vintner to grow vinifera grapes. The Oregon Winegrowers Association (P.O. Box 6590, Portland, OR 87228) has a list of wineries with their visiting times.

Old-fashioned ferries, operated by hand, still cross the Williamette River in a few places and are a great substitute to bridges if you have extra time. On the Labor Day weekend the Oregon State Fair is considered the largest in the Pacific Northwest.

Around Salem

Southeast of Salem, on the banks of the **North Santiam River**, are **Stayton's Santiam Historical Museum** and the **Jordan Covered Bridge** in Pioneer Park. Boaters head to the Detroit Reservoir while anglers find the scenic stretch right above the reservoir an especially challenging stream. In the winter, cross-county skiers and snowmobilers replace the anglers and hikers on the many Forest Service side roads and trails. Downhillers ski the **Hoodoo Ski Bowl** on the Santiam Pass.

Seven miles (11 km) south of Salem, take the kids to **Enchanted Forest**, a family-orientated theme park that has fairy-tale settings like Seven Dwarf's Cottage, an Alice in Wonderland rabbit hole, and other fun items. The historic Buena Vista Ferry, which carries a handful of cars and passengers across the Williamette, is 7 miles south of the Enchanted Forest.

Corvallis

Southwest of Salem, Corvallis is dominated by Oregon State University which provides the town with a more cosmopolitan flavor than you'd expect from a community of 45,000. Corvallis is Latin for "Heart of the Valley" and it's an apt description. The university specializes in agriculture and engineering and is often referred to a "Moss U". That's

Sandy Creek bridge, one of the many covered bridges in Albany.

more than just a bit unfair, especially since Hewlett Packard, the high-tech computer company came to Corvallis and around it has grown a sophisticated high-tech community.

The primary activity here is sports. The campus is perfect for walking and bicycling amidst the charming buildings. Corvallis Art Center is located in a renovated 1889 Episcopal church off Central Park. The **Horner Museum**, housed in the basement of Gill Coliseum, has an eclectic collection of items tracing Oregon's growth from the Indians and the Oregon Trail to the present.

Silver Falls State Park is Oregon's largest state facility and is located 25 miles (40 km) east of Salem on Highway 22, near the old mill town of Silverton.

Here you'll find 14 waterfalls in a series of cascading water. Seven of them are higher than 100 feet (30.5 m). Not only does it have the greatest concentration of waterfalls in the United States, but park paths allow you to go behind them. Throughout the valley between Albany and Roseburg to the south are numerous small communities like **Brownsville**, south of Albany, with its old-town that looks as though it came from a movie set. The **Linn County Historical Museum** co-ordinates wagon train tours called, Carriage me Back Days.

A pioneer cemetery on the east side of Kirk Street shelters the grave of the last Calapooya descendant and has headstones dating to 1846. **Sweet Home**, not far down Highway 34 from Lebanon, is the gateway into the Williamette National Forest. There, you can boat and fish at Foster and Green Peter Reservoirs. Brownsville hosts the state's oldest continuing community festival, the Pioneer picnic, a June event since 1887.

Albany

Albany is the place to arrange a covered bridge tour (see box p.293). They are covered because the roof protects the trusses from weather damage, thereby extending their live by decades. Of the one-time 300 plus in the state, 54 still survive. Albany has more historic homes than anywhere else in the state with more than 350 Victorian houses left over from Albany's golden age, which

Having a great time!

lasted from 1849 to the early 20th-century. It's also the home of the Albany World Championship Timber Carnival that takes place July 1-5, which encompasses speed climbing and other logging related competitions.

The **Albany Farmer's Market** is a treasureland of fruits wines, and other Williamette goodies from June through Labor Day. Museums include the Fire Museum, the Albany Regional Museum, and Monteith House, Albany's oldest frame building and the founding home of the Oregon Republican Party.

Eugene and environs

Eugene's industrial sister city is Springfield through which you drive on the way into the high Cascades ski country. Seven miles (11 km) east of Eugene, State Highway 58 leads past numerous small lakes and hot springs on route to Williamette Pass where you find skiing less than an hour from Eugene.

Head a few miles north of Eugene for historic **Coburg's** antique shop then continue on to **Junction City** which has a full-scale, four day Scandinavian Festival each August. Twenty miles south of Eugene is **Cottage Grove** where you can tour old gold mines and nearby mining towns by bus or car. There's also a two-hour locomotive ride offered.

The **Cottage Grove Historical Museum** documents the town's turn-of-the-century mining activity. An old miner's

Eugene

This is a city that never did decide whether it was urban or rural. In a sense it's neither one or the other, rather the best of both. With the Willamette National Forest to the east, the coast range to the west, and the river's rich fields between them, Eugene is a mixture of pastoral setting and cultured vigor. The 110,000 residents of Eugene combine with the 41,000 who live in nearby Springfield to make up the second largest residential region in the state, next to Portland.

The city offers sidewalk cafes, malled streets, upscale shops, one of the finest concert halls in the nation in the Hult Center, and the world renowned Oregon Bach Festival, plus the University of Oregon. The 250-acre university campus harbors an arboretum containing more than 1000 varieties of trees and the Museum of Natural History with its collection of fossil history, archeology, and Northwest Coast art.

The Museum of Art - with its colonaded sculpture court and pool - is one of the campus's architectural highlights. Permanent exhibits cover Northwest and international art and photography.

Eugene is a city that revels in its history, especially in the downtown area, the boundaries of which correspond roughly to the city's limits in 1876 when the railroad's arrival inspired confidence in its future.

At the **Fifth Street Public Market** are dozens of shops, 17 restaurants, and a courtyard that's a popular venue for the city's musicians, artists, and acrobats. Originally a feed mill, it's one of many innovative examples of Eugene's penchant for recycling and redesigning old commercial buildings.

You'll find the same kind of ambience at the Saturday Market, a weekly event that features entertainment between April and Christmas on Oak and Eighth Streets.

The Oregon Bach Festival at the university's music school in June/July is one of many events in and around the city during the year. Also staged are the Oregon Country Faire, Eugene Celebrations, Eugene Folk Festival, Bohemia Mining Days, and the Junction City Scandinavian Festival.

Historic sites

Eugene has 2,000 designated historic properties including the 1888 vintage **Shelton McMurphey House** (303 Williamette), an acqua-colored Victorian gem once known as the "castle on the hill". The McMurphey House is located in the East Skinner Butte Historic Landmark Area, the site of the city's first settlement. It contains a collection of period residential architecture including Queen Anne, Bungalow, Colonial Revival, and Classic Revival styles dating from the 1880s to the 1920s.

The **Italianate Smeed Hotel** (767 Williamette), with round arches over its windows, dates from 1885 and is one of the region's surviving hotels buildings. Today it houses retail businesses, restaurants, and professional offices.

Within the city are almost endless gardens, parks, and places where people and nature commiserate with one another. Owen's Municipal Rose Garden is in full bloom in late June. At the garden's center is the cherry tree planted in 1847, one year after the city's first plan was filed. Henrick's Park, the Profontaine Trail, Skinner's Butte, and the Spencer's Butte Trailhead provide places to sit or to hike.

The Eugene Hilton, River Valley Inn, and Campus Cottage are among the many lodging possibilities. Among restaurants are Chanterelle, Grape Vine, Ambrosia, and the Excelsior Cafe.

haunt, the Cottage Grove Hotel, has been restored to house specialty shops.

A loop drive leads through the old mining district and over covered bridges, including Oregon's only covered railroad bridge.

The MacKenzie River Valley offers access to the Three Sisters, Mount Jefferson, and Mount Washington Wilderness areas.

There's always a chance to see Roosevelt Elk in the Mount Washington
Wilderness Area.

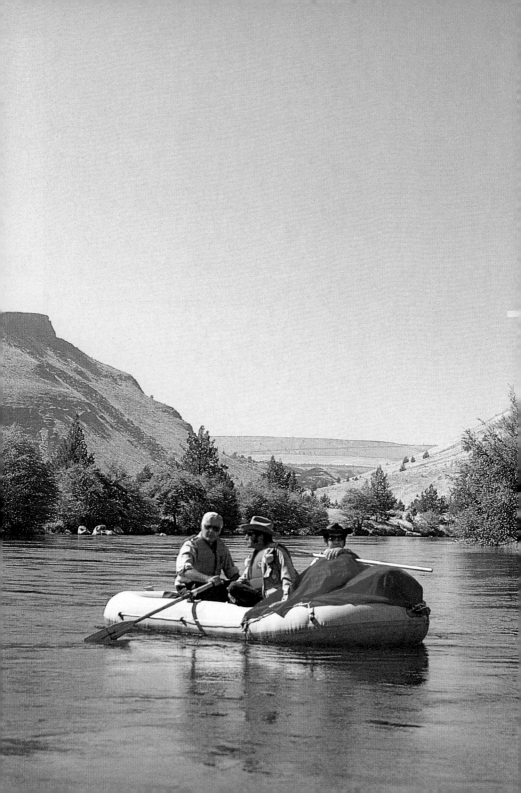

From Bend you can fan out to virtually any topographical area – east to the high desert county; west across the Cascades to the Williamette Valley; north to the Columbia River; south to the high Cascades and the numerous national forests.

In fact, the Bend and Central Oregon area is often called the state's "playground" with a dozen state parks, numerous golf courses, 150 lakes, more than 500 miles (805 km) of rivers and streams, and an evergreen forest twice the size of Rhode Island.

Quiet spot on the Deschutes River.

Expansive lava fields, caves, hiking trails, and resorts have given the region a tourism economy throughout the year. Yet, the area is so large and diverse, that it is seldom outwardly crowded.

Bend & Central Oregon

Ranching Settlement

Nestled against the east side of the Cascade Mountains, it's hard to believe that

The joys of camping.

town are galleries, specialty shops, restaurants, and the Des Chuites Historical Society that recounts the town's early days. In May, the Pole, Pedal, Paddle pentathlon draws international attention as does the July Cascade Cycling Classic. The Cascade festival of Music entertains each June and during a Fall/Winter series.

If you're coming in from the north along Highway 97, the information center at the edge of town is for the entire Central Oregon region and will help in planning. The building also houses the Bend Chamber of Commerce and the Central Oregon Reservation Center which provides lodging and reservation assistance.

If it's a view you want, drive to **Pilot Butte**, just east of town. This cinder cone with a road to the top offers spectacular views of the city and the Cascades beyond. Frankly, Bend isn't quite certain if it's made up of Cascades people, or desert people. They try to entertain both lifestyles.

The **Mount Bachelor ski area** is 22 miles (35.4 km) southwest in the Cascades that can be seen from the town's high points. This is the winter training ground for the U.S. National Ski Team and it draws skiers of all abilities from throughout the Northwest region. Because of its height at 9,000

Bend was a quiet high desert, sleepy little town in 1960, content to remain in its origins as a ranching settlement.

Called Bend because of a bend in the Deschutes River, it has a population of about 19,000. The city is a good fueling up place with decent restaurants and reasonable hotels. Developers saw the potential of its location and beginning about 25 years ago, in came the golf courses, the airstrip, river-rafting companies, the skiers, and rockhounds and tennis players. Down-

Eagle sculpture in Madras.

feet (2,743 m), skiing can run well into the summer.

Sunriver, once a stop for pioneers and a Second World War military installation, is a complete destination resort and called Sunriver Lodge. It has 5,000 residents and a couple of Robert Trent Jones golf courses, tennis ranches, and its own airstrip – all within a couple of miles of Mount Bachelor.

Warm Springs Indian Reservation

North of Bend are a collection of small communities, a mix of gas stops and memorable sites. The **Warm Springs Indian Reservation** is quite another matter, located on Highway 26 northwest of Madras.

The government gave the people there $4 million as compensation for the government interfering with their traditional fishing grounds. They immediately put the money into developing Kah-Nee-Ta, a luxury resort at the bottom of a canyon.

The arrow-shaped hotel is staffed by Reserve members, traditional foods are served including baked salmon cooked on wooden planks. There are tribal cultural events and the usual golf, tennis, and swimming.

The museum at Warm Springs opened in March 1993 to preserve the traditions and history of the Confederated Tribes of the Warm Springs Reser-

Warm Springs Indian Reservation is a tribute to the local Indian traditions and history.

Permanent mural in the Warm Springs Museum.

vations. In an aggressive program, the tribes purchased artifacts from individual members and families. As a result, the Warm Springs Museum – which cost more than $7.5 million – has one of the most complete material collections of family heirlooms, trade items, and bestowed gifts owned by an Indian tribe.

The building design, which resembles a traditional encampment, is made of native stone, heavy timber, and brick, all detailed to demonstrate the significance of art in everyday life.

One of the main attractions consists of three large scale recreations of traditional dwellings – of a Paiute family, Warm Springs teepee, and a Wasco plank house, each with their own displays of cultural heritage. Aside from the artifacts, the museum's collection includes 2,500 photographs that range from the 1850s.

Shaniko

Shaniko, founded in 1876, is a ghost town on Highway 97, but was once the self-proclaimed wool capitol of the-world. It enjoyed a decade of prosperity following its establishment as a rail terminus in 1900. But, it degenerated into a collection of gawdy hotels, sleazy saloons, and whore houses. Today it's a mix of honest restoration and tourism's excesses to reproduction.

South of Shaniko, on the junction of Highway 218, is the town of **Ante-**

Exquisitely beautiful Sparks Lake in the Sisters.

lope. Now once again a quiet, wayside town, it was once the center of a major confrontation between cultists and local citizenry.

This is where the late Indian guru, Bhagwan Shree Rajneesh bought a ranch and tried to take over the town and county after his entourage had settled in. He was eventually beaten off, but the legal and social upheavals turned the community into a battleground of conflicting attitudes and legalities for four years.

Sisters, on Highway 126 west of

Cowboys

Herding the cattle.

were grazing lands, though meager, and there were no fences. Texas Longhorns were brought into the region by the first Hispanics to settle in the northwest.

Today's rancher depends as much on his computer as on his horse. Keeping track of inventory, watching cashflow, following the latest beef futures, and estimating feed usage is the world of computer software and essential to modern ranching.

The dirty work still exists for the cowboy. Fences have to be fixed, horses ridden, and cattle branded. The lingering romance between the cowboy and the city dwellers has been formed as much by the likes of John Wayne and Randolph Scott, than by reality. The cattle drives across the prairies, the life under the stars, makes good movie material, but it's only sometimes true.

Today, chances are that, like at Dick Patterson's Arabian Ranch near Sisters north of Bend, Oregon, that you'll be driving llamas to the barn for shearing rather than cattle to slaughter.

Ranchers came into the Great Basin of Washington and Oregon in the 19th Century because it was perfect for cattle raising – there

Cattle barons

The cattle baron built huge empires much in the image of Ben Cartwright in the old Bonanza television series. They were two-fisted, hardheaded men who tolerated no nonsense and no interference from Indians, law enforcement officials, or homesteaders. And these ranches were huge. It has been said that rancher Henry Miller could ride from the Kern River in California up through Nevada to the Malheur River in Eastern Oregon without sleeping one night off his land.

The system was simple enough. You bought land and then hired someone to homestead a few acres around water. If you controlled a necklace of watering holes, you controlled the land around them.

The basic system of ranching remains much the same today. Three-quarters of huge Malheur County is still publicly owned and it is the seventh largest cattle country in the nation. The

Redmond, is a monument to the past, a town right out of the old west with wooden sidewalks, 1880s storefronts, and plenty of western hospitality. Some may find the tourist gimmick a bit hokey, but others will love it.

On a clear day, Sisters is exquisitely beautiful. Named after the three mountain peaks that dominate the horizon (Faith, Hope, Charity), it often seems a transplant from a movie set.

In June, the Sisters Rodeo brings in

private acreage is covered by irrigated crops. Sheepherding, which was in vogue during the late 19th and early 20th centuries, is no longer a big industry primarily because of a lack of labor.

These cold cattle barons were a ruthless, humorless lot who often had hearts of iron. One such was Pete French, an arrogant and forceful man whose empire included 100,000 acres on which there were 30,000 head of cattle and 3,000 horses.

While developing the ranch, he treated hundreds of local homesteaders the same way in which he treated cattle — evicting many of them from their squatters shacks. One of his enemies rode up to him one day and shot him dead. The killer was arrested and later acquitted by a jury of settlers.

Now, as with other industries, ranchers have to be flexible in what they raise and how they conduct their business. Some ranches, like Patterson's, have opened their gates to tourists and have turned some of the operations into dude ranches.

Llamas are seen fairly often around the Pacific Northwest. Patterson's llamas are used for pack animals on expeditions into the mountains as well as for pets and for wool production. Sheep ranchers in particular, like to have a llama or two around their stock because predators, like wolves and coyotes, hate their acrid smell.

The old French ranch empire still exists, though under a different name. Near Burns, the Roaring Springs Ranch is tucked under the west rim of the Steens Mountain. Originally homesteaded by Tom Wall, it was sold to Pete French. The dramatic backdrop, the well-kept ranch buildings, and the surrounding meadows makes the ranch seem as though it were built for a film.

about 50,000 people. Nearby is the world's largest llama breeding ranch at Dick Patterson's Arabian Ranch. A little more than 30 minutes away is the Hoodoo ski bowl, one of Oregon's most family oriented ski facilities.

Smith Rock, one of America's premier rock climbing areas.

Redmond

Redmond, the geographical center of Central Oregon, is the region's air gateway. It also has Eagle's Crest, a new resort with homes that rim an 18-hole golf course. To the north the spires of **Smith Rock** form sheer walls above the Crooked River.

Known as one of America's premier rock climbing areas, it draws an international standard of climbers. Smith Rock is surrounded by a 623-acre state park with several miles of hiking trails.

East of Redmond, following Highway 126 through the high desert to Prineville, a scenic rail trip offers dinner and brunch excursions into the Crooked

Pioneer days in the High Desert Museum.

Petersen's Rock Garden

Rasmus Petersen was an immigrant from Denmark who couldn't grow anything in the parched earth that passed for his farm near Redmond, Oregon. Born in 1883, he arrived in Central Oregon in 1906, built his home and gradually bought land until he had nearly 300 acres. But this was land that wasn't easily cultivated.

So, in 1935 he began scouring for pretty rocks and odd looking formations and found a lot of items he liked nearby and started building things. Soon, his idiosyncratic flight of fancy had produced a dramatic looking rock garden on four acres of his land.

Neighbors drove by and liked what they saw, dropped in to take a look, and had a meal and a coffee. Today, Petersen's Rock Garden is a tourist item, though Rasmus passed on some time ago, the victim of a heart attack in August, 1952. The garden consists of intricately detailed castles, towers, and bridges made of agate, jasper, lava, obsidian, malachite, petrified wood, and thunder eggs.

Petersen was both a nationalist and a religious man. There are numbers of miniature churches, the American flag, and the Statue of Liberty which a sculptor carved from a local boulder.

He maintained that the huge rock garden – handling all the stones and boulders – was nowhere near the amount of work he did in farming, year after year, plowing the fields and hauling off tons of rock.

Still owned and operated by his family, the gardens are located 2 1/2 miles (4 km) west of highway 97 between Redmond and Bend. Directional signs guide you.

A geology museum features a remarkable collection of crystals, local gemstones, and fossils. Free-roaming peacocks, chickens, antique farm implements and views of the snow-stacked Cascades add to the pleasant, down-home atmosphere.

All of it was culled from an 85 mile (137 km) radius of the garden. Ask the people who now operate the gardens and they'll tell you where to find some of the same items. In addition to the rock buildings, flags, towers, and arches, the grounds are adorned by flowers, fauna and placid ponds. There's a picnic area with tables, fireplaces and free-roaming peacocks, ducks and chickens to help you with lunch.

Admission is still by public donation, though a suggested "donation" of $2 for adults and $1 for children is recommended.

River Valley.

When coming from the west, you drop down to **Prineville** from tall bluffs into the valley that has hills dotted with junipers. The town is known as the gateway to the Ochocos, a heavily wooded mountain range that runs east and west for 50 miles (80.5 km). One of Oregon's least known recreational areas, the mountains are still pristine. If you continue along Highway 26, you'll eventually arrive at the John Day valley and the John Day Fossil Beds. (See: Box in Geography Chapter).

Desert country

While the mountain country is west of Bend, the desert lies to the east and south a short distance away. Six miles (9.6 km) south on Highway 97, the **High Desert Museum** includes, among other interesting things, a live animal education presentation. It has 20 acres of nature trails, and a variety of authentic period buildings.

The desert country contains some 90 mammals, 200 different kinds of

Lava River Cave.

birds, a dozen reptiles, and thousands of different plants. If you're planning to experience some of it, this is a good place to orientate yourself.

Across the highway the Lava Lands Visitor Center provides an overview of the region's volcanic features.

Middle and southern Oregon consists largely of lava. The interior of the state is essentially a plateau rising 4,000 feet (1,200 m).

Eruptions blanketed what was once forests to depths of hundreds of feet. As the mountains rose, they created a rain shadow.

The visitors center, though a small museum, is considered one of Oregon's geological showcases, the product of volcanic evolution.

A mesmerizing view of Mount Jefferson.

Winter in the Deschutes National Forest.

Lava caverns

Within the lava lands' 4,400 sq. miles is one of the most varied displays of volcanic features on the continent. The **Lava Cast Forest**, the result of eruptions from nearby Mount Newberry that covered the ponderosa pines. Lava casts of the trees remained after the wood had burned out or rotted.

The **Lava River Cave** is great for spelunkers. The tube, one mile (1.6 km) in length, was created when a river of lava began to cool, leaving a hard crust while molten material continued to flow underneath the surface. Once it drained away, it left a huge, walkable tube 50 feet (15 m) by 69 feet (18 m).

The lava lands are contained within **Deschutes National Forest** and within it are a variety of caverns with names like Wind Cave, Arnold Ice Cave, and Lava Icicle Cave, each with its own distinct formations. While the mountains and the lava have the most spectacular and most points of interest, it's the high desert that has the best stories of people who struggled there.

Lava Butte is one of over 400 cinder cones in a collection of more than 1,000 smaller volcanoes that comprise Newberry National Volcanic Monument, the West's newest offical Monument near the town of LaPine. Dedicated in 1961, the 56,000-acre park encompasses lakes, lava fields, and waterfalls. Cupped in the 5-mile (8-km)

Paulina Lake is one of Oregon's best fishing areas.

Guru Bhagwan

The ranch where Guru Bhagwan presided over.

religious movements during the preceding century, was to become a media event.

While he had studied the writings of Mahatma Gandhi, he shared little of the great India leader's

To some people the Bhagwan Shree Rajneesh was a nuisance, to others a great leader, and for some, just a glorified hoax. But, to most people in Oregon, he was the "Rolls Royce Guru".

In 1981, a red-clad group of people paid $6 million for one of the biggest cattle ranches in southern Oregon at Antelope. The rambling property was more than 100 square miles of dry hills and small gullies on the John Day River. Soon, the ranch was filled with 600 followers of Rajneesh from such scattered points as India and New Jersey. Some were well educated and monied, others not so.

The one element they had in common was absolute devotion to their leader, a 50-year-old, impish looking native of India. While denying his label as a spiritual leader or even as a founder of a cult, he said the colony – called Rajneeshpuram – was altruistic enough to be declared tax exempt.

So began the strange story of the Rolls Royce Guru who, in a land that had seen plenty of

philosophy. While Ghandi embraced poverty as a virtue, Rajneesh outwardly gathered luxury. By 1983 his follows had given him – and he had gratefully accepted – 21 luxury Rolls Royces. Two years later he had 90 of the cars.

Locals in the region – 135 inhabitants of nearby Antelope and the 2235 residents of Madras, 70 miles (113 km) away – looked upon the colony with controlled amusement.

Oregonians, used to strange wanderers and accepting of them as long as no one infringed on their neighbors, left them alone. While locals didn't particularly accept the sex, the smoking of pot, or the strange "family" collectives, no one took any action.

Rajneesh had been a character even in his own country. He liked to stir up people by making scandalous remarks and doing outlandish things. He had been fired from several prestigious teaching positions. But, Rajneesh made a mistake when he let it be known that he and his Rolls Royce driving group intended

caldera are Paulina and East Lakes, two of Oregon's best fishing areas. In the summer, naturalist-led walks and campfire programs are held at a small outdoor amphitheater.

Without doubt, the most scenic route between the Williamette Valley and the

Bend/Central Oregon region is via the MacKenzie Highway. If you drive in from Eugene, you pass through farm country alongside the McKenzie River.

At Foley Springs, after passing Proxy and Koosah Falls, you catch Highway 242 for the pass that takes you through

taking over the governments of nearby towns and the counties of Jackson and Waco.

He arrogantly flaunted his wealth. Accompanied by armed disciples he would drive one of his Rolls Royces to Madras where he would park near the supermarket, sit and smile imperceptibly while his guards bought him an ice cream soda.

The newcomers treated the locals with contempt, insulted them, and called them "rednecks" while threatening to take over their lives. The settlement was growing quickly with followers arriving every day. Plans were drawn for the building of a dam, a lake, an airstrip, a huge greenhouse, and vast farm fields. Ignoring prior water rights of the locals, Rajneesh demanded more water from the John Day River than they were entitled.

Rajneesh not only seemed to have access to endless amounts of money, but to legal minds as well. He discovered that to vote in an incorporated town in Oregon, one only needed to own a piece of property, spend 24 hours in town, and declare an intention to become a resident. So, Rajneesh bought an old building in which a number of members slept for one night, then demanded an election for which they would supply four candidates for the seven-member council.

The current council, in response, called for an election to unincorporate the town. Rajneesh supporters came to town and registered as voters. The final totals were 42 in favor and 67 against. Rajneesh had won. Calling a second vote for a city council, the Rajneesh faction won a 4-3 majority. The council then immediately voted to set aside a portion of the small municipal park for nude sunbathing. And the town's name was changed to Rajneesh. The situation deteriorated over time. Rajneesh opened his ranch to the masses and within a couple of months, 2,000 "homeless" including drunks, derelicts, and society's social rejects visited.

Degeneration of leadership

Lawsuits against Rajneesh and his group included a woman who claimed she had been swindled out of $310,000 – for which she was awarded $1.7 million in damages. At that point the leadership degenerated.

Rajneesh blamed the communes' problems with authorities – voter registration in the area was suspended and civil action taken in a number of disputes with the State – on his chief lieutenant, Ma Anand Sheela, also from India.

Sheela fled to Germany, and State and Federal investigators brought 35 charges against Rajneesh for a number of criminal offenses.

Eventually, Rajneesh was convicted of several charges including lying on his visa application and was given a 10-year prison sentence. It was suspended on his agreement to pay $400,000 in fines and to leave the country within five days, never to return.

To date none of the $55 million of cash and jewels listed in the commune's books have been found. The 93 Rolls Royces were sold at auction and bought by a Texas used car dealer. The property was sold at auction and bought for $4.5 million by Connecticut General Life Insurance Company, the mortgage holder.

Rajneesh died in India in January, 1990, and was cremated. The town's name is once again Antelope.

the mountains. Dee Wright Observatory, about halfway between ORE 126 and Sisters, offers views of Mount Jefferson, Mount Washington, and Three Sisters as well as the 8 mile-long (13 km) lava flow that bubbled out of nearby Yapoah a little less than 3,000 years ago.

Sawyer's Cave is on the right just past the junction of ORE 126 and U.S. 20. Classified as a lava tube, you can walk down through its cavern. You'll need a flashlight and a sweater. Watch both your head and your step.

This region is a mix of wildness and sophistication. It's dominated by the Rogue River, which begins at Boundary Springs, just north of Crater Lake National Park. It flows through a valley past the towns of Ashland, Medford and Grant's Pass, cuts through the Coast Range, and empties into the Pacific at Gold Beach. At several places it offers wild river rafting and high-speed jet-boat trips in a series of high adventure experiences. But, the region also offers Shakespeare at Ashland, and classical music at Jacksonville. It's a area where you can't experience just one kind of activity and still get an impression of what's available. If you're driving, carry a variety of clothing – some for going to the theater and some for water.

Redwood tree near the California border.

321

Corridor of the Northwest

This is the area that serves as the gateway to the Oregon Redwoods and to the coast. It's also the major funnel, via I-5, into

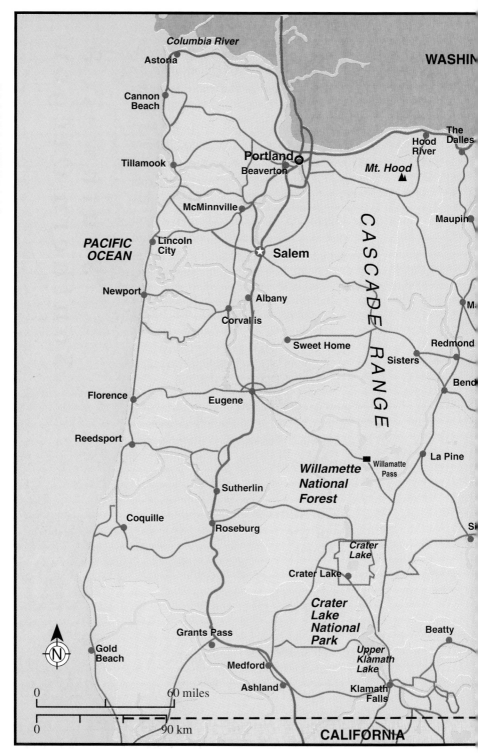

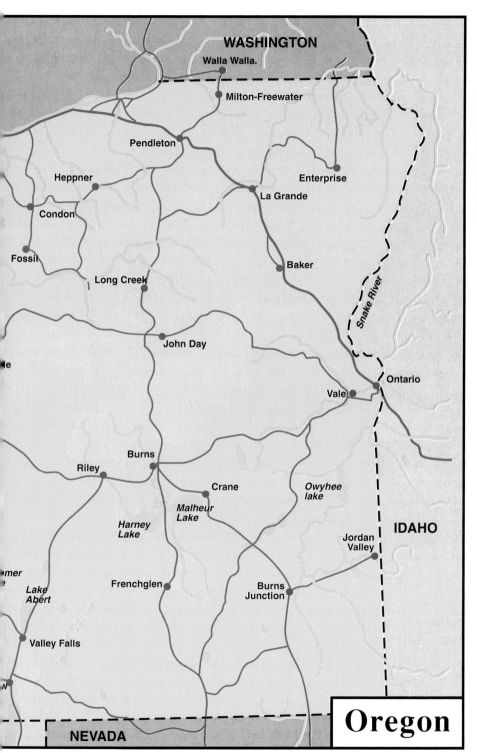

WASHINGTON

Walla Walla.

Milton-Freewater

Pendleton

Heppner

Enterprise

La Grande

Condon

Fossil

Baker

Long Creek

Snake River

John Day

le

Ontario

Vale

Burns

Riley

Crane

Owyhee
lake

Malheur
Lake

Harney
Lake

IDAHO

Jordan
Valley

mer
e

Lake
Abert

Frenchglen

Burns
Junction

Valley Falls

N

NEVADA

Oregon

Abandoned ranch in Southwest Oregon.

Northern California. South of the Williamette Valley and east of the Cascades, it is a corridor of the state marked by the V-shaped canyons of the Siskiyou Mountains.

As in other areas of the Pacific Northwest, white settlement in the 1850s led to bloodshed with the Rogue River Wars from 1851-56. In a pattern that was similar to the rest of the territories, the problems were resolved only when Indians were removed to a reservation in northwestern Oregon. That opened up the region for further white settlement.

Panning for gold, perhaps.

In the second half of the 19th Century, logging towns, farms communities, cattle ranches, and orchards sprung up in southwestern Oregon. But, the rural region also welcomed city culture. Vaudeville acts filled the saloons of Jacksonville in its earliest days and the Chautauqua movement brought lectures and entertainment to Ashland.

Applegate Trail

The old Applegate Trail is paralleled

today by I-5, linking the major cities of Ashland, Medford, Grant's Pass, and Roseburg leading up to Eugene and the Williamette Valley. A network of trans-Cascade routes cross the region, connecting cities and passing through some of Oregon's most scenic attributes.

There are eight scenic road tours available through the Southwest Oregon Visitor's Association ranging from a 24-mile historic drive from Ashland to Jacksonville, to a grand tour that literally circles the region from the California border up to Crater Lake, over to the coast, and then down coastal Highway 101 before looping back up to Grant's Pass and Medford.

If you arrive in the area by plane, commercial flights land at either Medford or Klamath Falls. The latter is also on Amtrak's main Pacific Coast line.

Medford/ Ashland

The Medford/Ashland area is easily reached via Highway 86 from Klamath Falls. Originally the home of the Rogue Indians and subsequently the corridor for the Oregon-California Railroad, it is steeped in history and has plenty of contemporary comforts.

Ashland is the home of the Oregon Shakespeare Festival (see: Arts and Culture Chapter) and from mid-February through October, produces 11 plays from the Bard to contemporary playwrights on three stages. "Festival of Plays" packages – which save you money without scrimping on amenities – are available from many of the area's 60 bed-and-breakfast inns. It's the highest number for a city of its size on the west coast.

While Ashland is relatively civilized during the non-summer months, be prepared for a human crush around June-September. The festival, now more than 50 years old, draws a total audience of more than 350,000 during the year and has a capacity of 94 percent.

Lately, Ashland has come into its own as a premier winter sports destination. In 1991, the owners of the Mount Ashland ski resort said they couldn't afford to keep up the ski lifts and runs. So, the town pulled together and raised enough money to buy the resort – mostly by donations and car washes.

While the permanent population is about 17,000, it often seems to be at least 10 times that in summer. Amazingly, however, the town never loses its charm. It seems like a small college town and has the atmosphere and appeal found in Cambridge or Oxford.

The theaters are remarkably open

to the public. For example, at the **Exhibit Center**, you can put on costumes from plays past and become an instant actor. There are lectures and concerts at noon daily, and excellent backstage tours in the mornings.

Music lovers combine theater with their specialty by attending Renaissance music and dance nightly in the courtyard. In addition, the marketing people of Ashland are astute enough to know that in the region is river rafting and picnicking and historical touring. So, packages for all these activities are easily available.

If you tire of Shakespeare, the **Actor's Theater of Ashland** is an experimental stage often called Off-Shakespeare. And the **Oregon Cabaret Theater** presents musicals and comedies through most of the year.

The best way to get tickets and information for the theater performances is by contacting Southern Oregon Reservation Center, P.O. Box 477, Ashland, OR 97520 or telephone (503) 488-1011 or (800) 547-8052.

The town's tour of art galleries, craft shops, boutiques, and restaurants is one of Oregon's most gentle and rewarding experiences. Thirteen of the town's Victorian homes are on the National Registry of Historical Places.

Ashland's **Southern Oregon State College** is the home of the Schneider Art Museum and the historical Chappell-Swedenburg House Museum.

The choices for lodging are numerous and include several attractive B&Bs like the Ashland Guest Villa, Edinburgh Lodge, Coach House Inn, Chanticleer, Romeo Inn, Fox House Inn, and The McCall House. Standard motels and hotels include The Palm Motel, Mark Anthony Hotel (National Landmark), Stratford Inn, Windmill's Ashland Mills Inn, and the Best Western.

The Mount Ashland Ski Area and the River Rogue Recreation Area, are nearby. Weisinger Ashland Winery, Ashland's Vineyards, and Rogue Brewery & Public House offer ample opportunity to sample Ashland products. The Weisinger winery is in a Bavarian-style building and the gift shop offers jams, jellies and wine. Out of town are the Royal Carter House, Neil Creek House, and Shute's Lazy S that caters to non-smokers and has a drama library where you can read up on the evening's Shakespeare presentation.

As you might expect, food in Ashland can be a delightful eating experience. At Chata, a few miles away from Ashland but worth the trip, a Paris-trained chef prepares sumptuous entrees. A huge chandelier hangs over the dining room. Traditional and nouvelle French fare can be had at Chateaulin, a restaurant in the most Shakespeare-looking interior in town with dark woods and stained glass windows.

Medford with a population of about 40,000 is the largest city in the region, a short trip up I-5 from Ashland. A more scenic route via Jacksonville is along Route 99. Oregon's pioneer past is carefully preserved in Jacksonville with about

90 original wooden and brick buildings dating back to the 1850s.

Surrounded by fruit-producing foothills, Medford is carved by Bear Creek. And along its shores are pathways, a nature trail, two city parks, tennis courts and facilities for outdoor summer concerts. The city is essentially a commercial and agriculture center and for years took a back seat to nearby Jacksonville whose boom-times ended in the 1880s. It's now a major retirement area because of its moderate weather and low cost of living.

The April Pear Festival and the Dixieland Jazz Festival in October headline the events calendar. A walk down Oakdale Avenue provides a tour past many of the city's original homes.

The new Southern Oregon Historical Society's History Center is downtown amidst antique shops, art galleries, and bookstores. **Railway Park**, a few blocks away from the Rogue Valley Mall, features miniature steam trains that run the second and fourth Sundays of every month. The town began as a stop on the California stagecoach route that connects Portland and Sacramento from the 1850s until the two states were connected by rail in the late 1880s.

The Visitor and Convention Bureau (1501 NE Sixth Street) provides information on boat and pack trips, many of which cover old mining territory. The **Schmidt House** was built around the turn of the century by Clauss and Hannchen Schmidt, German immigrants who homesteaded on the Rogue River in the 1880s. The house is preserved almost intact. In the vicinity are Jackson and Perkin's floral test Garden, and Harry and David's Country Store. The latter is an old-fashioned store that has fruit, veggies, and superb lines of cooked meats and delicacies famous throughout Southwestern Oregon.

Table Rocks

Table Rocks is 10 miles (16 km) northeast of Medford. The two eye-catching *mesas* are composed of sandstone with an erosion resistant lava cap. Over the years the wind and water have undercut the sandstone, with gravity pulling down the heavy basalt creating the nearly vertical slabs left today.

The site was where the decisive battle in the first of a series of Rogue Indian Wars in the 1850s was fought. A peace treaty was signed here. It became the center of the Table Rock Indian Reservation, but the reservation status was terminated soon after. The **Lower Table Rock Preserve** was created in 1979 near the westernmost mesa that towers 800 feet (244 m) above the valley floor.

Rogue River

You can take Highway 140 into the mountain lakes area or take Route 62 along the Upper Rogue River. Stop off at **Eagle Point** to see the historic Butte Creek Mill that has been grinding flour

Oregon Caves National Monument

It is not a place for anyone afraid of close spaces. For once you're deep down into the bowels of the earth, you can feel a bit closed in. Located about 50 miles (48 km) southwest of Grants Pass it's reached by taking US 199 to Cave Junction where the turnoff to Oregon Caves National Monument at ORE 46 takes you an additional 20 miles to the caves.

Now under restoration to clear rubble Depression era work left behind when workers diverted a river and cut trails in the Caves, the Monument has more than 3 miles of passageways lined with stalagmites, flowstone, translucent draperies, and cave coral. Tours take you through the Ghost Room, Paradise Lost, and the River Styx. But a lot of climbing is involved and not recommended for anyone with respiratory or heart problems.

Actually, the Monument is only one cave that opens into a succession of caverns formed over millions of years by the action of water. Simply put, they were created as rain and snowmelt seeped through cracks and fissures in the rock above the cave and percolated down into the underlying limestone. Huge sections of the limestone saturated and collapsed. When the water table eventually lowered, these pockets were drained and the process of cave "decoration" began. High in the Siskiyou Mountains, the caves have been attracting visitors since a local hunter, Elijah Davidson, chased a bear into them in 1874.

It's not a hot-spot of tourist activity and that's its charm. The cave is located at the head of an isolated and wooden canyon. That, plus the fact it's remote from population and sits at 4,020 feet (1,226 m), accounts for its late discovery. The tours are mandatory if anyone wants to explore.

Before entering the cave, the guide explains that visitors should dress warmly to offset the constant 45°F (5°C) temperature no matter how warm it is outside. Children under the age of 6 are not permitted inside the cave.

The gorgeous formations inside the cave were formed – and still are, for that matter – when limestone was dissolved by the water and carried in solution into the cave. When the water evaporated it left behind a microscopic layer of dust. This process was repeated countless times, gradually creating the wonderous formations seen inside today. When the minerals are deposited on the ceiling, a stalactite begins to grow. Limestone water that evaporates on the floor might become stalagmite. When they meet, they become a column.

Other cave sculptures include helicites – oddly bent formations that twist and turn in varied directions – and draperies, that look as their name implies and formed from water that flowed with more volume. As the tour progresses, there are vivid examples of every formation. The largest column in the cave is **The Grand Column** and **The Banana Grove** flowstone draperies resemble clusters of grapes.

Joaquin Miller's Chapel is named after a regional poet who visited the cave in its early days and then became involved in having it declared a national monument. The **Ghost Room**, is the largest of the cavities, about 250 feet (76 m) in length.

The tour exits at a spot a couple of hundred feet (61 m) higher than where you enter and the walk down is along a steep trail to the entrance. But you can also walk uphill to the **Cliff Nature Trail** which links up with a variety of trails in the region including the **Big Tree Trail Loop** which will provide spectacular views of the surrounding mountains and valleys.

The **Oregon Caves Chateau** is a rustic, six-story lodge that offers accommodation and food for anyone who wants to stay awhile. The chateau, open only June through September, itself is a wonder with a large, double fireplace in marble, big picture windows, a grand dining room and a creek that runs through it.

since 1873. Lost Creek Dam and Recreation Area features Oregon's largest fish hatchery and a fine state park. From here it's a gorgeous drive to Crater Lake.

Grant's Pass is the headquarters for licenced guides who lead expedi-

A worthy catch!

tions on the wild Rogue River. You'll often see and hear the river described in those terms – wild, scenic, scary. Those are accurate descriptions but nevertheless, thousands of people take the river tour without consequence.

Many first-time visitors introduce themselves to the Rogue by a jetboat tour over the water which brings them past wildlife and Indian burial grounds and under canyon walls, to arrive at Grave Creek where the "Wild and Scenic" stretch of the Rogue begins. Beyond this point, the river earns its reputation and there are 25 different outfitters waiting to take you through the wildest sections.

A paved road follows the length of the river from Agness to the ocean and south of the river to Agness from Grant's Pass. Southwest of Grant's Pass the Redwood Highway enters the Illinois Valley. Selma, Cave Junction, Kerby, and O'Brien are the valley's population centers.

Kerby

The Kerbyville Museum has displays of the area gold rush. Oregon's first gold strike was made on a tributary of the Illinois River in 1851. This is the route to Oregon Caves National Monument. Guided tours past the intriguing canyons are offered year 'round from April through Labor Day. The Oregon Caves Chateqau has accommodations and

Rogue River rafting – an unforgettable adventure!

dining in its old wooden lodge. Side trips are merited to the fishing resort at Lake Selmac and into the Kalmiopsis Wilderness, named after a shrub that has survived since the Ice Age.

Roseburg

Roseburg is the Northwestern gateway to Crater Lake and the center for tours into the Umpqua Valley. One of the Northwest's most scenic highways is ORE 138 which leads northeast from Roseburg into the high Cascades through the Umpqua National Forest and into Diamond Lake. While Roseburg might look like a community to pass through, it does have some hidden charm and

attractions. The area has five wineries open for tours and tastings – Davidson, Henry, Girardet, Callahan Ridge, and Hillcrest. The Roseburg Visitors and Convention Bureau offers three driving tours that take in much of the area's scenic attractions.

Wildlife Safari allows you to drive through rolling country to see a semi-natural wildlife preserve with predators separated from their prey. There are places from which you can watch baby animals closeup.

The **Douglas County Museum** displays logging, fur trapping, and pioneer items on an attractive, contemporary structure. And be sure that you stop off at K&R's Drive Inn where you get huge amounts of Umpqua ice cream. Located

In touch with nature, camping along the river.

20 miles north of Roseburg, you'll find the parking lot continually full.

The economic lifeline of the Douglas County region depends on the lumber activity in the Umpqua with 75 percent of the county's workers directly or indirectly dependent on the timber industry.

Umpqua

The North Umpqua and South Umpqua rivers join northeast of Roseburg to form the main branch of the Umpqua which continues through the forests to the Pacific. One of the star attractions of the north Umpqua is found at the Steamboat Inn, arguably the best of the re-

gion's lodging facilities. With only 15 units, the Inn is usually booked well in advance. But the restaurant alone is worth the stop.

The town itself is filled with historic homes, antique and collectible shops, B&Bs and a variety of attractions. On the way there from Medford on I-5, you'll pass the **House of Mystery** at the Oregon Vortex – a sort of inland Bermuda Triangle. Called the "Forbidden Ground" by the Rogue Indians because the place spooked their horses, the vortex is actually a repelling magnetic field where objects tend to move away from their alignment and move in funny directions.

In the same area is **Gold Gulch**, a recreated early-day gold mining town

Bigfoot

The legend of Bigfoot has been a part of Pacific Northwest lore as long as there have been people here. Essentially, it is considered by those who accept its existence to be a sub-human creature with an appearance and posture vaguely resembling those of a man and habits and mentality of an animal. In Canada, he is called Sasquatch while in the Northwest, including California, he's called Bigfoot.

It is thought to be omnivorous, possessed of an enormous physical strength, and to be generally non-aggressive to man though apparently curious about him. It has been called the Abominable Snowman of North America and indeed much of the reference to it and the descriptions of it are paralleled by those linked to the Yeti of the Himalayas. But, it also appears that the big fellow has been around for a while. Under a variety of names it is found in the culture of virtually all North American Indians and in many of Central and South America. Over the past 100 years, he has been seen in California, Washington, Oregon, and British Columbia and the sighting are uniformly similar.

While there are variations on the descriptions of hair color and length, of body bulk and height, the average description is uniform. It is of a hairy, brownish humanoid creature, upwards of 1,000 pounds (450 kg), walks upright and takes 6 to 8 foot (1.8-2.4 m) strides.

It communicates by way of a high-pitched whistling scream and leaves footprints up to 24 inches (155 cm) long and 8 inches (131 cm) wide. Many of the foot prints suggest a foot structure identical to the human foot and they leave impressions several inches deep on surfaces where a heavy man makes scarcely a mark.

Earliest references

The earliest known recorded references are found on the carved totem poles and masks of the coast Indians in British Columbia. But he also appears in legends of the Salish Indians in Western Washington.

The creature's intrinsic malevolence is contained in the legend about how a group of Indians burned alive a family of the creatures to whom they ascribed cannibalistic qualities. The ashes turned into mosquitoes and such was the beginning of that source of torment.

To the Indians, there was nothing terribly mythical about the creature. It existed in their day-to-day world and it was not something to be messed with.

It was an old man of the Salish People who said, when Bigfoot began to command attention in the media, "So, the white man has finally got around to that, has he?"

The artist Paul Kane, who chronicled in his paintings the western movement in the mid-19th century, mentions in his diaries that the local Indians at the mouth of the Kattlepoutal River, 26 miles (42 km) from Vancouver, Washington, reports the Indians never visited Mount St. Helens. The reason? The Indians knew it was the resident home of the big, furry creature. The legends have kept Bigfoot researcher, Rene Dahinden, busy for most of his adult life. For the past 30 years he has searched out people who have seen, heard, smelled, and even filmed the beast.

Sightings

Bigfoot's continuing saga is made more current by periodic sightings. The Deputy Sheriff of Grays Harbor County in Washington has provided one of the most detailed descriptions of the many night-sightings of Big Foot. The Sheriff of Skamania County in Washington made a cast of a footprint that was 22 inches (56 cm) long.

Even the Russians have done serious research on the creature. The late head of History at the Academy of Science in Moscow was convinced that his own evidence indicated the probable existence of what he called "the surviving remains of a branch of Neanderthals diverse regions of the world."

Just in case someone does capture one, there's a reward. Project Bigfoot in Seattle has posted an offer of $1,000 (a pittance for such a discovery, really) to anyone finding any verifiable remains.

Skull, hair, bones – anything – is eligible.

Stretch along the Umpqua river.

that can be either tacky or informative depending on your point of view. There are several unique displays outlining how mining was done on the frontier. There's also a gambling den, blacksmith shop and a walk into Millionaire Mine to see a real quartz gold vein.

And north of town is **Wolf Creek Tavern**, Oregon's oldest hostelery. Originally a hotel for the California and Oregon Stagecoach line, the property is now owned and operated by the State of Oregon as a restaurant and hotel. President Rutherford B. Hayes visited here in the late 1880s, and author Jack London stayed and wrote part of his novel, *The End Of The Story*.

The facility is a surprisingly wonderful and first-rate operation. The food feature locally-grown products and there's a wide selection of choice. The rooms are a delight for anyone who wants to combine contemporary standards with by-gone era style.

Southern Oregon – Sand & Mountains

One historian has called it the loneliest road in Oregon, Highway 20 out of Bend southeast to Burns and through Or-

egon's Old West. No major road rides the desert so completely and for so long. It is the bleakest, ghost-ridden, poignant, and yet is mysteriously awesome in its openness and parched drama.

Highway 20 cuts across the high desert that makes up Central Oregon, a vast plateau of unirrigated soil that settlers once tried to farm, not knowing when they bought their land from speculators and fast-buck artists, that it was utterly unsuitable for farming. They plowed up land meant to rest; put in crops that never had a chance to grow. Eventually most had to leave as dust storms and despair drove them out.

Today the desert lands are of little farm use except for cattle grazing. The occasional small windswept and sunbleached shack on the road is grim evidence of the broken dreams and the heartbreak that stalked everyone who tried valiantly to tame the cheerless landscape.

The names of the region tell a lot of the story – Hole in The Ground, Glass Buttes, Fort Rock, Devil's Garden, Fossil Lake, and Lost Forest. But the names and the failure of settlers to bring the land under control are only part of the story of this wonderfully stark land. It is, to many people, the most spectacular of Oregon's physical wealth.

Awesome frontier of the Oregon desert.

East of that line is an enormous openness and where travel is marked by caution. It's not easy to travel in that region, but the careful and prudent adventurer – during the summer months – can experience some of its grandeur.

Before you drive in this area, make certain your car is stocked with a cooler for soft drinks and snacks and take some camping gear because hotels and motels are few and far between. And, yes, there are rattlesnakes so you shouldn't overturn large rocks or go searching off into dark holes on your own.

In the winter, it can be cold and even dangerous with high winds and a mix of blowing snow and dust to confuse the inexperienced. Yet, there is skiing in the area and enough traffic on the highways to keep you company. Summer sports include whitewater rafting, hang gliding, and rockhounding.

Massive desert

How large is it? Well, the land encompasses nearly a third of Oregon's entire mass and the high-desert plateau has awesome geologic formations. Expect sheer cliffs, huge rocks, ponderosa pine and aspen, sagebrush and wildlife. The region averages less than 10 inches (24 cm) of rain a year and the temperatures range from 80-100°F (26.6-37.7°C) most summer days.

Three counties make up the southeastern-most corner of the state cover-

Solitude in the desert.

with a band of sheep and in time had the biggest herd of cattle and sheep in the state. It once covered 38,000 acres (15,380 hectares). He adored Mickey Hutton, one of the few women in the area. He made a diamond brooch in the form of his cattle-brand and placed it around her neck, announcing that anyone wearing his brand belonged to him.

Hutton didn't like the implication, took off the brooch necklace, threw it on the floor, and stomped on it. Brown never fully recovered from that rejection and his farm seems somehow the appropriate conclusion to his love.

Traveling the roads of southern Oregon can be smooth sailing on a paved highway or it can be an adventure along a dusty, never-ending dirt ribbon through the desert.

By all means, know where you're going before you turn off the main roads. But, if you're prepared with water and a full tank of gas, it's an adventure that can pay dividends in bringing you closer to the land.

The Lost Forest

The Lost Forest is found by driving along a dirt road intersecting Highway 20 at Buffalo Well between Brothers and Hampton. You'll find Lost Forest about 32 miles (51.5 km) later. It is lost because it's in a barren area with rainfall that supposedly can't sustain it.

Existing in a wasteland devoid of streams or springs, the 9,000 acre (3,640

ing 28,450 sq. miles. Yet there's a population of only 43,000 or so. The towns can vary in size from Burns – at the uppermost part of the region – with 7,000 population to the small town of Wagontire on Route 395, south of Riley, population seven.

Much of its charm is hidden, not to be discovered by those who race through it. Yes, there's the heat, the dryness, and the vast openness that sometimes frightens the senses, but there's also an eerie calm about the desert that caresses the imagination.

At the broken down, deserted remnants of **Gapp Ranch**, about 80 miles (129 km) out of Bend, the legend of Bill Brown is typical of the region.

Brown came to the drylands in 1880

One of the few hotels in the Oregon desert.

hectare) forest of ponderosa pine manages to thrive. The reason might be the layer of compact volcanic ash beneath the sandy soil, trapping what little moisture there is.

The Lost Forest is a remnant of the millions of acres of pine, hardwood, and palm trees that covered the then-wet, lake-rich plateau 10,000 years ago. Any change in the delicate ecological balance could wipe it out overnight.

And while you're in the neighborhood, stop off at **Fort Rock** with its Fort Rock Cave where 75 woven sagebrush

Jacksonville

Jacksonville,
historic gold-mining
town.

(One of the great contradictions of Oregon is that the heart of its cultural existence is not in its largest city, Portland, but in its heartland. So, unlike virtually every other state in America, two small communities – Ashland and Jacksonville – hold the key to Oregon's cultural richness.

Ashland, of course, has its Shakespeare festival for nine months of the year and even exports its staging to Portland for five months of theater activity in a separate package.

Jacksonville, on the other hand, not only has its fine Peter Britt Music Festival (held the ballroom of the U.S. Hotel and on the Peter Britt Estate) but is also one of the finest examples of early Oregon to be found in the state.

Located 5 miles west of Medford, this small town of 2,100 residents with 90 original wooden and brick buildings dating back to the 1850s, was the first designated National Historic Landmark District in Oregon and the third such site in the nation to be so named. The early history of the town, settled by gold miners in the 1850s, resembled that of other gold towns. The mines were rich, money was abundant, gambling rampant, and women in short supply.

An epidemic of smallpox, a flood, and a fire

devastated the city in the late 1860s and 1870s, but the rebuilt community – created in anticipation of a railroad that never arrived – managed to survive.

Early beginnings

Jacksonville had its beginnings in 1852 when two prospectors, passing through to California, discovered a gold nugget in a hoof print made by one of their horses next to the river by which they had camped the night before.

They continued onwards, but rushed back after discovering their secret had leaked out. Within a matter of weeks of staking claims along Rich Gulch and Daisy Creek, 2,000 men crowded the area. Tents and wooden shacks were quickly built and the town of Rock City was born, only to be changed to Jacksonville the following year in honor of President Andrew Jackson.

At one time it was the county seat and was even considered as a candidate for the state capitol. But the building of the railroad through Medford meant businesses moving eastward to that community and it becoming the county seat.

Oddly, the Great Depression meant a revival of the town with out-of-work families taking up

sandals were found in 1938. They were preserved and then carbon tested in 1949 and found to be 9,000 years old.

Nearby is **Devil's Garden**, likely

the most inhospitable section of the desert, a 4,200-acre area walled-in by a rim of lava. Here, among the juniper and sagebrush and broken lava, the

residence in the old buildings for cheap rent. Residents dug small shafts in backyards looking for gold and eventually interest in Jacksonville's gold heritage had its effect and old buildings began to be restored. The first was the Beekman Express and Banking Office, followed by the United States Hotel. Today, Jacksonville is a classic western town that seems right out of a Hollywood movie set. It has been used for several films including the television movie, *Inherit The Wind*.

In mid-June, Pioneer Days features a parade, a street fair, as well as an old time fiddlers competition. And the ongoing music festival produces world class classical, jazz, and bluegrass musicians such as Mel Torme, Jean Pierre Rampal, and B.B. King.

California Street, the heart of Jacksonville, is a walk back through time with the brick buildings beautifully restored.

But the first stop should be at the **Jacksonville Museum of Southern Oregon History** on Fifth Street where you'll find detailed exhibits of gold mining, Takelma Indian artifacts, and railroad history. In addition to the pioneer artifacts is a section on Peter Britt with a mockup of his studio. The stucco building next door used to be the county jail, but is now the **Children's Museum** where old toys are given hands-on inspection.

The **Jacksonville Doll Museum** – which used to be McCully House – contains nearly every doll contained in the Blue Book of Dolls with the oldest being a 1640 Italian creche doll with carved ivory head and hands.

The **McCully House Inn** (1861) is built in the classical revival style and is a Bed and Breakfast completely decorated in rugs and furniture of the time. Other B&Bs include the Touvelle House (1916), the Colonial House (1917), and the Reames House (1868).

At the Jacksonville Cemetery are the graves of Britt, C.C. Beekman, and other local notables.

only sound is the wind. Only one road enters it, 15 miles (24 km) northeast of Fort Rock. Ask at the local store in Fort Rock how to get there. In fact, this kind of exploration – word of mouth – is the most effective way of meeting locals and of finding the right routes in this part of Oregon.

The dry beds of Fossil and Silver Lakes have long been a favorite of fossil hunters and archeologists. The region is also good for rockhounds and photographers, especially at Four Craters and Crack In The Wall that is in the same general region as The Lost Forest and Fort Rock.

Blue Bucket Mine

No story is so enduring as the tale of the Blue Bucket Mine, because it was the old Blue Bucket that led to immigration of settlers in the region. Many versions of the story persist, but all talk of the finding of gold nuggets somewhere between the Snake and Deschutes rivers by one or more members of the disoriented Meek's Cutoff Party – the lost wagon train – of 1843, that was seeking a shortcut to the Williamette Valley.

Instead of a new route, they encountered starvation and death on a tortuous journey on the desert along the Ochoco Mountains. They eventually found the Crooked River and followed it north to The Dalles.

During the trip, children were sent to fetch water in a bucket and yellow metal was discovered in the bottom of the blue pail. A few of the larger pieces were flattened out and used as sinkers for fishing. The balance were simply left

Sandhill crane in the Malheur National Wildlife Refuge.

in the pail because the settlers didn't know what they had. It took the discovery of gold in California, three years later, for the lost wagon trailers to catch on to their find. But the route of the wagons were impossible to retrace. That there never was a mine, as such, hasn't diminished the importance of the story. Because of the search for the Blue Bucket, miners did come to the area, spread out, and gold was indeed found in places.

Miners searching for the location were the only ones in the desert prior to 1862 when the Homestead Law was passed. It gave any U.S. citizen 160 acres (64 hectares) of public land for $1.25 an acre. Later the acreage was doubled and redoubled.

The resulting march into the region produced a boom for hucksters and frauds. But, only three towns still remain along Highway 20 between Bend and Burns – Riley, Hampton, and Brothers.

In the late 19th-century there had been numerous small communities and many ranches, producing ranges wars of film fame. Battles between cattlemen and sheep herders were commonplace and thousands of sheep were slaughtered by angry cattlemen who claimed the animals were overgrazing on the native grasses.

Burns is the entry point into the 183,000 acre Malheur National Wildlife Refuge and is one of the largest in the 48 lower states. There are a staggering number of birds in the area – eagles, hawks, owls, cranes, ducks, geese, song-birds, about 250 species.

The city is named after the Scottish poet, Robert Burns, and today has few reasons for existing except for the Refuge. Malheur Lake and Harner Lake provide all of the water they need, so the wildlife, including deer, coyote, muskrat, beaver and weasal, thrive.

Beyond Burns, the land is a combination of dramatic vastness. If you have the time continue on Highway 20, crossing into Idaho at Ontario, then down to Boise before making the circle trip back on Highway 95. It's spectacular in its stark brightness.

Far East

Few major roads run through the furthest southeastern portions with Route 395 from California and U.S. 95 in from Idaho and south to Nevada being the most traveled. Unless you're comfortable driving dirt roads, you cannot drive east to west along the extreme southern portion unless you come in through Nevada on Route 140 through the Charles Sheldon Antelope Range and link up with Route 395 just north of Lakeview.

Burns Junction, at the intersection of Route 95 and ORE 78, if you're arriving from Idaho, is a decision point. Highway 87 takes you to Burns and from there you can follow Highway 20 to Bend. If you go left along Route 95, you end up in Nevada where you can

eventually link up with highway 140.

But this is an area that begs to ride the lesser established routes. In fact, the entire area is laced by the Southeast Oregon Auto Tour that takes in 170 geologic, historic, wildlife, ranching, and recreation activities. A guide of the many loops and routes is available at all offices regionwide.

Southeast of Burns are **Malheur Cave** and **Diamond Craters**, one of the most diverse basaltic regions in the country. A drive up the gradual slope of Steens Mountain will take you to 9,000 feet (2,743 m) above the desert floor.

Dry, Alvord Lake and the Alvord Desert can be seen a mile below. The 150-mile (241-km) Desert Hiking Trail is divided into six sections, with guided tours available with maps and information available at tourism offices in Burns.

Lake Owyhee

Lake Owyhee is Oregon's longest lake and the man-made water body - the result of Owyhee Dam – has miles of striking desert topography along its shores. It is near the Idaho border and reached by taking Route 201 south from Ontario and then a county road that stops at the lake.

Along the shores are bighorn sheep (they can actually be seen), secluded beaches and volcanic tuft formations at Leslie Gulch where Indian writings and artifacts are hidden within the canyon formations.

N ot far from Huntington, north of Farewell Bend, are deep ruts in the earth, part of what's left of the old Oregon Trail.

Nearby a small iron cross marks the spot where Indians killed immigrants in 1860. As at many other locations throughout Northeast Oregon, it's just another reminder of one of the most glorious and romantic adventures in the history of America.

Northeast Oregon is more than just the ongoing wasteland many people assume. This part of the state also has high mountains with offshoots of downhill skiing, cross-country skiing, and other outdoor activities amidst lakes, streams, and stunning scenery. The Pendleton Roundup and Hells Canyon Recreational Area are big tourist spots.

The region's economy is based on agriculture, cattle, and log- g i n g and,

Wallowa Valley in Northeast Oregon.

Northeast Oregon

345

The Oregon Trail passed through Fort Light in Northeast Oregon.

accordingly is susceptible to downturns in the economy. High unemployment rates are often a reality. So too is a sense of community spirit. People look out for one another and it's not uncommon for cars to stop if you've pulled over on a side road to ask if you need help.

But, the defining factor of this region – the one binding force that gives it identity is what folks here call simply, "The Trail". For the Oregon Trail was more than just a route. It was a migration; a movement west; an integration of peoples, ideas, and ideals.

It was the artery for 350,000 emigrants who settled the American West by walking and driving their covered wagons 2000 miles to the West Coast in the mid-1800s. More than 53,000 of those people settled in Oregon after traveling the route nicknamed "The Longest Graveyard".

Wagon ruts

The trail's route began in St. Joseph and Independence, Missouri and proceeded through a series of forts – Kearny, Laramie, Bridger, Hall, Boise – through the states of Missouri, Kansas, Nebraska and Wyoming to the final destination of Oregon City. Only about 300 miles of discernible wagon ruts and 125 historical sites are between St. Louis, MO and Portland. The old trail generally follows I-84 through Baker City, The Dalles, and Ontario and generally bisects the upper part of the state.

Summer temperatures are in the high 90s°F (30s°C), cooling quickly after sundown. Winter conditions vary regionally, from deep powder snow in the Wallowa mountains to chilly temperatures in the valleys. Relatively mild weather is the norm in Pendelton and the farming regions close to the Columbia River.

At Baker City's National Historic Oregon Interpretive Centre you can walk along the old wagon ruts for 15 miles. You can do the same around the Pendelton area in the mountain country of Northeastern Oregon. At **Farewell Bend State Park** on the Snake River, north of the Baker County line, the wagon trains left the Snake for the Columbia River. This section – over the Blue Mountains – was one of the toughest sections of the trip.

In Oregon City, **McLoughlin House** has exhibits at the official end of the trail, and downtown Portland's **Oregon Historical Center** has an overall presentation of what it all meant.

Nez Perce Indians

The northeast region of Oregon is unpopulated. It is cattle country, national forests, wildlife refuges, recreation areas, and small towns. The first immigrants to this part of America described it as looking poverty stricken and falling short of expectations. But the local native peoples, the Nez Perce, had a different view of the land and took advantage of its varied topography and weather patterns.

They spent winters in the canyons of the Grand Ronde, Imnaha, and Snake Rivers and summers in the Wallowa Valley and near Wallowa Lake. They fished for trout and salmon, hunted for big game like elk and bighorn sheep, and ate berries. The same land that provided them with sustenance, however, were a challenge to settlement with harsh conditions in the mountains, the rugged canyons, and the hot deserts.

It was gold in Idaho, Montana, and eastern Oregon in 1860/61 that brought massive immigration to the region and eventually led to war between the Nez Perce and the Federal Government.

Pressured by increasing white settlement, the government entered into a series of treaties and agreement with the Nez Perce, only to break many of them.

In 1877, Nez Perce Chief Joseph and his people trekked 1,800 miles (2,896 km) battling U.S. Army troops only to surrender in the Bear Paw Mountains of Montana. Today, the same natural attraction that the Nez Perce found both mystical and life-giving – at the John Day Fossil Beds, Hells Canyon Recreational Area, Malheur National Wildlife Reserve, and many others – draw naturalists, hikers, white-water enthusiasts, and skiers.

The region's towns are small, scattered, and centers for the local industries of cattle raising, lumber, and agriculture. Many ghost towns, remnants of

Remnants of the past – mail boxes in a ghost town.

the old gold trail settlements – dot the landscape.

Towns along the Trails

Ontario, the first town on the Oregon

side of the trail, was also a relocation center for Japanese Americans who were evacuated from the Pacific Coast during the Second World War. In one of America's darkest civil rights moments, President Roosevelt signed a declaration forcing 5,000 Americans of Japanese ances-

Howard Johnson Motel that accepts well-mannered pets.

While today it is now a logging and cattle town, **Baker City** was once the hub of the eastern Oregon gold rush. In 1890 its population swelled to 6,600, making it larger than Spokane or Boise, Idaho.

At the U.S. National Bank downtown is an 80.4 ounce gold nugget, the "Armstrong", that was found in 1913 and just one reminder of the riches the region gave up to prospectors.

The **Oregon Trail Regional Museum** and the **Eastern Oregon Museum** offer period artifacts. At Flagstaff Hill the 23,000 sq. foot National Historic Oregon Trail Interpretive Center, operated by the Bureau of Land Management houses a theater, artifacts, and recreations including a mining camp and encampment.

Eventually you come to the trail itself. In town, a 124-room Best Western Motel is better than average and A Domain B&B offers a pleasant alternative with legendary breakfasts.

Nearby are the old goldmining towns of Bourne, Sparta, Granite, Sumpter, Cornucopia and Copperfield, all ghost towns now with sagging buildings and abandoned equipment.

Copperfield

Copperfield was the toughest of the tough mining camps with saloons, whorehouses, dancehalls, gambling

try to liquidate their property and move into prison-like barracks in remote sections of the West.

Many of the internees stayed in the region after the war and are now well represented in the local business and agriculture communities. A museum documenting the internment is at Treasure Valley Community College. It has a

Snake River

The river is aptly named. Like a large serpent, it twists and slinks its way 1,000 miles (1,609 km) through four states. A chief tributary of the Columbia, it rises in Yellowstone National Park in Wyoming and flows south through Jackson Lake and southwest into Idaho where it is joined by Henry's fork and then runs southwest and northwest across Idaho and then bends into Oregon before turning north to flow into the Columbia near Pasco, Washington.

Its major claim to fame is the Hells Canyon, carved out by the Snake over millions of years and which averages 6,600 feet (2,011.6 m) in depth for 15 miles (24 km) and 5500 feet (1,676 m) for 40 miles (64.3 km). The Snake River Gorge portion is 20 miles (32 km) long and averages 6,000 feet (1,828 m) in depth.

In 1975, Congress established the Hells Canyon National Recreation Area, a region that provides stunning vistas, native ruins, and the thundering flow of the Snake.

The rush of the Snake River through the gorge is indeed impressive, flowing at twice the volume of the Colorado River's journey through the Grand Canyon. Rapids occur with incredible frequency and from river level it seems like a ribbon of foaming energy. Slowed somewhat now by the backwaters of three Idaho Power Company dams – Brownlee, Oxbow, and Hells Canyon – there was a time when the Snake between Farewell Bend and Lewiston was the west's wildest river.

Since boats ran on its lower reaches, the federal government classified it as a navigable river, but in Hells Canyon that was only due to superhuman efforts. Those who did were searching for gold. In its history, only one man ever succeeded in bringing a craft upstream. Many died.

The Nez Perce Indians never even tried, giving the canyon a wide berth in their journeys. One look at into the barren gorge still generates a sense of respect and fear. The somber hue of the rock-faced lava walls, the endless gorges slicing into the trench, the barren and impassable hills, and the meandering sea of mountains combine to form an overpowering portrait of desolation and sterility.

Yet, these are the elements that also make it one of the most starkly beautiful places in Oregon. The silence is overwhelming, the purity of light casts a deceiving crystalline softness.

Exploring Snake Country

While it's one of the great natural wonders of the Pacific Northwest, it's also one of the most dangerous to anyone tempted to explore on their own. Weather conditions dictate most activities and this is rattlesnake country. Wise hikers takes a snake bite kit, water, and some food when walking in the region.

From Joseph, recently paved Route 129 is the most scenic route. Well maintained, you can drive for miles along it – even in summer months – without seeing another car. It joins Route 86 at the southern end of Wallowa National Forest where you have the choice of heading west to Baker City or taking a sidetrip to the Snake River and the Oxbow dam.

From Baker, Route 86 is the easiest, paved all the way to halfway where you should stock up on groceries and gasoline. By crossing the Snake into Idaho, you drive another 30 miles (48 km) to Hells Canyon Dam, the last one before the most rugged canyon stretch is reached. But, locals take a little known, more difficult route through Cuprum, Idaho to Kinney Point and ultimately to Sheep Rock for the best views from overhanging shelves into the folded hills.

In the Wilderness, vehicles are prohibited but are allowed in the Recreation Area. Most float trips begin just below Hells Canyon Dam and jet-boat trips start at Lewiston, Idaho or in Clarkson, Washington.

dens, and with gun fights the daily norm. There were no jails and the local law was a joke, unable to maintain order.

The governor in Salem threatened to impose martial law, but was told that if he showed up in town he'd be shot.

Sumpter, an abandoned gold-mining town.

Eventually, the town burned to the ground, several months after a sprightly diminutive woman, Fern Hobbs, confronted the town officials and demanded their resignation.

They laughed at all 105 pounds (47.5 kg) of her. But she had brought along her own assemble of burly prison guards, the state penitentiary warden, and an order from the governor imposing martial law. The resignations came quickly and the town began to civilize itself.

John Day

The town of **John Day** was named after a scout of John Jacob Astor's overland expedition in 1811. The town prospered as a pony express station on the route from The Dalles to Canyon City during the gold strikes in Idaho, Montana, and Eastern Oregon. It eventually became the ranching center it is today.

The **Kam Wah Chung & Co. Museum** in a restored building that served as a trading post in the late 1860s, records the history of the town and of the Chinese community in the gold rush. The entire region was developed on gold. Hundreds of Chinese came to work the mines and towns like Canyon City, Burns, and Prairie City owe their existence to the yellow stuff.

The **John Day Fossil Beds National Monument**, encompassing more than 14,000 acres, contains fossils of vegeta-

John Day Fossils contains fossils up to 45 million years ago.

tion and animals that flourished in the area up to 45 million years ago. It's 40 miles (64 km) away.

Joseph

Joseph was named for the two great Nez Perce Chiefs, Old and Young Joseph. The town is the site of the **Wallowa County Museum** containing displays on the Nez Perce and early pioneer days. Old Joseph's grave is marked by a stone shaft in the Nez Perce Indian Cemetery. **Nez Perce Crossing** is a museum full of Indian and western memorabilia.

Chief Joseph Days (July), Hells Canyon Mule Days (September), and the three-day Alpenfest (September) are re-

gional rodeos and festivals.

The town is becoming somewhat of an art colony. Just opened is the Manuel Museum and Studio on Main Street, the working address of sculptor David Manuel who was Oregon's official sculptor for the 1993 Oregon Trail Celebration. And Valley Bronze of Oregon has built a foundry and a showroom.

Wallowa Lake Lodge and Chandler's Bed, Bread, and Trail Inn are popular inns while Vali's serves fine Wiener schnitzel.

Pendelton

On the route of immigration on the Oregon Trail, **Pendelton** became a town in the 1880s and the center of wheat and cattle raising. Today its major industry is sheep raising and wool keep the area vital. The process of weaving, spinning, and carding can be seen at the Pendleton Woolen Mills.

The **Pendleton Roundup** brings in rodeo competitors and cowboys from around the region and is recognized as one of the top rodeos in the nation since 1910. (See: Box on Pendleton in Festivals Chapter).

Right outside of town, the **Blue Mountains** offer every form of outdoor recreation. The **Umatilla National Forest** offers camping and fishing along the Umatilla River.

Milton-Freewater is the site of the Frazier Farmstead Museum, a premier restoration of a 19th-century farm; and in Echo, Fort Henrietta Days re-enact local history every September.

During the 1860s, some 10,000 miners camped in the vicinity of Canyon City and conducted business on the town's main street. The **Grant County Historical Museum** displays artifacts and the restored Joaquin Miller Cabin is a major exhibit.

Switzerland of America

Called the "Switzerland of America", the **Wallowa Mountains** are in the furthest northeast corner of the state. The 10,000 foot (3,048 m) mountains and the wilderness terrain was once claimed by the Nez Perce.

Wallowa Lake

The region's jewel is Wallowa Lake, which at 5,000 feet (1,524 m) is the highest body of water in eastern Oregon and part of Wallowa Lake State Park. Ringed by lodges, the classic Moraine-held glacier lake is a few miles south of Joseph and supposedly the home of the Wallowa Lake Monster, a creature with a gentle disposition varying from 30 feet (9 m) to 100 feet (30 m) long depending on sighting and the amount of beer consumed.

A ride in the Mt. Howard Gondola – the steepest and longest in North America – takes you to the 8,200 feet (2,500 m) elevation of Mt. Howard and offers a spectacular summertime view.

Hells Canyon

Carved by the Snake River, the Hells Canyon is the deepest gorge in America and is surrounded by a massive recreation region, the largest of which is the 215,000 acre Hells Canyon Wilderness. A 67.5 mile (108.6 km) stretch of the Snake River is protected under the National Wild and Scenic Rivers System. Tours are available to Hat Point Lookout, 5,770 feet (1,758 m) above the canyon floor.

A jet boat trip down the river takes you close up to the petroglyphs and other archeological remains of an Indian tribe that once lived there.

Cascade Lakes to California

The south Cascades region consists primarily of high mountains, lakes, and a series of strung-together wilderness areas. In this area people are scarce, the landscapes are dramatic, and what little human activity can be found is usually linked to outdoor activity – water and hiking activities in the summer months, skiing in the winter.

The number of sizable towns can be counted on one hand. Surrounding them, however, is what often appears

The remote wilderness of the Cascades.

to be an inexhaustible number of pine trees of the Deschutes, Winema. Fremont, Rogue River, and Ochoco National Forests, high mountains, many deep lakes, a wide variety of flora and fauna species, and many unusual land features the result of lava flows during the Micocene epoch.

If you take Highway 97 along the eastern border of the region,

Mount Jefferson Wilderness is one of the designated wilderness areas protected against over-development.

you're essentially following the route taken by explorer John C. Fremont in 1843 and 1846. Unlike other regions of the state, settlement proceeded quite slowly in the southern Cascade Lakes region. Some of that hesitation was due to the U.S. Army who stopped immi-

grants from settling east of the Cascades because of Indians refusing to leave their land.

Ironically, in recent decades, wilderness areas were established by the federal government as a buffer against over development. Mount Jefferson Wil-

straddles Oregon and California, **Upper Klamath Lake**, **Lower Klamath** (California), **Aspen Lake**, and, of course, **Crater Lake**. It is also, by necessity, a land of lodges and resorts catering to those who drive through to see the spectacular views and who want to spend time in the lakes region.

Elk Lake Resort, for example, is a remote lodge at **Elk Lake**, a small mountain body of water about 30 miles (48 km) west of Bend on the edge of the Three Sisters Wilderness Area. You reach the lodge by snow cat or cross-country skiing in the winter. Getting a reservation is as tough as getting there as there is only a radio phone.

Much easier to get to is **Cultus Lake Resort**, 50 miles (80 km) southwest of Bend, alongside a lake in the Deschutes National Forest that's a popular destination with boaters and fishermen.

Oregon's tallest town

Lakeview is just north of Goose Lake and its recreation area. At an elevation of 4,300 feet (1,311 m), it calls itself Oregon's Tallest Town, but it's a claim that many others assert so take it merely as a local boast.

More to the point, it's a place better known for its geyser, Old Perpetual, than it's elevation. That it doesn't really rival Yellowstone Park's, Old Faithful, isn't important. It is Oregon's only geyser.

Located at **Hunter's Hot Springs**, a 47-acre property with hot water pools 2

derness Area, Mount Washington Wilderness Area, and the Three Sister Wilderness Area are the major shields.

Lake Resorts

On the Oregon side of the border are numerous lakes – **Goose Lake** which

Ski trail on Mount Hood.

miles (3.2 km) north of town on Highway 395, it erupts every 30 seconds, shooting 75 feet (22.8 m) in the air for 3 to 5 seconds.

It has been shooting off for the past 60 years, apparently the result of a driller tapping a hot water stream. The resort at Hunter's Hot Springs was built in 1920 and includes a small restaurant and a motel.

The **Schminck Memorial Museum** in Lakeview has more than 5,000 antiques assembled by the Oregon chapter of the Daughters of the American Revolution. Indian Village boasts the West's largest collection of arrow heads.

Lakeview is Lake County's business center, shipping point for the region's cattle ranches, and the major entry point either into the desert areas or the High Cascades of south-central Oregon. It's a physical area with a wide variety of activities being its charm and one of the major reasons for its popularity as a tourist destination.

Abert Rim

Ten minutes from town **Warner Canyon Ski Area** features 14 runs and 3.5 miles (5.8 km) of cross country trails. A half hour north of town along Route 395 is 30-mile-long (48 km) **Abert Rim** that towers 2,000 feet (607 m) over Lake Abert with its shore-lined petroglyphs. Abert Rim is the largest fault escarpment in the United States, rising 2,000

Flowering beauty in the Cascades.

Mountain with its 275,000-acre National Antelope Refuge.

If you're heading south into California or to the Goose Lake Recreation Area on Highway 395, stop off at Stringers, 15 miles (24 km) from Lakeview for their wild plum wine which the owners claim is the only such wine in the world. The wild plum jam is first rate.

North of Lakeview on about 20 miles (32 km) on U.S. 395 is Summer Lake, the site of a wildlife refuge that attracts thousands of visitors and wildlife every year. To get there from Lakeview you pass through Abert Rim, some 15 miles (24 km) north of Lakeview.

Driving on Highway 140, west of Lakeview on the way to Klamath Falls will take you through the **Gearhart Mountain Wilderness Area**. Forget the car if you want to explore the region. It's accessible only by foot or by horse with two major trails cutting through it.

feet (610 m) above Lake Abert. The lake is one of the most unusual in the area, having no outlet and rich in brine shrimp. The food attracts countless birds and other wildlife.

Because of its high salinity, it's unsafe to swim in it. The Lakeview Ranger Station can provide information about hiking up the back side of Abert Rim. It's not an easy hike – after first driving along bumpy back roads – but the view from the rim is spectacular.

The area is a rock collector's paradise with jasper, agate, fire opal, thundereggs, sunstone, feldspar, petrified wood, obsidian, and obsidian needles, especially in the area along Hogback Road.

Towering over the rock fields is **Hart**

Klamath Falls

The town of **Klamath Falls**, with 19,000 population, is the largest human habitat within 100 miles (161 km). Located at the southern end of Upper Klamath Lake, the biggest body of water in the lower Cascades, the town's economic base is determined by how many tourists come through the area.

But it is also the home of the Oregon Institute of Technology. And, with a self guided walking tour of 21 historic points, there's plenty within the town bounda-

Fossils

Nature's diary — fossil beds in the John Day area.

Fossils are nature's way of keeping a diary, just in case someone forgets who was at her party. Through fossil evidence that has survived time, we've been left nature's guest list. Fossils are the remains or imprints of plants or animals which are preserved from prehistoric time by natural methods.

The John Day fossil beds are just one of many collections found around the world, but no less wonderous. In Alberta, Canada, dinosaurs left behind their remains in a number of places; the evidence of early man is found in Africa and China; and small fossils of sea life and vegetation is found along the shores of Washington's Olympic Peninsula.

Fossils are found in sedimentary rock, asphalt deposits, coal, and sometimes in amber and other materials. Fossilization of skeletal parts and other hard parts is most common; only very rarely are flesh and other soft parts preserved.

Conditions conducive to the formation of fossils include quick burial in moist sediment or other material that prevents weathering and excludes oxygen and bacteria, thereby preventing decay. Shells and bones embedded in sediment in past geologic time, left perfect specimens of internal and external structures.

Sometimes, after these specimens were enclosed in the rock formed from the hardened sediments, water percolating through the ground dissolved out the shell and other structures, leaving behind a space in which only the form was preserved. This is known as a natural mold. Casts can then be made from them by pouring in plastic materials. And if these molds are filled with mineral by subsurface water, natural casts are formed.

Molds of insects that lived millions of years ago are sometimes found in amber. These were formed by the enveloping of an insect in the sticky resin that became amber. Through the years, the delicate tissue dried until little remained except the mold.

So minutely detailed are these molds, that detailed microscopic studies can be made. In

ries to keep a visitor occupied for the best part of a couple days. Klamath Falls, however, is so isolated from any other community that it once attempted to secede from Oregon and become the state of "Jefferson". Now the city's economy is secured at least during the

summer by the numbers of bird watchers, anglers, and sports people who come from both Oregon and California which is only 25 miles (40 km) away.

The **Klamath County Museum** features exhibits on local geology, history and wildlife. The museum's annex is

some case, scientists have been able to recreate dinosaurs from the impressions of dinosaur skin. Coprolites are fossilized excrement material, and if it's possible to determine their source, they are useful in revealing the feeding habits of these animals.

At times, entire animals have been preserved. In Siberia, some 50 specimens of wooly mammoths and a long-horned rhinoceros have been found preserved in ice with even the skin and flesh intact. Several specimens of the wooly rhinoceros have been found in oil-saturated soil in Poland. The skeletal remains were intact because the animals were engulfed in ancient tar pits, asphalt bogs, and quicksand.

At Rancho La Brea, outside Los Angeles, asphalt deposits have yielded a rich variety of birds and mammals. And in regions of Washington and Oregon, volcanic ash has performed the same process.

Petrification is another form of fossilization. This can occur in several ways. Mineral matter from water can penetrate porous material such as bones, making the material more compact and stonelike, protecting it from deterioration. Sometimes, the entire organic material can be replaced by the process and only the form of the original is retained.

The scientific study of fossils is called Paleontology. It wasn't until the year 1800 that fossils were generally regarded as remains of living things and accepted as a valuable record of the past.

The study of paleontology has financial as well as scientific purposes. The discovery of oil deposits, for example, is often dependent on the finding of fossils – indicating the possibility of subsurface oil saturated strata.

Cozy comfort in winter.

the restored Baldwin Hotel Museum. The four-story brick structure, built in 1904, first housed the hardware business of a civic leaders and was converted into a hotel in 1911. Among the hotel's guests have been presidents Theodore Roosevelt, William Howard Taft, and Woodrow Wilson. Many of the hotel's original furniture pieces remain. At the **Favell Museum of Western Art and Indian Artifacts**, including a collection of arrowheads. The **Ross Ragland Museum**, a onetime art deco movie theater, now presents plays, concerts, an impressive 130 nights a year.

North of town is the **Fort Klamath Museum**, on Route 62 south of Crater Lake, on the site of a fort established in 1863 to protect white settlers. A replica of the guardhouse contains military clothing, equipment, firearms, and exhibits on the Modoc War.

Upper Klamath Lake, at roughly 64,000 acres, offers prime fishing because of its shallow waters. One of the best birdwatching areas in the Pacific

Lava Beds National Monument

Centuries ago, a group of volcanoes erupted in the Klamath Basin, near the Oregon/California border. The surrounding 72 square-mile area was covered by molten rock, forming a rugged landscape that is now the Lava Beds National Monument.

It's on the California side of the border, but isn't particularly difficult to reach. Driving south of Klamath Falls on ORE 39 or US 97 you meet California 161 just across the border and, after turning either east or west (depending on how you approach it) take Route 139 south past the Tule Lake National Wildlife Refuge and drive until you reach the Forest. This is fairly desolate country without much in the way of facilities except for a series of campsites. The hub of the region is Lassen Volcanic National Park, site of a now calm volcano and a showcase for lava flow tubes, mud pots, and hot springs. Then lava action from the volcanos left varied formations, some of which rising 4,000 to 5,700 feet (1219-1737 m), providing a glimpse of what much of California and southern Oregon must have looked like in Primordial times.

Cinder and spatter cones and miles of undulating, hardened flows – some with such fanciful names as Devil's Homestead and Black Lava – show the viscosity of once molten rock, flow patterns, lava tubes, and honeycombs of caves created by sudden cooling. The caves are a once-in-a-million spot with 20 lava tube caves, a crater, Indian pictographs, and wildlife. It's remarkable that anything can live in this region, but life does persist.

Nearby Klamath National Wildlife Refuge is the largest Bald Eagle wintering area in the lower 48 states. An interpretive center is available to explain why.

The Tule Lake National Wildlife adjoins the lava beds immediately to the north and the Klamath Basin Refuge is next to that. Both are easily accessible via Highway 97.

A major war was waged against Native American Indians in this rugged country. After several years of disputes with settlers in the Klamath Basin, a band of Modoc Indians, led by their chief, Captain Jack, took refuge in the lava beds where they held out against federal and volunteer troups for six months in 1872- 73.

The Modocs

The ancestral home of the Modocs was in the area now occupied by the southern portions of the wildlife reserve and they have been removed to share lands, in the 1860s, with the Klamaths in Oregon. When they couldn't get along with one another, the Modocs tried reoccupying their ancient lands and the U.S. Army decided to return them to the Klamath region. The Modocs retreated to the lava beds and held off an army force of 600 men with only 60 warriors. The loss eventually meant the end of the tribe and a monument has been erected to commemorate the battle.

The park preserves Captain Jack's stronghold, a network of caves in which Kientpoos (his Modoc name) and his men took shelter. Also marked are the spot where General Edward Canby who was gunned down by the Modoc during a peace parley and the site of Colonel Alvan Gillem's camp, near which he buried many of the 46 soldiers killed in the siege.

The irony of General Canby's killing is that he desperately tried stopping the return of the Modocs. His objections were over-ruled, eventually ending in the siege and removal of the Modoc survivors to Oklahoma territory.

Lassen Volcanic National Park

If you've taken the time to reach these lava beds, you might as well continue south to **Lassen Volcanic National Park**, where you'll see more of the same, but with other attractions along the way. The region is rich with reminders of a romantic, but harsh history with museums and historic parks. In Alturas, due east 10 miles (7 km) from where highway 139 joins 299, the Modoc County Museum features collections of indian basketry. And about 7 miles (4.5 km) north on Highway 395 is the intriguing, Chimney Rock. When settler Thomas Denson built a cabin there in 1870, he used this pyramid-shaped rock for his chimney, carving the hearth and flue through the rock.

Family outing in the Cascades.

Northwest, the marshes and westlands on the water's north end are home to otter, beaver, and muskrat. One of the best ways to visit the Klamath Lake region is via the Upper Klamath Lake Tour Route which, in effect, circles the lake. If you're approaching from Crater Lake take Route 62 south, or Highway 97 if you're going north. Several state parks, botanical areas, nature sites, and waterfowl observation points make the trip a good one.

Klamath Basin National Wildlife Refuge

The Klamath Basin National Wildlife Refuge is the region's best known attraction. The complex consists of six separate parcels of open water, marshes, meadows, and forests. Good viewing can be had at **Lower Klamath** and **Thule Lake Refuges**.

There are plenty of lodging facilities in the Klamath area. The Klamath Manor in Klamath Falls is a converted turn-of-the-century with period furnishings. The Stone House is another B&B that offers charm and a great view from the porch which fronts on Klamath Lake.

Klamath Falls has a variety of motels among which are the Thunderbird, and Best Western Klamath Inn. At the north end of the lake, adjacent to the Upper Klamath National Wildlife Refuge is Harriman Springs Resort and Marina, and the Rocky Point Resort.

A view of the south side of Mount Hood from Trillium Lake.

As for food, well you won't find more than basic "cuisine" though some restaurants offer pleasurable eating. Try Alice's for a San Francisco fare; Fiorella Italian Ristorante which specializes in pasticcio; Malatore's for basic Italian; Wongs and King Wah's for Chinese; and Grampa Bailey's for family style.

The Cascades Lake Highway is a Forest Service scenic highway winding past Mount Bachelor and into the high lakes region. This 100-mile (161-km) tour needs several hours and a picnic lunch. For the most information, use the

Osprey in the Crane Prairie Reservoir.

Crane Prairie Reservoir

The most notable wildlife in the southern lakes region can be found at **Crane Prairie Reservoir**, the site of the first Osprey management region in the United States. Because of the damming of the Deschutes River in the 1930s, much of the trees remain above the water levels creating perfect nesting habitat for the hawks.

The Crane Prairie Resort rents canoes or powerboats for those keen on exploring this unusual scenery. You can also see great blue herons and sandhill cranes nesting near the reservoir and maybe catch a baldeagle or two soaring overhead.

National Forest Service's booklet, Casades Lakes Discovery Tour.

Davis Lake, at the southernmost point of the highway, offers some of the most unusual topography in the area with its northern end blocked by a huge lava dam. The water flows underground through lava channels and emerges at Wickiup Reservoir, due west of La Pine.

The National Parks system is as much an industry as it is a sight-seeing exercise.

Whole towns, resorts, restaurants, touring companies, and car rental agencies make a healthy business from the thousands who arrive every year to experience them.

While the parks themselves are exceptional destinations, they aren't an end in themselves. A peripheral experience is available enroute and in the neighborhood.

With all the wilderness areas, protected coastlines, National Forests, and wildlife refuges throughout the Pacific Northwest there are just four National Parks – The Olympic, North Cascades, Mount Rainier, and Crater Lake. Of those, only Crater Lake is in Oregon.

Nature's bounty to mankind.

National Parks

367

Olympic National Park

The Olympic National Park was one of only 100 parks worldwide designated a

Prepare yourself for an unsurpassed forage into God's creation.

World Heritage Park by the United Nations in 1981. Paved roads only skirt around the 908,720 acres of mountains and rain forest except for very short extensions into visitors areas. This allows the largest coniferous forest in the United States, with its 180 species of birds and 50 species of animals to remain undisturbed.

Sequim

The main northern entry into the park is through Port Angeles which also serves as the embarkation point for the privately owned Black Ball ferries to Victoria, British Columbia. Nearby is one of the peninsula's more unusual towns.

Located on the Strait of Juan de Fuca the town of **Sequim** (pronounced squim) has a climate that's dry enough to attract golfers during the rainy season. The Olympic Game Farm – whose tigers, lions, and buffalos are trained for films – is just north of town and offer driving tours.

In Sequim, the Sequim-Dungeness Museum preserves the native and pioneer heritage of the area. Opposite the mouth of the Dungeness River is one of the peninsula's great natural features, the 7-mile (11-km) **Dungeness Spit**.

It's the longest natural sand hook in the United States. The adjacent Dungeness Recreation Area provides access to a national wildlife refuge, an area swarming with sea life.

Rain forest in the Olympic Peninsula.

well known lodgings.

If you take the Hills/Hurricane Ridge Road from Port Angeles into the Olympic National Park, you'll climb 5,200 feet (1,585 m) in just 17 miles (27 km).

From the Hurricane Ridge Lodge you have a breathtaking view of Mount Olympus, the highest in the Olympics Range at 7,965 feet (2,428 m). Visitors to Hurricane Ridge can eat in the day lodge. In winter, it serves as a ski lodge for the downhillers and cross county skiers. **Hurricane Ridge** is one of the most popular destinations in the park. From there you can walk through meadows atop the mountain while deer, for which the ridge is famous, wander nearby.

The annual snowfall of 400 feet (122 m) is how the area's 50 glaciers stay icy during the summer. Down below, the Bogachiel, Hoh, Queets, and Quinault valleys are the park's rain collectors with between 150-200 inches (381-508 cm) falling annually. In the park are eight wildflower species found nowhere else, the continent's largest elk deer population, and world-record trees. There are no poisonous reptiles or insects, and the only problem plant is the stinging nettle.

For rain forests, the Hoh, Queets, and Quinault Valleys are the ones into which you can drive at least a short distance. Because of the Park Service Interpretive Center, the Hoh is the most popular.

The Lake Quinault Lodge, the Sol Duc Hot Springs Resort, and the Lake Crescent Lodge and Log Cabin Resort

Port Angeles, even though a major port and the peninsula's largest community, is not a tourist trap. A major attraction is the City Pier, adjacent to the ferry terminal. It has an observation tower, promenade decks, and the Arthur D. Feiro Marine Laboratory where you can touch samples of local marine life.

While you're waiting to get into the National Park, Casoni's is a fine Italian restaurant west of Sequim. Four miles (6.4 km) east of Port Angeles is C'est Si Bon, a fine restaurant in modern decor for dinner only. The Greenery in Port Angeles and the First Street Haven is home for large breakfasts.

The Red Lion Bayshore Inn, the Sequim Bay Resort, Groveland Cottages, Tudor Inn, and Lake Crescent Lodge are

Pinetrees near Lake Crescent in the Olympic National Park.

are popular places to stay.

The only way to completely cross the park is on foot. Backcountry use permits are required for trail or beach camping. Pick one up at the ranger station closest to your point of departure. For a north to south 44-mile (71 km) hike, start at the north Fork Ranger station. This is the route followed by James Christie, leader of the Seattle Press expedition across the then-unexplored Olympic Peninsula in 1890.

It took him six months to complete the route. Your journey should take but four days. There are other shorter hikes.

The most popular trail approaches are from the Hoh Valley and the Soleduck Valley. The trails between them join a system converging at High Divide, close

to Seven Lakes Basin.

The latter is a huge, glacier formed valley that is usually crowded by backpackers and fishermen.

Climbing is possible, but you better know what you're doing as the better routes require clampons, rope, ice picks, and skill. The pamphlet, *A Hiker's Guide To The Olympics*, provides details of the various routes. The book and maps can be had from the Pacific Northwest National Parks and Forests Association, 3002 Mt. Angeles Rd., Port Angeles, WA 98362.

North Cascades

It really doesn't exist as a single desig-

Ross Lake National Recreation Area.

Mount Rainier

Whenever anyone within 100 miles (161 km) of Mt. Rainier refers to it, it's simply, "The Mountain". Located 74 miles (119 km) southeast of Tacoma, the 14,410 feet (4392 m) high mountain is the fifth highest in the lower 48 states and is so big that it creates its own weather system.

Local Indians called the mountain, Tahoma – the mountain that was God. And indeed, there are moments when anyone living within the influence of its potential anger sometimes think the Indians, just might be right. It got its current name when Captain George Vancouver named it after his friend, Admiral Peter Rainier although the Admiral had never seen it.

It's the tallest of the Cascade volcanoes. While it's quiet now – not dead, but sleeping – it wasn't always so. It is estimated that it was once 16,000 feet (4877 m) tall about 75,000 years ago, but that glaciers later stripped about 2,000 feet (650 m) off its top. Even today 26 glaciers slowly crush the mountain sides and the mountain is host to the single largest glacier system in the continental United States.

While on clear days, Mount Rainier can seem a cuddly, coned giant, its gentleness is deceiving and every now and then you can see the hidden power deep in its bowels.

Steam hisses from fumaroles high on the glacier-clad cone, where stranded hikers have survived by gathering around the steam vents for warmth. Even the first white climbers to make it to the top, in 1870, gathered around a vent. Geologist claim that it will again erupt, but they claim that day is not soon. The bigger worry is mudslides which can happen if the steam vents melt the snow surrounding the cone, releasing massive slides. There's ample evidence this has happened before, at the 1947 Kautz Creek mudflow.

Geologists also claim that about 5,800 years ago, such a mudslide buried the site of present day Enumclaw 70 feet (21 m) deep and almost reached the present day suburbs of Tacoma.

Climate Influence

Because Rainier towers over the other mountains in the Cascades – with the other peaks guarding its flanks – it helps force the incoming ocean air to drop moisture on the west face of the mountain. Thus, Rainier's influence on Washington's climate is clearly obvious with the western part of the state being wet and the east, in the rainshadow of the Cascades, dry.

The mountain's height also accounts for its lenticular clouds, the upside down and saucer shaped clouds that just above the summit on clear days. The largest amount of snowfall ever recorded anywhere was on Rainier in 1972 when the Paradise ranger station snowpack reached 93.5 feet (28.5 m).

A lot of climbers get to the top the hard way, though it can be extremely dangerous. Every year, there's an "incident" and many knowledgeable climbers have lost their lives over the years. It takes three days for a good party to hit the top. Serious groups start at Paradise station for Camp Muir at 10,000 feet (3048 m).

There are two ways to do it; with Rainier Mountaineering or on your own. Unless you're an experienced climber with a long list of credits you must climb with the guide service. If you plan to climb with your own party, you have to register at one of the Ranger stations in Mount Rainier National Park. They will make sure you have adequate experience and the proper equipment and will tell you about routes, avalanche conditions, and weather forecast. You must also check in with them when you come down.

nated area. Rather, the **North Cascades National Park** is a interconnected series of national forests, parks, and wilderness areas in a rambling, indistinguishable design.

The park comprises all of the Mount Baker National Forest, Wenatchee National Forest, part of the Okanagan National Forest, and a section of the Snoqualmie National Forest. In addition, it is joined on its southern and eastern side by Glacier Peak Wilderness and Pasayten Wilderness, respectively.

To simplify it, the 505,000 acres expanse is divided into two units. The northern unit runs from the Canadian border to Ross Lake National Recreation Area. The southern unit continues on to the Lake Chelan National Recreation Area. Much of its eastern boundary is the summit of the Cascade range, and the western boundary is the **Mount Baker-Snoqualimy National Recreation Forest.**

It's not a park that's easy to penetrate. It is the most rugged of Washington State's national parks, the most remote, and it has the fewest roads. All visitor facilities in the northern portion are inside the **Ross Lake National Recreation Area.** On the southern end, the Lake Chelan area is the heavy use region, including the town of Stehekin.

Route 20 is the most spectacular way to traverse the park. But, this isn't a park to drive through. The most spectacular points can best be experienced either by hiking or on horseback. So take along your hiking books, map and a malleable schedule. Since Highway 20 is closed during the heavy snow months, plan to drive the park in summer. Be sure to make at least two stops along the Highway 20 (the North Cascades Scenic Highway), at Diablo Lake,

for lunch at Diablo Lake Resort. While in the region take the Seattle Light tour of the power generating facilities.

The tour begins with a slide presentation at the Skagit Tour Center in Diablo followed by a 560 ft. (171 m) ride up Sourdough Mountain on an antique incline railway used to haul supplies during construction of Diablo Dam. Then you cruise across Diablo Lake and back to an all-you-can-eat dinner.

Washington Pass Overlook

The second stop off Highway 20 is at 5,447 ft. (1,660 m) Washington Pass Overlook where a short paved trail will take you to viewpoints at Liberty Bell Mountain. From that point it's downhill to the Methow Valley. Remember that there are no gas stations or refreshment facilities for the miles (121 km) between Ross Dam and Mazama on the dry side of the range.

On the eastern side of the park, the towns of Tt and Winthrop, in the Methow Va, are tourist towns with Winthrop h1g a western theme. Sun Mountain Le is set on a hill that overlooks the Methow Valley and has the Cascade behind it.

Mount Baker

Elk is abundant in the Mount Baker National Forest.

another and seem part of the same large mass. But, it does throw a fright into residents of the Puget Sound every now and then when it decides to belch steam from its cone.

By any standard, Mount Baker is a impressive piece of real estate. The northernmost of the Cascade volcanoes, it towers drantically over the surrounding hills. Ironically, can best be seen from the Canadian side of th border even though it is 56 miles (90 km) ue east of Bellingham. For that reason, it's o of the most popular skiing and hiking areas both those living in the upper Puget Sod area, and Vancouver, British Columbia.

It was discovered by Captain Vancouver's first mate, Joseph Baker in the 1792 voyage and was thus named although for centuries it had been know to local Indians as Komo Kulshan, meaning "Broken One". That was a reference to an eruption that had blown out part of its summit.

In 1843, it erupted after centuries of being dormant, causing a huge forest fire on the east shore of Baker Lake. After that, it was quiet until 1975 when it again began to give every indication of exploding. Seismologists began to think it would, but then Mount St. Helens did blow in spectacular fashion. But the long term danger from Mount Baker is still quite real, evident every time she lets loose a belch of steam.

Baker is part of the Mt. Baker-Snoqualmie National Forest. The foothills, forests, streams, and country villages you pass through on the

Photographer's ream

It's a photographers dream, bed in glaciers and snowfields and always se to be clearly visible on even marginally cle ays. Standing side by side with Mount Shu at 9038 feet (2755 m), the pair seem flow into one

Steheki

The only way to reach resort town of Stehekin at the nor n tip of Lake Chelan, is by air, boa by hiking. It's like trave ling to ano world. One of the most pleasant w o reaching the

town is via the boat, *Lady Of The Lake*, from the town of Chelan.

If you plan to stay a couple of days, try it the old fashioned way at the Stehekin Valley Ranch where the Courtney family will drive you from the boat landing in Stehekin and take you to the furthest end of the valley for a

Mount Baker

Elk is abundant in the Mount Baker National Forest.

another and seem part of the same large mass. But, it does throw a fright into residents of the Puget Sound every now and then when it decides to belch steam from its cone.

By any standard, Mount Baker is an impressive piece of real estate. The northernmost of the Cascade volcanoes, it towers dramatically over the surrounding hills. Ironically, it can best be seen from the Canadian side of the border even though it is 56 miles (90 km) due east of Bellingham. For that reason, it's one of the most popular skiing and hiking areas for both those living in the upper Puget Sound area, and Vancouver, British Columbia.

Photographer's Dream

It's a photographers dream, bathed in glaciers and snowfields and always seems to be clearly visible on even marginally clear days. Standing side by side with Mount Shuksan at 9038 feet (2755 m), the pair seem to flow into one

It was discovered by Captain Vancouver's first mate, Joseph Baker in the 1792 voyage and was thus named although for centuries it had been know to local Indians as Komo Kulshan, meaning "Broken One". That was a reference to an eruption that had blown out part of its summit.

In 1843, it erupted after centuries of being dormant, causing a huge forest fire on the east shore of Baker Lake. After that, it was quiet until 1975 when it again began to give every indication of exploding. Seismologists began to think it would, but then Mount St. Helens did blow in spectacular fashion. But the long term danger from Mount Baker is still quite real, evident every time she lets loose a belch of steam.

Baker is part of the Mt. Baker-Snoqualmie National Forest. The foothills, forests, streams, and country villages you pass through on the

Stehekin

The only way to reach the resort town of **Stehekin**, at the northern tip of Lake Chelan, is by air, boat, or by hiking. It's like traveling to another world. One of the most pleasant ways to reaching the

town is via the boat, *Lady Of The Lake*, from the town of Chelan.

If you plan to stay a couple of days, try it the old fashioned way at the Stehekin Valley Ranch where the Courtney family will drive you from the boat landing in Stehekin and take you to the furthest end of the valley for a

and Pasayten Wilderness, respectively.

To simplify it, the 505,000 acres expanse is divided into two units. The northern unit runs from the Canadian border to Ross Lake National Recreation Area. The southern unit continues on to the Lake Chelan National Recreation Area. Much of its eastern boundary is the summit of the Cascade range, and the western boundary is the **Mount Baker-Snoqualimy National Recreation Forest**.

It's not a park that's easy to penetrate. It is the most rugged of Washington State's national parks, the most remote, and it has the fewest roads. All visitor facilities in the northern portion are inside the **Ross Lake National Recreation Area**. On the southern end, the Lake Chelan area is the heavy use region, including the town of Stehekin.

Route 20 is the most spectacular way to traverse the park. But, this isn't a park to drive through. The most spectacular points can best be experienced either by hiking or on horseback. So take along your hiking books, map and a malleable schedule. Since Highway 20 is closed during the heavy snow months, plan to drive the park in summer. Be sure to make at least two stops along the Highway 20 (the North Cascades Scenic Highway), at Diablo Lake,

for lunch at Diablo Lake Resort. While in the region take the Seattle Light tour of the power generating facilities.

The tour begins with a slide presentation at the Skagit Tour Center in Diablo followed by a 560 ft. (171 m) ride up Sourdough Mountain on an antique incline railway used to haul supplies during construction of Diablo Dam. Then you cruise across Diablo Lake and back to an all-you-can-eat dinner.

Washington Pass Overlook

The second stop off Highway 20 is at 5,447 ft. (1,660 m) Washington Pass Overlook where a short paved trail will take you to viewpoints at Liberty Bell Mountain. From that point it's downhill to the Methow Valley. Remember that there are no gas stations or refreshment facilities for the 75 miles (121 km) between Ross Dam and Mazama on the dry side of the range.

On the eastern side of the park, the towns of Twist and Winthrop, in the Methow Valley, are tourist towns with Winthrop having a western theme. Sun Mountain Lodge is set on a hill that overlooks the Methow Valley and has the Cascades behind it.

road from Bellingham provide an almost end-less series of sight seeing opportunities.

Among the pleasant mountain towns along Highway 542 are Deming, Kendall, Maple Falls, and Glacier, all with the assortment of shops and cafes.

The mountain and its accompanying forest cover an area far larger than just the peak and its immediate vicinity, spreading east to the bor-der of North Cascades National Park and past the towns of Concrete and Darrington.

Near Deming is the small Mount Baker Vine-yards on Mount Baker Highway, is open to the public with daily tours and a tasting room. Be sure to try the plum wine, a local favorite.

Skiing is a favorite recreation on Baker with a season that opens in November and some-times runs into June with at least one of the runs open. That gives it the longest ski season in the entire state. The runs have an elevation range from 3,500 feet (1067 m) to 5040 feet (1536 m) and a vertical drop of 2,200 feet (670 m). There are seven double chairs, three rope tows, a day lodge, and restaurant.

During the summer, the mountain is popu-lar with day hikers and backpackers who often walk over Austin Pass between Mount Shuksan and Mount Baker to Baker Lake which exists because of a Seattle City Light's Lower Baker dam.

The mountain has four zones supporting different varieties of vegetation and animal life, from sea-level forests to alpine meadows. Coyo-tes, bears, black-tailed deer, elk, porcupines, and mountain goats stalk the land. And five species of salmon spawn in the rivers.

hearty meal at their ranch. Open in the summer months, the ranch's tent-cabin offer a place to bunk and enjoy the basics of a camping lamp and showers in the main building. Cascade Corrals arranges horseback rides and moun-tain pack trips.

A more contemporary lodging is

Recreational possibilities abound in Mount Rainier National Park.

found at the Silver Bay Inn in a spec-tacular setting near a 700-foot (213-m) waterfall and a green lawn that rolls to the lake. The North Cascades Lodge is nearby and is a popular spot.

Mount Rainier

Whether you arrive from the east or the west, the park is buffered by national forest wilderness areas. You could spend weeks in the area and never exhaust its recreational possibilities.

Arriving by Route 706, you have to pass through the town of Elbe which has the **Mount Rainier Scenic Railroad**. It makes a 14-mile (23 km) trip, huffing and steaming, through the forests to

Crater Lake National Park, Oregon.

Mineral Lake.

The Morton Dinner Train makes a 4-hour, 40 mile (64 km) round-trip ride from Elbe to Morton. Passengers travel through gorgeous scenery in a restored, 1920s passenger train. The dinner is surprisingly good. The drive from Seattle takes about 3 hours. A network of roads encompasses the Park as well as a complex 305-mile (491-km) trail system.

The area was first settled by the Longmire family in the 1880s. An interpretive center at the town of **Longmire**, near the Park entrance, acquaints you with the family and the area. The National Park Inn is a basic lodging facility that has recently undergone renovation. The Paradise Inn, just below the visitors center is a massive, 1917 lodge complete with exposed beams.

Paradise is the most popular point of the park. On the way to the 5,400 ft. (1,646 m) center, you'll get fantastic views of Narada Falls and Nisqually Glacier. Sunrise, open only during the summer, is the closest you'll get to the peak. The old lodge, at 6,400 ft. (1,951 m) doesn't have overnight facilities, but it does have a snack bar and exhibits about the mountain.

In the vicinity of Mount Rainier are several major resort and tourist areas including Crystal Mountain Resort, just outside the Park's north boundary on Highway 410. The major ski facility has no gas station.

Chinook Pass

Chinook Pass, the highest of the mountain passes at 5440 ft. (1658 m) has lovely Tipsoo Lake, one the most easily accessed alpine lakes.

Double K Mountain Ranch, Crystal House Motel, and Whistlin' Jack Lodge are three overnight facilities. The Summit House restaurant, accessible only by chairlift at Crystal Mountain, is the highest restaurant in the state and offers a fabulous view of Mount Rainier and the exhausted but jubilant climbers approaching the summit.

Crater Lake

Oregon's only National Park, Crater Lake, is rimmed by a 33 mile (53 km) drive circling the lake. With more than 50 turnouts, it's the best way to see a region laced with vertical lava flow patterns. Rim Drive's highest viewpoint is at Cloudcap. This is the best place to see how part of Mt. Mazama was sliced by the Caldera's collapse.

Sixteen miles (26 km) west of Crater Lake is the Rogue River Gorge. This large river is channeled here in a lovely, small canyon that is easily accessible on foot. In the same area, a mile west of Union Creek, is Natural Bridge where the Rogue flows into a lava tube for a short distance before reappearing. In summer months, you can approach Crater Lake either from the north, off ORE 138 or from the south from ORE 62. The northern option is closed during the winter.

First of all, if you cannot get a room at the Mazama Village's 40 modern rooms, plan to either tent at one of the campgrounds or to stay in one of the towns on the Park's slopes. The Crater Lake Lodge is undergoing major renovations and is scheduled to open in the summer of 1995.

Diamond Lake Resort, seven miles (11 km) north of Crater Lake; Singing Pines on the road from Bend; and a number of lodges and resorts in Klamath Falls are your best bets for comfortable nearby lodging.

I f you can define a region by its sporting activities, the Pacific Northwest is decidedly singular. In the rest of the country, team sports dominate the landscape either because of the climate or the inclination of the population. In the Pacific Northwest the climate and the terrain invite a physical communion that encompasses virtually every kind of activity.

In the major cities, joggers brave the early morning rains; bicyclists ride to work; and golfers can be seen teeing off on New Year's Day regardless of the weather just to thumb their noses at relatives in snow-bound Cleveland.

Gearing up for a good time in downtown Portland.

Sports & Recreation

379

City and country activities

There are not many divisions between city and country activities. Because the mountains and the water are within easy striking distances, they continually draw activity to

Scout crossing along Timberline Trail in Mount Hood.

them. The same bicyclists who drive the many paths in Portland can be seen cycling along the Columbia. That's not to suggest people here are indifferent to the local team sports. On the contrary, loyalty and enthusiasm are intense. It's simply that they have their place in the grand sports scheme.

Skiing

You'll find skiing virtually all along the Cascades and on the Olympic Peninsula. Next to jogging, it's probably Portland's favorite activity and ranks high among Seattle residents.

In Portland, the Mount Hood Express van service gets skiers to and from the ski resorts at Mount Hood and from the airport to Timberline Lodge. The airport service can take you from the Portland International Airport baggage area to the slopes in about one hour.

Timberline Ski Area, with its Timberline Lodge is popular with locals because it offers skiing through to Labor Day high on the mountain.

Mount Hood Meadows is the largest ski area on the mountain with more than 2,000 skiable acres and nine chair lifts that can carry 14,400 skiers an hour.

The closest area to Portland is Multorpor SkiBowl, offering 61 runs to challenge skiers of all skills even though it has more expert runs than any other ski area on Mount Hood.

In the southern Cascades, near

Skiing ranks high as a sport among Seattle residents.

Bend, **Mount Bachelor** is considered by many to be one of the finest ski facilities in American and certainly the finest in the Pacific Northwest.

There are nearly 120 miles (193 km) of cross-country ski trails in **Mount Hood National Forest** with the best being on the mountain's northeast flank. The Deschutes National Forest, surrounding Bend, is even richer in Nordic trails with more than 165 miles (266 km).

In Washington, **Hurricane Ridge** on the Olympic Peninsula, **Mount Baker** near Bellingham, **Mount Rainier, Crystal Mountain** outside Tacoma, **Stevens Pass, White Pass**, and **Snoqualmie Pass** all have multiple skiing facilities (see: Cascades Chapter box on Skiing).

Hiking is probably the best way to experience the scenic trails.

Sea Kayaking

Enthusiasts swear that the only way to experience the real Northwest is by sea kayaking. In that way, they claim, the Northwest comes to you. They have a point. If you're on the water in a power boat the animal life is frightened away. But, if you're in a kayak in one of the many isolated inlets along Puget Sound– or anywhere on the coast, for that matter – you're part of the environment.

Sea kayaking has a long past. The first were built by the Native Indians about 10,000 years ago and many traveled as far south as San Diego with animal skins stretched tightly across their light, wooden frames.

The same technology is used today, though the materials have changed. Instead of animal skins, today's seagoing kayaks are made of fiberglass and plastics. They are extremely light, durable, and efficient.

Sea kayaks are also surprisingly available to anyone. You needn't be greatly experienced in either boating or canoeing. The sport is safe for anyone who can heed the safety measures.

They can carry 100 or more pounds (45 k) of goods and anywhere up to three kayakers. They can be easily carried by one person and can be launched or beached in a couple of inches of water. Their beauty is that they required no moorage, trailer, or fuel.

Puget Sound is home to many species of sea mammals ranging from seals and otters to whales. In between those extremes are hundreds of small animals and birds that no one on a power boat or from shore ever sees or hears.

There are a number of sea kayaking tour companies around Puget Sound, offering inexpensive trips for experts and novices. Most are geared to the beginner since advanced kayakers tend to drift off on their own. While the larger communities like Port Townsend along the Sound offer rentals you'll find the Seattle area the best place for finding tours that range from one-day along Lake Union to week-long adventures in the San Juan Islands.

Getting started

If you've not done this before, the Northwest Outdoor Center on Westlake Avenue offers kayak or canoe rentals from their Lake Union dock. It's an inexpensive and different view of Seattle and the water traffic is minimal.

The center's urban tour is a great way to learn the fundamentals of kayaking. The tour circumnavigates houseboats, shipyards, parks, and there's a stop for refreshments. You'll have the advantage of traveling in a group. And you can get moonlight trips and dinner tours to Lake Union restaurants.

It's when you get away from Seattle and into the upper Puget Sound region that kayaking takes on a special meaning. Experienced kayakers will find the Bellingham region a good departure point that is usually calm during the summer. Northern Lights Expeditions, Northwest Sea Ventures, and Shearwater Kayak Tours offer a variety of excursions into the islands.

Being at eye level in the bays and inlets of the San Juans or along the edges of other islands in the middle Puget Sound, offers unique chances to see wildlife. The advantage of the organized tours is that they provide the camping and cooking equipment. Organizers also have access to the latest weather reports and seasonal opportunities for seeing flora and fauna. What you'll need is warm clothing, a sleeping bag, and a willingness to get wet now and then.

Saltwater Kayaking

Saltwater kayaking has become one of the most popular of individual sport activities in the Seattle area. It is a novel and ideal way to experience the vast abundance of sealife in the Northwest. The region is perfect for it with inlets and passages all the way up the coast to Alaska. Several shops along Union Lake specialize in kayaks and sponsor in-

Seattle Mariners

When Seattle was first awarded a baseball franchise, in 1969, it signaled that the city had finally become "Major League".

That the original American League team, the *Seattle Pilots*, lasted for only one year before folding its tent and moving to Milwaukee to become the Brewers, did upset a lot of residents of the Pacific Northwest.

For Seattle's first major league team didn't really belong just to one city – nor more than the current *Seattle Mariners* baseball team that occupies the Kingdome.

The team did then, and still does, really belong to the whole region – Seattle, Portland, and even Vancouver, British Columbia.

Baseball

Baseball is a long time tradition in Seattle, going back to 1890 when the first professional team was organized. Called the *Seattle Reds*, it played in the Class-C Pacific Northwest league (PNL). Two years later, the *Reds* won the PNL Pennant when the Portland club declined to enter the playoffs because of financial problems. The Reds were renamed "*Braves*" and moved into their first real stadium in 1896, Athletic Park at 14th and Yesler.

Baseball got a little confusing in the region between 1903 and 1919. In 1903, the Pacific Coast League was formed and Seattle was a Charter member. Thus, Seattle had two professional teams for one season. The *Braves* were once in the Pacific National League but folded one year later.

Three years later, Seattle ended its membership in the PCL and joined the Class-B Northwestern League, where it remained until 1910 when it rejoined the PCL. It was renamed the "*Indians*" and played a 225 game schedule.

In 1937, Emil Sick bought the team for $115,000 and immediately changed the name to the "*Rainiers*", a natural move seeing as he was the owner of the Rainier Brewing Company. A year later the *Rainiers* moved into the newly built Sick's Stadium, with its seating capacity of 11,500. That year, local sports hero Fred Hutchinson began his rookie season and posted a 25-7 pitching record. "Hutch" would go on to a major league pitching and managing career with the *Detroit Tigers* after helping lead the *Rainiers* to three consecutive PCL Pennants.

Two things happened in 1955 to change the direction of Seattle baseball – Hutch returned to the Rainiers as manager and led the team to another PCL crown; and the first official proposition for a domed stadium was made. For the first time, Seattle began to seriously consider becoming major league.

It was encouraged when the Brooklyn Dodgers and the New York Giants moved to the West Coast – to Los Angeles and San Francisco, respectively. But, were they willing to pay for it? Not likely. Two bond issues to support construction of the domed structure failed – in 1960 and 1964.

In 1960, Sick sold the club to the Boston Red

struction and outings.

Bicycling

Bicycle trips in and around Portland and Seattle are a great way to see the two cities. Any book store has books outlining popular routes. During the summer, a 6 mile (9.6 km) stretch along Lake Washington is closed to auto traffic from 10 a.m. to 5 p.m. every third Sunday. Other popular routes include the **Burke-Gilman Trail**, **Green Lake Ride**, **Lake Washington Ride**, **Magnolia View**, **Queen Anne Hill**, **Shilshole Bay/Salmon Bay**, and **West Seattle Beach Ride**.

A variety of bicycle clubs throughout the state of Washington and Oregon

Sox and Seattle became the Red Sox AAA affiliate, staying with the organization until it was sold to the *California Angels*. No one knew it at the time, but manager Bob Lemon would guide the team to its last championship in 1968. In 1967, the population at last gave permission to raise funds to build the domed stadium due for completion prior to the 1972 season.

Alas, Seattle was left with a stadium-in-waiting. Between 1972-76, the city fielded a team, all right, but it was again minor league – in the Class-A Northwest League.

Then, on April 6, 1977, Major League baseball came back to Seattle for good when the new *Seattle Mariners* played the *California Angels* in the Kingdome before a crowd of 57,762. The M's starting pitcher that night was Diego Segui, a member of the 1969 *Pilots*.

Seattle has had good and hard times over the years, but has seen its share of success in the American League including two no-hitters from their pitching staff.

Long term plans call for the team not only to play games in Seattle but also up in Vancouver, where there is also a domed stadium. The team might also be shared with Portland, though the bulk of the games will be played in Seattle.

The team has been successful in the past three years setting franchise attendance and television ratings records. Majority ownership of the team is held by Jeff Smulyan who also owns the largest radio broadcasting corporation in the United States, Emmis Broadcasting of Indianapolis, Indiana.

provide information. The City of Seattle Engineering Department publishes a Bicycle Guide map. In addition, the Washington State Bicycle Association (call 329-BIKE) has a list of biking associations; and the Washington State Highway Department has 61 different routes for cyclists and publishes maps.

In Oregon, for the past 20 years, highway funds have been set aside for the development and maintenance of bicycle paths. The Oregon Coast Route parallels Highway 101 and the coastline from Astoria to Brookings. The **Oregon Dunes National Recreation** Area near Florence is a popular mountain biker's challenge.

Write to the Oregon Dept. of Transportation, Room 200, Transportation Building, Salem, OR 97310 and ask for the Oregon Bicycling Guide.

Fishing

Fishing is popular in winter and summer, along the coast and in the mountains. Fishery biologists claim that there are 150 species of fish in Puget Sound and another 36 in Lake Washington. Fishing piers around the Sound are plentiful. The fishing seasons vary according to species. The best way to sort out when it is is to stop off at a sporting goods store and ask for information about seasons, licence fees, and tips on where they're biting.

Watersports and boat rentals are relatively common. In Puget Sound especially, every waterside community has power boats, skiffs, and sailboats available on a daily, hourly, or weekly rental basis and a variety of charters for fishing or sightseeing.

Team Sports

Professional, college, high school, and a

A quiet fishing spot.

Windsurfing along the Columbia Gorge.

variety of amateur sports are available for spectactors throughout the Pacific Northwest although spectator sports activities in Seattle and Portland are the most intense.

Outside of Seattle and Portland and the major university towns like Eugene, Oregon Pullman and Washington, spectator sports are generally local in nature. But, in the college towns, the pageantry of athletic competition takes on heroic dimensions with the Homecoming Game in football often the year's major event.

Baseball and football

University sports, especially football,

draw spectators from throughout the two states and at times create near-fanatical devotion. No event, for example, is more enthusiastically awaited than the rival football matchup between the University of Washington Huskies and the Washington State Cougars for the Apple Cup.

It's the classic wet-sider/dry-sider matchup and the intensity of the rivalry can be seen in the results of the games between 1961 and 1993.

The much larger and more monied University of Washington holds only a two-game edge, seven to five over their cross-state competition.

For days prior to the event, newspapers devote much of their entire sports sections to the game between the PAC-

10 rivals. Not only are the teams analyzed, but psychologist explain why the intense rivalry is positive and life-styles pages explain how to get the most fun from the weekend game.

Major League baseball, football, and basketball are, of course, the glamor sports that draw gigantic crowds and big dollars.

Popular teams

The *Seattle Seahawks*, the National Football League franchise, has been the city's most popular team for several years though in recent years the team has fallen on hard times. Home games are played in the Kingdome and the games are usually sold out.

The *Washington Huskies* have generated about as much loyalty as have the Seahawks. They've played in many post-season bowl games including the Rose Bowl.

The *Mariners* is Seattle's American League baseball team and has been an annual "also-ran" though periodically the team has had a good run. Unlike the *Seahawks*, finding tickets is a relatively easy matter.

During the 1990 season, the club made major league history when it acquired all-star outfielder, Ken Griffey, Sr. to join his son Ken, Jr. in the *Mariners'* outfield. They built on that "first" with another, by being the first-ever father and son combination to hit back-to-back home runs.

The Kingdome itself is worth a visit. It covers 9.1 acres and is 250 ft. (76.2 m) high and 660 ft. (201. m) in diameter. It seats 64,772 for football and for baseball, 59,623. Personality shows draw 80,000.

For the trivia-minded, the King County Multipurpose Stadium (its official name) has 17 washrooms for men, 15 for women; 87 waterfountains, two freight elevators, and 51 concessions. There's a sports museum and space for 2,700 cars in the parking lot.

Basketball

The natural rivalry that you'd expect between Seattle and Portland hasn't materialized except in one professional sport, basketball – the only major league professional sport found in both cities.

The *Seattle SuperSconics* (abbreviated to the *Sonics*) became an American household name when it won the National Basketball Association (NBA) title in 1979. Unfortunately, that was the only time the team – which plays in the Coliseum on the Seattle Center grounds – won it.

Like the *Sonics*, Portland's NBA franchise, the *Trail Blazers*, have won a single NBA title, in 1977, and have been trying ever since to repeat. But they've come closer than their neighbors to the north, having been finalists twice since 1990. The Memorial Coliseum, where they play, is usually sold out.

Portland's lineup of teams includes

Golf

Northwest Washington is experiencing a golfing boom, especially with the area serving the population of Vancouver, B.C. Among the finer courses are the Palmer course at **Semiahmoo Resort** in Blaine; **Sudden Valley Golf and Country Club** and the **Lake Padden Municipal Golf Course** in Bellingham.

Spokane is one of the best kept secrets for golfing in Washington State, combining the lushness of tree-lined valley courses, and desert courses laid out across dry hills.

There are 10, 18-hole courses and one nine-hole course within easy driving distance of the downtown area. The furthest are just 25 minutes away, while the closest are 10 minutes journey away.

Indian Canyon, the location for the Spokane Open each August, is one of the top public courses in the United States and always ranked high in Golf Digest Magazine's "best" lists. Others include the **Meadow Wood Golf Course** that opened in 1988 and the newly opened Creek at Qualchan.

Across the border, just minutes away in Idaho, the new **Coeur d'Alene Resort Golf Course** is unique because it boasts the world's only floating green, a par three hole designed to change position daily. The green floats in Lake Coeur d'Alene and golfer reach the green via boat after teeing off.

The Portland area has 43 courses –– all but nine of them public. The costs remain among the lowest of the Northwest. To list all of the areas available for golf isn't practical. Write to the tourism regions listed in the Directory for a complete list in their regions.

The problem when golfing the Northwest is not which courses to play, but which of the almost 400 to ignore.

The same values that make the region a unique sightseeing experience, also provide varied golfing opportunities. There are seaside links courses, uphill and down mountain courses, desert courses, and courses that meander through vineyards.

While some of the courses are private and open to members only, most have reciprocal agreements with other clubs. If you're a member of a private club, it's often worth a telephone call to find out if they'll offer tee times.

Generally speaking, the coastal areas and the Williamette Valley in Oregon are the only year round golfing zones, though you should be prepared for rain and chilly weather. Those who want desert courses will have to wait for late spring and summer.

The Puget Sound area has some of the newest and most sophisticated public courses. **McCormick Woods**, on the Kitsap Peninsula, ranks among the finest in the entire Northwest. Located southwest of Port Orchard, the 18-hole venue is an intregal part of a self-contained development totaling 1,300 acres of which 500 are devoted to natural woods, wetlands, and parks. Along the fairways and greens is landscaping work that includes Japanese gardens and ground cover. The course is developed over gentle, rolling landscape.

In touch with nature.

the Western Hockey League Winter Hawks, and the Minnesota Twins' AAA farm team, the *Portland Beavers*.

Spectator Sports

In golf, Portland's Fred Meyer Challenge, and the Cellular Ping Golf Championship attracts many of the world's great players. Portland International Raceway hosts racing events including the Indy car World Series race.

Greyhound racing is held at Multnomah Greyhound Track in Fairview, while horse racing is at Portland Meadows Race Track in the city.

Oregon State University in Corvallis and the University of Oregon in Eugene, both field PAC-10 teams in football, baseball, soccer and other events.

The *Tacoma Stars* indoor soccer team play 26 home games from October through April at the Tacoma Dome; and the *Tacoma Tigers*, a Pacific Coast League AAA baseball team play 72 games at 8,000 seat Cheney Stadium.

Hydroplane race on Lake Washington

Each summer Seafair sponsors an unlimited hydroplane race on Lake Washington, usually in late August. It's one of the most popular events in the city and always garners nationwide media interest.

S hopping in the Pacific Northwest is both a practical and a cultural experience. In the large shopping centers like Portland's new Pioneer Place, located in the heart of downtown on SW Fifth and Yamhill, there are clusters of stores selling women's apparel and fashion, sporting goods, gifts, books, and specialty items.

These malls are monuments to merchandising, different in character, say, than Milan's Galleria Vittoro Emanuele in Italy, which is really an old street.

In one of the many downtown specialty stores.

Instead these shopping palaces are new and fresh and while they sometimes lack character, the better ones will provide you with an ample choice of domestic and imported goods.

Shopping & Cuisine

393

Factory outlets

Factory Outlets are becoming tourist destinations all by themselves. Several are located throughout the Northwest, usually near busy Interstate Highways.

Name brand mer-

chandise is offered at discounts from 20-60 percent and each center has different stores.

Outlets are located at North Bend off I-90; Lincoln City on the Oregon Coast; Burlington north of Mount Vernon on I-5; Post Falls east of Spokane over the Idaho border; Centralia just off I-5 in Washington; and at Troutdale, Oregon.

Both Seattle and Portland have large shopping centers and malls that cater to a multitude of desires. And a few are architectural gems – all day destinations where you can stroll and window shop.

Portland

Downtown Portland is Oregon's largest shopping destination with over 1,200 stores. The tempo is upbeat, stock is ample, and parking is plentiful. The Galleria, New Market Theater, Lloyd Center, Mall 205, and Pioneer Place are the biggest of the shopping centers.

Pioneer Place in particular is a massive center of glass and art objects, and is connected to Saks Fifth Avenue. In a different style, the SW Montgomery Street Espanade (RiverPlace & SW Montgomery) is on the waterfront and a broad walkway with benches and tables allows for leisurely walking. In the development are small shops, restaurants, and a marina.

Portland's retail core radiates from Pioneer Square in all directions. Just off the square are Nordstrom and Meier & Frank, two northwest-based stores. Pioneer Place is an 80-store pavilion including the Pacific Northwest's only Saks Fifth Ave.

Specialty shops fill the street-level storefronts of Portland's office buildings. When you enter **Nike Town** via the futuristic Star-Trek-like sliding door on the corner of Sixth Avenue and Salmon Street, you enter a two-story museum and gallery, where you find equipment from some of the greatest professional sports stars (all Nike clients, of course).

The **Portland Saturday Market** is the city's artisan-version of Seattle's Pike Place Market. Every weekend from March to Christmas, 280 independent artists and craftspersons gather in the open air at the marketplace, 108 West Burnside, to sell their wares. Located in the Historic Old Town area, it is positioned under the shelter of the west end of the Burnside Bridge. Admission is free.

Riverplace Esplanade, the **Skidmore Fountain Building**, and **Yamhill Marketplace** are other shopping centers where you can get arts, crafts, clothing and books.

Books

Books are a big business in both Portland and Seattle. In Portland, **Powell's** has three large facilities. The main bookstore is at 1005 W. Burnside and it bills itself as the largest in north America. It

Customers are part of the window display at a Portland bookstore.

also has two specialty stores – a technical bookstore at 32 NW 11th Ave., and a travel store at 701 SW Sixth Ave.

The **University of Oregon Bookstore** (734 SW Second), the **U.S. Government Bookstore** (1305 SW First), **Portland State Bookstore** (1880 SW Sixth), **Oregon Historical Society Bookstore** (SW Broadway & Mission), and the **Old Oregon Bookstore** (1128 SW Alder) have a wealth of regional and national information. Rare & used books can be found at the **Great NW Bookstore** (1234 SW Stark St.).

Whatever sporting goods, bicycle or hiking equipment you need can be found in Portland's downtown area at The **Nike Store** (920 SW Sixth), **Lightening Speed Cyclery** (90 NW Second), **Oregon Mountain Community** (60 NW Davis St.), **Portland Outdoor Store** (304 SW Third), and the **US Outdoor Store** (219 SW Broadway). Bike rentals can be had at **Ankeny Re-Cycle Bikes** (1227 SW 11th).

There are an endless number of shopping malls throughout the region and in the suburbs of both Seattle and Portland. In Portland's western region there's great shopping at Washington Square, Beaverton Mall, and Beaverton Town Square.

Throughout the rest of Oregon, shopping is plentiful and in keeping with community character. You can expect, for example, less choice in small communities, but also specialties that you normally won't find in Portland.

Portland's 23rd Street

The northwest corner of Portland is one of the city's most colorful districts with elegant older homes and with residents that include numerous artists, published writers, and a comfortable blend of ages and income brackets. It's also the home of Northwest 23rd – your street if you're a confirmed shopaholic.

It's the "happening" place in Portland beginning at West Burnside. Along this stretch of road you'll find antique stores, boutiques, card shops, design studios, ethnic restaurants, florists, galleries, home furnishing stores, interior decorators, pubs, and all of the peripheral attributes of a Bohemian district gone upscale.

The shops are located in a series of buildings and homes that have been renovated from their previous existence to a series of multi-floored shops, restaurants, and galleries.

Northwest 23rd and its extensions encompass an area referred to as Nob Hill, a sort of San Francisco reference because it's the most expensive real estate in the city. And many of Portland's portliest are witness to the claim that more calories are consumed in the area's restaurants than anywhere else in town.

On the south side of Burnside at 23rd you'll find a fine woman's store, **The Towne Shop**, and one for men, **Estes**. At the turn of the century, this was the newest fashionable place to be and the Gothic Victorian homes along 23rd have now been turned into shops much in the same way as San Francisco's Union Street.

The Uptown Shopping Center has an excellent array of small shops and nearby is the **Foothill Broiler**, long known for its hamburgers and homemade pies. **Westover Place** is an old Tudor-style home now filled with small shops. The **Nob Hill Exchange**, a former garage, has been tiled and restyled to high-Deco with a selection of specialty boutiques inside. The **West End Ltd**. across the street, is a well established women's wear shop.

At the corner of Everett and 23rd is the **Everett Street Market** with a wide selection of foods. Next door, **Ron Paul Catering & Charcuterie** offers sandwiches made to order.

One of the most concentrated shopping areas is the 700-block. Here the intensity of the shops increase and you'll find no shortage of ways to spend money and to intake calories.

If announcing where you've been is part of your shopping style, stop off at **Myra's**. She sells a giant canvas tote bag imprinted with "I'd rather be shopping on NW 23rd Avenue".

If you get tired of shopping you're generally in the same neighborhood as the Pittock Mansion, Forest Park, the Pittock Wildlife Sanctuary, Audubon, and Collins Sanctuary.

Seattle/Tacoma

In Seattle/Tacoma, there's no end to it. The major stores are all centrally located with distinctly different shopping styles, and neighborhoods offer their own style of small shops and intimate art galleries.

The suburban areas have large shopping centers – Northgate, Bellevue and Tukwila – with retail shops in a convenient location. In Seattle, the leading downtown department stores are within easy walking distance of the major hotels.

Northwest Indian art can be found throughout the city, but the major outlets are the **Burke Memorial Museum**, **Daybreak Star Art Gallery**, the **Legecy**, **Sacred Circle Gallery of American Indian Art**, and **The Snow Goose**.

For outdoor equipment and clothing you'll find everything from sleeping bags to freeze-dried food and down jackets at **REI** (Recreational Equipment Inc.,

Eddie Bauer, and **The North Face**.

Bergman's is the area's leading luggage store in five locations around the city, and if its raining you can find rain gear at **Peter Storm Inc.**, and at **Weather or Not**, both of which sell nothing but rain paraphernalia.

The **University Bookstore** claims it is not Portland's Powell's but is the largest in the Northwest. Who knows and who cares? The point is you'll generally get whatever you want at either. **Shorey's** is one of the world's largest antiquarian bookstores with more than 250,000 volumes in stock.

For imported goods look along the waterfront, in the International and University districts, Pike Place Market, and along Broadway. **Gilman Village** in Issaquah is a charming collection of restored vintage houses connected by wooden sidewalks with shops in them selling everything from shoes to plants.

Westlake Center is at the heart of Seattle's shopping district. Located on Pine Street between Fourth and Fifth Avenues, the newly completed mall features a variety of upscale specialty shops. It is surrounded by Westlake Park and Downtown Seattle's major department stores. **Pike Place Market** is an easy 10 minute walk away.

Nordstrom, founded in Seattle, is noted for its contemporary fashions. It's said that no one matches the store in service and display technique. The Bon Marche is a traditional department store with unusual sections such as a model railroad and crafts departments.

Rainier Square is an elegant cluster of shops at the base of Security Tower in downtown near the Hilton and Olympic hotels. **Broadway** on Capitol Hill, is where young Seattle goes for its upscale and avant garde clothing and fashion. In the Pioneer Square district – not to be confused with Portland's Pioneer Place – is where you'll find small bookstores, art galleries, and specialty stores of all kinds.

Seattle was one of the nation's pioneers in covered shopping malls. Some of the major one are **Alderwood Mall** (136 stores), **Bellevue Square** (198 stores), **Northgate** (116 stores), **Sea-Tac Mall** (106 stores), **Southcenter** (127 stores).

While most of the Pacific Northwest isn't old enough to have its own antiques, most have to be imported, there are numerous shops with excellent collections at reasonable prices. Shops are opening and closing rather quickly, so any specific listing is pointless, but they tend to cluster in the downtown area, Pioneer Square, University, Capitol Hill, Queen Anne Hill, and near the Pike Place Market.

The gallery business is a tough one and some galleries that seemed to have been highly successful have closed with owners citing burnout as a reason for getting out of the business. You'll find the bulk of them in the Pioneer Square region, but not exclusively.

If you're from New York or Chicago, you'll find few galleries that sell works by the international stars. Instead you'll see much by Northwest artists, national

Oyster bar in the Old Town in Portland.

and contemporary print makers, ceramics, and wood-carvers.

If you're in Tacoma, the **Tacoma Mall** with its 140 shops is one of the most complete centralized shopping experiences in the Northwest. Nordstrom, Bon Marche and other large stores are represented here. Just north of the mall are smaller shopping centers. A similar shopping area can be found at the **Lakewood Mall**. Though not as large as the Tacoma Mall, it has the major stores.

Procter District

A small, mostly upscale cluster of shops called the **Procter District**, runs along the 2700 block area of North Proctor. It has several shops including the Proctor District Antique Mall with more than 40 dealers, and the Pacific Northwest Shop that stocks only goods produced in the region. While the major malls and shopping centers may be the most obvious places to shop, the small intimate shops of the major cities are where the action really is.

Regardless of where you are – Portland, Seattle, Tacoma, Ashland, Yakima, Spokane – you'll find regional art and crafts, outdoor items, and local specialties to take home when you leave.

Cuisine

It wasn't long ago that if you mentioned

Thoroughly Japanese in a Seattle restaurant.

gourmet cuisine and the Pacific Northwest in the same breath, your comments would be met with a raised eyebrow or a sneer.

That has changed in recent years even though some converts to the style and content of Northwest food and wine have noted that Northwest cuisine is more of a melting pot of styles than something unique to the world.

That's somewhat true. What makes the cuisine of the Pacific Northwest is not just its freshness, but its diversity. There is no specific food that is grown or caught that personifies the entire region. Still, it is a combination of a land capable of growing virtually anything, mixed with art, tradition and culture.

Like its topography, Northwest cui-

sine varies both with distance and the seasons. And in the major centers of Seattle, Olympia, Tacoma, and Portland, foods are not only regionally based, they enjoy a heavy influence from ethnic communities.

Seattle, in particular, is a international gourmet's delight with large Japanese, Thai, Vietnamese, Chinese, French, and Italian communities and numerous other samplings of the world's population within close reach.

And the Native Indian cuisine, with its emphasis on specially prepared salmon, is always popular fare though your best chances of authentic Native Indian food is along the coast on or near native villages. In Seattle, people come not just to see the sights, but to sample the seafood and there are plenty of choices. Kasper By The Bay, Salty's On Aki, Satsuma, Takara, and Hirams At The Locks are among the most popular and highly rated.

Micro-breweries

At Noggin Brewery Bar & Restaurant and at Jake O'Shaughnessy's they also come for the beer. For Seattle – and to a lesser extent, Portland – is a micro-beer capital with many pubs and small breweries marketing local brews within a small retailing area, much like England. The micro-breweries are a combination of a brewery with an attached drinking establishment. You needn't buy a brew to enjoy them as they sell non-

Wine in Washington

In Washington State, wine is a growth industry in more ways than one. While it had long had the potential to be a major grape growing region, it wasn't until the mid-1970s that the industry expanded from a minor one to its current, formidable status. Its best products are now recognized as able to compete with the best on the continent.

Together, Washington and Oregon are the second largest producers of wine in the United States behind only California. The premium European varieties – Cabernet Sauvignon, Pinot Noir, Chardonnay, and Reisling – make up the bulk of the Pacific Northwest's grape harvest. The region had only 10 wineries in 1975, and today has more than 140.

Washington State has 80 wineries, and by far has the most production with 15,000 acres (6,000 hectares) in premium vinifera production.

If just one-third of the potential premium grape acreage (which experts estimate at 150,000 (60,000 hectares) were to be developed, Washington's wine industry would equal California's Napa/Sonoma wine region in size.

Washington also supplies wine-grapes to wineries in northern California, southern British Columbia, and eastern Canada.

Most of the vineyards are in Eastern Washington which is on the same latitude as some of France's great grape growing regions, at just north of 46 degrees latitude, similar to Bordeaux and Burgundy.

There are three viticultural areas; the Columbia Valley, Yakima Valley, and the Walla Valley region. But, it's the Yakima region that's the state's wine center with 40 wineries between Yakima and Walla Walla.

And, like the Napa and Sonomas regions in California, they have helped create a tourism industry that has encouraged the growth of country inns and bed and breakfasts.

The increase in wine production coincided with a relaxation of the state's liquor laws. For years, the state's laws were so protective to the small wine industry that anyone wanting an extensive cellar had to smuggle in their stock. In fact, you were unable to buy wine outside the state controlled liquor stores.

But that has all changed and you can now find a number of excellent wine shops in Seattle and throughout the state. The climate of the Washington vine-growing districts is at least as good as the best of California's. The valleys are cool, with relatively little frost, and the growing season is usually sufficient to produce well-ripened grapes with an acceptable balance of sugar and acidity.

These conditions make Washington State vineyards particularly suitable to the best of classic European varieties. Some of the best vineyards in Eastern Washington are on south-facing slopes above the Columbia, Yakima, and Snake rivers where they get as much as 16 hours of sun daily. As with all wine-producing areas, many wineries have been built in palatial settings.

Among the Columbia wineries are Bookwalter Winery, Gordon Brothers Cellars, Preston Wine Cellars, and Quarry Lake Vintners all in Pasco, and the Columbia Crest Winery in Paterson - the most dramatic and built on a hill overlooking the Columbia River. The Columbia crest winery produces more than a million gal-

alcoholic drinks and offer food.

The **Pacific Northwest Brewing Company** is located in the heart of Pioneer Square and produces six mild beers for its British owner.

Trolleyman, near the north end of Fremont Bridge, is the birthplace of Seattle's popular Ballard Bitter and Red Hook Ale. Big Time Brewery is near the university and resembles a typical rowdy

lons annually and has a reflecting pool, fountain and courtyard, a luxurious lobby, and a tasting and sales room. **Champs de Brionne** is built into the jagged cliffs overlooking the Columbia just above Vantage, a site chosen for growing Pinot Noir. During the summer, concerts by international stars are given in the natural amphitheater on the property.

Klona Vineyards (Benton City), **Hogue Cellars** (Prosser), **L'Ecole No. 41** (Lowden), **Hunter Hill Vineyards** (Othello), and **Kiona Vineyards** (Mattawa) are all small, family operations that produce well known proprietor labels.

Oddly, the majority of Washington State wine production facilities are located near the state's metropolitan centers which means the grapes have to travel an average of 200 miles (321 km.) from the vineyards to the winery. But it also means that you can take a complete wine tour of the state without traveling far from downtown Seattle.

The **Columbia Winery** is the oldest in the state and is located just east of Seattle in Woodinville. And just across the street from the Columbia Winery is the Northwest's largest winery, **Chateau Ste. Michelle**. In a clever replica of a French chateau, the winery offers daily tours and concerts during the summer. Also in the Woodinville area are the **French Creek Cellars**, **Tegaris**, and **Salmon Bay wineries**. Located in Seattle's south end is the small, family operated **E.B. Foote Winery**; a newcomer to the area is the **Salmon Bay Winery**, also in the south end. **Covey Run**, which makes wine in eastern Washington, has a tasting room in Kirkland.

Around Puget Sound are **Snoqualmie Winery** (Snowqualmie Falls), **Quilceda Creek Winery** (Quilceda), the **Bainbridge Island Winery** (Bainbridge) and **Neuharth Winery** (Sequim) on the Olympic Peninsula.

One of the many micro-beers produced in Portland.

the Pacific coast and the staff is incredibly knowledgeable about each one's subtle difference. There's an increasing number of small, intimate restaurants bordering scenic Commencement Bay in Tacoma, many featuring clams and oysters as well as salmon.

In downtown Tacoma's Engine House No. 9, at Sixth and Pine, the former firehouse offers close to 50 quality beers including the recreation of Tacoma's original beer, Tacoma Brew. Once the premier label of the Pacific Brewery, the factory was converted to a soap factory during prohibition.

And in Yakima, the Grant's Pub Brewery that opened in August, 1982, is one of the most popular watering holes in inland Washington. With seven dif-

student pub.

The Mecca of all Northwest micobreweries is **Coopers Northwest Alehouse**, also near the University. Twenty-one of its 22 beers are specialties from

A conservation-attuned hamburger joint.

Fresh seafood is a must along the Northwest.

ferent brews – Scottish Ale, Imperial Stout, Celtic Ale, Wheat Beer, Yakima Cider, and Spiced Ale – it also has a music program of jazz, blues, and folk groups.

Food in the northwest is regional. For example, while seafood is indigenous to the coast, chances are that in central Washington or in eastern Oregon any seafood you get on a plate will have been frozen.

Local food writers insist that, yes, there is a Pacific Northwest cuisine. But traditionalists insist there are really only two – French and Chinese – and anything else is merely good eating.

But there is simply too much activity in food creation here to justify such as closed attitude. Chefs in the various

regions don't simply cook, they create – making the presentation as much a feast for the eyes as for the mouth.

But, for the Indians around Puget Sound, fish is still central to their culture, providing not just sustenance, but spiritual significance. Many communities still hold first-salmon ceremonies to honor the first fish caught each season and to "ensure" future runs.

Court decisions have given tribes power over fish habitat and management decisions, so their relationship with the salmon is now a new political power.

Seafood is the main cuisine of the coastal northwest, and it's with this specialty that chefs make their reputations. They produce simple and complex recipes including such creations as

Seafood

There are countless ways of cooking salmon.

Sea cuisine is not a simple matter of cooking a fish. In a world defined by water and what lives in it, the Pacific Northwest has almost as many appetites as there are different peoples.

Not all sea life is eaten. Whales for example are not, though they were a staple for the Coastal Indians from the Neah Bay area. Nor are seals and and most other mammals on the menu. But, generally speaking, if it swims or crawls, it's a potential meal.

The common salmon has a pedigree. The King, or chinook, is the largest, most prized, and is generally considered the best tasting; the

Silver, or coho, is coveted by Europeans for smoking; Sockeye or red salmon is most frequently seen in fish cans; and Chum, is often used for feed.

Salmon can be prepared in a myriad of ways. The Native Peoples often wrapped them in leaves and baked them over hot coals, steaming them in their own juices. It's still made that way in many restaurants around the Pacific Northwest, especially in the Seattle/Portland regions. The influx of Asians have produced their own procedures and techniques ranging from drying the fish, smoking it, or eating the meat raw.

If the King Salmon is the Rolls Royce of the Pacific Northwest, bottom fish are the compact cars. Actually, bottom fish is a generic catch-all term encompassing all edible fish that live near the ocean floor. Caught either commercially or for sport, Northwest bottom fish categories include rockfish, flatfish, ling cod, sculpin, and bass.

The rockfish family is the most prolific with more than 60 species, size ranging from six inches (15.2 cm) to three feet (91.4 cm). They aren't the prettiest fish around, though are often quite colorful. With their compressed bodies, large mouths, and spiny head, rockfish can also be pinkish red, orange red, black and blue, orange and gray, yellow and black.

Flatfish are given that name because both eyes are on the same side of their body, they lie around on the bottom of the ocean, and often bury themselves in the bottom with just their eyes exposed.

The flatfish group includes halibut, sole, flounder, and turbot. Halibut, caught off the Oregon coast can weigh more than 100 pounds (45 kg) causing more than one person to compare catching a halibut to pulling a refrigerator off the ocean floor. Culinary classics in the group are petrale and Dover sole.

Dungeness Crab with Columbia River Caviar or pickled Sturgeon with toasted garlic paste.

In Autumn, mussels and oysters are

at their peak flavor as the waters of the Pacific Ocean cool down from summer's warm temperatures. Inland, mushrooms – such as the trumpet-shaped

The ling cod is a highly prized catch because it not only cooks up tastily white and firm, it can be fried, baked, sauteed, broiled, or poached and works well with any seasonings.

Compared to the ling cod, the bass-like snapper doesn't adapt as easily to all recipes. But, the darker-fleshed red snapper is a favorite among cooks, especially the cost conscious ones. It works up well with heartier seasonings.

Among trendy diners, the cabazone, a member of the sculpin family, is becoming a favorite. The flesh can be greenish, but turns white when cooked. Don't eat the eggs; they're poisonous.

Mussels have only recently gained popularity in the region although they have always been prominent in Europe. In the past, travelers coming back from Europe were the ones seen plucking them off rocks and dock poles at low tide.

Cooking them in their own juice is popular as is placing the meat in a chowder mix. Crawfish, sidestripe shrimp, Dungeness crab, and gooseneck barnacles have their own supporters and sea food restaurants throughout the Puget Sound area have them on their menus.

Getting some of these items is becoming difficult. Clamming is restricted in many parts of Puget Sound and diving for geoduck, the prime ingredient of great chowder, is regulated.

The razor clam that was once a mainstay of the Pacific coastal beaches is infected with a disease that does not affect humans but which will, in time, likely wipe out the creatures.

The rare and tiny Olympia Oyster lives only in some reaches of Puget Sound in Big Skookum, Little Skookum, Oyster and Mud bays. The population was almost wiped out by pollution and the importation of Japanese Pacific oysters which brought their own disease. Today, only a few hundred bushels are harvest yearly and finding them on a menu is rare indeed.

chanterelle, appear along foggy forest trails in the Cascades.

Other fungi, like shiitake and enoki are also hand gathered in the wood.

Morels grow as well and fetch $16 a pound. The mushroom has enough significance to generate a yearly mushroom festival in Falls City, Oregon.

Fruit harvests are celebrated throughout the two states, in the Williamette, Hood River, and; valleys. But it's not enough to simply ask for apples or pears or even grapes.

Among the apple varieties are Granny Smith, Gravenstein, Rome Beauty, Golden Delicious, Jonagold, Fujis, Akane, Gala, Liberty, Melrose, Mitsu/Crispin, Pippin, Spartan, King, and Idared; cherries include Bing, Lambert, Rainier, Royal Ann, Van, Olivette, North Star, and Montmorency; and pears encompass Bartlett, Bennett, Bosc, Comice, Conference, d'Anjou, Forelle, Rescue, Seckel and at least five varieties of newly imported Asian pears.

In winter, the ocean produces the finest of Northwest clams, the Geoduck (pronounced gooey-duck). At three to seven pounds (1.3 to 3.2 kg) they are big and generally used in the making of clam chowder.

Dungeness Crabs weighing in at about three pounds (1.3 kg), are best in winter and considered a delicacy. Cooks sometimes serve them with a delicate blackberry butter, but in general leave them alone.

In spring, pencil-thin sweet asparagus thrives in most fields and rhubarb blooms and stays until the end of summer.

The sour rhubarb stalk is used for more than just a tart pie. It also shows

Apple blossoms between Hood River and Parkdale.

up as a glaze on poached salmon or fresh halibut, two springtime standards.

Small, thin-skinned potatoes make their debut in spring as farmers markets begin to open throughout the Pacific Northwest.

You can split the Northwest into a series of nine regions and each produces its unique crops or catches.

In Washington's Northwest corner, agriculture is the dominant industry with more than 2,000 commercial farms and thousands more backyard enterprises. Dairy products include many

carrots.

Northern Oregon and southern Washington State from around Portland to the ocean supports 150 cash crops. Berries of all types, apples, melons, cherries, peaches, and other fruit; and sweet corn, cucumber, tomatoes and asparagus. The blossoms mean a productive honey industry.

The valleys also support prize winning vintages from Oregon's wine belt and ranchers market spring lamb, rabbits, chicken, and beef. From the coast comes a variety of sea foods. Local restaurants use their closeness to items to produce Alder-smoked sausage pate and smoked duck with blackberry sauce.

The Williamette Valley holds the majority of the Oregon's 34,000 farms and reaches from the Cascades to the coast. Besides the traditional crops are the grapes that produce some of Oregon's newer wine labels, plums, bush beans, hazelnuts, peppermint, pumpkin, and a wide variety of fruit jams.

Apples are the big crop in northern Washington with relentless sunshine and well irrigated fields. Wheat, oats, pears, barley, sweet corn, potatoes, hay for beef cattle and dairy cows are products of the area.

From the Yakima and north-central Oregon come pears and apples and wine while the Great Basin of the dry lands produces cattle and wheat, lamb and small boutique crops like asparagus. Melons, strawberries, pears, and specialty potatoes – as well as crawfish come from the Southwest Oregon.

varieties of cheeses. Raspberries, bottom fish, and apples are foods grown and caught here.

From the Olympic Peninsula come salmon, mussels, seaweeds, and sea urchins. At the southern end of Puget Sound come oysters and virtually every kind of truck crop vegetable including squash, tomatoes, French beans, and

Nightlife

As with most countries, nightlife in America's Pacific Northwest is largely determined by where you are. In the large cities, there's something for everyone. In small communities, nightlife could well be defined by the local motel pub.

One good way to establish what's available is to co-ordinate your stay with the large numbers of festivals that take place throughout the region and by the time of the year. Action along the coast will be different in the summer than in the winter. And in Jacksonville, the music festival determines the kinds of nighttime entertainment that is available.

Generally speaking, though, if you're looking specifically for a wide range of activity, stay in the large cities – Portland and Seattle.

There's no entertainment ghetto in Seattle. The Pioneer Square area is busy with pubs, bars, restaurants, and jazzjoints. But it's not the only

Portland bar scene.

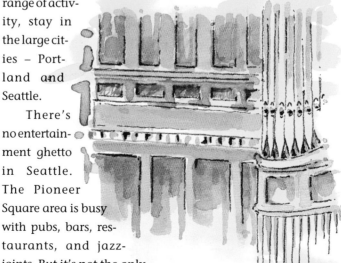

Cozy Places

Seattle has cosy, out of the way places that are acknowledged refuges against hectic city life. These are places where you'll simply want to nurse your drink, eat slowly, and either talk, read, or simply unwind.

At **Oliver's** in Seattle's Mayflower Hotel, in the heart of downtown, you can find nine different martinis, all with fanciful names and with the choice of Tanqueray Gin or Stolichnaya vodka and a touch of vermouth.

You'll want to sample the "Glacier Blue", a drink invented by the Four Season's Hotel and the winner in 1992 of the annual Martini Challenge. It's a mix of Stolichnaya Cristall, Bombay Gin and Blue Curacao.

At **Adriatica's**, above Union Lake, the bar is set high enough for a sweeping view across the lake. There are enough appetizers to keep you busy for the entire evening, but try the four-cheese pizza with grilled prawns adorning the blend of Feta, Mozzarella, Asiago, and Provolone.

Deep in the heart of the Pike Place Market, **Place Pigalle** is an elegant and cool contrast to the hustle and high energy of the market. It's the perfect little bar, overlooking Elliot Bay, that specializes in premium and unusual spirits.

There's a wide choice of French and Swiss wines, and assorted beers from many countries. Most of all, it has a relaxed, continental feel.

The **Bookstore** in the Alexis Hotel is aptly named. It's a favorite stopping off spot for office workers in the neighborhood who like to drink, talk, and look at the titles among the floor-to-ceiling bookshelves and the racks of international newspapers and magazines.

An added bonus is the pub fare that is made in the same four-star kitchen that produces the food for The Painted Table, that yearly makes somebody's "best" list, and is at the other end of the lobby.

The **Cloud Room** atop the Westcoast Camlin Hotel reminds the casual drop-in of the dark, New York style bars of the 1950s. The piano player is first rate and can play any of those ballads you used to dance to. The garden terrace lounge is a great hand-holding, look-into-those-eyes kind of place that offers a lovely view of the city.

The Sorrento Hotel's **Fireside Room** has a roaring fireplace to keep both the body and the romance warm. It has soft, cushiony chairs that you sink into and an elegance that's reflected in the drawing room atmosphere. Light entrees and an international menu varies in style and texture from simple to sublime, seared rare tuna to burgers.

It's especially good as a late evening place with a wide selection of cognacs and armagnacs and a variety of coffee extravaganzas.

Adjacent to the Four Seasons Olympic Hotel lobby, the **Georgian Terrace** is a cosmopolitan place that has whispers of chic. A broad selection of wines are available by the glass.

place in town. Along Broadway and in the University area you'll find much of the same and in the city's hotels are some of the best lounges and music acts in the city.

It's important to understand that the mood is created by a number of decors and atmospheres ranging from austere to opulent. In many of the clubs you'll find that many owners have tried to create a sense of local charm by any number of ways – by lining the walls with memorabilia or by using art from Native Peoples and local artists.

Bars and restaurants come and go quickly as owners search for some magic formula that will establish a loyal following. Theater is popular in Seattle with many venues offering a wide choice. **A Contemporary Theater** (ACT) is one of Seattle's most respected theaters, producing important and significant plays.

Bathhouse Theater has a six-play yearly schedule of contemporary and classical works presented in a small, 140 seat space on the northern edge of Green Lake.

The **New Theater and Art Center** is located on Capitol Hill and is the city's most daring theater venue. The productions here are designed to keep the locals talking – a mix of traditional, contemporary and a bit of cabaret.

Seattle Repertory Theater is the city's oldest equity company and produces six plays a year. The **Group Theater** is the resident company of The Ethnic Theater at the University of Washington, producing new scripts that deal with social problems in either a humorous or serious fashion.

Civic Light Opera, The Empty Space, The Good Companions, Intiman Theater Company, Seattle Gilbert and Sullivan Society, and the Seattle Children's Theater all mount a series of plays during the year. Movie theaters are sprinkled throughout the city, but for something unusual try one of the specialty house like the Toyo Cinema with its Japanese films (subtitled), or The Market Theater behind the Pike Place Market that specializes in high-quality flicks. The Grand Illusion Cinema is a small art house that show documentaries and unusual films.

For music, there's an enormous selection available from rock to classics. The Philadelphia String Quartet, Seattle Opera Association, Seattle Symphony, Seattle Youth Symphony, Cascade Symphony, Collegium Musicum, Contemporary Group, Northwest Chamber Orchestra, the Washington Jazz Society, **Seattle Classical Guitar Society**, Early Music Guild – among many others – produce regular concerts.

For rock, try the **Ballard Firehouse** (Russell & Market), the **Central Tavern & Cafe** (207 First Ave.), **Doc Maynards** (610 First Ave.), or **The Far Side Tavern** (10815 Roosevelt Way NE). For jazz few spots can compare with **Dimitrou's Jazz Alley** (6th & Lenore) or the **New Orlean's Creole Restaurant** (114 First St.) , both of which feature name performers. The ethnic clubs include **China Gate** (516 Seventh St.) with Korean, Filipino and other music; **George's Bar & Grill** (1901 4th Ave) with Greek music and belly dancing; and **The Backstage** (2208 NW Market) with blues and rock. A couple of comedy clubs have sprung up in recent years including **Seattle Improv** (1426 First Ave.) that comes with laughter and Northwestern food. **Comedy Underground** (622 S. Main) is an underground nightspot where local and nationally known comics hone their talents.

Gooey's (Seattle Sheraton), **Pier 70 Restaurant and Chowder House** (2825 Alaskan Way), are two disco/dance clubs popular with the singles set. Bars are around for every taste. Sports bars include Sneakers (567 Occidental) across from the Kingdome where the walls are covered with celebrity photos and signatures; and F.X. McRory's whose restaurant has an old-fashioned saloon bar attached. You'll find plenty of eat-

Night activity in Puget Sound.

Movie Scene

Aside from the skyscraper, no building type is more clearly representative of 20th-century architecture than the movie palace.

Their heyday is still a part of the Pacific Northwest. In the age of multiple theaters in shopping malls and downtown, the Egyptian on East Pine in Seattle and Harvard Exit, on Broadway, are gorgeous survivors from the era of individual movie theaters.

The Egyptian hosts films from the Seattle International Film Festival each May. And downtown Seattle features several old theaters that were saved from the wrecking ball and conversion to parking lots.

Seattle has indeed been fortunate because it has always had good theaters in which to hold concerts and films. Part of the reason is because Alexander Pantages founded his vaudeville empire here at the turn-of-the-century. At one time his theaters graced every west coast city, though much of what he built has been torn down. One of the grandest of his buildings was in Vancouver, B.C., but it was removed for a parking lot in the 1960s.

In their day, the movie palace architects were faced with a building program almost unrivaled in complexity, requiring a vast collection of rooms under one roof and they were frequently situated on odd-shaped pieces of land.

Built decades before Hollywood created the movie picture extravaganza, the theaters were spectacles in their own right. They were built not as romantic extremes, but to serve a financial purpose – to draw people to the box office.

Throughout America, even the smallest town could boast of regally outfitted movie houses often built by the same people who designed the big-city movie palaces.

B. Marcus Priteca, a Seattle native, was a master theater designer and was kept busy in his home town building theaters that were both functional and attractive. Though much of what he constructed has been torn down, there are still examples of his work.

The **Colisem Theater** at 5th and Pike is a Priteca-designed house that was one of the first giant movie theaters in the country. Built in 1915 it was the largest theater in the west – including Los Angeles – for years.

The **Paramount Theater** at 907 Pine, is another Priteca design. It was opened in 1927 and is still considered one of the most acoustically perfect theaters on the coast. Now used for a variety of shows, though mostly for rock, it has a wonderful Wurlitzer pipe organ that has been restored to original condition.

The **Fifth Avenue Theater**, 1308 Fifth, is one of the most favored buildings in Seattle. The gaudy old hall is probably the finest example left of the old theater tradition. Today it's used primarily for long-stay Broadway shows.

It's also the most faithful to its origins. Built in 1926, the highly ornate auditorium is a near-perfect duplication – at twice the original scale – of the Imperial Palace in Beijing's Forbidden City. The only detail designer R.C. Reamer changed was the color scheme, giving the carver "wooden" beams (plaster) a green hue for a Northwest flavor.

---

ing places in and around your hotel. But for a unique experience, try the restaurants specializing in Northwest cuisine. **Cafe Sport**, at the north end of the Pike Place Market, features fired oysters and grilled tuna brushed with soy, sage, and sesame. The **Alexis Cafe**, in the Alexis Hotel, emphasizes seafood and Northwest wines.

If you're the type who scoffs at hotel restaurants, you're in for a surprise at **Fullers** in the Seattle Sheraton. The seafood and appetizers are considered among the finest in the city. **F.X. McRory's**, just across from the Kingdome, is known for its bourbon-soaked beef and lamb, oyster bar and fresh fish selections.

Not all of Seattle's movie theaters are old. Like all cities, it has its share of shopping-center and multi-plex theaters. The **Bay Theater** (2044 NW Market runs Disney films in their original and is great for children.

The **Cinerama Theater**, 4th and Lenora, is one of Seattle's best technological efforts with fine sound. The **Egyptian**, 801 E. Pine, used to be a Masonic Auditorium and hosts the International Film Festival every summer. It has lots of space.

The **Market Theater**, 1428 Post Alley, is in an alleyway behind the Pike Place Market and has a good auditorium and pleasant lobby.

Seattle has two IMAX theaters that show IMAX films on wraparound screens – Eames/IMAX Theater at Pacific Science Center, and the Omnidome at Pier 59.

The most eclectic programming can be found in the University District at the Grand Illusion, Seven Gables, and Neptune.

One of the most pleasant movie house concepts in the northwest is at Portland's **Bagdad Theater and Pub**, 3702 SE Hawthorne Blvd. The owners, the McMenamin Brothers, restored a classic Arabian Nights movie palace to its original size after it had been split up into a multiplex theater. They now show second-run films and pour some 20 microbrews at the bar.

The **Fox Theater** on SW Broadway is a lovingly rendered roaring twenties motif. The **Roseway Theater** on SW Sandy Blvd., is another well-preserved screen gem featuring contemporary films as well as musicals of the 1940s and '50s.

Portland's night scene is scattered throughout the city. The **Dakota Cafe** (239 SW Broadway) is acknowledged as the hottest spot in town for the under-'30s crowd with live rock, pop, and blues on weekdays and a disco on weekends. The **Dublin Pub** (3104 SE Belmont) offers live entertainment with an emphasis on Irish music. If you don't want to spend the money for **Atwater's** (111 SW Fifth Ave.) food, the view from the bar atop the 30th floor location in the US BanCorp building is romantic and spectacular. **Shanghai Lounge** (309 SW Montgomery) is where downtown working boys and girls from the office buildings come to mingle and introduce themselves. **Champions** (1401 SW Front) is Portland's premiere sports bar. The **Last Laugh** (426 NW Sixth) is the city's grandest and most popular comedy club. **Key Largo** (31 NW First) has been packing in nightclubbers for a decade. Local rock, reggae, blues, and jazz performers all find their way onto the stage with local R&R bands a mainstay.

Roseland Theater (8 NW Sixth is a couple of blocks from Key Largo and has the same style; **Satyricon** (125 NW Sixth) is a block away from Roseland and leans heavily on punk and heavy metal; and the Dakota Cafe is Portland's largest nightclub and popular with the college kids and young professional. **Maxi's Lounge** (Lloyd Center), is where to go for top-40 dancing and **Embers** (110 NW Broadway) is primarily a gay disco though straights are being attracted to it as well.

For movies, **Cinema 21** (616 NW 21st) is located on Nob Hill and is a reliable foreign film house; the **Northwest Film & Video Center** is affiliated with the Oregon Art Institute and there's no telling what will appear on any given night. Here you get art films, old standards, animation, and funky B-flicks.

TRAVEL TIPS

Getting There

The two major ports of entry are through Seattle's SeaTac Airport or Portland International Airport. Major commercial airlines serve each. While SeaTac has been the major international departure airport for years, Portland is increasing its offshore service dramatically, especially to Japan and Mexico.

Airports are located in most strategically placed communities and are served by a network of feeder lines, most of which are operated by the major airlines.

The Black Ball Ferry sails between Victoria and Seattle and the Washington State Ferry operates between Port Angeles and Victoria. A new service is beginning in 1994 to link Seattle with Victoria, with B.C. Ferries Corporation replacing recently lost passenger/car service.

Greyhound and Trailways provide bus service in the Northwest including Canada. Amtrak connects Portland with Seattle and Chicago; and Seattle with Los Angeles. The major highways are well maintained. Winter driving can be treacherous in the mountains and in the open deserts.

Accommodation

There's a wide range of accommodation throughout the Pacific Northwest with more than enough choice to meet everyone's budgets. The major cities, like Seattle, Portland, and Spokane, have expensive international named hotels like Hilton, Sheraton, and Westin. Motels are easily available in and out of large and small towns. But they also have upscale B&Bs that include breakfast and sometimes dinner in their prices. Resorts outside the city often have specialties to which they cater such as skiing, golf, or fishing. Farmstays, pensions, and youth hostels are available.

Accidents Or Emergencies

The emergency number in most communities is 911. If the number isn't available, dial O for operator. The American Automobile Association is available throughout the Northwest with outlets through a number of gas stations in small communities.

Business Hours

Opening times vary. Office hours in major cities are generally 9-5pm, but stores have different hours, sometimes opening at 10 a.m. Saturdays stores are open all day. On Sundays, it varies from town to town. In Seattle, most stores open at noon on Sundays. Museums and Galleries are sometimes close on Mondays, but that varies from town to town.

Climate

The climate is complex due to the influence of the Cascade range. East of the chain, the weather is drier and warmer in the summer, colder in the winter. On the west side, it is milder and wet in winter, and during the summer generally clear, sunny, and moderately warm. In the mountains, bring enough clothing to insulate against sudden weather changes.

Consulates

Foreign Consulates in the Pacific Northwest are located in Seattle. Countries represented are Austria, Bolivia, Canada, Chile, Denmark, Ecuador, Finland, France, Germany, Great Britain, Guatemala, Iceland, Japan, Korea, Luxembourg, Mexico, Norway, Paraguay, Peru, Philippines, South Africa, Sweden, and Switzerland.

Crime

Be prepared for it, but don't expect it. The Northwest is generally safe and in most areas it is okay to walk at night. Use common sense in locking up personal items in the trunk of your car. Never leave money or jewelry in your hotel room, using instead the hotel's safe deposit boxes.

Currency

American currency is always the means of exchange although close to the Canadian border most areas will accept Canadian dollars at their current exchange rate. Foreign exchange is available at major Seattle and Portland downtown banks and at major hotels.

Customs

There are no restrictions the movement of goods between states. From overseas there are restrictions on the importation of alcohol, cigarettes, and money. Contact the nearest U.S. consulate or a travel agent for the newest regulations as they do changes from time to time.

Liquor laws

The minimum age for buying alcoholic beverages in Washington and Oregon is 21 and proof of age is often required. Liquor is sold by package in state liquor stores and licensed outlets. Packaged wine or beer may be purchased in grocery stores.

Local Transportation

Portland and Seattle have excellent bus service, Tri-Met in Portland and Metro in Seattle. Buses are free in specified downtown areas in both cities. Otherwise you must have exact change when boarding a bus. Taxi stands are at the airports, major hotels, the train station, and some street corners. Fares are regulated. In Seattle, fares are $1.20 initial charge with each additional mile being charged at $1.40. In Portland meter rates are $1.30 plus $1.40 a mile.

Motoring

A car is needed if you're to see the Northwest. The official national speed limit is 55 mph (89 km), but on Interstate Highways, the speed is sometimes greater. City speeds are 25-35 mph (40-56 km). Right turns are permitted on red lights.

　　Car rental companies will demand a valid driver's license. Off shore visitors might want to carry an International Driver's license though few companies require them. Always carry insurance against accident and personal liability. If your own insurance doesn't cover you, buy the package from the car rental agent.

Postal Services

Post office hours are usually between 8:30 a.m. and 5 p.m. Monday-Friday. These hours can change, however, in small towns. Letters for delivery in the U.S. is 29 cents. Overseas depends on the destination.

Time

The Pacific Northwest is on Pacific Time. Without Daylight Savings Time adjustments when it is noon in Seattle it is 10 a.m. in Hawaii, 2 p.m. in Chicago, 3 p.m. in New York, and 8 p.m. in London.

Tipping

It should reflect the kind of service you get. The accepted rate for porters at airports and hotel bellboys is 50 cents a bag. In restaurants tip 15-20 per cent of the bill. Unlike in many countries, a service charge is not included in the bill. No tipping is necessary in cafeterias. Taxi drivers, barbers, and bar tenders should be tipped 10-15 per cent.

Tourist Information

Both Washington and Oregon provide statewide tourist advisories. SeaTac and Portland International have in-house tourist information centers.

Weights & Measures

The United States is one of the few countries not using the metric system. Foreign visitors should carry a small pocket conversion calculator. They are inexpensive and highly useful.

DIRECTORY

HOTELS
Portland (503)
The Benson,
422 SW Broadway,
(97205), Tel: 228-2000.

The Heathman,
1009 SW Broadway,
(97205), Tel: 241-4100.

Governor Hotel,
611 SW 10th,
(97205), Tel: 224-3400.

Hotel Vintage Plaza,
422 SW Broadway
(97205), Tel: 228-1212.

RiverPlace Hotel,
1510 SW Harbor Way,
(97201), Tel: 228-3233.

Marriott Residence Inn,
176 Multnohah,
(97232), Tel: 228-1400.

Oregon - Coast (503)
Astoria Franklin Street Station
(B&B),
1140 Franklin Street, (97103)
Tel: 325-4313.

Astoria Inn, 3391 Irving Ave.,
(97103) Tel: 325-8153.

Crest Motel,
5366 5366 Leif Ericson Dr.,
(97103) Tel: 325-3141.

Bandon Inn at Face Rock,
3255 Beach Loop Rd.,
(97411) Tel: 357-9441.

Lighthouse B&B,
650 Jetty Rd.,
(97411) Tel: 357-9316.

Windermere Motel,
3250 Beach Loop Rd.,
(97411) Tel: 347-3710.

Cannon Beach Hotel,
1616 S. Hemlock, Box 943,
(97110) Tel: 436-1392.

Coos Bay Coos Bay Manor
(B&B),
955 S. 5th St.,
(97420) Tel: 269-1224.

Depoe Bay Inn At Otter Crest,
Otter Crest Loop, Box 50, Otter
Roch,
(97369) Tel: 765-2140.

Channel House,
35 Ellingson St., Box 56,
(97341) Tel: 765-2140.

Surfrider Oceanfront Hotel,
Box 219,
(97341) Tel: 764-2311.

Whale Cove Inn,
SRSBox 1-X,
(97341) Tel: 765-2255.

Holiday Surf Lodge,
Box 9,
(97341) Tel: 765-2133.

Gleneden Beach Salishan Lodge,
Hywy 101, Box 118,
(97388) Tel: 764-3600.

Lincoln City Palmer House
(B&B),
646 NW Inlet,
(97367) Tel: 994-7932.

Inn At Spanish Head,
4009 South Highway 101,
(97367) Tel: 96-2161.

Shilo Inn,
1501 NW 40th St.,
(97367) Tel: 994-3655.

Nendels Cozy Cove,
515 NW Inlet Dr.,
(97367) Tel: 994-2950.

Siletz Bay Inn,
861 SW 51st St.,
(97367) Tel: 996-3996.

Edgecliff Motel,
3733 S. Highway 101,
(97367) Tel: 996-2055.

Manzanita The Inn At
Manzanita,
67 Laneda,
(97130) Tel: 368-6754.

Newport Sylvia Beach Hotel,
267 N.W. Cliff St.,
(97365) Tel: 265-5428.

The Hotel Newport,
3019 N. Coast Highway 101,
(97365) Tel: 265-9411.

B.W. Windjammer Hallmark
Resort,
744 S.W. Elizabeth,
(97365) Tel: 265-8853.

WILLIAMETTE VALLEY (503)
Corvallis Hanson Country Inn,
795 SW Hanson St.,
(97333) Tel: 752-2919.

Madison Inn,
660 Madison Ave.,
(97333) Tel: 757-1274.

Shanico Inn,
1113 NW 9th St.,
(97333) Tel: 754-7774.

Nenbels Inn,
1550 NW 9th St.,
(97333) Tel: 753-9151.

New Oregon Motel,
1655 Franklin,
(97403) Tel: 683-3669

Salem Phoenix Inn,
4370 Commercial St. SE,
(97302) Tel: 445-4498.

Chumaree Hotel & Convention
Centre,
3301 Market St. NE,
(97302) Tel: 370-7888.

Salem Grand Motel,
1555 State St.,
(97302) Tel: 581-2466.

SOUTHERN OREGON (503)
Ashland Chanticleer Bed and
Breakfast Inn,
120 Gresham St.,
(97520) Tel: 482-1919

Mount Ashland Inn,
550 Mt. Ashland Rd.,
(97520) Tel: 482-8707

Stratford Inn,
2350 555 Siskiyou Rd.,
(97520) Tel: 488-2151

Country Willows,
1313 Clay St.,
(97520) Tel: 488-1590

Arden Forest Inn,
261 Henry St.,
(97520) Tel: 488-1496

Grant's Pass Paradise Ranch Inn,
7000-D Monument Dr.,
(97526) Tel: 479-4333

Riverbanks Inn,
8401 Riverbanks Rd.,
(97527) Tel: 479-1118

Morrison's Rogue River Lodge,
8500 Galice Rd.,
(97523) Tel: 476-3825

Jacksonville Old Stage Inn (B&B),
833 Old Stage Rd.,
(97530) Tel: 899-1776

McCully House Inn (B&B),
240 E. California,
(97530) Tel: 899-1942

Medford Under The Greenwood
Tree (B&B),
3045 Bellinger,
(97501) Tel: 776-0000

Red Lion Inn,
200 N. Riverside,
(97501) Tel: 779-5811

OREGON CASCADES (503)
Bend Sunriver Lodge,
15 Miles south of Bend, Hywy
97, Sunriver,
(97707) Tel: 593-1221

Inn Of The Seventh Mountain,
18575 Century Dr., 7 miles west
of Bend,

(97709) Tel: 452-6810

Mount Bachelor Village,
19717 Bachelor Dr.,
(97702) Tel: 452-9846

The Riverhouse,
3075 N. Hywy 97,
(97701) Tel: 389-3111

Rock Springs Guest Ranch,
64201 Tyler Rd.,
(97701) Tel: 382-1957

Entrada Lodge,
19221 Century Dr.,
(97702) Tel: 382-4080

Best Western Woodstone Inn,
721 NE Third St.,
(97701) Tel: 382-1515

Klamath Falls Thompsons By The
Lake (B&B),
1420 Wild Plum Court,
(97601) Tel: 882-7938

The Klamath Manor (B&B),
219 Pine, (97601) Tel: 883-5459

Sisters Black Butte Lodge,
Hywy 20, (97759) Tel: 595-6211

Western Ponderosa Lodge,
505 Hywy 20, (97759)
Tel: 549-1234

The Fourth Sister Lodge,
Box 591, (97559) Tel: 549-6441

Sisters Motor Lodge,
600 W. Cascades,
(97759) Tel: 549-2551

WASHINGTON
Seattle (206)
Alexis Hotel,
First & Madison Streets,
(98104), Tel: 624-4844

Edgewater Inn,
2411 Alaskan Way, Pier 67,
(98121), Tel: 728-7000.

Four Season Olympic,
411 University,
 (98115), Tel: 621-1700.

Holiday Inn Crowne Plaza,
Sixth & Seneca,
(98101), Tel: 464-1980.

Inn At The Market,
Pike Place Market,
(98101), Tel: 443-3600.

Mayflower Park Hotel,
Fourth Ave. & Olive,
 (98101), Tel: 623-8700.

Seattle Hilton,
Sixth & University,
(98101), Tel: 624-0500.

Sheraton Seattle Hotel & Tower,
1400 Sixth,
(98101), Tel: 621-9000.

Stouffer Madison,
515 Madison St.,
(98104), Tel: 583-0300.

Warwick,
4th & Lenore,
(98104) Tel: 443-4300

Westcoast Roosevelt Hotel,
1531 Seventh,
 (98101), Tel: 621-1200.

Westin Hotel,
1900 Fifth Ave.,
(98101), Tel: 728-1000.

GREATER SEATTLE (206)
Bainbridge Island The Bombay
House (B&B)
8490 Beck Rd. NE,
(98110) Tel: 842-3926

Bellevue Holiday Inn,
11211 Main,
(98004) Tel: 455-5240

Hyatt Regency at Bellevue Place,
900 Bellevue Way
(98104) Tel: 462-1234

Edmonds Edmonds Harbor Inn,
130 W. Dayton,
(98020) Tel: 771-5021

Issaquah The Wildflower (B&B),
25237 SE Issaquah-Fall City Rd.
(98027) Tel: 392-1196

Kirkland Woodmark Hotel,
1200 Carillon Point,
(98033) Tel: 822-3700

Sea-Tac Seattle Airport Hilton,
17620 Pacific Hywy S.
(98188) Tel: 244-4800

Seattle Marriott at Seat-Tac,
3201 s. 176th,
 (98188) Tel: 241-2000

Westcoast Sea-Tac Hotel,
18220 Pacific Hywy S.
 (98188) Tel: 426-0670

Wyndham Garden Hotel,
18118 Pacific Hywy S.
(98188) Tel: 244-6666

PUGET SOUND - (206)
Anacortes Channel House
(B&B),
2902 Oakes Ave.,
(98221) Tel: 293-9382

Majestic Hotel,
419 Commercial Ave.,
 (98221) Tel: 293-3355

Bellingham Best Western Heritage Inn,
151 E. McLeod Rd.,
(98226) Tel: 647-1912

Schnauzer Crossing (B&B),
4421 Lakeway Dr.,
(98226) Tel: 733-0055

The Resort at Sudden Valley,
2145 Lake Whatcom Rd.,
(98226) Tel: 734-6430

DeCann House (B&B),
2610 Eldridge Way.
(98225) Tel: 734-9172

Blaine Inn At Semiahmoo,
9565 Semiahmoo Pkwy,
(98230) Tel: 371-2000

La Conner La Conner Channel
Lodge,
 209 N. 1st,
 (98257) Tel: 466-1500

The Heron,
117 Maple,
(98257) Tel: 466-4626

Lopez (San Juan Islands) Inn
At Swift's Bay, Rt. 2,
(98261) Tel: 468-3636

Edenwild Inn,
Lopez Village,
(98261) Tel: 468-3238

Lummi Island The Willows,
2579 W. Shore Dr.,
(98262) Tel: 758-2620

Lynden Dutch Village inn,
655 Front St.,
(98264) Tel: 354-4440

Olympia Westwater Inn,
2300 Evergreen Park Dr.,
(98802), Tel: 943-4000

Tyee Hotel,
500 Tyee Dr.,
(98502) Tel: 648-6440

Harbinger Inn (B&B),
1136 E. Bay Dr.,
Tel: 754-0389

Orcas (San Juan Islands)
Deer Harbor Lodge and Inn,
Deer Harbor,
(98245) Tel: 376-4110

Turtleback Farm Inn (B&B),
Rt. 1 (98245) Tel: 376-4914

Beach Haven Resort,
Rt. 1 (98245), Tel: 376-2288

Kangaroo House (B&B),
North Beach Rd.
(98245), Tel: 376-2175

North Beach Inn,
at North Beach,
(98245), Tel: 376-2660

Orcas Hotel,
Ferry Landing,
(98280), Tel: 376-4300

San Juan (San Juan Islands)
Duffy House (B&B),
760 Pear Point Rd.,
Friday Harbor
(98250), Tel: 378-5604

Lonesome Cave Resort,
5810 Lonesome Cove Rd.,
Friday Harbor
(98250), Tel: 378-4477

Roche Harbor Resort,
Roche Harbor,
(98250), Tel: 378-2155

Tacoma Sheraton Tacoma Hotel,
1320 Broadway,
(98402), Tel: 572-3200

Best Western Executive Inn
and Convention Center,
5700 Pacific Hywy,
(98424), Tel: 922-0080

Whidbey Island Inn At Langley,
400 First, Langley,
(98260) Tel: 221-3033

Captain Whidbey Inn,
2072 W. Captain Whidbey Inn
Rd., Coupeville,
(98239) Tel: 678-4097

OLYMPIC PENINSULA (206)
Port Angeles Domaine
Madeleine,
146 Wildflower Lane,
(98362), Tel: 457-4174

Lake Crescent Lodge,
20 miles west of Port Angeles on
Hywy 1010,
(98362), Tel: 928-3211

Tudor Inn,
1108 Oak,
(98362), Tel: 452-3138

La Push Ocean Park Resort,
La Push Rd.,
(98350), Tel: 374-5267

Kalaloch Lodge,
Hywy 101,
(98331), Tel: 962-2271

Lake Quinault Lake Quinault
Lodge,
S. Shore Rd.,
(98575), Tel: 288-2571

Moclips Ocean Crest Resort,
Hywy 109,
(98571), Tel: 276-4580

Sandpiper Beach Resort,
2 miles south of Pacific Beach,
(98571), Tel: 276-4580

Casa Del Oro Apartments Hotel,
Point Brown Ave. NW,
(98569) Tel: 289-2281

Port Ludlow
The Resort at Port Ludlow,
9483 Oak Bay Rd.,
(98365), Tel: 437-2222

Port Townsend
The James House (B&B),
1238 Washington,
(98368) Tel: 385-1238

Hastings House/Old Consulate
Inn,
313 Walker, (98368)
385-6753 Fort Worden,
200 Battery Way,
(98368) Tel: 385-4730

Ravenscroft Inn,
533 Quincy,
(98368), Tel: 385-6724

The Tides Inn,
1807 Water,
(98368), Tel: 385-0595

Poulsbo Manor Farm Inn (B&B),
26069 Big Valley Rd.,
(98370), Tel: 779-4628

Sequim Juan De Fuca Cottages,
561 Marine Dr.,
(98382), Tel: 683-4433

**SOUTHWEST WASHINGTON
(206)**
Long Beach Peninsula
The Shelburne Inn,
Pacific Hywy & 45th, Seaview,
(98644), Tel: 642-2442

Vancouver Nendels Suites,
7001 NE SR 99,
(98665), Tel: 696-0516

Westport The Chateau Westport,
W. Hancock & S. Surf,
(98595), Tel: 268-9101

Glenacres Inn,
222 N. Montesano,
(98595), Tel: 268-9101

**WASHINGTON CASCADES
(206)**
Cle Elum Hidden Valley Guest
Ranch,
Hidden Valley Rd.,
(98922), Tel: 857-2322

The Moore House (B&B),
526 Marie St.,
(98943), Tel: 674-5939

Leavenworth All Seasons River
Inn (B&B),
8751 Icicle Rd.,
(98826), Tel: 548-1425

Enzian Motor Inn,
590 Hywy 2,
(98826), Tel: 548-5269

Mazama Country Inn,
14 miles west of Winthrop,
(98833), Tel: 996-2681

Snoqualmie The Salish Lodge,
37807 SE Fall City/Snoqualimie
Rd.,
(98065), Tel: 888-2556

EASTERN WASHINGTON (206)
Chelan Campbell's Lodge,
104 E. Woodin,
(98816), Tel: 682-2561

Ellensburg Best Western
Ellensburg Inn,
1700 Canyon Rd.,
(98926), Tel: 925-9801

Kennewick Quality Inn on Clover Island,
435 Clover Island,
(99336), Tel: 586-0541

Pasco Red Lion Inn,
2525 N. 25th,
(99301), Tel: 547-0701

Pullman Paradise Creek Quality Inn,
1050 Southeast Bishop,
(99163), Tel: 332-0500

Richland Red Lion Hanford
House,
802 Goerge Washington,
(99352), Tel: 946-7611

Spokane Waverly Place,
709 W. Waverly,
(99205), Tel: 328-1856

West Coast Ridpath,
515 W. Sprague,
(99204), Tel: 838-2711

Shilo Inn,
923 E. Third Ave.,
(99202), Tel: 222-2244

Yakima
The Tudor Guest House (B&B),
3111 Teiton Dr.,
(98902), Tel: 452-8112

Rio Marada Motor Inn,
1603 Terrace Heights Dr.,
(98901), Tel: 457-4444

RESTAURANTS
Portland (503)

Genoa (Northern Italian)
Tel: 238-1464

Heathman Restaurant (American)
Tel: 241-4100

L'Auberge (French)
Tel: 223-3302

Zefiro (Seafood)
Tel: 226-3394

Cafe des Amis (French)
Tel: 295-6487

Indigine (Pacific Northwest)
Tel: 238-1470

McCormick & Schmick (Seafood)
Tel: 224-7522

Al Amir (Middle Eastern)
Tel: 274-0010

Berbati (Greek)
Tel: 226-2122

Brasserie Montmartre (Continental)
Tel: 224-5552

Chen's Dynasty (Chinese)
Tel: 248-9491

London Grill (Continental)
Tel: 295-4110

Opus Too (American)
Tel: 222-6077

Oregon - Coast (503)
Astoria Columbian Cafe (Vegetarian)
Tel: 325-2233

The Ship Inn (Casual Seafood)
Tel: 325-0033

Bandon Seastar Bistro (low fat cuisine)
Tel: 347-9632

Brookings Hog Wild Cafe (Cajun/American)
Tel: 469-3733

Rubio's (Chiles)
Tel: 469-4919

Cannon Beach Cafe de la Mar (Pacific Northwest)
Tel: 436-1179

The Bistro (Pacific Northwest)
Tel: 436-2661

Florence Blue Hen Cafe (Funky American)
Tel: 997-2907

Gleneden Beach Chez Jeannette (French Country)
Tel: 764-3434

Salishan Lodge Restaurant (Pacific Northwest)
Tel: 764-3600

Lincoln City Bay House (Pacific Northwest)
Tel: 996-3222

Road's End Dory Cove (Oregon Coast)
Tel: 994-5180

Manzanita Blue Sky Cafe (Pacific Northwest/Asian)
Tel: 368-5712

Jarboe's (Seafood)
Tel: 368-5113

Newport The Whale's Tail (American/Continental)
Tel: 265-8660

Oceanside Roseanna's Cafe (Seafood)
Tel: 842-7351

Seaside Dooger's (Family)
Tel: 436-2225

WILLIAMETTE VALLEY (503)
Corvallis The Gables (American)
Tel: 752-3364

Nearly Normal's (Mexican)
Tel: 753-0791

Eugene Ambrosia (Pizza)
Tel: 342-4141

Chanterelle (Continental/Pacific Northwest)
Tel: 484-4065

Hilda's (Latin American)
Tel: 343-4322

Mekala's (Thai)
Tel: 342-4872

Chez Ray's (Eclectic)
Tel: 342-8596

Salem La Margarita (Mexican)
Tel: 362-8861

McGrath's Public Fish House (Seafood)
Tel: 362-0736

Morton's Bistro (Northwest Italian)
Tel: 585-1113

Alessandro's Park Plaza (French)
Tel: 370-9951

SOUTHERN OREGON (503)
Ashland Chateaulin (French)
Tel: 482-2264

Winchester Country Inn (American/Vietnamese)
Tel: 488-1113

Green Springs Inn (Italian)
Tel: 482-0614

Primavera (Pacific Northwest)
Tel: 488-1994

Bella Union (American/Cajun)
Tel: 899-1770

Medford Genessee Place (Continental/American)
Tel: 772-5581

OREGON CASCADES (503)
Bend Scanlon's (Seafood)
Tel: 382-8769

Pescatore (Pacific Northwest)
Tel: 389-6276

Westside Bakery & Cafe (Western)
Tel: 382-3426

Deschute Brewery & Public House (Casual)
Tel: 382-9242

Klamath Falls Fiorella's (Northern Italian)
Tel: 882-1878

Sisters Hotel Sister Restaurant & Bronco Billy's Saloon (Old West/Mexican)
Tel: 549-7427

EAST OREGON (503)
Echo The Echo Hotel Restaurant (American)
Tel: 376-8354

Ontario Casa Jaramillo (Mexican)
Tel: 889-9258

Joseph Vali's Alpine (Hungarian/German)
Tel: 432-5691

La Grande Golden Harvest (Chinese/American)
Tel: 963-3288

Mamacita's (Mexican)
Tel: 963-6223

Pendelton Raphael's (Native American)
Tel: 276-8500

WASHINGTON Seattle (206)
Assaggio (Italian)
Tel: 441-1399

Dahlia Lounge (Eclectic)
Tel: 682-4142

Fullers (Pacific Northwest)
Tel: 447-5544

Place Pigalle (Seafood)
Tel: 624-1756

Ray's Boathouse (Seafood)
Tel: 789-3770

Union Bay Cafe (Continental)
Tel: 527-8364

Chau's (Chinese)
Tel: 621-0006

El Puerco Lloron (Mexican)
Tel: 624-0541

Huong Binh (Vietnamese)
Tel: 720-4907

The Pink Door (Pacific Northwest)
Tel: 443-3241

Maximilien-in-the-Market (French)
Tel: 682-7270

McCormick's Fish House (Seafood)
Tel: 682-3900

Viet My (Vietnamese)
Tel: 382-9923

GREATER SEATTLE (206)
Bainbridge Island Four Swallows (Pasta)
Tel: 842-3397

Pogacha (Croatian)
Tel: 455-5670

Tosoni's (American)
Tel: 644-1668

Edmonds Provinces Asian Restaurant (Asian)
Tel: 744-0288

Ciao Italia (Italian)
Tel: 771-7950

Issaquah Mandarin Gardin (Chinese)
Tel: 392-9476

Nicolino (Italian)
Tel: 391-8077

Yarrow Bay Grill & Beach Cafe (Seafood)
Tel: 889-0303

PUGET SOUND - (206)
Anacortes La Petite (French)
Tel: 293-4644

Janot's Bistro (Pacific Northwest)
Tel: 299-9163

Bellingham Thai House (Thai)
Tel: 734-5111

Blaine Inn At Semiahmoo (Seafood)
Tel: 371-2000

La Conner Palmer's (American Country)
Tel: 466-4261

Gardner's (Seafood/Pasta)
Tel: 786-8466

Orcas (San Juan Islands) Christina's (Northwest)
Tel: 376-4904

Ship Bay Oyster House (Seafood)
Tel: 376-5886

Bilbo's Festivo (New Mexico)
Tel: 376-4728

San Juan (San Juan Islands) Roberto's (Italian)
Tel: 378-6333

Springtree Eating Establishment (Seafood)
Tel: 378-4848

Tacoma Pacific Rim (Asian)
Tel: 627-1009

The Lobster Shop (Seafood)
Tel: 927-1513

Harbor Lights (Seafood)
Tel: 752-8600

OLYMPIC PENINSULA (206)
Port Angeles Downriggers (Seafood)
Tel: 452-2700

Port Ludlow The Resort at Port Ludlow (Eclectic)
Tel: 437-2222

Port Townsend The Public House (Casual)
Tel: 385-9708

Cafe Piccolo (Italian)
Tel: 385-1403

Fountain Cafe (Greek)
Tel: 385-1364

Sequim The Buckhorn Grill (Seafood/Continental)
Tel: 681-2765

Casoni's (Italian)
Tel: 683-2415

WASHINGTON CASCADES (206)
Cle Elum Mama Vallone's (Steaks)
Tel: 674-5174

Leavenworth Reiner's Gasthaus (Austrian/Hungarian)
Tel: 548-5111

Terrace Bistro (Continental)
Tel: 548-4193

EASTERN WASHINGTON (206)
Ellensburg Giovanni's on Pearl (Seafood/Pasta)
Tel: 962-2260

Valley Cafe (Eclectic)
Tel: 925-3050

Kennewick Casa Chapala (Mexican)
Tel: 586-4224

Pullman The Seasons (Pacific Northwest)
Tel: 334-1410

Swilly's (Eclectic)
Tel: 334-3395

Richland Emerald Of Siam (Thai)
Tel: 946-9328

Spokane Clinkerdoggers (Pacific Northwest)
Tel: 328-5965

Marrakesh (Moroccan)
Tel: 328-9733

Milford's Fish House (Seafood)
Tel: 326-7251

Walla Walla Jacobi's (Pacific Northwest)
Tel: 525-2677

PHOTO CREDITS

INDEX

INDEX

431